STRATEGY, POLITICS, AND

DEFENSE BUDGETS

STRATEGY, POLITICS, AND DEFENSE BUDGETS

WARNER R. SCHILLING

PAUL Y. HAMMOND

GLENN H. SNYDER

COLUMBIA UNIVERSITY PRESS

NEW YORK AND LONDON

Copyright © 1962 Columbia University Press

First printing 1962
Second printing 1966

Library of Congress Catalog Card Number: 62-17353

Printed in the United States of America

Institute of War and Peace Studies

Strategy, Politics, and Defense Budgets is one of a series of publications sponsored by the Institute of War and Peace Studies of Columbia University. Other books from the Institute are: Alfred Vagts, *Defense and Diplomacy: The Soldier and the Conduct of Foreign Relations* (1956); Seymour Melman, editor, *Inspection for Disarmament* (1958); William T. R. Fox, editor, *Theoretical Aspects of International Relations* (1959); Kenneth N. Waltz, *Man, the State, and War* (1959); Samuel P. Huntington, *The Common Defense: Strategic Programs in National Politics* (1961); Samuel P. Huntington, editor, *Changing Patterns of Military Politics* (1962).

Foreword

As the three studies in this volume eloquently demonstrate, finding the best way to protect the United States against external military threats is not just a technical problem. The threats are multiple, and there is no automatic calculus to determine what percentage of our defense effort ought to be allocated to any one of them. Neither is there any automatic calculus to determine how much national sacrifice is enough to support an "adequate" level of defense mobilization. Although public oratory and expert recommendations appear to reflect a contrary belief, everyone who has seriously reflected on problems of national security knows that what appears "wholly adequate" to one man appears "dangerously inadequate" to another. There is now general agreement among those in and out of uniform, in the White House and on the Hill, in the Pentagon and in the universities, in Washington and in the rest of the country, that perfect security cannot be purchased at any price.

We want the greatest security at the least human and material cost; but beyond this, we have to recognize honest differences of opinion. Men equally concerned to preserve and promote national security differ greatly in their views on how much and what kind of defense expenditures are essential. They differ partly because they are unequally expert in dealing with the various military and nonmilitary considerations that enter into policy calculations, and they differ because they are unequally concerned about the impact of a given defense policy on particular domestic groups or domestic policy objectives. President Eisenhower's call for "security and solvency" and his fear of a great and growing "military-industrial complex" reflect his concern that military problems be solved in a way that least harms domestic policy objectives which seem particularly important to him.

The myth that questions of national security are above or at any rate somehow apart from politics has died hard. A more rational choice of defense policies and levels of defense expenditures requires that we recognize and come to understand the political process as it operates to define national security policy rather than that we ignore or deny that process.

These studies by Professors Schilling, Hammond, and Snyder, presently or formerly members of the Institute of War and Peace Studies of Columbia University, all throw light on that political process in a critical period of transition after 1948—from the period of American atomic monopoly to one in which there are thermonuclear weapons on both sides, from American suspicion of Soviet objectives to certainty of implacable Soviet-American confrontation, from fear that Germany and Japan might again develop military power to fear that they might not develop enough military power to bear their share of the burden of restraining the Soviet bloc, and from belief in the temporary necessity of high peacetime defense expenditures to acceptance for many years to come of a level of expenditure several times higher. The three studies deal in turn with the three main phases of this transition—the warning phase of 1948–49; the phase of reaction to dramatic events beginning in 1950; and the phase in which the course of military policy is reset in the first years of the Eisenhower administration.

The three analyses in this volume are part of a series of studies of national security policy made possible by a Carnegie Corporation grant for research by members of the Institute of War and Peace Studies. I am happy to record our gratitude for this support. The Carnegie Corporation, however, bears no responsibility for the form which the studies have finally taken.

June, 1962 WILLIAM T. R. FOX, *Director*
Institute of War and Peace Studies
Columbia University

Contents

THE POLITICS OF

NATIONAL DEFENSE: FISCAL 1950

by Warner R. Schilling

Acknowledgments

It is a pleasure to acknowledge the stimulation I have received from conversations with Richard E. Neustadt and Edward L. Katzenbach, Jr., and the comments that Bernard C. Cohen, Roger Hilsman, and Samuel P. Huntington have made on one or another of the drafts of this study. To William T. R. Fox, whose criticism and counsel have attended every stage of my work, my debts are as numerous as they are great.

I wish also to thank Barbara Turlington, Barbara Rapoport, and Norma Schilling for research assistance; Ann Hohri and my wife for their patience and skill with me, copy, and proof; Edwin G. Nourse for his courtesy in permitting me to quote from his personal papers and diary; the Viking Press for permission to quote material from *The Forrestal Diaries*, edited by Walter Millis, with the collaboration of E. F. Duffield; the Council on Foreign Relations for affording me the use of their clipping files; and the estate of James V. Forrestal and the Princeton University Library for permission to quote from papers in the personal part of the Forrestal Collection. Parts of Chapters I and II were earlier incorporated in my "The H-bomb Decision: How to Decide Without Actually Choosing," *Political Science Quarterly*, March 1961, pp. 24–46, and the editors have kindly permitted some of the language to do double duty.

Certain additional acknowledgments are made in Chapter I, footnote 16.

Contents

Contents

1 Introduction

There has been a revolutionary change in the security position of
the United States since the end of World War II and with it a revolutionary change in the pattern of American defense expenditures.[1]
During the first half of the century the industrial superiority of the
United States provided it with a military potential that completely
overshadowed that of the other Great Powers. In 1918, for example,
the United States produced 58 percent of all the steel made in the
world, nearly twice as much steel as was produced by England,
Germany, and France combined. Similarly, in 1944, the United
States produced 45 percent of all the combat munitions made that
year, nearly twice as much as that produced by the sum of its
enemies and 50 percent more than that produced by the sum of its
allies.[2] The weapons of World Wars I and II and the distribution
of the people, skills, and resources necessary to make and use those
weapons were such that no single foreign nation could conceivably
muster enough power from inside its own frontiers to threaten the
continental security of the United States.

[1] The following discussion of these two changes owes much to the points
made in William T. R. Fox, "American Foreign Policy and the Western European Rimland," *Proceedings of the American Academy of Political Science*,
January 1948, pp. 71–78, and his "Civilians, Soldiers, and American Military
Policy," *World Politics*, April 1955, pp. 402–18.

[2] Witt Bowden, Michael Karpovich, and Abbott P. Usher, *An Economic
History of Europe Since 1750* (New York, American Book Company, 1937),
p. 389, and Raymond W. Goldsmith, "The Power of Victory: Munitions Out-
put in World War II," *Military Affairs*, Spring 1946, pp. 71, 75.

More strictly speaking, America's industrial superiority was not per se the
equivalent of superior war potential. The military utility of America's industrial
economy was also dependent on the willingness of Americans to turn it to
military purposes and their skill in doing so. For these points see the analysis
of the concept of war potential and its components in Klaus Knorr, *The War
Potential of Nations* (Princeton, Princeton University Press, 1956).

Foreign nations, by converting a higher proportion of their military potential into force-in-hand, could and did maintain at times armed forces much larger than those of the United States. But two factors ruled out the possibility that through such an effort a foreign nation could secure a sufficient edge in striking power to assault successfully the American continent. The first was the character of the logistical and technical problems that would be met in attacking across wide oceans even a poorly armed United States. The pre-1945 weapons systems could not promise a quick victory, and in the face of the vastly superior American potential a long war was out of the question. The second restrictive factor was the overseas balance of power. The interests and arms of the other Great Powers were so committed one against the other that none was free to direct its strength against the United States. In time of peace they did not dare turn their backs on more immediate enemies; in time of war their hands were full fighting them. In sum, so far as continental interests were concerned, the American security position during the first half of this century was doubly insured. By virtue of its superior potential, the United States had no need to fear any nation; by virtue of the character of military technology and the balance of power abroad it could afford to leave that potential largely unmobilized.[3]

There was only one possible flaw in this security position. No single nation could threaten the United States, but what if by conquest and alliance the people, skills, and resources of all of the Great Powers in Europe should be combined? The United States would confront in such a combination a military potential roughly equivalent to its own. Would such a combination have occurred had not the United States entered World War I or World War II?

[3] This analysis excludes the military problem of defending extra-continental territory and interests, in particular the Philippines and the Open Door in China. This is not to denigrate the importance of these problems. (Indeed, as the analysis indicates, they were normally the only serious ones the nation faced. In this case, it was the United States which had the problem of employing force across an ocean. Moreover, whenever general war occurred in Europe, the Far Eastern balance of power collapsed, and the United States was left alone to confront Japan.) The point is, rather, that with respect to security problems of this order, there has been no real qualitative change between the first and the second halves of the century.

Would such a combination have been able to assault successfully the American continent? Was the threat of such a combination of sufficient gravity to justify the costs of going to war to prevent it? Americans differed on the answers to these questions in the years immediately preceding the nation's entry into both world wars. In any event, the result, if not in all instances the intent, of American intervention was to remove the contingency from the realm of reality.

The pattern of American defense spending during the first half of the century broadly reflected the outlines of this security position. With the major exception of naval expenditures preceding World War I, defense spending was "crisis-oriented." [4] During years of European peace, the armed services were allocated only a small fraction of the resources they would require in event of war. Even with the outbreak of general war abroad, the threat to American security was not immediate. In both world wars the distribution of power among the belligerents was such as to make total victory neither immediate nor certain. This condition gave Americans time and allies. There was time to debate the dimensions of the threat, and time to begin to arm. In both instances these initial military preparations were quickly followed by American intervention. But if Americans had not yet fully mobilized their potential, neither had their enemies completed the conquests necessary to match that potential. There were allies to hold the line until the conversion of American potential to power was complete, and with that conversion the road to victory, however bloody, was certain.

This historic pattern of American defense expenditures has been aptly characterized as a "feast or famine" cycle. During "peace" the services received practically nothing. The nation's income was

[4] The Navy was maintained as a permanent force-in-being partly to meet the extra-continental problems noted in footnote 3 and partly because naval and civilian policy-makers did not fully appreciate the security that the European balance of power provided against an overseas attack from that quarter. In the case of naval planners, there was still a third consideration: they were fearful that the American public, if presented with the fait accompli of a European conquest in the Caribbean, would be unwilling to mobilize the power required to reconquer the area. See the present author's forthcoming study, "Admirals and Foreign Policy."

spent primarily in the private sector, and that part available for government expenditure was allocated almost exclusively to what, in contrast to security needs, may be called welfare goals. Once "war" occurred, however, the stops were pulled, and by and large the services had to compete only with each other's claims on the nation's income.

It is not necessary to enter into judgment on the past to note that the conditions which gave some sense to this pattern are no longer present. The American security position following World War II was undermined by two concurrent developments: the collapse of the European balance of power and the advent of nuclear weapons systems. These two developments have completely changed the strategic significance of the earlier components of American security: allies, time, the overseas balance of power, oceans, and industrial superiority. The new weapons systems are so cheap and so destructive, relative to the old, that the Soviet Union, a single nation of inferior industrial capacity, can muster from inside its own frontiers enough power to devastate the American continent. Given a sufficient edge in striking power, the Soviet Union could mount from across and under the oceans an attack that would produce victory in a matter of minutes. Nor are there any other nations of sufficient military magnitude to balance the might of the Soviet Union and give her pause before making such an attack. Finally, unlike the case of the Kaiser's or Hitler's Germany, the conquest of the peoples, skills, and resources of the Old World is not a necessary first step in a Soviet attack on the United States. Accordingly, the United States can no longer count on the unfolding of such a conquest to provide time for Americans to alert themselves to danger and to arm to meet it, or to provide allies to preoccupy the enemy until they are ready.

This revolutionary decline in the security position of the United States did not, of course, take place overnight at the end of World War II. Nor were the true dimensions of the transition, as it occurred, immediately and equally apparent to all. The defense budget which will here be the object of study, that for the fiscal year 1950, is a case in point. It was formulated in the midst of this transition. The first of the two developments noted above—the collapse of the European balance of power—was both evident and very much in the minds of those who fashioned the fiscal 1950 budget. The second development—the advent of Soviet nuclear weapons systems —had yet to occur. When the budget went to Congress in January 1949, the Soviet Union had not even exploded its first A-bomb, much less did it have a stockpile of H-bombs and the ICBM's to deliver them. Russian intercontinental striking power, although anticipated by those who made the fiscal 1950 budget, was nonetheless a prospect, not a fact, and it belonged to a future that they did not, in all instances, accurately foresee.[5]

Still, if the deterioration in the American security position had not yet run its full course at the time of the fiscal 1950 budget, the fact that that position was undergoing a change for the worse was clear. Equally clear was the fact that the change in the American security position required a change from the previous pattern of American defense spending, that the United States could no longer afford to follow the "feast or famine" cycle of the first half of the century. In face of the new conditions, existing and impending, defense spending had to be oriented toward a situation of "permanent crisis." Thus, in June 1948, the State Department advised the Secretary of Defense that, given the character of the Soviet threat, a defense policy "based on the maintenance of a permanent state of adequate military preparation is better than an effort pointed toward a given peak of danger." Similarly, the first Chairman of the Joint Chiefs of Staff, General Omar N. Bradley, warned the nation in October 1949 that it was "in for a long pull" and that defense budgets would have to be designed accordingly.[6]

The budget for fiscal 1950 was so based and so designed. It was also the first postwar budget in which the participants, Congressional

---

[5] The literature marking these two developments is by now quite extensive. Especially valuable for their historical perspective, however, are Hajo Holborn, *The Political Collapse of Europe* (New York, Alfred A. Knopf, 1951), and Bernard Brodie, *Strategy in the Missile Age* (Princeton, Princeton University Press, 1959).

[6] Bradley, "This Way Lies Peace," *Saturday Evening Post*, October 15, 1949, p. 33, and Walter Millis, ed., *The Forrestal Diaries* (New York, The Viking Press, 1951), p. 508.

as well as Executive, had an opportuntiy to reach their decisions, from beginning to end, through the new organizations provided by and attendant to the National Security Act of 1947.[7] The fiscal 1950 budget thus provides a bench mark from which to appraise the concepts and the institutional arrangements with which the nation has since endeavored to meet the new pattern in its defense spending, a pattern which is likely to be as characteristic of the second half of the century as was the "feast or famine" cycle of the first half.

II

It is easy enough to conclude that government spending for defense can no longer be oriented toward either of the earlier extremes: all for welfare or all for defense. It is quite another matter to decide just where, in budgeting for the "long pull," the balance should be struck. In general, the question can be conceived as one susceptible to a rational solution: it is a question of knowing the dimensions of the security problem at hand, the relative importance of the national ends involved, the nature of the means available, and the consequences that would follow for those ends from the alternative ways in which the available means can be employed to secure them.

Once the question is broached in particular, however, it is immediately apparent that there are a number of subproblems connected with the defense budget which make it extremely difficult to find a rational answer to the question of how much to spend.[8] It is

[7] In addition to providing a formal charter for the Joint Chiefs of Staff and their Joint Staff, the 1947 act established the National Security Council, the Central Intelligence Agency, and a "unified" National Military Establishment under the Office of the Secretary of Defense. For this legislation and its development, see Walter Millis, Harvey Mansfield, and Harold Stein, *Arms and The State* (New York, The Twentieth Century Fund, 1958), chap. 4. Congress, on its part, merged its formerly separate committees for War and Navy Department affairs and appropriations into single armed services and military appropriations committees. See Elias Huzar, *The Purse and The Sword* (Ithaca, Cornell University Press, 1950), pp. 27–29.

[8] For stylistic convenience, the phrase "how much for defense" will be frequently used instead of the more explicit "how much for what kind of defense." The thoughts that follow on rationality and defense budgeting were set in motion some time ago by Bernard Brodie's "Strategy as a Science," *World Politics*, July 1949, pp. 467–88.

further apparent that, despite the susceptibility of the question to rational investigation, the answer must be determined as much through the interplay of power and interest as through the interplay of information and reason. An appreciation of these two central aspects of defense budgeting—the inordinate intellectual difficulty of the problems involved, and the fact that they are resolved through the medium of politics as well as that of analysis—is essential for an understanding of the post-1945 budgeting process and the kind of budgets produced by that process.

The intellectual difficulty of determining on a rational defense budget can largely be attributed to five of the more salient subproblems associated with it. The first is the problem of purpose. Defense preparations have no meaning except in their relationship to the foreign policy purposes of the nation, but this relationship is not always easy to establish. In the first half of the century, except just before and during time of war itself, civilian statesmen demonstrated very little interest in how the plans and preparations of the armed forces were related to the nation's foreign policy. Military planners were left to guess at the course of the nation's foreign policy as best they could.[9] With the end of World War II, the need for a much closer relationship between foreign policy and defense preparations than had heretofore prevailed was formally recognized with the creation of the National Security Council in 1947. But the existence of such an agency guarantees only that a forum is available for the discussion of the problem. It is not a guarantee that the problem will be resolved to the satisfaction of everyone concerned. Civilian statesmen may find themselves so uncertain or divided regarding the nation's foreign policy purposes and problems as to be unable to give military planners the guidance they would like. Statesmen may also at times be unwilling to do so, for there is a basic conflict between the two groups in their orientation toward the common problem. For the military, a "rational" defense policy requires their sharpest possible definition of foreign policy goals, so that their preparations can be made in full knowledge of the

[9] See Millis, Mansfield, and Stein, *Arms and the State,* Chap. 1, and the present author's "Civil-Naval Politics in World War I," *World Politics,* July 1955, pp. 572–91.

ends to be served. But for statesmen, a "rational" foreign policy may on occasion call for a calculated ambiguity regarding certain purposes or may require holding fast to a latitude of choice with regard to future courses of action.[10]

The second subproblem in rational defense budgeting is that posed by the existence of alternative means. And if it is not always easy to identify the foreign policy purposes for which preparations may be required, it is even more difficult to specify the means which will best serve those purposes. There exists a wide variety of weapons systems from which to choose, both among those in hand and among those capable of future development. Here, too, choice is complicated by basic conflicts in orientation, this time among military planners themselves. Military science is not normally so exact as to rule out all but one school of thought on the question of how battles are to be fought and wars won. As a result, military planners frequently find themselves uncertain or divided regarding the kinds of preparations necessary to support the foreign policy purposes of the nation. There is, moreover, the additional complication that some purposes might alternatively be met through nonmilitary means, that is, through economic or diplomatic arrangements, or through the allocation of American resources to advance the military power of other nations.

The determination of the size and kind of forces required would be easier if it were not for the third problem: that caused by the fact that the future is normally uncertain and indeterminate. It is impossible to predict with assurance which of the nation's purposes will be challenged or how and when.[11] Nor is there any ready

[10] On the conflict in general, see Fox, "Civilians, Soldiers, and American Military Policy," *World Politics*, April 1955, pp. 416–17. For complaints that the military receive insufficient and imprecise guidance, which are disparate enough in time and circumstance to suggest that the problem is chronic, see "Civil-Naval Politics in World War I," *World Politics*, July 1955, pp. 578–79; *National Security Organization*, A Report With Recommendations Prepared For the Commission on Organization of the Executive Branch of the Government by The Committee on National Security Organization (Washington, 1949), p. 37; and General Maxwell P. Taylor, *The Uncertain Trumpet* (New York, Harper and Brothers, 1960), pp. 82–83, 87.

[11] This problem may be considerably eased for a nation which is planning to initiate the use of force in pursuit of one or more of its objectives.

calculus through which probabilities of occurrence can be safely related to quantities of preparation. An estimate that there is only one chance in three of war does not mean that security can be purchased by providing only one-third of the force that would be required to fight it. In the face of uncertainty regarding the intentions and actions of possible opponents, military planners may responsibly press for preparation in full against problematical contingencies. In this respect, military defense is often likened to insurance. As one Senator phrased it during the debate on the fiscal 1950 budget, the nation was paying "an insurance premium on democracy." [12] But there is more than one point to the parallel; for nations, as with individuals, there is no way to determine objectively how much insurance it is rational to carry.

The defense budget is also very much unlike life insurance. The amount purchased of the latter normally has no influence on the health of the insured. In contrast, the kind of armament a nation carries may have a most significant influence on the course of its political life. The need to estimate this influence in advance constitutes the fourth major problem in defense budgeting. Nor is it always an easy matter to tell whether additional arms will have a provocative or a deterrent effect, whether they will serve to ease or to exacerbate security problems with other nations.

Last but not least, there is the problem of cost. Security is not the only national goal, nor is defense the only activity that lays claim to the government's budget. Resources allocated to defense are resources no longer available for the satisfaction of other values. Where is the balance to be struck, what constitutes a rational allocation of national resources? Again, there are basic conflicts in orientation to this question. Officials responsible for serving the range of national values will take quite a different view of costs than that taken by those responsible for servicing only one value, whether military security or some other. In addition to differences in approach, there will also be basic conflicts in judgment. People who differ in the value they attach to welfare goals will necessarily differ

---

[12] *Congressional Record*, 81st Cong., 1st Sess., Vol. 95, pt. 9 [hereafter cited as *C.R.*, 95], p. 12250.

in their sense for the "cost" of a given defense budget to those goals. The same will hold for those who differ in the value they assign to foreign policy goals. Needless to say, these judgments are not made any easier by the four problems discussed above. Both singly and in combination they make it extremely difficult to estimate the costs of alternative military budgets for foreign policy goals. As a result, even people with common evaluations of security and welfare goals may find themselves in conflict regarding the size of the defense budget.

The point to these five problems is simple. A multiplicity of answers, all of them "right," must be admitted to the question of how much it is rational to spend for defense. The opportunities for reasoned and intelligent conflict with regard to the factual premises involved are legion. The questions of value involved are, in the final analysis, matters of personal preference. Inevitably, then, there will be differences and uncertainty—regarding the foreign policy goals to be served; regarding the relative utility of the various means available to implement those goals; regarding the shape of the future; regarding the impact on that future of the means under consideration; and regarding the costs it is desirable to incur for defense. Uncertainties and differences of this order can have but one result. Good, intelligent, and dedicated men will be found on all sides of the question of how much and what kind of defenses the nation should buy. They will disagree on the answer to this question, and they will dispute it with a passion appropriate to the seriousness of the choices involved.

The fact that questions of value are at stake insures that there can be no one determinate answer to the problem of how much to spend for defense. The inevitability of equally plausible but conflicting factual premises insures that there will not even be determinate answers to questions regarding the consequences for this or that value if one or another alternative course of action is followed. There are, accordingly, no individuals who can provide determinate answers: not in the Defense Department, in the State Department, in Congress, or in the Office of the President. Choice is unavoidable: choice among the values to be served, and choice among the divergent conceptions of what will happen if such and such is done.

It is for this reason that the defense budget, while susceptible to rational analysis, remains a matter for political resolution. Choices of this order can be made in only one place: the political arena. There the relative importance of values can be decided by the relative power brought to bear on their behalf. There the distribution of power can decide matters that the distribution of fact and insight cannot.

III

Recognition that the defense budget is necessarily a problem for political choice, that even in theory there is no one "right" budget, points directly to the importance of exploring the process through which these choices are made. Such an inquiry is obviously in order for an understanding of the manner in which these complicated and consequential problems are actually resolved. Less obvious, perhaps, is the fact that knowledge about how these choices are made can also contribute to an understanding of the kind of choices that are made. There are, then, two questions to be asked about the budgeting process: how are these choices made? and what kind of choices are made as a result of the way in which they are made?

The phrasing of the second of these two questions is by no means meant to suggest that the content of a defense budget can be mainly explained in terms of the working of the political process through which it was determined. The kind of defenses a budget provides will be primarily a reflection of the kind of ideas people have about the political-military world in which they are living, the kind of answers they have in mind for the five problems discussed above.[13] But the influence exercised on the content of the budget by the character of the political process, while definitely subordinate, is not insignificant. The political process is the medium through which differing ideas about the world are affirmed or rejected as a basis for policy, that choice is made among divergent answers to the

[13] For a general discussion of the relationship between the "fund of ideas" policy-makers have and the policy-making process, see Bernard C. Cohen, "Foreign Policy-Making: Modern Design," *World Politics*, April 1953, pp. 377–91.

policy problems of the budget, and it is through this selective function that the political process can exercise an influence on both the content and the form of policy.

The kind of influence exercised by the political process will depend on the nature of the policy biases that are built into it. No political process is ever entirely "neutral" with regard to the kind of policies it will produce. As American politicians recognized when they met to design their Constitution, to change the way in which policy is made is often as good a route toward a desired change in policy as a direct attack on the particulars of the policy.[14] It is for this reason that the structure of the political process—how power and responsibility are distributed among the participants—is itself a "political" issue. Accordingly, just as there is no one "right" budget, so, too, there can be no one "right" budgeting process. So long as the participants differ in their conception of what constitutes the "right" budget, they should also be expected to differ in their conception of how power and responsibility should be distributed among those who determine that budget.

What is true for the structure of the political process generally is equally relevant to administrative structure in particular. If administrative organization is conceived, as Arthur Macmahon has suggested, as a device for arranging minds to work on a given problem, the opportunities for affecting a change in policy through a change in organization are readily apparent.[15] The design of an organization involves a choice as to the kinds of minds to be arranged (what values and what skills they are to represent) and a choice as to how they are to be arranged (what influence they are to exercise in the resolution of the problem). Changes in organizational design, by

[14] The insistence, for example, of the southern states at the Constitutional Convention that the Senate be required to ratify treaties by a two-thirds vote (rather than some other arrangement) reflected a very definite policy objective. They wanted to make certain that, whatever else the new Federal government might do in foreign affairs, there would be no further negotiation with Spain to enlist her help against the British in the north in return for the concession to Spain of American claims to the Mississippi. See Samuel Flagg Bemis, *A Diplomatic History of the United States* (New York, Henry Holt and Company, rev. ed., 1942), pp. 78–80. The phrasing of the "neutrality" point is Richard E. Neustadt's.

[15] Arthur W. Macmahon, *Administration in Foreign Affairs* (University, Alabama, University of Alabama Press, 1953), p. 1.

changing the kind of values and skills brought to bear on a problem or the relative order of their influence in its resolution, can therefore have a decided effect on the content of policy. Hence the opportunity to practice "politics through reorganization." However, as in the case with variations in the political process generally (where the consequences for policy are likely to be far less than those which would result from variations in the body of ideas the participants have about the political-military problems with which they are engaged), the opportunity to change policy by reorganizing those who make it is definitely limited. Organization can bring minds together, but it cannot make them think.

These points—that there is no determinate answer to the question of how much to spend for defense, that the budget is necessarily a problem in political choice, that the kind of budget chosen, while primarily a result of the ideas policy-makers have about the problems involved, will also be influenced by the kind of political process in which their choices are made, and that the character of this process is itself a matter of political choice—constitute the central points of departure for this analysis of the fiscal 1950 budget. It will be the purpose of the chapters that follow to describe the political process through which that budget was determined; to examine the relationship between that process and the content and form of the budget; and, using this specific case as a point of reference, to discuss in more general terms the prospects for affecting changes in the character of American defense budgets through changes in the character of the budgeting process. The reader should bear in mind that, although considerable attention will be given to the relationship between the content of the fiscal 1950 budget and the policy ideas of those who determined it, the primary focus will be on what was, in reality, the less consequential relationship, that between process and choice. The reason for accenting the less influential relationship is that many of the policy ideas current in 1948 and 1949 are today mainly of historical interest and relevance, whereas the conditions under which the fiscal 1950 choices were made closely approximate those under which present and future defense budgets will be determined.

A word of caution is in order about the factual picture which will be presented here of the issues at stake in the fiscal 1950 budget and the manner in which they were resolved. The information available from the public record, while extensive, is far short of that necessary for a complete account of these matters. There is, for example, very little evidence with which to illustrate one of the more outstanding features of the political process: the multiplicity of informal communications among the participants. Equally restrictive is the fact that many of the documents which would illuminate the fiscal, foreign policy, and military issues connected with the budget are still classified. These limitations impose serious handicaps on the narrative and the analysis it can support. Thus, an account of Congressional action on the budget must be made in the absence of information bearing on the informal contacts Congressmen had with each other and members of the Executive and without reference to such documents as may exist indicating the content of the formal but off-the-record testimony received by the concerned Congressional committees.

An additional handicap is involved in the case of Executive action on the budget. Here most of the available evidence is provided by Walter Millis' edition of *The Forrestal Diaries*. This is a very valuable source, and without it the present study would not have been feasible. The difficulty with this source, however, is that it presents primarily a picture of events as seen and interpreted by the Secretary of Defense, James Forrestal. As a result, an account based on it runs the risk of being one-dimensional in its presentation, for it can be safely presumed that each of the major participants had a significantly different picture of the events in which they were jointly engaged and a different conception of the considerations that prompted their own and each other's actions.

The present author has made a modest effort through interviews and other sources to add to the information heretofore available about the fiscal 1950 budget and to secure a sense for how its development appeared from institutional vantages other than Forrestal's. It should be clear, however, that the narrative which follows will not be a detailed and documented history. It is presented rather as an outline of events and perspectives which will be sufficient to sustain an analysis in terms of the points advanced in this Introduction.[16]

Before the discussion of the fiscal 1950 budget is undertaken, one final introductory task remains to be accomplished. This is to delineate briefly the nature of the political process through which American foreign policy is made. The "budgeting process" is a particular manifestation of this more general process and will be better understood if seen in this context. There are, in addition, certain consequences for the form of policy that follow from the character of this general process, and it will be useful to have these in mind when examining the relationship between the budgeting process and the form of the defense budget. Finally, barring a major revolution in the American political system, the characteristics of this general process set the limits within which possible changes in the budgeting process can be realistically discussed.

IV

The key components of the foreign policy process, following closely the terminology and concepts of Gabriel Almond, can be broadly described as follows: an elite structure characterized by a large number of autonomous and competing groups; and a mass structure characterized by a small, informed stratum, attentive to elite discussion and conflict, and a much larger base normally ignorant of and indifferent to policy and policy-making.

The condition responsible for the competitive character of the elite structure is obvious; members of the policy elite normally differ and differ significantly about both the ends and the means of foreign policy. The autonomy of the elite structure is the result of

[16] I would like to express here my great appreciation for the time and consideration certain past and present government officials gave to my research inquiries. Some have requested that they remain anonymous. I have also omitted reference in the text or footnotes to the use of interview material in the case of central participants in the determination of the budget; they are few, and I alone am responsible for the use and interpretation I have made of the information and insight they so kindly provided. In all other instances, the text or footnotes will indicate the use of interview data, some of which was secured in connection with my study of the H-bomb decision of 1950.

the fact that power is both widely dispersed among the participants in the policy process and drawn from a variety of sources independent one from the other. The group character of elite politics reflects both of these circumstances. The diffusion of power means that various members of the policy elite must group together on the basis of some amalgam of interest if they are to have any prospect of seeing their individual preferences compete successfully against the goals and programs advanced by others. The absence of a single locus of power or a base from which it can be monopolized also means that policy, once formulated, must continue to depend upon the voluntary coordination of elite groups if it is to be effective.[17]

It is this dependence of the elites, one upon the other, for both the formulation and the conduct of policy, and the absence of any single chain of command whereby their cooperation can be assured, that Roger Hilsman has highlighted with his description of the policy process as one of "conflict and consensus-building." For the would-be policy advocate must do more than contend with the opponents of his program; he must develop support for it throughout the relevant parts of the elite structure and, on occasion, the mass structure as well. If, by means of persuasion and judicious accommodation to the interests of others, he is able to bring the weight of opinion to his cause, the resulting agreement will probably insure the adoption of his policy and its effective implementation. Failing such support, or lacking the political skills and prestige prerequisite for an opportunity to secure it, or confronted from the beginning by a wide and politically unassailable consensus to the contrary, the realistic policy advocate will turn his political energies to more promising issues. For however wise his idea and cogent his argument or extensive his personal influence, his will remain a voice in the policy wilderness.[18]

---

[17] Gabriel Almond, *The American People and Foreign Policy* (New York, Harcourt, Brace and Company, 1950), pp. 136–45.

[18] For Hilsman's analysis, which has contributed much to that which here follows, see his "The Foreign-Policy Consensus: An Interim Report," *Conflict Resolution*, December 1959, pp. 361–82, and his "Congressional–Executive Relations and the Foreign Policy Consensus," *The American Political Science Review*, September 1958, pp. 725–44. Samuel P. Huntington's "Strategic Planning and the Political Process," *Foreign Affairs*, January 1960, pp. 285–99, is

The characteristics of elite structure and elite relations just outlined are general to all policy-making situations, although the number, size, and kind of elite groups necessary for the formulation and conduct of policy—and, therefore, the kind of consensus required—will, of course, vary greatly with the issues and circumstances involved. The policy process is by no means confined to the structure of government, and the policy elite includes a very large number of people who are not government officials. However, since the issues and circumstances with which this study will later be concerned involve mainly government elites and government structure, it will be useful to continue the development of the above concepts primarily in this context.

It is, to begin with, important to note that there are two basic causes for policy conflict among government elites and that these lead to two different kinds of groupings among them. Many of these conflicts simply reflect the diversity of opinion Americans are likely to hold, in the absence of sanctions to the contrary, regarding the state of the world and what America should do in it. The groups that coalesce in support of one or another of these views appear, for the most part, to cut across formal institutional and organizational lines (Congress, Executive, State, Defense).[19]

In contrast, some policy conflicts are "institutionally grounded." These are differences that result from the peculiar responsibilities (with respect either to values or to skills) of various government institutions and organizations. Not sharing the same responsibilities (or, put the other way, not charged with the representation of the same values or skills), government organizations will necessarily bring divergent interests and approaches to common problems. When conflicts of this order occur, the lines of battle are more likely to conform to the boundaries of the organizations involved. These are also the more enduring of the two kinds of group conflict. Specific ideas about what to do in the world will change, and with them the ad hoc groupings that once espoused them. But divergent

_____

reasoned from a somewhat different conceptual framework, but reaches several of the same conclusions.

[19] See Hilsman, "The Foreign-Policy Consensus: An Interim Report," *Conflict Resolution*, December 1959, pp. 365–66, 379.

responsibilities are built into the structure of government. The allocation of responsibility may be changed, but the effect is usually to shift the location of battle rather than to bring it to an end.

Conflicts caused by divergent institutional interests and approaches are an integral part of the policy-making process. They are especially evident, as will be seen, in the budgeting process as it takes place among the "quasi-sovereign powers"—the departments, bureaus, and agencies—that make up the Executive branch of the government. The general character of conflict between such "powers" is in many respects comparable to the diplomatic struggle among contending nations.[20] Each endeavors to isolate the other, to secure "allies" for itself, and to gain the favorable opinion of "neutrals"— activities of great importance given the dispersion of power among elite groups. Discussions between the contending parties are negotiatory rather than analytical in character. The object is to persuade the opponent that his position is unreasonable (either by arguments designed to show that it will not really serve his interest or by appeals to other interests alleged to be both common and more important), or, failing that, to search for grounds on which a satisfactory settlement can be made. This may take the form of a direct compromise on the issue concerned (where the incentive to accommodate stems from the desire to avoid the costs of even a winning fight) or of a bargain reached by bringing into negotiation another issue in dispute and thereby permitting each (provided they evaluate the two issues disproportionately) to give up something of less value than that which it receives. In inter-institutional as in international relations, however, not all negotiations terminate in settlements, and the course of conflict is therefore marked by the postponement of disputes and by truces as well as treaties.

There is, of course, a very important difference between the conflicts of nations and those of government organizations: the coercive options available to the latter do not include the infliction of death. As a result, although the elements of conflict and accom-

---

[20] The comparison was first called to the present author's attention by William T. R. Fox, and it has heavily influenced the research and writing of this study. The analogy is also discussed by Hilsman, *ibid.*, pp. 367–71.

modation are present in both relationships, the basic orientation of the two is quite different. The diplomacy of nations is ever oriented to the prospect of war, and conflict is marked by a high propensity to arm and prepare for the worst. The negotiations of government elites, in contrast, are oriented to the prospect of agreement, and conflict is marked by a high propensity to search for a way of resolving it. In sum, the general pattern of these quasi-sovereign relations is marked by two dominant characteristics. Conflict most certainly is one. The other is the "strain toward agreement," the need to build a consensus that includes, as it were, one's enemies as well as one's friends.

The imperative to strive for agreement, to reach some sort of accommodation, is a logical derivative of the condition noted earlier: the autonomy of the elite structure. Power is diffused among Executive organizations no less than among other elite groups. The dispersion of power means that the contending groups will need the support of each other, as well as that of allies and neutrals, in order to translate their goals into policy—if not today on this issue, then tomorrow on some other. The opportunities to compel this support are minimal. It must be given, and it is unlikely for long to be given for nothing. The major motive for accommodation is necessity; there are simply not very many occasions when the policy elites can afford the luxury of letting their conflicts terminate in "war." A secondary motive, but one not to be overlooked, is desire. Competing elites not only need to accommodate, they want to. They do have interests in common, and one is the desire not to see the nation without any policy at all on an issue of consequence. To be sure, there will be occasions when "no" policy seems preferable to "wrong" policy, but there will be others when what seems to be a pressing necessity for action will produce some scratch formula for accommodation that the parties would otherwise have dismissed as neither rational nor expedient.[21]

The policy elites are drawn together, then, by the same conditions

[21] As many observers of American foreign policy have marked, American politicians sometimes have a regrettable tendency to carry this "strain toward agreement" out of the domestic political arena and into the international.

that permit them to fall apart: the fact that they are many in number and the fact that power is widely diffused among them. For those interested in the parallel with international relations, it should be noted that the same two conditions (many states, none of which has a hegemony of power) are responsible for the "strain toward equilibrium"—the effort to maintain the balance of power—in the conflict among nations. Equilibrium is thus the functional analogue of agreement. Here, too, dependence provides the motive, so long as the diversity of interests pursued by the nations making up the system makes plausible the expectation that today's ally may be tomorrow's enemy, and vice versa.

The existence of this "strain toward agreement" does not mean, of course, that the policy process puts Humpty Dumpty back together again. There are conflicts, and they do persist. Accommodation does not always have the effect of resolution. The life expectancy of "treaties" among Executive agencies is probably no greater than it is for those made in international relations, and many accommodations are mere makeshifts made for the moment. Indeed, as Samuel Huntington has pointed out, in some instances the necessary minimum of voluntary coordination is secured only by an agreement to postpone the occasion for disagreement, that is, by postponing decision. In this case the strain toward agreement produces the façade, not the substance, of agreement. The conflict is put off, but so too is the policy problem at issue and the opportunity to reach a consensus as to what to do about it.[22]

This last point is a proper introduction to the question of the relationship between the characteristics of the policy-making process and the form of the policy produced by that process. American foreign policy is, in fact, subject to a variety of symptoms as a result of the way in which it is made. The symptoms that make up this "policy syndrome" derive, in one way or another, from the autonomous and competing character of the policy elites and the resultant necessity for voluntary coordination among them.

Most of the consequences of such an elite structure have been

[22] Huntington, "Strategic Planning and the Political Process," *Foreign Affairs*, January 1960, pp. 291–92.

well marked by Almond. There is, to begin with, the clear possibility that the policy elites may produce "no policy at all." Their conflict can result in pure stalemate. Equally obvious are the possibilities for "compromised policy," where alternatives may be so watered by accommodation that the direction of choice is hardly evident; "unstable policy," where changes in the ad hoc groupings of elites point policy first in one and then in another direction; and "contradictory policy," where the quasi-sovereign power and responsibility of government institutions and organizations permit them independently to follow different policies.

Additional symptoms derive from the need to achieve a consensus for the support of policy, especially if the consensus has to be a wide one. Here there is the possibility of "paper policy," the case where policy has been duly and officially promulgated, but the support necessary for effective implementation by all concerned is simply nonexistent. Where policy problems happen to be new or technical in nature, those members of the elite perceptive and informed enough to recognize them may find it difficult if not impossible to secure this recognition from others, much less build a consensus for action. The result is what they at least would characterize as "blind policy."

Other symptoms mark the style of the policy process itself. It is "slow." Competition and consensus-building cannot take place overnight, and the delay between the recognition of a problem and the development of a policy for it may sometimes take longer than the exigencies of the situation seem to warrant or, in fact, permit. The policy process also has a tendency to be "leaderless." [23] The diffusion of power and responsibility places the initiative everywhere with the result that it is sometimes exercised nowhere; the elites

[23] The ability of the President to impose his will on the quasi-sovereignties that make up the Executive is limited. In terms of the international relations analogy used here, the President is more like a Super-Power, in that he is the most important ally to be enlisted. On occasion, however, the power of the President is not unlike that of that imaginary entity, "the United Nations"; his ability to enforce his will is more a function of his capacity to mobilize the power of his constituents than it is of his own personal resources. See Richard E. Neustadt, *Presidential Power* (New York, John Wiley and Sons, 1960), especially chaps. 2 and 3.

assume a "radar approach" to policy-making, each watching and waiting upon the other. The absence of a single source for coordination may also permit the process of accommodation to produce such a composite of everyone's interests that the rationale of the final result will not be apparent to anyone. A third stylistic symptom is the tendency of the policy process to be "indecisive." As previously noted, the desire to avert conflict may easily take the form of avoiding choice.[24]

Finally, as William Fox has observed, the policy process exercises a "gyroscopic" effect on policy. Policies once set in motion tend to go on and on, without much regard, at times, for changes in the circumstances that first occasioned them. In part this is related to the need for agreement; the best way to maintain a consensus is not to disturb it. It also reflects the fact that the time and energy of the policy elites are limited. Most policy problems are very difficult; so, too, is the process of reaching an agreement on what to do about them. The combination of the two difficulties can easily lead the policy elites, once they have thought and fought their way through to an operational consensus, to adopt an attitude of leaving well enough alone. And so they do, until some drastic change occurs in their environment which sharply and dramatically challenges the wisdom and feasibility of the previous course of action. The policy consequence is "outmoded policy," and the stylistic consequence is "crisis-oriented" diplomacy.[25]

The tendency of policy change to wait on crises is reinforced whenever the required consensus necessitates the participation of the general public. Being, as noted, normally ignorant of and indifferent to policy events, the masses can be spurred to action (that is, to part with their blood, treasure, or votes) only when the elites

[24] The preceding points are a modified version of those listed by Almond, *The American People and Foreign Policy*, pp. 144–46. For what is here called "blind" policy and "leaderless" and "indecisive" policy, see also the characteristics listed by Hilsman, "The Foreign Policy Consensus: An Interim Report," *Conflict Resolution*, December 1959, pp. 362, 373, and Huntington, "Strategic Planning and Political Process," *Foreign Affairs*, January 1960, pp. 292–95. The reference to the "radar approach" is from Fox, "Civilians, Soldiers, and American Military Policy," *World Politics*, April 1955, p. 414.

[25] Fox, "American Military Policy," *World Politics*, April 1955, p. 415.

confront them with what seem to be the gravest of problems. But once aroused, since the public's response is emotional rather than intellectual in content, its participation may produce such policy symptoms as "over-reaction" (more apprehension or belligerence than the elites may find appropriate) and "short-reaction" (where the public sense of crisis disappears before the problem is actually resolved).[26]

All this is not to say that the defense budget for fiscal 1950, because it was fashioned in the policy process, will necessarily be found to have been made up of compromised and contradictory policies, with some areas where there was no policy at all, others where policy kept changing, and still others where it was ineffectual or blind. Nor is the preceding discussion necessarily meant to predict that little leadership controlled the content of the budget, that it had no central rationale, that it deliberately avoided major choices, that it was either fashioned in crisis or made more with reference to precedent than to the world about it, or that it proved out of date by the time it was complete. But should the budget prove to have some, several, or all of these characteristics, the burden of the preceding discussion is that it will not have been by accident of the time, the problems, and the people involved. The burden further is that, in this event, no matter how unattractive or inappropriate from hindsight may seem the form of the budget's choices or the style in which they were made, considerable caution must be exercised in any discussion of how things might have been different.

[26] On the general character of the public's response and participation in foreign policy, see Almond, *The American People and Foreign Policy*, Chaps. 3–4, especially pp. 53–54, 85–86.

The emotional rather than intellectual character of the public's response to the elite discussion also makes possible "under-reaction," for not all policy problems can be presented as crises (for example, the question of civil defense). Other consequences follow for the style of the elite-mass discussion. There is a constant temptation for the elites to engage in "simplistic" or "demagogic" statement or to practice outright "duplicity."

II *The Budget*

The security position of the United States at the beginning of 1948, when work on the defense budget for the fiscal year 1950 was about to commence, was midway through the revolutionary change described earlier. Russian nuclear weapons were still for the future. The balance of power in Europe, on the other hand, was already a thing of the past. The lands west of the Iron Curtain were militarily enfeebled, economically distressed, and politically, in several cases, besieged by domestic Communist parties. The once mighty nations of western Europe were in no condition, singly or collectively, to contain the military power of the Soviet Union, even in the face of the severe material and personnel losses that nation had itself suffered as a result of the war. There was, in short, nothing the Europeans could do to prevent the Russians from achieving at their will what had just been so painfully wrested from the hands of the Germans: an empire embracing all the peoples, skills, and resources of the Old World.

By January 1948 American policy-makers were alert to the problem and at work on it. Symbolic of the developing consensus regarding the extent and dimensions of the Soviet threat, George Kennan's famous analysis—which had been circulated confidentially among government officials in February 1946—appeared publicly in the July 1947 issue of *Foreign Affairs*. Action, as well as analysis, had been developing. In March 1947, with the Truman Doctrine, a beginning had been made to substitute American for European power along the periphery of the Soviet Union, and in June of 1947 Secretary of State George Marshall took the first step in the plan to revitalize European power itself.

The "objective of our policy from this point on," Marshall had declared at a Cabinet meeting in November 1947, "would be the restoration of the balance of power in both Europe and Asia and . . . all actions would be viewed in light of these objectives." Although the formal commitment of American power to help make up the balance in Europe was, in 1948, still a year away, the de facto commitment was present in the Mediterranean, in the form of a naval task force, and in Germany, Austria, and Trieste, where some 113,000 American troops stood providing the function that under later NATO strategy was to be glorified as "plate glass." To deter the Red Army from breaking it, there was the industrial superiority that had twice defeated Germany, together with several hundred medium-range bombers and some unknown number of atomic bombs to put in them.[1]

The change in America's security position was similarly reflected in the level of defense expenditures since the end of the war. Expenditures on the armed services under President Truman's first peacetime budget, that presented to Congress in January 1946 for the fiscal year 1947, were $11.8 billion out of a total budget of $39.2 billion. The sums for fiscal 1948 were $10.5 billion and $33.7 billion, and the budget just presented to Congress in January 1948—for fiscal 1949—estimated defense expenditures at $10 billion out of a total of $39.6 billion. These figures stand in some contrast to those for the years immediately preceding the attack on Pearl Harbor: $1.4 billion out of a total of $8.7 billion for fiscal 1939; $1.8 billion out of $9.1 billion for fiscal 1940; and $6.3 billion out of $12.7 billion for fiscal 1941. Expressed in terms of a percentage of gross national

[1] For the circulation of Kennan's memorandum, Marshall's statement, and the disposition of American ships and troops in Europe, see Millis, ed., *The Forrestal Diaries*, pp. 135–40, 302, 341, 375.

The Truman administration was to be notably unsuccessful in its effort to "restore" the balance of power in Asia. Although the march to power of the Chinese Communists was still a third development of great consequence for American foreign policy that was under way on the eve of the fiscal 1950 budget, it was not of the same revolutionary character as the two discussed above. The problems occasioned by the rise and expansion of China during the second half of the twentieth century are likely to be more serious for American foreign policy than those occasioned by Japan during the first half, but they are not strategically dissimilar.

product, military expenditures for the calendar years 1939, 1940, and 1941 had been 1.4, 3.9, and 13.1 percent, respectively. The figures for the calendar years 1946, 1947, and 1948 were 13.6, 5.3, and 4.7 percent.[2]

The point to these figures is not just that the United States came out of World War II spending much more money for defense than it had been spending before it went into the war. The same thing had happened following the war with Spain and, again, following World War I. What marks the post-World War II situation from these earlier cases is the magnitude of the increase involved. In the case of both the war with Spain and World War I, the postwar level of defense expenditures was about three times as high as the prewar level, whether measured by current or constant dollars. Following World War II, however, the postwar level (pre-Korea) was twelve times higher than the prewar level, measured in current dollars, and eight times as high in constant dollars.[3] Both the order of this increase, compared to that in the earlier wars, and the absolute differences in the size of the sums involved seem great enough to be considered a qualitative change from the earlier pattern of prewar-postwar spending. They would also appear to testify to the American sense that something was amiss in the nation's power relationship to the Old World.

The budgets for the fiscal years 1947, 1948, and 1949 were, then, fabulously large compared to the prewar defense budgets. But mere size, while suggestive, is not very meaningful. What did budgets of this particular size have to do with the' security problem at hand?

[2] See United States Bureau of the Budget, *The Budget of the United States Government for the Fiscal Year Ending June 30, 1954* (Washington, 1953), p. 1136 [hereafter cited as *U.S. Budget, FY*]; *U.S. Budget, FY 1949,* p. M11; *U.S. Budget, FY 1947,* p. 777; and M. Slade Kendrick, *A Century and a Half of Federal Expenditures* (New York, National Bureau of Economic Research, Inc., 1955), pp. 12, 77.

The government's fiscal year commences in July of the preceding calendar year. The fiscal 1950 budget, for example, provided the funds for government expenditures and the authorizations for government contracts for the period July 1, 1949, through June 30, 1950.

[3] Kendrick, *A Century and a Half of Federal Expenditures,* pp. 11–12, 82. The "level" or plateau character of spending between wars can be easily seen in Kendrick's complete tables.

By what strategy did the United States plan to cope with its new military position? And how were the forces provided by these budgets related to that strategy? These are questions to which, as will become apparent during the course of this study, different Americans gave different answers. Within the administration, however, the dominant conceptions of the time were those summarized by James Forrestal in a letter written in December 1947.

Forrestal, who had earlier, in July, been appointed the nation's first Secretary of Defense, wrote the letter to Senator Chan Gurney, Republican of South Dakota and then Chairman of the Senate Armed Services Committee. The purpose of the letter was to provide the Senator with a private comment on a newspaper editorial which had suggested that the United States really had only two alternatives in Europe: either to raise enough American troops to hold it or to pull out altogether. Forrestal rejected both alternatives.

Certainly we can not default Europe to Russia. To do so would mean that within the next two decades North America would be open to successful attack by a totalitarian land power augmented by the naval and air power which the resources of all Europe are capable of producing if brought under a single authoritarian management.

On the other hand, while the United States could mobilize sufficient force to hold Europe against a Russian attack, the effort would press the American economy to its limits. Nothing would be left to finance European economic recovery and European rearmament. This, too, Forrestal thought an undesirable alternative.

As you know, I hold that world stability will not be restored until the vacuum created by the destruction of German power and the weakening of the power of Western Europe has been filled—in other words, until a balance of power has been restored in Europe.

To restore this balance, "to follow a course which offers a prospect of eventually achieving national security and also long-term world stability," Forrestal was willing to accept what he called a "calculated risk" for American security in the short term. It was perfectly true, he admitted, that the current level of defense spending kept American forces below "the minimum which would in

themselves ensure national security." But doing so made available
the money with which the United States could assist the economic
and military recovery of western Europe. As for the risk the United
States would meanwhile run, there were for the moment "certain
military advantages which go far toward covering the risk." Russia
had predominant land power in Europe and Asia, but the United
States had predominant sea power, exclusive possession of the
atomic bomb, and the superior industrial plant.

As long as we can outproduce the world, can control the sea and can
strike inland with the atomic bomb, we can assume certain risks otherwise unacceptable in an effort to restore world trade, to restore the balance
of power—military power—and to eliminate some of the conditions
which breed war.

The years before any possible power can achieve the capability to
attack us with weapons of mass destruction are our years of opportunity.[4]

II

This was a good strategy, even a very good strategy. But time
and circumstance can deal harshly with the best of plans, and they
were to show little respect for this one. It had four fundamental
flaws. Two were errors of commission: (1) it greatly overestimated
the difficulty the Russians would have in developing the capability
to deliver an intercontinental nuclear attack and the time it would
take them to do so; and (2) it greatly underestimated the difficulty
the United States would have in rearming the western Europeans
and hence the time it would take "to restore" the European balance
of power.[5] The other two errors were those of omission: (1) the
strategy did not provide for the possibility that the United States
might meet formidable military problems that in their immediate

---

[4] Millis, ed., *The Forrestal Diaries*, pp. 349–51. The additional text quoted
is from the copy in the Forrestal Collection, Princeton University Library.
[5] What Marshall and Forrestal meant by "restoration" is not made explicit
in the available documents, but it is a fair reading that they had in mind
the development of a *European* force able to cope on its own with a Red Army
attack. Once accomplished, however, "restoration" was not to be the occasion
for the withdrawal of the United States from a commitment of its own power
to the defense of western Europe. It was expected that the United States
would continue to back up the Europeans with at least the A-bomb.

origin and character, at least, would involve neither Europe nor Soviet nuclear weapons; and (2) the strategy showed no appreciation for the fact that, once the Soviet Union *had* achieved the capability to attack the United States with nuclear weapons, American security would cease to pivot on the presence or absence of a European balance of power.

This last was intellectually the most serious error of all. By tying the prospect of "long-term world stability" to the restoration of the European balance of power, this strategy had confused the fact that the two revolutions in the American security position were occurring sequentially in time with the idea that they were aggregative in their significance. The first, the disappearance of the European balance of power, had seemed to italicize the importance of Europe for American security. The nation was now obliged to act towards Europe in time of peace in a manner that had heretofore been necessary only in time of war: the United States had to choose sides and commit its power. By 1948 this choice and commitment had been all but made, and it was duly ratified a year later in the North Atlantic Treaty. This was a truly revolutionary act, the first time that the nation had committed itself in advance of a European war to the terms and side on which it would fight since the ill-fated "permanent" alliance with France in 1778.[6]

Under these circumstances it was perhaps natural that the prospect of Russian nuclear weapons would be dimly seen as compounding but not altering the problem at hand. The fact of the matter, however, was that the effect of the second revolution would be to reduce the military significance of the first. The more developed Russian intercontinental nuclear striking power, the less important would be the addition of western Europe's people, skills, and resources for an attack on the United States and, perforce, the less significant the issue of the distribution of power on that Continent

[6] In essence, the United States changed from a strategy of no prior commitment, which, historically, had never prevented America's participation in the general wars of Europe, to a strategy of prior commitment, which, hopefully, would prevent a European war in the first place. See William T. R. Fox, "American Foreign Policy and the Western European Rimland," *Proceedings of the American Academy of Political Science*, January 1948, p. 74.

for the military security of the United States. This is not to say that
the import of the second revolution was that Europe would cease to
be an area of military and political interest for the United States
and the Soviet Union.[7] It is to say, however, that the import of the
two revolutions for American relations to Europe was to point those
relations in different directions; that the two revolutions represented
qualitatively different problems, not the unfolding of one steadily
worsening problem; and that in the preoccupation with the meaning
and meeting of the first, the strategy of Marshall and Forrestal had
not really faced up to the implications of the second.

The approach of the administration to the second revolution was
not an instance of "blind policy." A policy had been formulated to
meet it: international control of atomic energy by the United Nations.
By the fall of 1947 it was obvious that this policy had failed.[8] Yet
relatively little attention, compared to the plans made for Europe,
had been given to the development of another to take its place. The
priority given to the balance-of-power problem can be explained by
a variety of causes. To begin with, *this* problem was at hand; the
other was then thought to be quite distant. The time and energy
of government planners are limited, and in the absence of compelling
conditions to the contrary, planning which *has* to be done (because
of the pressure of clearly visible and immediately pressing events)
will normally take precedence over planning that *should* be done—
if planning priorities were set solely by a review of the full range
of foreseeable events and a dispassionate judgment among them
regarding the order of their importance.[9]

A second cause was the fact that the problem of the European
balance of power was a familiar one; analysis could be undertaken
against a background of both historical and personal experience.
The nuclear revolution, in contrast, had no precedent, and many
seemed to consider its analysis the prerogative of only those with

[7] For a discussion of the reassessments of the NATO commitment that the
advent of Soviet nuclear power was later to force, see Klaus Knorr, ed.,
NATO and American Security (Princeton, Princeton University Press, 1959).

[8] For the administration's recognition of this fact, see Millis, ed., *The Forrestal Diaries*, pp. 338–39, 424.

[9] Cf. Richard E. Neustadt, *Presidential Power* (New York, John Wiley and
Sons, 1960), pp. 155–58.

specialized and esoteric skills. A third cause, and one not to be dismissed lightly, was the extreme difficulty of the nuclear problem. Analysis simply did not bring forth strategies that had anywhere near the promise that was possible in the case of the European balance of power. The two problems were, after all, quite different in character. The European balance of power could, in theory at least, be restored, and with it a return to some semblance of the happy past would be possible. But with the collapse of the negotiations at the United Nations it was apparent that the nuclear genie was out of the bottle for good and that, whatever the strategy designed to cope with it, the nation was in for a time of change and peril.

The perplexing character of such strategy as existed can be seen in the contents of the report submitted in January 1948 by the President's Air Policy Commission. Bluntly entitled "Survival in the Air Age," the so-called Finletter Report grimly proclaimed January 1953 as the date by which the nation should be ready to deal with an atomic attack. Such an attack could come without warning, and if it came it would be with a violence calculated to destroy the cities and factories that had spelled victory in the last two wars. To meet this problem, the report declared, the United States required a "new strategy."

As outlined by the commission, there was nothing in this new strategy about the European balance of power, and very little about the Army or the Navy. What was required was a 70-group Air Force which, among other items, would provide for 700 very heavy bombers instead of the 580 bombers the Air Force then had under its budgeted strength of 55 groups. The strategic purpose of this force would be twofold: to win the atomic war if it came, and, hopefully, by confronting the Russians with "the prospect of a counterattack of the utmost violence," to persuade them not to attack in the first place.

The Finletter Report contained the threads of a strategy, but nowhere in the pages of the report were they united in a meaningful pattern. In one place the report stressed the need for an Air Force capable of smashing Russian cities and factories. The prospect

of having to pay such a "devastating price" would make them "hesitate to attack us." In another place, the emphasis was on the importance of a continental air defense system to protect American
cities and factories and on the need to launch a counterattack against
the Russian delivery forces "at the earliest possible moment." This
would "silence the attack on the United States mainland and give
us the time again to build up our industrial machine and our manpower to go on to win the war." The discussion of enemy strategy
was similarly divergent. One page affirmed that if the enemy had
learned anything from World Wars I and II, it had been the importance of not letting "United States industrial power get under way;
they must destroy it at the outset if they are to win." Yet on another
page, the report predicted that the targets for the enemy's first
bombardment would be the American air defense and counterattack
forces. Finally, nowhere in the report was an effort made to confront and answer a most uncomfortable question: if the United
States could achieve a counteroffensive blow of the magnitude described against Russian cities and delivery forces, why could not the
Russians do the same or better with their attacking blow? And, in
this event, against what and with what would the United States
launch its counterattack? [10]

What was advanced in the Finletter Report, clearly, was not a
"new strategy," but rather the problems and choices around which
the discussion of strategy was destined to revolve for years thereafter. The report did not appear to recognize the possible conflicts
between a strategy designed to deter an atomic attack and a strategy
designed to win an atomic war. Much less had it resolved those
conflicts into a coherent strategic doctrine. Yet without such a confrontation and resolution, the "new strategy" was something less
than complete. It would lack any criteria by which to allocate resources between defensive and offensive forces or to assign targets
(cities or delivery forces) to the latter.

For the moment, the ambiguities of the new strategy were of no
consequence. The Russians had yet to develop any bombs, and

[10] *Survival in the Air Age,* A Report by the President's Air Policy Commission (Washington, 1948), pp. 6, 10, 12, 14, 20, 23–25.

even after they began to do so there was every reason to expect that they would have far fewer bombs and bombers than the United States. The pinch of resources, and with it the hard choices and the need for clear doctrine, was in 1948 something for the distant future. The size and composition of the 70-group Air Force, the program endorsed by the Finletter Commission, could be, and obviously was, largely pulled out of the blue. It had, in fact, been first advanced early in 1945, before the disappearance of the Alamogordo tower had even so much as demonstrated the feasibility of the fission bomb.[11]

These, then, were the two basic strategic conceptions which had been evolved to meet America's new security position, and the two were to guide the formation of the fiscal 1950 budget. Neither strategy, it is important to note, took account of the other or of the problem that occasioned it. The "Forrestal" strategy failed to provide for the time when American security would no longer turn on the stability of the European balance of power. The "Finletter" strategy, while correctly anticipating that the future pivot would be the stability of the Soviet-American balance of terror, made no provision for the possibility that the United States would continue to have a political and military stake in the independence of western Europe.

Time was shortly to overrun both strategies. Ironically enough, so far as the fiscal 1950 budget was concerned, a major flaw in each was to show in 1949—before Congress had passed the budget, but well past the time when the Executive had prepared it. In the spring of that year, a State-Defense mission to Europe returned with the sobering news that the theoretical opportunity to create a balance against the Soviet Union did not exist as a practicality. The nations of western Europe were simply not prepared, at least for the time being, to make the expenditures that would be required. The mission suggested as an alternative that an effort be made to build enough power in western Europe to prevent the Russians

[11] For the background of the 70-group program and the Finletter Commission, see Walter Millis, Harvey Mansfield, and Harold Stein, *Arms and the State* (New York, The Twentieth Century Fund, 1958), pp. 147–48, 203, 205–8.

from overrunning it with the forces which they then had stationed in eastern Europe. By obliging the Russians to gather additional forces before attacking, the West would at least receive some warning that an attack was coming. During the next ten years NATO was to experience a variety of plans and postures: the abortive effort to rearm the Germans in 1950; the commitment of American troops in 1951; the plans for a 96-division force in 1952; the cutbacks of 1953; the admission of Germany and the decision to use nuclear weapons, regardless of whether or not the enemy did, in 1954—but by the end of the decade, NATO's military strength was still incapable of accomplishing any more than the task suggested in the spring of 1949.[12]

The second shock came in August 1949, when the Soviet Union exploded its first fission bomb. According to the Alsop brothers, the Joint Chiefs of Staff had not expected the Russians to make their first bomb until 1952 and were further planning (in contrast to the estimate of the Finletter Report) on the premise that it would take the Russians until 1955 to accumulate a stockpile of military significance. In October 1948 an account in the New York *Times*, which similarly reported 1952 as the year the Joint Chiefs anticipated the first Russian A-bomb, stated that a longer range JCS plan had estimated 1977 as the date when the Soviet Union would have "intercontinental rockets equipped with atomic warheads." As for an H-bomb, in 1948 this was a technical possibility known only to a handful of physicists and soldiers. It was considered by most to be a scientific puzzle, deserving of continued study, but one for which the prospects of a solution were hardly promising.[13]

The Russian explosion failed to force a clarification of the "new strategy," but it did lead to the American decision in January 1950 to make a more determined effort to explore the feasibility of an

[12] See *ibid.*, pp. 237–38, and Roger Hilsman, "On NATO Strategy," in Arnold Wolfers, ed., *Alliance Policy and the Cold War* (Baltimore, The Johns Hopkins Press, 1959).
[13] Joseph and Stewart Alsop, *The Reporter's Trade* (New York, Reynal and Company, 1958), p. 135; New York *Times*, October 3, 1948; and United States Atomic Energy Commission, *In the Matter of J. Robert Oppenheimer*, Transcript of Hearing before Personnel Security Board (Washington, 1954), pp. 18, 77, 228.

H-bomb. The decision was made partly in the hope that if the United States could develop such a weapon it would be able to maintain its qualitative lead over the Soviet program and thereby minimize the political and military disadvantages that would result from the loss of its fission monopoly. An even more compelling motive was the fear that, if the United States did not move more energetically to explore this possibility, the Soviet Union might be the first to achieve the weapon.[14] The second motive proved to be the more realistic. The pace of Soviet military technology was relentless and continually unexpected. The Soviet thermonuclear explosion of 1953 occurred only ten months after the American test of 1952, and it was said to have been of a better design. Beyond a doubt, the Soviet ICBM of 1957 both preceded in time and was of superior performance to its 1958 American counterpart.

Thus did events foreclose on both strategies. Far from having restored the European balance of power before the Russians secured the weapons of mass destruction, the United States found itself fully caught up in the balance of terror and still without a balance of power on the Continent. As for the "new strategy," the weapons had come far quicker to hand than had the necessary ideas to mind. By 1958 the hard choices had arrived, and the pinch of resources was everywhere constrictive of alternatives. The conflicts between win-the-war and prevent-the-war strategies and forces were by now clearly apparent; not so the strategic doctrine through which they could be resolved. Two-way thermonuclear war was an everyday possibility, but the nation was still without a clear or common strategy to guide its choices among deterrent and fighting capabilities, defensive and offensive weapons, city and delivery-force targets, or even between striking first or striking second.[15]

[14] The relationship between the H-bomb decision and the strategic considerations of the time is outlined in the present author's, "The H-Bomb Decision: How to Decide Without Actually Choosing," *Political Science Quarterly*, March 1961, pp. 24–46.

[15] For a discussion of the conflicts and choices involved, see Bernard Brodie, *Strategy in the Missile Age* (Princeton, Princeton University Press, 1959), especially Chaps. 6–8.

III

In January 1948 this future was completely veiled. These were to be the "years of opportunity." The year soon began to fill with opportunities, although some could be equally well characterized as emergencies. On February 24 Czechoslovakia fell to a Communist coup; on March 5 a telegram arrived from General Lucius Clay in Berlin reporting a shift in Soviet mood which led him to feel that war might come with "dramatic suddenness"; on March 8 the American Embassy in Nanking warned that the policies of Chiang Kai-shek would shortly lead him either to defeat or to the necessity to negotiate a peace with the Communists; on March 12 Ernest Bevin, the British Foreign Secretary, proposed a meeting to discuss a plan for "Atlantic security"; and on March 31 a conflict over Russian traffic controls led to a temporary halting of the trains into Berlin, a harbinger of the Berlin blockade which on June 24 was to begin in earnest.

The events of the "March crisis" served to expedite Congressional action on the administration's request for $5.3 billion for European economic recovery and to lead the State Department, by late April, to begin talking about the necessity of at least $3 billion in military aid as well. These reactions were quite in keeping with the strategy to rebuild the balance of power in Europe. But what of the "calculated risk" that was being run with the size of America's own armed forces in order to provide the financing for these programs? The March crisis seemed to indicate that the risk was greater than had heretofore been appreciated, and on March 14 the Joint Chiefs of Staff recommended that the President ask Congress to renew the draft and provide a supplemental appropriation to the fiscal 1949 budget for the purpose, as Forrestal later described it, of bringing American strength "up to the point where it more nearly met the realities of the world situation." [16]

The realities of American strength were grim enough, the advan-

[16] For the above events, see Millis, ed., *The Forrestal Diaries*, pp. 382, 387, 392–93, 397, 409, 425, and Millis, Mansfield, and Stein, *Arms and the State*, pp. 211, 213.

tages of the atomic monopoly, naval supremacy, and industrial superiority notwithstanding. From a strength of 12.3 million on VE-Day, the armed services had been reduced by February 1948 to a total of 1.3 million. The services did not have enough men to implement their joint war plan, and the strength of the Army was below that considered necessary to perform even its routine occupation and training missions. The situation had been carefully outlined before President Truman on February 18, including the difficulties that would be faced in the event of local, limited emergencies. If more than a division should have to be sent to any of the "possible explosive points in the world"—the briefing officer listed Greece, Italy, Korea, and Palestine—partial mobilization would be necessary. The problem had been aptly described by Marshall at a meeting of the National Security Council the week before: ". . . we are playing with fire while we have nothing with which to put it out." [17]

Spurred by what appeared to be a gathering crisis in Soviet-American relations, President Truman personally went before Congress on March 17 to recommend the reenactment of the draft and to reaffirm his earlier requests for a universal military training program. He was silent, however, on the size of the increase he proposed to make in his defense budget. His original budget for fiscal 1949, presented in January, had asked for $10 billion in new obligational authority for the armed services. The new program submitted by the services on March 24 would have almost doubled the size of the budget; it called for a 70-group Air Force and a total strength of more than two million men and would have required at least a $9-billion supplement. Truman, who had been thinking in terms of a $1.5-billion supplement, consented to a $3-billion supplement, which Forrestal presented to Congress the next day. This provided for a 55-group Air Force and an increase to 1,734,000 men from the March strength of 1,384,500.[18]

[17] *U.S. Budget, FY 1947*, p. LVIII, and Millis, ed., *The Forrestal Diaries*, pp. 373–76, 393.

[18] See, in part, Millis, ed., *The Forrestal Diaries*, pp. 397–98, 436, 401. The original budget for fiscal 1949 had projected an increase to 1,423,000 men. See *U.S. Budget, FY 1949*, p. M15.

The defense budget figures previously discussed have been in terms of "expenditures," the sums the government will actually spend in a given fiscal year

Of the 349,500 new men, 72 percent were to go to the Army and the Marines. Previewing a budgetary conflict (although not its outcome) that was to preoccupy the services during the Eisenhower administration, Forrestal had chosen not to press for the 70-group Air Force, but to strive instead to meet the Army's manpower shortage. Additional men for the ground forces, he explained to the Senate Armed Services Committee, were badly needed in order to make possible "an alert force to meet emergency situations. . . ." Although the Air Force was to remain at 55 groups, 15 of those groups had been maintained in only skeletonized strength. With its share of the supplement, the Air Force would be able to bring those 15 groups to peacetime strength and place 6 of its groups at wartime strength.[19]

The original defense budget for fiscal 1949 had been prepared before Forrestal took office. "It had been my hope," he told the House Armed Services Committee in April, "that I would be able to keep from having to make judgment on budget matters until the formation of the 1950 budget. But events have dictated otherwise." The Secretary soon had cause to regret his premature involvement. In subsequent testimony before the committee, the Air Force Chief

---

to meet its obligations. All "expenditures" result from obligational authority provided by Congress, but not all the obligational authority that Congress provides during a given fiscal year will require expenditures during that same year. Congress provides authority to incur obligations when it enacts appropriations and contract authorizations (permission to incur obligations which will require later appropriations to liquidate). The "new obligational authority" provided in a budget represents (a) new contract authorizations and (b) net new appropriations (total appropriations minus those required to liquidate earlier contract authorizations).

Unless otherwise noted, all budget figures used hereafter will be in terms of "new obligational authority" for the reason that the services considered this figure the more accurate measure of the resources they were being provided by a given budget. The new obligational authority provided in fiscal 1947 and fiscal 1948 was $11.1 billion and $10 billion, respectively. See *U.S. Budget, FY 1949*, pp. A7–A8, and *National Military Establishment Appropriation Bill for 1950*, Hearings before the Subcommittee of the Committee on Appropriations, House of Representatives, 81st Cong., 1st Sess. (Washington, 1949) [hereafter cited as *HCA, Hearings 1950 Budget*], I, 20.

[19] Millis, ed., *The Forrestal Diaries*, p. 401, and *Universal Military Training*, Hearings before the Committee on Armed Services, United States Senate, 80th Cong., 2d Sess. (Washington, 1948) [hereafter cited as *Senate UMT Hearings, 1948*], pp. 34, 393.

of Staff, General Carl Spaatz, flatly challenged Forrestal's decision against a 70-group Air Force and declared it to be the "minimum" necessary to defend the United States in view of existing world conditions. The Air Force Secretary, Stuart Symington, told the committee that American security would be better served by taking the money the President had asked for universal military training and spending it on a 70-group Air Force. The Army Chief of Staff, General Bradley, was not one to be left behind. (He had already felt obliged, in testimony before another committee, to assail those who believed "that the atom bomb and other weapons of mass destruction have all but eliminated the need for an army in any war which may come.") Bradley followed Symington to the stand the next day and declared that the alternative to universal military training was not a 70-group or even a 1,000-group Air Force, but rather 800,000 more men in the Army.[20]

Commenting on these proceedings in the New York *Times*, Hanson Baldwin proclaimed unification a "joke." His column also indicated what he thought to be the point of the joke. The Air Force thought that Russia could be defeated through use of the A-bomb alone and from bases 2,000 miles away. The Army and the Navy, on the other hand, did not believe that Russia could be defeated through the bomb alone and further thought that bases much closer (and thereby requiring more land and sea defense) would be required for the bombing part of the campaign.[21]

The butts of the joke were James Forrestal and Harry Truman. They had visibly lost control of the services and of the budget.

[20] *Selective Service,* Hearings before the Committee on Armed Services, House of Representatives, 80th Cong., 2d Sess. (Washington, 1948) [hereafter cited as *House Selective Service Hearings, 1948*], pp. 6082, 6159–60, 6138, 6216, and *National Military Establishment Appropriation Bill for 1949,* Hearings before the Subcommittee of the Committee on Appropriations, House of Representatives, 80th Cong., 2d Sess. (Washington, 1948) [hereafter cited as *HCA, Hearings 1949 Budget*], III, 2–4.

[21] New York *Times,* April 15, 1948, and Millis, ed., *The Forrestal Diaries,* pp. 414–15.

The only planes the Air Force had in any number at this time that could carry the A-bomb were the B-29's and the B-50's (a postwar modification of the B-29). These planes did not have an intercontinental range unless they were refueled in the air, a technique with which the Air Force was then still experimenting. See *Senate UMT Hearings, 1948,* pp. 381, 420.

Forrestal labored mightily to restore some semblance of agreement within the administration on the crucial matter of the national defense. There is no need to detail here the strategy and tactics of his negotiations; they were but a preview of his later efforts during the preparation of the fiscal 1950 budget. The end product of his bargaining was an agreement reached on April 19 whereby, in return for a $3.5-billion supplement (the Air Force getting 66 groups and most of the additional $481 million) and permission to tell Congress that what they really needed was $9 billion, the Joint Chiefs of Staff promised to back unanimously the new $3.5-billion supplement. The formula with which the Chiefs bridged the difference between $9 billion and $3.5 billion was an expression of their recognition that the budget, in addition to their "solely military considerations," had also to be responsive to the needs of the economy, the capacity of the aircraft industry, and the "calculated risk which can be accepted in light of changing world politico-military situations."

With the President's approval, although Truman indicated that the new sum would have to be reviewed by the Budget Bureau, Forrestal went again to Congress, this time with a $3.5-billion program, but armed now with the signed statement of the Chiefs in support of it. This represented the first time, he proudly told the Senate Subcommittee on Military Appropriations, "that the Joint Chiefs of Staff as a body have supported any budget request; and I may add . . . that it is the first time that they have considered [jointly] any budget request." [22]

So far as Congress was concerned, this was a case of too little and too late. The House had already passed a bill that provided $822 million more for the Air Force than Forrestal had requested under his $3-billion supplement, and the Senate was subsequently to do the same. The House's action was in response to earlier testimony by Symington that the Air Force's share of the supplement

[22] Millis, ed., *The Forrestal Diaries*, pp. 402–3, 412, 415–19, and *Supplemental National Defense Appropriation Bill, 1948,* Hearings before the Subcommittee of the Committee on Appropriations, United States Senate, 80th Cong., 2d Sess. (Washington, 1948) [hereafter cited as *SCA, Hearings 1948 Supplemental Budget*], p. 6.

would leave it, with regard to aircraft procurement, about $850 million short of where it should be, given the 70-group program endorsed by the Finletter Report.[23] An Air Force of this size had also been endorsed on March 1 in the report of the Joint Congressional Aviation Policy Board, a study group Congress had established to parallel the investigation of the Finletter Commission into national aviation policy. The 70-group program had quickly won wide support on the Hill, but what appears to have captured the attention of Congresss was not the picture of two-way atomic war that the Finletter Commission (and to a much lesser extent the Congressional Board) had endeavored to forecast. More dominant appears to have been the image of one-way atomic war, with the 70-group Air Force eliminating the need for the large American land army that had been required to defeat Germany. The response to the 70-group program was thus closely associated with Congress' decision to reject Truman's proposal for universal military training.[24]

With President Truman, Forrestal's program turned out to be a case of too much and too often. Early in May, Forrestal learned that the review of the Budget Bureau had reduced the $3.5-billion program to $3.1 billion, and that the Director of the Bureau, James Webb, had advised the President to cut the program even further, to $2.5 billion. Truman stood by Webb's recommendation. With evident

[23] The Air Force's agreement to the $3.5-billion supplement was made on the understanding that its share of this new supplement would be *in addition* to whatever it secured as a result of Congress' independent action. The $3.5-billion supplement would raise the services to 1,795,000 men, and the Air Force was to receive 53,000 of the 61,000 man increment. See Millis, ed., *The Forrestal Diaries*, pp. 414–15, 419. For Symington's testimony, see *Senate UMT Hearings, 1948*, p. 383.

Symington had earlier testified that the total funds needed by the Air Force in fiscal 1949, if it was to achieve 70 modernized groups by 1953, would be $5.4 billion. In contrast, under the $3.5-billion supplement, the Air Force would receive $4.9 billion. The $5.4-billion figure also included the cost of 27 National Guard groups and 34 Air Reserve groups, 22 special squadrons that the Air Force considered necessary to support the 70-group force. See *HCA, Hearings 1949 Budget*, II, 10, 44, 180.

[24] *National Aviation Policy*, Report of the Congressional Aviation Policy Board (Washington, 1948), pp. 3–4, 6–7. The basis for Congressional support of the 70-group program is discussed in Chaps. III and IV of the present study. For the connection between universal military training and the 70-group program, see Millis, ed., *The Forrestal Diaries*, pp. 378, 388, 412–13, 426–27.

exasperation, he observed that, although he had first thought a supplement of $1.5 billion would be adequate, he had nevertheless consented to a $3-billion program, but when Forrestal had come forward with the $3.5-billion program, he had made it clear that his final approval would be dependent on the findings of the Bureau of the Budget. These now showed that it would be necessary to keep the defense budget for fiscal 1950 and succeeding years at the level of $15 billion, and Truman announced that he was in agreement with this conclusion.

The $15-billion ceiling was actually $14.4 billion so far as the armed services were concerned, since the Bureau's figure included $600 million for the stockpiling program. While the budget Forrestal and the Chiefs then had before Congress amounted to only $13.5 billion (the original $10 billion for fiscal 1949 plus the $3.5-billion supplement), the forces the services had programmed under this budget were, in Forrestal's own estimate, expected to lead to a $16-billion budget for fiscal 1950 and one of $17.5 billion for fiscal 1951. Accordingly, Truman pointed out that, given the ceiling, a reduction in the $3.5-billion supplement was mandatory, unless the services were to be subjected to a "demoralizing demobilization" at the end of fiscal 1949. Truman therefore proposed that, although Forrestal could defend a $3.1-billion program before Congress (his third), it was to be understood that the services would not actually spend all of it. They were, in fact, told in June not to permit their build-up to exceed a force greater than 1,539,000 men—a limit which provided less than half the increase which had been scheduled under the $3-billion program first proposed in March.[25]

The fiscal 1949 budget, as finally passed by Congress (along with the draft), totaled $13.8 billion: $4.7 for the Air Force, $4.9 for the Navy, and $4.2 for the Army. The Air Force share included, however, the extra $822 million that Congress had provided to bring aircraft procurement in line with the 70-group program. The Pres-

[25] Millis, ed., *The Forrestal Diaries*, pp. 430–31, 435–38, 498, and *SCA, Hearings 1948 Supplemental Budget*, p. 12. The original fiscal 1949 budget also included $500 million for universal military training and $660 million for stockpiling, making a total of $11.2 billion in new obligational authority for all defense purposes. With the $3.5 supplement this total had become $14.7 billion.

ident disposed of these extra funds by the simple expedient of not spending them, and the Air Force was cut back to 59 groups for the fiscal year.[26]

IV

It was against this background and in the face of the $14.4-billion ceiling that planning began on the defense budget for fiscal 1950. The subsequent deliberations of the Executive were given fairly detailed coverage by the press, and the content of these reports is worth summation. Although not without error, they will provide a reasonably accurate introduction to the issues and alternatives involved. More importantly, they will also serve to indicate the kind of information potentially available to Congress in January 1949 when that body began its formal hearings on the budget finally submitted by the President.

The existence of the ceiling was public knowledge by the fall of 1948. According to an account in the New York *Times* in September, one reason why Truman had set the ceiling was his expectation that if the Republicans were victorious in the November election their President would certainly not want a higher budget and would probably propose a lower one. Later, in October, the *Times* related the ceiling to a statement Truman had made the previous May when he had signed a supplemental appropriation bill for the Air Force: ". . . our national security requires that the total national defense program be based on a strong economic system and depend on a level of expenditures which can be supported in subsequent years." [27]

This picture was supplemented by two columns in the New York *Herald Tribune* written by the Alsop brothers in December. They identified Webb, Secretary of the Treasury John Snyder, and Presidential Assistant John Steelman as the chief advocates for the ceiling within the administration. Their motive was said to be the

[26] *HCA, Hearings 1950 Budget,* I, 20, II, 118. The final total for defense expenditures in fiscal 1949 was $11.9 billion. See *U.S. Budget, FY 1954,* p. 1136.
[27] New York *Times,* September 10, and October 24, 1948.

desire to avoid either new taxes or economic controls, and Edwin
Nourse, the Chairman of the President's Council of Economic
Advisers, was said to have provided the analysis which pointed to
the necessity for such taxes and controls if the defense budget were
to exceed the ceiling. In contrast, a second group, identified with
Clark Clifford and Leon Keyserling (respectively, the White House
Counsel and another member of the Council of Economic Advisers),
was reported to be urging Truman to ask Congress for additional
taxes and controls. But this group was pressing for about $1 billion
in new welfare programs (housing, education, health insurance,
public power), not for higher defense expenditures.[28]

The New York *Times* reported on several occasions that the effect
of the ceiling would be to compel the services to cut back the
programs they had commenced under the supplemental budget for
fiscal 1949, since these had been based on the assumption that more
than $15 billion would be available for fiscal 1950. In December
the Alsops provided a grim description of the consequences of such
a cutback. If the ceiling was maintained, the rearmament program
launched in the spring to meet the deterioration of the international
situation would be "publicly gutted." In addition to a drastic reduction in Army manpower, they predicted that the Air Force would
be reduced to about 50 groups, which would be tantamount to
"abandoning plans for any effective air striking force," and that
the Navy would have to reduce its strength in the Mediterranean.
All this would have the short-run result of killing "the last slender
hope of a Berlin settlement" and the long-run result of putting the
nation vis-à-vis Russia in the same position in which Stanley Baldwin
had placed England vis-à-vis Nazi Germany.[29]

According to the New York *Times,* some members of the military
were asking for a $17-billion budget in order that the services
could sustain the force levels contemplated in their spring programs. Other members were said to be arguing the need for a $30-

[28] Joseph and Stewart Alsop, New York *Herald Tribune,* December 3 and 17,
1948.
[29] See New York *Times,* September 10 and October 24, 1948, and J. and S.
Alsop, New York *Herald Tribune,* December 3, 1948.

billion budget. An omnivorous reader might have believed that he had gained some sense of what the services expected to accomplish with a $30-billion budget from an article the Alsops had written in September for the *Saturday Evening Post*. This article purported to outline the strategy that the Joint Chiefs had recently agreed upon for war with the Soviet Union.[30]

The plan, as described, called for the formation of 45 European divisions, in contrast to the 15 understrength divisions the western European nations were said then to have. The mission of this force would be to hold the Rhine against the first assault of the Red Army. Its success, in the face of a much superior foe, was expected to result from the damage that the American Air Force would produce with its atomic strike against the Soviet Union. Some 300 to 500 bombers were to be used for this mission, and its success would require a network of overseas bases in the United Kingdom, North Africa, and the Middle and Far East. The article was not very explicit about the role of American troops, but the implication was that the success of the whole operation would depend on the rate at which they could be moved across the Atlantic to reinforce the Europeans. This accomplished, the combined forces could then move forward in victorious counterattack against the Red Army.

The Alsops reported that the services still had a few unresolved conflicts regarding this plan. There was some dispute regarding the targets to be bombed in the Soviet Union: whether population centers as well as key industrial cities [sic] or just the latter. Also, the Navy was said to be intent on taking part in the atomic strike (and therefore on building a super-carrier that could launch planes big enough to carry the A-bomb), although the other services thought its hands would be full securing the Atlantic against Russian submarines in order to permit the movement of men and munitions from the United States to the zone of combat. A report in October by Hanson Baldwin in the *Times* indicated that this might not be a complete listing of the differences to be resolved. He

[30] New York *Times*, October 24, 1948, and J. and S. Alsop, "If War Comes," *Saturday Evening Post*, September 11, 1948, pp. 15–17, 178, 180, 182–83.

advised his readers of a debate within the Pentagon about whether to plan on a stand at the Rhine or at the Pyrenees, the point being that many believed that a stand on the Rhine would require German and Spanish manpower. He further reported an even more basic division of opinion between those who thought the war could be won through atomic bombing alone and those who believed that these weapons could not by themselves stop the Red Army. Assuming that the two stories were referring to something approximating the same plan, a reader of both might well have wondered just what the Chiefs had found to agree upon.[31]

Both Baldwin in the *Times* and the Alsops in the *Herald Tribune* expressed doubt that the President would actually stick by his $14.4-billion ceiling. A "broader review of all the facts seems certain to make him change his mind," was the conclusion expressed on December 3 by the latter. The nature of the review to which Truman might be subjected was outlined on December 10 in the *Times*. At a "future conference" the military planned to brief the President on the security alternatives involved in each of three budgets: the $14.4-billion budget; one for $21 billion, which was identified as their top figure; and a compromise budget at $17-18 billion. It was hoped that at this conference civilian experts would, on their part, spell out the implications of each of these budgets for the state of the economy.[32]

The public received its briefing on these alternatives through the means of an unsigned article in the December issue of *Fortune*. The article was described as the result of two months of discussion with "responsible military experts" and "foreign policy strategists," and its burden was a comparison of the strategic consequences that would result from a $14.4-billion defense budget with those that would follow from an $18-billion budget. To this end, the differences between the two budgets in numbers of heavy bomber groups, divisions, and aircraft carriers were enumerated, but the

[31] H. Baldwin, New York *Times*, October 10, 1948.
[32] See Baldwin in New York *Times*, October 31, 1948; J. and S. Alsop, New York *Herald Tribune*, December 3, 1948; and New York *Times*, December 10, 1948.

been anticipated under the $3.5-billion April program. The Navy was to have 8 heavy carriers and some 527,000 men, which would be 5,000 less than it had in December 1948 and 25,000 short of the April goal. The strength of the Air Force was to be around 412,000 men, a bare thousand more than its number in December 1948 and 41,000 short of the April level. The Air Force was, moreover, to be reduced to 48 groups, which put it organizationally worse off than it had been before the March crisis began.[35]

What were the considerations actually responsible for the $14.4-billion ceiling? What was the relationship between the forces provided under the fiscal 1950 budget and the strategies through which members of the Executive hoped to meet the nation's foreign policy problems? Through what process of analysis and choice was it decided to request this particular budget of Congress rather than one of the alternatives which were apparently considered: $30 billion? $21 billion? $18 billion? These are questions which will be answered in a later chapter dealing with Executive choice and the budget. These same questions, however, confronted Congress in 1949, and before exploring the evidence now available on how the Executive made up the budget, it will be instructive to see what Congress made of it at the time—what questions Congressmen asked, what answers they received, and what the relationship was between the information they got and the choices they made.

[35] See *U.S. Budget, FY 1950*, pp. M6, M13–M15, M18–M23, 693–94; *HCA, Hearings 1950 Budget*, I, 8–10; and Millis, ed., *The Forrestal Diaries*, p. 419.

III   *Congressional Choice and Rationality*

The multiplicity of figures that the Executive branch was reported to have considered prior to the presentation of the $14.2-billion budget—$30 billion, $21 billion, $17-18 billion, $14.4 billion— generated an understandable amount of confusion in the minds of some Congressmen. Thus, during the House debate on the budget in April 1949, Representative Frank Keefe, Republican of Wisconsin and a member of the parent Appropriations Committee, observed that Congress knew the military had wanted larger sums than those finally requested and had reduced their estimates only after repeated "prodding and pressure" from the President. Yet these same men, since they were appointees of the President, had not been "permitted to come out and support [before Congress] any-thing other than the Bureau of the Budget estimate." The problem, exclaimed Keefe, was this: "Whom are we going to believe in this matter; that is the thing that bothers me."

Keefe's own answer was that the House should support the decisions of its Subcommittee on Armed Services Appropriations. They had "given this thing very great study." Representative George Mahon, the Texas Democrat who was the Chairman of the Subcom-mittee, said nothing to disabuse him of the wisdom of this answer. It was up to Congress, he had declared on the floor of the House the day before, to reach its own decisions about the size of the budget and how it was to be allocated among the services. This was their responsibility, and it should not be abdicated to the Bureau of the Budget or anyone else. When another Congressman asked if they were really to believe that the five members of the subcommittee who acted on the bill "are better informed than the

President and the Secretary of Defense in determining what should be the over-all figure for national defense?" Mahon replied:

I say that Congress should not abdicate its functions. I say that after eleven weeks of hearings and hundreds of hours of study the members of the Committee are vastly better informed about some provisions of this bill than some of the people in the executive branch. Congress must not abdicate; we must stand firm in our Constitutional function to legislate.[1]

Mahon was here echoing a conception of Congressional responsibility that had been advanced during the hearings of his subcommittee by Representative Carl Vinson, Democrat of Georgia and the Chairman of the House Armed Services Committee. In his testimony before the Appropriations Subcommittee, Vinson had declared that there was nothing "holy" about the President's budget and that they had not been sent to Congress to become "stooges of the budget." It was the responsibility of the House and the Senate, Vinson avowed, "to take whatever action is deemed proper to get the required defense for the least money—even if that requires increasing the budget recommendations—or even if it requires reshuffling the funds the budget proposes." These sentiments were fully shared by the ranking Republican member of Vinson's committee, Representative Dewey Short of Missouri, who asserted during the House debate: "It is the Congress of the United States, and particularly the two Committees on Armed Services [Appropriations] of the Senate and the House that are to determine what is necessary for our national defense." [2]

The purpose of this chapter is to examine the performance of Congress in the light of the role prescribed by Mahon, Vinson, and others: that of making an independent analysis and choice with regard to the size and composition of the budget. In practice, as both Keefe and Short observed, if Congress is to perform such a role it must be primarily through its committee structure, since there is no real opportunity for extended analysis through the means of floor debate. In the case of the fiscal 1950 budget, for example, the House debate was limited to parts of two days, and the more

[1] *C.R.*, 95, pp. 4524, 4509.
[2] *HCA, Hearings 1950 Budget*, I, 206, 222, and *C.R.*, 95, p. 4500, cf. 4509.

leisurely Senate had the bill before it for only three days. In contrast, Mahon's subcommittee met mornings and afternoons for two months considering the defense budget and heard the testimony of 402 witnesses from the National Military Establishment. The record of its hearings was 2,971 pages in length and was accompanied by a 59-page report.

The analysis of the Senate Subcommittee on Military Appropriations was much less extensive. Hearings were held for only eight days and resulted in a 427-page record and a 35-page report. The difference is largely accountable to two facts. The Senators, to begin with, had less time for the job than their counterparts in the House; they had obligations to other committees as well, whereas members of the House Appropriations Committee were by rule prevented from serving on any other committee. Moreover, since appropriation bills must originate in the House, the Senate's custom was not to begin its own hearings until the budget had passed the House, and the Senators by and large restricted their attention to the issues in dispute between the House and the Executive. Accordingly, in the examination that follows, most of the illustrative material will come from the record of Mahon's subcommittee. The extent and character of its analysis can be considered typical of the best that was developed by the two committees concerned with the determination of the fiscal 1950 budget.[3]

Both subcommittees were in the first year of their existence. Prior to 1949, each house had maintained two separate subcommittees for military appropriations, one for the Army's budget and one for the Navy's. Stimulated by the establishment of the Department of the Air Force and the reorganization of the services into the National Military Establishment, Congress had decided to consolidate its own structure, and the new "unified" committees became effective with the organization of the 81st Congress. The fiscal 1950 budget thus marked the first time in the twentieth century

[3] For details on the House and Senate debates and committee hearings, and the reasons for the more dominant role of the House committee, see Stephen K. Bailey and Howard D. Samuel, *Congress at Work* (New York, Henry Holt and Co., 1952), pp. 363–64, 366, 369–73, 377–79, and Elias Huzar, *The Purse and the Sword* (Ithaca, Cornell University Press, 1950), pp. 29, 36–39, 70, 73.

that single committees of Congress undertook to consider the whole military budget.

It should also be noted that the activity of these committees that will be here considered—their effort to reach an independent judgment on the size and composition of the defense budget—was only one of their two major responsibilities, and a relatively new one at that. During the years of "feast or famine" budgeting, the jurisdiction of the service and appropriations committees had been delimited on the basis of a distinction between "policy" and "costs," with the result that the appropriations committees had concerned themselves with the financial details of military programs rather than with the policy premises from which those programs had been derived.[4] Whatever its former utility, such a division of labor was obviously poorly suited to the post–World War II budgeting problem. The size and composition of the annual budget had become a policy choice of great consequence. Since the armed services committees had no established procedures for reviewing the content of the budget, the task of deciding whether its allocations were indeed "necessary" seemed to fall, if only by default, to the appropriations committees.

As indicated by the statements quoted earlier, this development in the responsibilities of the appropriations committees was neither shunned by the members of Mahon's committee nor contested by those of Vinson's. The change did, however, leave a certain area of confusion regarding the responsibilities of the two sets of committees. Thus, while the hearings held by the House and Senate Armed Services Committees during the spring and summer of 1949 were for the most part not directly concerned with the major issues of the budget, the members of those committees, as will be seen, were far from indifferent or inactive with regard to those issues. On the other hand, while the members of the appropriations committees undertook to pass judgment on the military posture that the fiscal 1950 budget would provide, they also continued to devote

---

[4] For the reorganization of the appropriations committees and their traditional conception of their responsibilities, see *HCA, Hearings 1950 Budget,* I, 1, and Huzar, *The Purse and the Sword,* pp. 28–29, 398–402.

the greater part of their time to discharging their traditional responsibility as a watchdog over the financial details of the budget's programs.

II

The House Subcommittee on Armed Services Appropriations opened its hearings on January 31, 1949. In addition to Mahon, the Democrats on the committee were Harry Sheppard of California and Robert Sikes of Florida. The Republican members were Albert Engel of Michigan and Charles Plumley of Vermont. Sheppard and Plumley had both served as chairmen of the former Subcommittee on Naval Appropriations. Mahon and Engel had been members of the former Subcommittee on Military [War Department] Appropriations, and Engel had been its last chairman. Sikes had served for several years on the former Military Affairs Committee and in the preceding year on the Armed Services Committee, but he had not heretofore served on an appropriations committee.[5]

The hearings were the beginning of the committee's formal opportunity "to learn" about the budget, but the members were by no means in a position of having to start from scratch in their inquiry. Well in advance of the President's budget message, they had had an opportunity to amass a good deal of intelligence regarding the budget's content and the considerations that had produced it. Intelligence of this sort could be, and presumably was, gathered from three main sources: a knowledge of previous budget policy; informal contacts with members of the Executive; and press reports. It is, of course, no longer possible to determine what information the members of the committee actually had about the budget when their hearings began. But the content of the news stories that were written during the fall of 1948 can be taken as illustrative of the kind of information that was available.

The quality of the stories to be found in the New York press and in various national periodicals was not unimpressive. There were, as previously noted, reports about the reasoning responsible

[5] *C.R.*, 95, p. 4427, and Huzar, *The Purse and the Sword*, p. 33.

for the $15-billion ceiling (including an accounting of both those against it and those for it); about the effect the ceiling would have on the rearmament program of the preceding spring; about the size of the various defense budgets that had been developed by the services; about the content of the basic war plan of the Chiefs; and, finally, about the strategic difference between the two budgets which were allegedly the major alternatives placed before the President.

Given information of this order, and given a determination to reach their own judgment regarding what was "necessary for national defense" and to avoid being mere "stooges of the budget," the members of the subcommittee might well have been expected to have started their hearings armed with a very provocative list of questions. They could have interrogated State Department witnesses regarding what had happened on the international scene to justify cutting back the defense program of the preceding spring. They could have cross-examined witnesses from the Bureau of the Budget and the Treasury Department regarding the fiscal premises responsible for the $14.4-billion ceiling, and they might have explored with advocates of various welfare programs the case to be made for spending additional sums for those purposes instead of for national defense.

There were, above all, a variety of questions which invited discussion with representatives of the military establishment: the relationship between the forces provided by the $14.2-billion budget and what were believed to be the nation's two major military problems (the defense of Europe and the prospect of two-way atomic war); the consequences for military security that would have been expected if one of the other budgets reported to have been under consideration had been chosen (including a follow-up on such matters as the importance of holding on to the Mediterranean, and the issue of whether the division of funds among the services should remain proportionately the same regardless of which size budget they received); and, last but not least, the question of which, among the variety of conflicting theories the military had about how to fight and win wars, had furnished the criteria used in determining on the number and kind of forces provided by the President's budget.

Questions such as these could not only have been stimulated through a reading of the public press or through private conversation with Executive officials. They were, in their general form at least, equally capable of being derived from a logical and inquisitive approach to the question of how much to spend for defense. The asking of such questions and the receipt of answers to them was imperative if the members of the subcommittee were to provide themselves and Congress with the kind of information necessary to reach an independent judgment on the size and composition of the defense budget.

Yet these were precisely the kinds of questions that the members of the committee did not ask, and to which as a result they received no answers. The 3,000 pages of the committee's record not only failed to add anything to the information already developed in the press about the major policy issues involved in the budget; the committee's record actually fell far short of containing even that much information.

The intellectual poverty of the committee's record can be illustrated by the character of its inquiry into one of the more obvious issues that faced it: the question of what military capabilities the services would have under the fiscal 1950 budget. If Congress was to make a rational choice of its own on this matter, the committee had to secure, first, information about the kinds of military problems the services were likely to confront, and, second, information about the consequences for their ability to meet those problems if this, that, or some other sum of money was made available. The committee had to learn more than what the services could accomplish with the funds provided by the President's budget. The committee had also to secure some knowledge of what could be accomplished with other budgets, for unless it established alternatives to the President's budget, it would have nothing from which to choose.

In appraising the committee's performance in developing such alternatives, it must be recognized that this was not a task on which it received much help from the members of the Executive. For them the consideration of alternatives was finished; their choices had been made or made for them. They came to the committee not for the purpose of reminiscence or second-guessing, but to secure Congressional approval for the President's budget and to support it, if necessary, against its critics. While their support might be something less than whole-hearted, and they might on occasion permit the face of their dissatisfaction to show, they were reluctant, for reasons which will be examined later, to engage in a detailed documentation of that dissatisfaction.

The administration witnesses came to the hearings, then, intent on discussing one figure, not several. Not even this figure, the $14.2-billion budget, was discussed in terms calculated to give the committee much understanding of what the military consequences would be if Congress chose to endorse it. Thus, Forrestal soberly proclaimed that the "military forces provided under this budget are for a national defense position of relative military readiness, coupled with a higher degree of mobilization preparedness with proper balance between manpower and material, consistent with our traditional concept of military strength for purposes of defense." In the absence of considerable elaboration, it is doubtful if this statement could have had much meaning, but the committee accepted this and similar descriptions without complaint or question.

At times administration witnesses described the budget as if it would permit them to meet in a satisfactory manner just about any problem the nation might face—as if, that is, the choice of the $14.2-billion figure involved no costs at all to military security. When Mahon asked Forrestal if "the program submitted here in the budget for air power is reasonably adequate under all circumstances?" the Secretary replied: "Under all circumstances; yes." This assurance was a considerable advance over the forcefulness, if not the candor, of the testimony he had given in connection with the fiscal 1949 supplement. At that time he had said, "The term 'adequate' itself is relative, and must mean 'adequate for what circumstances?'" The nation could not be ready for war and "run a democratic economy at the same time." The "inevitable conclusion" was that "It is not possible for us—at present, if ever—to maintain in peacetime anything approaching what might be called an adequate military establishment." [6]

The press reports made it impossible for Forrestal to hide the fact that, however "adequate" the $14.2-billion budget, the services *had* considered other and higher figures. Forrestal confirmed that two other figures ($30 billion and $16.9 billion) had been involved in the making of the budget, but he made no effort to dwell on their significance. The $30-billion figure, he explained, was merely the sum of the initial requests of the three services. (In an appended statement, he noted that the Joint Chiefs of Staff had later reduced this total to $23.6 billion and that further study would probably have cut it to $21 billion.) There has never been the "faintest idea," Forrestal declared, of submitting the $30-billion figure to Congress or to the President. "That was the total in the event we had to be ready for instant war, but we were not planning for that." [7]

Except for an expression of shock at the size of the figure, the committee accepted this statement without further comment. Neither then nor on the subsequent occasions when the $30-billion figure was mentioned did members of the committee ask for an explanation of what the difference was between $30 billion (or $23.6 billion) and $14.2 billion in terms of the ability of the nation to fight. They made no effort, that is, to pin down just what things, given the lower figure, the services would not now be able to accomplish in the event of war and what consequences would therefore follow for the course of such a war if it came.

Later in the hearings, Symington gave a somewhat different explanation for the $30-billion figure. The word had "got around" that, after each of the services submitted their estimated needs, "we were all going to be cut proportionately because there was no

[6] *HCA, Hearings 1950 Budget,* I, 17, 21, and *HCA, Hearings 1949 Budget,* I, 13.

[7] *HCA, Hearings 1950 Budget,* I, 16–17. Two days later in a public speech, he described the $30-billion estimate as "not unwise or ill-advised at the time," since it was advanced shortly after the events of the spring of 1948. The news story received a headline stating that the improved international situation was responsible for the reduction to $14.2 billion. See the New York *Times,* February 2, 1949.

agreed upon strategic plan against [which] to buy." He had, therefore, arbitrarily increased the estimate developed by the Air Force
from $8 to $11 billion in order to make certain that their request
would be the equal of those submitted by the Army and the Navy.
Symington added that he had also hoped, by making the total figure
larger, to make it look "ridiculous" and thereby force the services
to operate "on the basis of an integrated plan." This story did stir
two members of the committee to make some pointed, unhappy
references to interservice rivalry. But no one asked whether his
strategy had been successful and if an integrated plan was behind
the $14.2-billion budget.[8]

Forrestal's discussion of the $16.9-billion figure was, if anything,
even more terse than his description of the $30-billion figure. He
simply stated that $16.9 billion was the "figure that we finally
requested of the President," because the amount available under
the $14.4-billion ceiling "was not sufficient to provide all the forces
which the Joint Chiefs of Staff, from a purely military standpoint,
considered necessary." This was all Forrestal volunteered on the
subject. The National Military Establishment, he affirmed, recognized that the President had to take "all relevant factors" into consideration in formulating his budget, and because he had given this
consideration, the military establishment supported the final result.[9]

If Forrestal was less than completely informative about the
policy consequences of the $14.2-billion figure or the reasons behind
his $16.9-billion request, it must also be said that the members of
the committee were far from demanding in their cross-examination.
Not a single question was put to Forrestal about the $16.9-billion
budget. No one asked when he had submitted it or why it was
rejected. Nor were there any questions put to him or anyone else
during the 3,000-page hearings about the particulars in which the
Chiefs had found a $14.4-billion budget wanting: about the kinds
of things the services would be unable to accomplish, if war came,

[8] *HCA, Hearings 1950 Budget,* II, 16–18. For an excellent analysis of the
procedures through which service estimates are compiled, see Arthur Smithies,
The Budgetary Process in the United States (New York, McGraw-Hill Book
Company, Inc., 1955), pp. 243–56.
[9] *Ibid.,* I, 12, 16.

on Truman's $14.2-billion that they would have been able to accomplish for $2.7 billion more. The committee did gather, as will be seen, some information about what the dollar difference between various figures meant in terms of numbers of men and machines. But information of this sort revealed nothing per se about what difference these alternative numbers would make in terms of the services' performance on particular problems, and it revealed, therefore, essentially very little about the security consequences involved in the choice between such figures.

It is possible that the difference between the Chiefs' $16.9-billion request and Truman's $14.2-billion budget, as expressed in terms of the actual ability of the armed forces to accomplish certain objectives in time of war, was discussed by the committee off the record. Witnesses went off the record frequently during the course of the hearings when they touched on what they or members of the committee considered classified information. One such occasion was the briefing given the committee at the start of the hearings by General Alfred Gruenther, the Director of the Joint Staff. This was completely off the record. It is possible that he presented at that time an outline of the kind of war the Chiefs planned to fight with Russia and indicated, as he did so, the kind of performance the services would be able to deliver on that strategy with the $14.2-billion budget. It is further possible that, in this context, the committee asked what difference a $16.9-billion budget would have made. This is not, however, likely. There are three specific references to Gruenther's testimony on the record, and none suggest that it was at all of this character. These three references are, moreover, in agreement in suggesting what the content of that testimony was: an "intelligence" briefing on the strength and deployment of Russian forces.

In addition to Gruenther's statement on behalf of the Joint Staff, the committee also received presentations from the plans and operations divisions of each of the three services. The presentations of the Air Force and the Army were partly off the record; the Navy's was completely so. Again, it is possible that during these presentations comparisons were made between the $16.9-billion and the

$14.2-billion budgets in terms of the ability of the services to carry out particular missions planned for war. This, too, seems unlikely. Nowhere in the 3,000 pages of the printed record is there one reference to suggest that the committee received such information, and it seems plausible to suppose that there would have been.[10]

The only public consideration the subcommittee gave to the $16.9-billion request was on March 28 when Vinson, accompanied by several other members of the Armed Services Committee, came to testify before Mahon's group. It was on this occasion that Vinson enjoined the subcommittee not to be "stooges of the budget." Vinson himself came to advocate a $1.6-billion increase over the President's budget: $800 million for the Air Force, $545 million for the Navy, and $254 million for the Army. The order of his Air Force increase was obviously designed to repeat the effort Congress had made the previous spring to accelerate it toward the 70-group program. In the case of the Navy and the Army, his increases were designed to prevent them from falling below their January 1949 manpower levels and to raise their budgets in certain selected areas to the amounts requested in the Chiefs' $16.9-billion budget.

Vinson's total increase would have left the budget still $1.1 billion short of the Chiefs' budget, but he pinned his argument nevertheless to their request. "Now, where," he asked, "do we look mainly in this country for the best judgment on what is needed for an adequate defense?" His answer was: to the Joint Chiefs of Staff. The subcommittee could arrive "more soundly at our national defense needs," he declared, if they undertook to compare the President's budget, "which is compounded of a number of extra-military considerations," with that advanced by the Chiefs, "which is exclusively military in nature."

The comparison Vinson gave the subcommittee showed the benefit of considerable informal communication with the services, for much

---

[10] For the service presentations, see *ibid.*, II, 36–41; III, 62; IV, 17–26; for Gruenther's briefing, see *ibid.*, II, 36; IV, 17, 567. The point about Gruenther's briefing would seem clearly made by Bradley's reference (IV, 567): "Our present planning in the Joint Chiefs—and consequently the Army planning— is based on this [Gruenther's statement] same intelligence estimate that you have heard."

of the information he presented about the $16.9-billion budget was not elsewhere available on the public record. Analytically, however, his comparison had little to recommend it. In the first place, he never explained the reasons why he had decided to recommend certain of the items in the Chiefs' $16.9-billion budget, but not others. Secondly, in discussing the increases he did recommend, the comparisons he made with the amounts requested in Truman's budget were either purely numerical in character or on such a high level of generality as to convey little sense for the operational consequences involved. In the case of the Army increase, for example, one of the additions he urged the subcommittee to make was $48 million for the modernization of medium tanks. The totality of his argument was to point out that this would permit 743 such tanks to be modernized (as the $16.9-billion budget would have provided) instead of the 250 tanks that would be modernized under the President's budget. Similarly, in comparing the Chiefs' budget with Truman's, he reported that under the latter the Army would have two less divisions in its "mobile striking force." This, Vinson argued, "materially lessens our readiness in the event of an emergency here or elsewhere in the world." His point was logical enough, but hardly incisive. The question still remained, just what would happen without those troops (or tanks) in the event of what kind of emergencies? [11]

The Army's own conception of its needs had been described to the subcommittee the week before by General Bradley. He labeled as "wishful thinking—and unrealistic thinking" the idea that a war with Russia could be won through strategic bombing alone. Equally unrealistic was the expectation that strategic bombing could be accomplished by means of a single strike at intercontinental distances. A number of bases close to the enemy would be needed from which

[11] See *ibid.*, I, 206–18, 221. The $254-million increase for the Army was composed of (a) $105 million to keep manpower at the January 31, 1949, level (an increase of 34,668 men over the President's budget) and (b) three additions which would bring the budget, in these respects, up to the funds requested in the $16.9-billion budget. These last were: $84 million for 350 more anti-aircraft guns; $48 million for 493 more modernized tanks; and $17 million for placing 191,314 more reserves on pay drill status.

repeated raids would have to be launched, and for their protection these overseas bases would be dependent on the Army and the Navy. Having thus disposed of what he considered the major misconceptions about World War III, Bradley had next turned to the task of delineating its true shape.

The war, Bradley predicted [his time span was not indicated], would take place in three phases. The strategic air offensive would constitute only the first. During this offensive, phase two—the mobilization and build-up overseas of American troops—would be under way. All this was preparatory to phase three: "the conclusive land battle, which must eventually take place if we are to be victorious over an enemy nation." The key point, he stressed, was the necessity during phases one and two for American troops to hold on to an overseas base from which phase three could be launched. (Secretary of the Army Kenneth Royall had warned the committee that if this base were lost it might then take 15 to 30 years to win the war.) Bradley declared that an island, such as Great Britain, was not too desirable for such a base. "A toehold on the same continent with the enemy is much more desirable." [12]

The questions to be asked, then, about the differences in the numbers of men and machines provided by the $16.9 and the $14.2-billion budgets were what difference they would make for the Army's ability to secure and protect overseas air bases, to keep a toehold on the Continent, or to undertake the build-up necessary for the final, conclusive land battle. In January, before Vinson's own committee, Bradley had testified that an 800,000-man Army, the size contemplated by the $16.9-billion budget, would be necessary to defend and support a 70-group Air Force and that, with the 677,000 men scheduled by the fiscal 1950 budget, the Army would be able to defend and support only about 50 groups.[13] But what

---

[12] *Ibid.*, IV, 7–8, 567–70. This represented a stronger case for the Army than Bradley had made in his testimony on behalf of the fiscal 1949 budget. At that time he stressed only the need for land forces to secure and protect air bases and made no reference to the need for a final, conclusive land battle. See *Senate UMT Hearings, 1948*, pp. 350–51, and HCA, *Hearings 1949 Budget*, III, 2–4, 1220–23.

[13] See *Hearings on the Bill to Authorize the Composition of the Army of the United States and the Air Force of the United States and for Other Purposes,*

difference the two budgets would make in the Army's ability to maintain a foothold on the Eurasian mainland was established in neither Vinson's nor Mahon's hearings, although if Bradley's conception of World War III were correct it was, perhaps, the more significant difference. Unexplored also were the consequences of each budget for the Army's rate of build-up and for the kind of performance the "mobile striking force" might make in the event the "emergency" turned out to be of a local, limited character.

Vinson's comparison of the $16.9 and $14.2-billion budgets was similarly numerical when he discussed the Navy. Under the President's budget the Navy would be able to procure 843 aircraft during the fiscal year. Vinson labeled this "far insufficient for the needs of the fleet today," and he recommended an additional $343 million in order to permit the Navy to procure 1,361 aircraft as scheduled under the Chiefs' budget. He also urged the subcommittee to provide an additional $98 million for the operation and maintenance of the fleet. This, he pointed out, would permit the Navy to operate 10 heavy carriers (as scheduled by the $16.9-billion budget) instead of the 8 permitted by Truman's budget. Even 10 heavy carriers, Vinson asserted, would not meet the Navy's "minimum needs" in the initial stages of a war. These references to "needs" were a promising beginning, but they turned out to be the sum total of the discussion concerning the relationship between the number of carriers (or aircraft) and the Navy's performance in time of war.

Vinson's statements were in some contrast to the testimony the subcommittee had received from the Secretary of the Navy, John Sullivan. He had said that the President's budget would "maintain the minimum active naval power consistent with our national needs." Even more damaging to Vinson's argument, given his effort to contrast Truman's budget with the considered military judgment of the Joint Chiefs of Staff, was the testimony of General Hoyt Vandenberg, who in April had succeeded Spaatz as Chief of Staff

---

Committee on Armed Services, House of Representatives, 81st Cong., 1st Sess. (Washington, 1949) [hereafter cited as *HCAS, 1949 Authorization Bill*], pp. 109, 115.

for the Air Force. Vandenberg had earlier informed Mahon's committee that the only major difference the Chiefs had been unable to resolve, when they determined the forces to be maintained under Truman's budget, had been the number of heavy carriers. The Air Force had recommended 4, the Army 6, and the Navy 9, and the final choice of 8 had been made by Forrestal.[14]

Vinson did not refer to the Chiefs' $16.9-billion request when he discussed the additional $800 million he was proposing for the Air Force. The reason for his lack of parallel treatment may have been the fact that the $16.9-billion budget had scheduled the Air Force at 59 not 70 groups. Vinson was one of the main advocates of the 70-group program and had been among those who had led the House to vote the extra $822 million for the Air Force in the fiscal 1949 budget. Mindful of the fact that Truman had refused to spend the $822 million, and of the press reports indicating that the fiscal 1950 budget would put the Air Force even further away from its goal, Vinson had announced shortly after the November election that he would introduce a bill in the new Congress authorizing the 70-group program. Vinson was here trying to use the Constitutional power of Congress to place an upper limit on the size of the forces that can be maintained by the President as a device for mobilizing opinion behind an effort to increase forces to that limit. To this end, Vinson had held hearings in January (during which he was able to entice Symington, without much difficulty, into testifying that a 70-group Air Force was "the minimum required for national security"), and the authorization bill

[14] See *HCA, Hearings 1950 Budget*, I, 210–11; III, 8; II, 99. The $545-million increase Vinson proposed for the Navy was composed of (a) $87 million to keep manpower at the January 31, 1949, level (an increase of 28,367 men over the President's budget) and (b) three additions which would bring the budget, in these respects, up to the funds requested in the $16.9-billion budget. These last were: $98 million for the operation and maintenance of the fleet; $343 million for the procurement of naval aircraft; and $17 million for research and development.

In his testimony before the subcommittee, Vinson on several occasions stated that these figures totaled $645 million, and as a result he kept referring to his total increase as $1.7 billion instead of $1.6 billion. Whether this is indicative of the amount of time and analysis that had gone into his proposals is not clear.

had passed the House six days before he appeared before Mahon's committee.

In contrast to the $799-million increase he recommended for the Army and the Navy, which he described as his own idea, Vinson's $800-million Air Force increase was proposed in the name of his whole committee. Given this backing and the recent expression of sentiment in the House, Vinson probably considered it unnecessary to dwell on the desirability of the measure. Whatever the reason, he contented himself with a numerical analysis: with $800 million more the Air Force could be increased from 48 to 57 groups. This could be accomplished, he pointed out, without even having to exceed the President's total budget. The budget had allowed $800 million for universal military training, and this, he correctly predicted, Congress would once again reject.[15]

Mahon's committee proved as persuaded of the importance of increasing the Air Force budget as Vinson's. The subcommittee's report was submitted on April 9. It recommended a variety of cuts in the President's budget which totaled $237 million for the Army, $120 million for the Navy, and $13 million for the Air Force. The committee then further recommended that an extra $800 million be added to the Air Force budget for the purpose of permitting it to procure additional aircraft and to expand from 48 to 58 groups. In contrast to the President's request for $13.4 billion (the committee did not have the $830 million request for housing and pay raises before it, since this had not received the required legislative authorization), the committee's budget was, thus, $13.8 billion, which, as it happened, was the same amount Congress had finally appropriated in fiscal 1949.

[15] On the size of the Air Force under the $16.9-billion budget, see Millis, ed., *The Forrestal Diaries*, p. 538. For Vinson's authorization bill, see New York *Herald Tribune*, November 27, 1948, and *C.R.*, *95*, p. 2936, as quoted in Paul Y. Hammond, "The Missions of the Services." (A later version of this manuscript, entitled "Super-Carriers and B-36 Bombers: Appropriations, Strategy and Politics," is at this writing in the press of the Twentieth Century Fund.) The device of using the power to impose a "ceiling" as an attempt to raise the "floor" is discussed in Huntington, "Strategic Planning and the Political Process," *Foreign Affairs*, January 1960, p. 288. For Symington's testimony, see *HCAS, 1949 Authorization Bill*, p. 154, and for Vinson's, *HCA, Hearings 1950 Budget*, I, 212–14, 225.

When the budget was debated on the House floor, Vinson made no reference to his earlier proposal to add $799 million to the Army and Navy budgets. An amendment was introduced by Sheppard to add $300 million to the Navy's funds for aircraft procurement, but although it was supported by Vinson, Plumley, and Sikes (Sheppard and Plumley, it will be recalled, were former chairmen of the old Subcommittee on Naval Appropriations, and Vinson had been for decades the patriarch of the old Committee on Naval Affairs), the Navy increase was defeated. The House passed the appropriations bill on April 13, 1949, exactly as the subcommittee had reported it.[16]

III

Since the Air Force increase was the major change the subcommittee made in the President's budget, the kind of information which the subcommittee secured about that change is deserving of special attention. Certainly neither Symington nor Vandenberg said anything to discourage the committee from increasing their budget. Symington had followed Truman's budget message within a week with his first Annual Report, in which he again asserted the need for a 70-group Air Force by 1952. This obliged Truman to insist at a subsequent press conference that 48 groups were adequate. It also led the President and Forrestal to discuss, and not for the first time, the matter of Symington's dismissal. Before the subcommittee, the words of the Secretary and his Chief were guarded, but pointed. They spoke, respectively, as follows:

We believe that this country can be beaten in two ways, however; one would be in battle, and one would be economically; and, therefore,

[16] House Report No. 417, *National Military Establishment Appropriation Bill, 1950*, 81st Cong., 1st Sess. (Washington, 1949) [hereafter cited as *House Report, 1950 Budget*], pp. 4, 31; Senate Report No. 745, *National Military Functions Appropriation Act, 1950*, 81st Cong., 1st Sess. (Washington, 1949) [hereafter cited as *Senate Report, 1950 Budget*], p. 5; and Bailey and Samuel, *Congress at Work*, pp. 369–70.
The Air Force increase was $222 million in appropriations and $577.7 million in contract authority for aircraft construction and related procurement. Given the $13 million cut elsewhere, the net increase over the President's budget was $786 million. See also the table in Section V.

inasmuch as we have nothing to do with the amount of money available, we are backing the President's budget because he says there is not enough money to go through with this 70-group program.

Not taking into consideration the other factors which I realize must be taken into consideration, but speaking purely from a military point of view, it is my opinion that the minimum defense forces as far as the Air Force is concerned—and with world conditions as they are—would consist of a 70-group Air Force.

The strategy of the Air Force was to challenge, not the President's ceiling, but rather the budgets of the other services. Thus, Vandenberg affirmed his belief that "adequate national defense" could be obtained for $15 billion. So, too, did Symington. "Frankly," he said, "I think you can get the United States secure for $15,000,000,000, and I have felt that way for some time, for a good many months." These statements could be taken as endorsements of the President's budget. On the other hand, given their repeated assertions that the national defense required a 70-group Air Force, their words could also be taken as a suggestion that overall security would be maximized if Congress took money out of someone else's budget and made it available to the Air Force.[17]

The failure of the subcommittee to secure information about the strategic consequences of alternative force levels was very much evident in the discussion of the Air Force budget. Referring to Symington's statement that the Air Force's original request had been for $8 billion, Mahon asked for "whatever you can give us as to approximately what made up the things you might have been able to do with the $8,000,000,000 plus which you cannot now do with the amount you are now requesting [$4.5 billion]." To this Symington replied: "Since this decision on the money we have now changed our program from a 70-group program to a 48-group program. That is basically the largest difference in the money." The difficulty with Symington's answer was that he was essentially saying only that if the Air Force had more money, it could buy more

[17] *HCA, Hearings 1950 Budget,* II, 18, 104, 236. On the matter of Symington's report and discussed dismissal, see Millis, ed., *The Forrestal Diaries,* pp. 544–46.

airplanes. It revealed nothing about the security consequences involved in the difference between 48 and 70 groups.

On another occasion Mahon asked General Vandenberg what sort of Air Force program could be supported with an additional $600, $800, and $1,000 million dollars. The General replied that he could maintain 54, 57, or 60 air groups. Although in this instance Mahon appears to have been looking for an answer in groups, it is nevertheless noteworthy that the answer revealed nothing about the kind of additional groups to be added: troop carrier groups, heavy bomber groups, jet fighter groups, or what. In neither of these instances, nor on similar occasions, was there any sign that Mahon or his fellow committeemen felt at all dissatisfied with such answers. No members went on to state that, while this was all very interesting, what they really wanted to know was just what kind of airplanes would be in these groups and exactly what the Air Force would be able to do with them.[18]

The whole discussion of the 70-group Air Force had been heavily clouded since the publication of the Finletter Report by the fact that its composition was treated as classified information. No one, as a matter of public knowledge, was supposed to know how many and what kind of planes were to be in it. It had, in short, all the attributes of a "magical" number. The first break in the overcast of secrecy occurred in January 1949 when Vinson coaxed Symington, during the authorization hearings, to put the composition of the force on the public record.

Mahon considered this a great breach in the nation's security and exchanged some sharp words with Vinson on the subject when he came before the subcommittee. Mahon felt so strongly about the matter that he would not permit the figures to appear in his own record. The composition of the 48-group force scheduled under the President's budget had also been published by Vinson's committee, and this Mahon did include in the record, protesting as he did so the wisdom of the earlier disclosure. (The next year he kept the comparable information out of his hearings on the fiscal 1951 budget.) Mahon's record also contained the number of planes that

---

[18] *HCA, Hearings 1950 Budget,* II, 17, 107.

were in theory to make up the various kinds of groups. It did not, however, contain the composition of the 59 groups into which the Air Force had been finally organized under the fiscal 1949 budget. This information was later released by the Air Force on May 1, 1949.[19]

The issue was somewhat ironic. Although it had obviously been forgotten by, or had escaped the attention of, Vinson, Mahon, Symington, and apparently everyone else (except perhaps Russian intelligence), the fact of the matter was that all the information necessary to discover the composition of the 70-group Air Force (and that of the 66-group and the 55-group forces as well) had already been published in one or another of the voluminous hearings held during the spring of 1948 on the fiscal 1949 budget.[20]

From these various sources it would be clear to the diligent Congressman who consulted them that the 70-group Air Force would include 20 strategic bombardment groups: 4 heavy and 16 medium. The heavy bombardment groups (18 planes each) were made up of intercontinental-range bombers (B-36's at this time). The medium bombardment groups (30 planes each) were made up of planes requiring overseas bases or aerial refueling to reach their targets (B-29's and B-50's at this time). The 70-group Air Force would additionally contain: 6 strategic reconnaissance groups; 4 tactical reconnaissance groups; 5 light bombardment groups; 22 day fighter groups; 3 all-weather fighter groups; 4 heavy troop carrier groups; and 6 medium troop carrier groups.

In contrast, the 48-group Air Force planned for fiscal 1950 would include only 14 strategic bombardment groups: 4 heavy and 10 medium. The remainder of the force was to contain: 6 strategic

[19] See HCAS, *1949 Authorization Bill*, pp. 174–75; HCA, *Hearings 1950 Budget*, I, 218–19; II, 21, 23, 131–33; *Department of Defense Appropriations for 1951*, Hearings before the Subcommittee of the Committee on Appropriations, House of Representatives, 81st Cong., 2d Sess. (Washington, 1950) [hereafter cited as HCA, *Hearings 1951 Budget*], p. 1352; and New York *Times*, May 2, 1949.

[20] See HCA, *Hearings 1949 Budget*, II, 55, 171–73, and *Senate UMT Hearings, 1948*, p. 392. The March data did not, however, break down the strategic bombing groups between heavy (B-36) and medium (B-29) bombardment groups, and one of the "January" strategic reconnaissance groups was listed in March as a strategic bombardment group.

reconnaissance groups; 1 tactical reconnaissance group; 1 light bombardment group; 17 day fighter groups; 3 all-weather fighter groups; 4 heavy troop carrier groups; and 2 medium troop carrier groups.[21]

In the case of the 59 groups into which the Air Force had been finally organized during fiscal 1949, the number of strategic bombardment groups had been 15, of which 2 were heavy and 13 were medium. There was, then, very little difference between the 59-group force and the 48-group force in so far as strategic bombing was concerned. (Indeed, the 48-group force would be two groups stronger in intercontinental bombers.) With regard to the rest of the 59-group structure, it was apparently overextended, and General Vandenberg told the subcommittee that when the 59 groups were reorganized they would just about make 48 full groups.

The scheduled cutback from the 59 groups maintained in fiscal 1949 to the 48 groups planned for fiscal 1950 was, therefore, more symbolic than real. As for the difference between the 48-group force and the 70-group goal, this, in so far as strategic bombing was concerned, was not 22 groups but 6, none of which consisted of intercontinental bombers. Testimony before Mahon's committee revealed, moreover, that the Air Force had only about 40 B-36's anyway, by no means enough to constitute the 4 groups anticipated in the 48- and 70-group programs. How soon the then current procurement rate would fill out these 4 groups, the public record did not reveal.[22]

[21] The December 1948 version of the fiscal 1950 budget had scheduled the mix between heavy and medium bombardment groups at 2 and 12. In January 1949, acting on the recommendation of General Curtis LeMay, the Commanding General, Strategic Air Command, the Air Force decided to change the mix to 4 and 10. In March 1949, again at LeMay's request, the number of planes in a heavy bombardment group was increased from 18 to 30. Both changes were approved by the Joint Chiefs of Staff, and they reflected the Air Force's increased confidence in the B-36 and its interest in reducing its dependence on overseas bases. See *HCA, Hearings 1950 Budget*, II, 21, and *Investigation of the B-36 Bomber Program*, Hearings before the Committee on Armed Services, House of Representatives, 81st Cong., 1st Sess. (Washington, 1949) [hereafter cited as *HCAS, B-36 Hearings*], pp. 50, 82–90, 143–48.

[22] *HCA, Hearings 1950 Budget*, II, 118, 137. The 48-group force would require a total of 180 B-36's, not counting spares. (In addition to the 4 heavy bombardment groups, 2 of the strategic reconnaissance groups—also increased

These figures, once a curious and determined Congressman had gathered them, still told him very little about the differences between the 48-group force and the 70-group force in terms of what they could accomplish in time of war. On this point, Mahon did manage to secure one relatively meaningful statement during the course of the hearings. This at least made explicit what could be inferred from the difference in the group structure of the two forces. In scaling down from 70 to 48 groups, an Air Force witness explained, the Air Force had tried "to preserve the striking power necessary for a retaliatory offensive and the minimum defensive capability for the security of the United States" at the expense of its missions in support of the other services. As a result,

[The 48-group force] . . . would have definite capabilities in the strategic air-offense field, and would have a respectable defensive power. It would be deficient in its means to exploit the offensive, because it is shy in the essential close support of ground-force elements and in the pursuing of the tactical advantage with fighter bombers and light bombardment.[23]

All these points were by no means highlighted in the record of the subcommittee's hearings or its subsequent report. Neither had they apparently impressed themselves too clearly on the minds of the committee members. On March 31, in anticipation of their final recommendation, the committee recalled several witnesses from the Air Force for the purpose of asking them what they would do if the Air Force received an $800 or $1,000-million increase over the President's budget. The committee was told that with an $800-million increase the Air Force would organize into 57 groups. The breakdown of the 9 additional groups to be added was: 4 medium

---

in March to 30 planes each—were to be equipped with the B-36.) As of the summer of 1948, the Air Force had received contract authorization for a total of 95 B-36's. In March and April 1949, as a result of the two decisions described in footnote 21, the Air Force ordered an additional 75 planes. The funds for these planes were not, however, to come from the fiscal 1950 budget. They were made available out of the fiscal 1949 budget through the cancellation of contracts for other aircraft. See *HCAS, B-36 Hearings*, pp. 82–90, 463–68.

[23] *HCA, Hearings 1950 Budget*, II, 151. The witness was Major General F. H. Smith, Jr., Assistant for Programming, Deputy Chief of Staff for Operations.

bombardment; 1 light bombardment [used for the support of ground troops]; 3 day fighter; and 1 medium troop carrier. With the $1,000-million increase, the Air Force would provide, additionally, the final 2 medium bombardment groups required to give it the full 20 strategic bombardment groups of the 70-group program. (An inquisitive Congressman would not have found all of these figures in the record, but he could have deduced them from the information in it and that provided in January by the Armed Services Committee.) [24]

Thus, of the 9 groups to be added for $800 million, only 4 were for strategic bombing. The breakdown of the actual airplanes that could be manned and supported with this increase was off the record, but the frustrated comment of Representative Sikes revealed that the increase would not provide for the procurement of so much as *one* bomber, heavy or medium. This, apparently, was not quite what the committee had had in mind, and Sikes exclaimed:

General, many of us feel the need for implementing our long-range striking force so that in the event of an emergency we could strike positive, powerful blows anywhere in the world.

As I interpret the breakdown you have given us, I do not see that you are going to materially strengthen your long-range striking force.

On the one hand [the $1,000-million increase] you plan to add a small number of bombers but they are not the planes we have been taught to believe are our most effective long-range planes [that is, not B-36's]. The other program [the $800-million increase] does not carry any bomber procurement.

To this Symington replied that the Air Force, under the 48-group program, had already "taken care of what we thought was the most important aspect [the strategic striking force]." An Air Force budget officer explained that "We have already augmented our bomber program and our strategic striking force to the extent possible in the production schedules." The virtue of the projected increases, he pointed out, was that with them, aside from adding to the number of groups in the strategic bombing force, "we have balanced

[24] *Ibid.,* I, 228, 240.

off as far as we can the ground support, and so forth, we are providing the Army." [25]

The report of the subcommittee did not make this point clear. On the contrary, it obscured it. The report did not itemize the groups that would be added by the $800-million increase, but presented instead an abbreviated breakdown of the 58 groups the Air Force would have as a result of it. This identified 20 groups as "bombardment groups." This statement did not distinguish between heavy and medium bombardment groups, and the figure, while suggestive of the 20 strategic bombardment groups called for under the 70-group program, actually included the 2 light bombardment groups for ground support. The subcommittee's total of 58 groups was one group higher than that projected by the Air Force in March. The additional group was a day fighter group, and it presumably represented a second thought on the part of the Air Force about what could be accomplished with the $800 million.[26]

The conclusions to be drawn from the preceding pages are these: (1) the subcommittee had determined on increasing the Air Force's budget before they had any clear idea of what the dollars would actually buy; (2) the Air Force itself believed that the major strategic deficiency of the 48-group program was its ability to support ground combat, and it planned to use the additional funds largely to meet this deficiency; (3) the committee had by no means developed the information necessary to permit it to make a rational judgment as to whether the ability of the Army to fight a war would be better served by increasing its air support or by increasing the men and machines it could employ on the ground; (4) the committee's questions were in general not such as to make the strategic issues at stake in the increase very clear to themselves; and (5)

[25] *Ibid.*, I, 235–36. The witness was Colonel J. A. Brooks III, Chief, Program Analysis Division, Office of the Comptroller.

[26] *House Report, 1950 Budget,* p. 31. By the time the 10-group increase was described to the Senate subcommittee in June, the Air Force had dropped this extra fighter group and had substituted for it an additional medium bombardment group. See *National Military Establishment Appropriation Bill for 1950,* Hearings before the Subcommittee of the Committee on Appropriations, United States Senate, 81st Cong., 1st Sess. (Washington, 1949) [hereafter cited as *SCA, Hearings 1950 Budget*], p. 336.

the committee's record and report were not such as to make either the facts or the issues very clear to others.

The end result was a Congressional choice made without any real understanding of the alternatives involved and which had little to recommend it even in terms of its own rationale. The quality of analysis in the House debate was that of the subcommittee's magnified. The major speech on behalf of the $800-million increase was made by Representative Clarence Cannon, Democrat of Missouri and Chairman of the Appropriations Committee proper. Cannon had sat in on many of the subcommittee's meetings, and he took charge of Mahon's bill when it came under attack from Sheppard and Vinson for failing to provide additional funds for the Navy as well. With scant regard for the three-phase war outlined by General Bradley and identified by him as the basis for the Joint Chiefs' own strategic planning, Cannon proclaimed that atomic bombardment might end a war with Russia in three weeks. And, if not, the United States could let Europeans fight Europeans.

We will not necessarily have to send our land army over there in the next war, as in the last war. Let us equip soldiers from other nations and let them send their boys into holocausts instead of sending our own boys. That is what long-range planes mean.

With equal disregard for the fact that the 10-group increase he was sponsoring provided 6 groups for the support of a land army that planned to fight "over there" and for the procurement of not a single B-36, Cannon urged his colleagues to put their "money in the only place that counts, and that is on long-range, land-based bombers." [27]

IV

A serious effort to reach a rational judgment about the desirability of the administration's defense budget would have involved the subcommittee in a consideration of the five matters noted in the

[27] *C.R.*, 95, pp. 4500–4501. Cannon's statements are from the New York *Times*, April 14, 1949. He subsequently edited his remarks for the record. See Bailey and Samuel, *Congress at Work*, p. 371. The statement that all 6 groups were for ground support is partly inference, but they were so described by the Air Force to Mahon's committee. See *HCA, Hearings 1950 Budget*, I, 228.

Introduction: (a) the nation's foreign policy purposes; (b) the alternative means available to serve those purposes; (c) the possible shapes of the future; (d) the effect that budgets of various size might have on these futures; and (e) the costs such budgets would entail for other national values. In actuality, the subcommittee's "study" failed to come to grips with any of these subjects.

With regard to the budget's relationship to the nation's foreign policy objectives, the committee did receive an off-the-record briefing from George Kennan, the Director of the State Department's Policy Planning Staff. But this briefing appears to have been the foreign policy counterpart to that given by General Gruenther on behalf of the Joint Staff. Just as Gruenther had catalogued Russian capabilities, so Kennan presented a general review of Russian intentions—the goals, strategy, and tactics of Soviet foreign policy. Neither together nor separately did these briefings provide the committee with what it needed most if it was to undertake an independent review of the administration's budget: a politico-military analysis of the American security position; an outline of the general strategy through which the administration planned to maintain and improve that position; and a demonstration of how the forces provided under the budget would help to implement that strategy. Gruenther and Kennan had talked about Russian forces and Russian intentions, but not about the relationship between American forces and the defense of western Europe, the prospect of "local emergencies," or the shape that international politics might take after the advent of Russian nuclear weapons systems.[28]

The poverty of the subcommittee's consideration of these matters is easily illustrated: only once in 3,000 pages was an effort made to relate the budget to the North Atlantic Treaty then before the Senate. This occurred when Vinson was summarizing his recommendations for a $1.6-billion increase in the President's budget. Sheppard interrupted to observe that the United States was about "to take on additional military responsibility."

[28] For references indicating the character of Kennan's briefing, see *HCA, Hearings 1950 Budget*, II, 36; IV, 17, 567.

The degree to which the increase in our military aspect should be considered in accordance with the [North Atlantic] compact is an unknown factor so far as I am concerned at the moment. I know that it is pertinent, but as to the degree of pertinency, I don't know. I want to ask you if you have had any conference with the State Department or any other military echelon that would indicate to you the percentage of increase that might be necessitated because of the North Atlantic compact and its ramifications.

Vinson replied that he had not.

I can just use common sense, and from a common-sense viewpoint, I know the obligations that the Atlantic Pact is going to impose upon this country. And I know nothing will contribute more to strength and the power of the pact than to let . . . the world . . . know that we are not diminishing our forces when we sign the pact.

Sheppard was not completely satisfied with this analysis.

In order for me to have my thinking straightened out on several aspects of our military requirements, I want to find out if I possibly can through the proper source as to what degree, mathematically speaking, our military obligations can become effective under this pact, because it is extremely interesting.

Vinson said: "I cannot answer. Perhaps Mr. Short can." There was no answer from Mr. Short.[29]

Similarly unanswered was the question of whether the administration believed that the international situation had so improved since spring that the rearmament started then could be safely cut back. Although this question had received considerable discussion in the press during the fall of 1948, the subcommittee made no effort to secure an answer to it. Symington told Vinson's committee in January that he thought the international situation looked about the same as it had in the spring of 1948, and Bradley told Mahon's committee in March that he had been more worried last year than he was now, and that was about the sum of the public record on the subject.

In consequence, Congressional debate was grounded on individual appraisals, and these were varied. Speaking in favor of Sheppard's

[29] *Ibid.,* I, 221–22.

and Vinson's move to add $300 million for the Navy to Mahon's bill, Plumley admonished the House in April that every man in it "knows down to his shoes that the [international] situation is definitely worse and more critical than as of a year ago." Plumley cited the Berlin blockade, the new responsibilities of the Atlantic Pact, and the looming victory of communism in China. "God knows," he warned, "we will need all we can have or get if I see what I think I see ahead."

The vision of Senator Elmer Thomas, Democrat of Oklahoma and Chairman of the Senate Subcommittee on Military Appropriations, was quite different. Speaking in August on behalf of a bill that cut that of the House by $1.1 billion, Thomas explained to the Senate that recent months had seen a definite improvement in the international situation and that the earlier "feverishness" was no longer justified. What the State Department thought of all this no one knew. Neither committee had solicited its views on the matter, and the State Department did not volunteer them.[30]

The quality of the analysis given by Mahon's committee to the problems posed by the existence of alternative military means has already been examined. As for the possibility that some of the purposes the budget was designed to serve might be equally well or better promoted through nonmilitary means or the military power of others, this the committee did not broach at all. All members of Congress were, of course, aware of the fact that the budget contained a $4.9-billion appropriation for European aid and that, as Mahon pointed out in the House debate, this was properly regarded as a part of the national defense program. But neither his committee nor anyone else's undertook to examine whether American security might be better served by a shift of funds from this program to the military budget or vice versa. The absence of examination did not, of course, inhibit the expression of opinion. Thus, in the House the advocates of Sheppard's naval increase insisted that money spent in this fashion would "do us a great deal more good" than the same amount spent on foreign aid, and in the Senate the proponents for

[30] *HCAS, 1949 Authorization Bill*, p. 157; *HCA, Hearings 1950 Budget*, IV, 577; and *C.R.*, 95, pp. 4432, 12252.

restoring the cuts in the House's Air Force increase advanced the same argument.[31]

The problem of considering American military needs in light of the military power of allies was interjected just once into the considerations of the subcommittee. Engel told Symington that he could make up his mind about how many groups the Air Force needed a lot better if he knew something about the kind of air forces the European nations were creating. Engel thought "that the real defense has to consist of the joint forces of all the Allies and in building them up so we will have an overwhelming balance of military power." Symington replied he would try to get some figures for him, although he indicated that it would be rather difficult. Whether the committee received the information is not revealed by the record, but unless it was accompanied by some statement about the contribution European planes would make to the problems the Air Force expected to meet in war, the figures could not have had much meaning. The issue was also introduced once into the record of the Senate subcommittee. There Louis Johnson, who had succeeded Forrestal as Secretary of Defense in March, assured the economy-minded Senators that the funds the President had recently requested for European military aid in no way reduced the requirements of the American armed forces for fiscal 1950.[32]

Mahon's committee did give considerable attention to the possible shapes of the future. Its inquiry was limited, however, to two questions: when would the Russians get the A-bomb, and what was the likelihood of general war? The information received on both of these questions was almost entirely off the record, but the sum of it was probably indicated in Symington's testimony. He stated that most of the civilians he had talked with in the military establishment did not believe the Russians would start a war until they had the A-bomb, and although a variety of dates had been advanced for this, in his own opinion it would not be before 1952. When Mahon

[31] See *C.R.*, *95*, pp. 4428, 4431, 12302. The words quoted are Vinson's.
[32] *HCA, Hearings 1950 Budget*, II, 27–28, and *SCA, Hearings 1950 Budget*, p. 5.

reported his bill on the House floor, he listed the numerous witnesses with whom his committee had discussed the likelihood of war and announced that there was no anticipation that it would come in the near future.

The difficulty in knowing what to do with such information was well illustrated in an exchange between Sikes and Major General S. E. Anderson, the Air Force Deputy Chief of Staff for Operations. Referring to the earlier briefings by Kennan and Gruenther, Anderson said that the substance of their remarks had been that "fiscal year 1950 is a period in which no major power is likely deliberately to resort to force of arms." Sikes commented that this was "only an estimate" and that intelligence had been fooled before. "Since this is the case, we cannot guarantee that we are not going to be attacked; we have to be ready to defend ourselves and take retaliatory action." General Anderson's rejoinder was to note that the Kennan-Gruenther briefings had also made the point that fiscal 1950 was "a period through which the danger of unplanned hostilities as a result of miscalculation will continue." [33]

Did this mean that the only rational course was to plan for the possibility of Russia's irrationality? Mahon told the House "If war comes soon, we are appropriating too little. If we have miscalculated the dangers, if the threat of war is just a deceptive mirage on the horizon, we are appropriating too much." What Mahon did not tell the House, however, was what criteria his committee had used to arrive at the size of the appropriations bill he did recommend. How had the committee chosen a sum of this order rather than some other that could be equally well described as too much for peace and too little for war? The answer is obvious. Mahon's committee had not made any choice, except the choice not to review the choice the Executive had made.

The committee did not attempt to explore the problem of what the effect might be on the shape of the future from changes in the size and composition of the President's budget. Had the committee given more attention to the question of what foreign policy considerations had been responsible for the cutback from the rearmament

[33] *C.R.,* 95, p. 4427, and *HCA, Hearings 1950 Budget,* II, 36, 39, 41.

program begun in the spring of 1948, it might have been led to examine whether and how changes in the budget might affect the future course of Soviet foreign policy. As it was, the only references to the problem of estimating the provocative and/or deterrent effects of the budget were a few that occurred during the floor debates, such as that made by Mahon. He asserted that the reason there had not already been a war with Russia was, in all probability, because the nation had atomic bombs and planes to carry them. He also claimed that the extra funds his committee recommended for the Air Force would further diminish the likelihood of such a war. But Mahon, given his interest in the 70-group program, presumably did not mean to imply that an even larger increase in the Air Force's budget would not have had an additional deterrent effect.[34]

The subcommittee inquired not at all into the considerations responsible for the $15-billion ceiling. No effort was made to follow up the suggestions in the press that the ceiling was the work of the Bureau of the Budget and the Treasury Department and to explore with witnesses from those agencies the premises on which they were supposed to have argued for it. Far from undertaking to discover whether there might be some other sum which would strike them (if not the President) as more desirable to spend on defense, the committee seemed content to let the administration witnesses discuss the ceiling as if it involved no choice at all. Consider, for example, the following statements advanced, respectively, by Forrestal, Sullivan, and Bradley.

The impression that the military are not conscious of economic considerations is unfair and inaccurate. They are deeply conscious of the fact that our military power rests fundamentally on the will and spirit of the people, and upon our capacity to produce. That capacity to produce can only be maintained if you have a sound and thriving economy.

We accept it [the budget] because of the overriding necessity for a military budget consistent with the needs of our national economy, which is the indispensable basis of all our military strength.

[34] *C.R., 95*, pp. 4429, 4528.

And I may also assure you that we are fully cognizant of the fact that our country can only afford so much and that we of the Army fully and and wholeheartedly support the budget under the limitations imposed by our Commander-in-chief.[35]

All three of these statements implied that the dollars allocated to defense in the fiscal 1950 budget were limited by a fixed condition (what the economy could stand) rather than determined through the interplay of competing demands on the national income. The members of the committee did not challenge this perspective; indeed, as will be seen, they fully shared it. As a result, the committee tended not to see even the theoretical possibility of spending significantly larger sums for defense than those which the Executive had determined the nation should bear; much less did it try to find out what the costs of such higher budgets might actually be.

Just as the committee gave no attention to the possibility of spending a much larger sum than that requested by the President, so too it made no effort to investigate the consequences of spending a much smaller sum. The scope of the House's choice was, accordingly, restricted to the realm of making changes, not in the gross size of the budget, but in the manner in which this gross had been allocated among the services. Here, the major change rejected (the proposal to add $300 million to the Navy's budget) was of the same form as the major change voted, the Air Force increase. In both instances, the House appears to have made its choice without any real understanding of the alternatives involved.

v

The performance of the House subcommittee can be easily summarized. Its "very great study" came nowhere near developing the kind of information necessary to permit the House to make its own decision about what was "necessary for national defense." The performance of the Senate subcommittee was no different. The bill it

[35] *HCA, Hearings 1950 Budget,* I, 15; III, 2; IV, 575.

reported in July contained three major changes from that voted by the House in April. First, the Senate committee restored $132 million of the $357 million that the House had cut from the Army and Navy budgets, and it imposed cuts of its own elsewhere in the budgets of those services totaling $30 million. The result was a net increase of $89 million for the Army and one of $13 million for the Navy. Secondly, the committee recommended a general reduction in the budget of $434 million which was to be made by the Secretary of Defense where he saw fit. Finally, the committee recommended that the Senate reject the extra $800 million that the House had voted the Air Force. The considerations responsible for these last two changes will be discussed in Chapter IV. The quality of the analysis behind them was, if anything, even lower than that associated with the choices made by the House committee.[36]

The Senate committee's bill had a much stormier passage than had Mahon's in the House, but it was ultimately voted with these particulars unchanged on August 29, 1949. By this time the fiscal year 1950 was already two months under way, and Congress had been obliged in the interim to provide the Executive with temporary appropriations in order to make possible the meeting of payrolls and the conduct of other essential activities. In October the representatives of the two chambers met in conference to resolve the differences between their two bills. The bargaining was complex and long. In the end, with regard to the Army and the Navy, they agreed to a budget that provided $3 million more for the Army and $96 million more for the Navy than had the House bill.

The Senate also agreed to drop its provision for a $434-million cut to be made at the discretion of the Secretary of Defense. The House had particularly objected to this provision, both because it seemed an evasion of Congressional responsibility and because the Senate, while willing to grant this discretion to the Secretary, had at the same time seen fit to restore so many of the specific cuts the House had made. The Senate's concession was, however, largely

[36] Figures from Huzar, *The Purse and the Sword*, pp. 203–4, and *Senate Report, 1950 Budget*, pp. 3–4. See also the table on p. 89.

a formal gesture. Both chambers knew that Secretary Johnson was planning further reductions, and the final bill contained the request that he keep them informed of their extent and nature.

The President's announcement on September 23 that the Soviet Union had exploded its first A-bomb, three years in advance of the date the Finletter Report had used as a "pessimistic" planning estimate, provided whatever additional incentive the House required to stand fast in its determination to appropriate the extra $800 million for the Air Force. The Senate extracted from the House an agreement to cut these funds by $63 million, and then, having received from the President unmistakable signs that he would not spend the extra money, agreed to a bill containing the remainder of the increase. In return for this concession, the Senate secured a bill containing a lower appropriation for the stockpiling of raw materials than had been desired by the House. Neither side was particularly pleased with these compromises, but the pressure to reach some form of agreement was great. Congress wished to adjourn, and the Executive wished to have its appropriations for the fiscal year finally determined.

The bill was passed on October 18 and signed by the President on October 29. Excluding the Air Force increase, its total provision for the armed services ($13.8 billion) was only $269 million short of what the President had requested in January. As for the Air Force increase itself, the President disposed of this in the manner expected. These funds, he announced when he signed the bill, would be placed "in reserve." [37]

The development of the budget can be seen in the table on the next page. All figures are in new obligational authority.

Congress clearly failed to act the part in which Mahon, Vinson, and others had cast it: that of a coordinate budget-maker intent on reaching its own determination of what was necessary for national defense. It is also evident that the failure of Congress was that of its committees written large. They made no effort to review the considerations responsible for the President's budget or to develop

[37] These events are described in Bailey and Samuel, *Congress at Work*, pp. 371–81, and Huzar, *The Purse and the Sword*, pp. 191–92, 204–6.

alternatives to it. Without such information, Congress was in no position to make a rational, independent judgment on the size and composition of the defense budget. Nor did it. In essence, Congress appears to have accepted the Executive's choice of a budget in the vicinity of $15 billion without question and to have gone on to endeavor, with very little reason to guide it and rather limited success, to make a few changes in the way the President had allocated this sum.

Congressional action on the budget

	Pres.[a]	House[b]	±Pres.	Senate[c]	±House	Conference ±House[d]	Final I[e]	Final II[f]
USAF	4.554	5.340	+786	4.541	−799	−63	5.277	5.289
USN	4.347	4.227	−120	4.240	+ 13	+97	4.324	4.313
USA	4.498	4.261	−237	4.350	+ 89	+ 3	4.264	4.263
	13.399	13.828		13.131	−434		13.865	13.865
				12.697				

[a] *HCA, Hearings 1950 Budget*, I, 20.   [b] *House Report, 1950 Budget*, p. 4.
[c] Figures derived from *ibid.*, p. 4, and *Senate Report, 1950 Budget*, pp. 3–4.
[d] *C.R.*, 95, pp. 14136–38, 14920–21.
[e] The "Final I" figures are the arithmetic results of those previously cited. The present writer cannot account for the difference between these and those of "Final II."
[f] For the Air Force and the Navy, see *HCA, Hearings 1951 Budget*, pp. 1313, 1769. The Army figure is derived from *U.S. Budget, FY 1951*, pp. A95, A96, 605.

The gap between Congressional pretensions and Congressional performance is striking. A plausible explanation for this gap is to be found in still another disparity: that between the formidable character of the task to which Mahon and his colleagues had dedicated themselves and the resources they had to carry it out. There were, after all, only five men on the House subcommittee and they had but two staff assistants to help them. As one Representative sympathetically put it to the House: "There were these seven men pitting their knowledge and their skill, their insight and their vision, against this great array [from the Executive] that comes up before them one after another." [38] Under these circumstances, may not the committee have concluded that it was not only an unequal contest

[38] Quoted in Bailey and Samuel, *Congress at Work*, p. 304. The staff of the Senate subcommittee appears to have been no larger.

but essentially a hopeless one, that a rational review of the President's budget, however desirable, was for all practical purposes beyond their means?

The opportunity of the subcommittee to develop meaningful alternatives to the President's budget was obviously restricted by limitations in ability, in staff, in time, and in information. Many of the problems associated with the budget must have struck the committee as being open only to professional analysis. Moreover, even though a committee member might consider himself as capable of grappling with these problems as the Chiefs, there was still no escape from the fact that the Chiefs had far more "Indians" than the committee had. What is more, the vast apparatus of the Executive had had eight months to analyze and reflect on the budget, whereas only two months were available to the subcommittee. Finally, if the alternatives involved in the budget were to be developed effectively, the committee's analysis would have to extend into a consideration of war plans. These, however, were matters of highly classified information, and it could hardly be expected that the administration would lightly make them available.

The sum of these limitations may well have been sufficient to persuade some members to give up before they started and to forego an analysis of the budget. But they do not in themselves afford a satisfactory explanation for the performance of the subcommittee as a whole. What makes many of the problems associated with the defense budget difficult is the fact that they have no determinate answer, not that the answers can be determined only through the application of complex and esoteric professional techniques. They are hard to decide, not hard to understand. The failure of the committee to come to grips with the major foreign-policy and strategic assumptions of the budget must, then, be explained more by the way the members exercised their abilities than by the character of those abilities.

The same point can be made with regard to staff. There is no evidence to suggest that the committee was dissatisfied with the size of its staff. When a Representative suggested during the House debate that they give Mahon's committee more money in order to equip it with a larger staff, the members of the committee did not rise to affirm the pressing necessity for such action if they were to cope with the high policy problems of the budget. As previously noted, the committee did not even make use of the rather extensive preliminary analysis developed in the press with regard to the background and implications of the budget.[39]

Few people are so pressed for time as an energetic and dedicated Congressman. As Senator Brien McMahon, Democrat of Connecticut and then Chairman of the Joint Committee on Atomic Energy, once graphically described it: ". . . we are so burdened, so harried, with forty times more than we can do, that unless someone comes up and pounds on us, it is just not possible for us to be looking for things to do, to say nothing of doing them." In consequence, it is not unknown for a chairman to gavel his committee to order knowing no more about the subject at hand than the formal purpose of the hearings, and to have learned this only by virtue of the piece of paper that a staff member has just passed to him. Another chairman may count himself lucky if his staff has had the time to prepare at least a few intelligent questions with which to start the hearings, but even so he must confront the Executive witnesses during the remainder of the session completely cold and in the dark. Under these circumstances, there are Congressmen whose sense of frustration with their performance yields to no one's.[40]

[39] Engel did allow that there was "no question" that a larger staff would be useful, but it is to be noted that the dialogue was concerned with the need for additional staff to help discover instances of extravagant funding, not to help develop the major issues of the budget. See *C.R.*, 95, p. 4513. For a discussion of the committee's staff practice at that time, see Huzar, *The Purse and the Sword*, pp. 386–93.

With regard to the use made of the press, not one of the periodical and newspaper articles summarized in Chapter II was inserted in the *Congressional Record*.

[40] See the transcript of an interview with McMahon printed in the *Bulletin of the Atomic Scientists*, January 1952, p. 7. The two instances cited are based, respectively, on personal interviews with (a) the Staff Director of one of the major Senate committees in the national security field (December 2, 1955), and (b) with the Chairman of a major House subcommittee in this field (March 29, 1957). Neither committee was an appropriations committee. The same general point is made in Huzar, *The Purse and the Sword*, pp. 383–84.

But while the time of Mahon's committee was limited, a great deal could still have been learned in two months if the committee had spent this time questioning the major political and military premises of the budget. Instead, the committee allocated the bulk of its time to an examination of the minutia of the budget's programs. The possible relationship of the budget to the North Atlantic Treaty occupied but a few puzzled paragraphs in the 3,000 pages of the hearing. Even the price of the oats the Army expected to buy for horses received as much attention as this, while a more consequential item like the appropriation for the National Board for the Promotion of Rifle Practice managed to occupy the committee for 15 pages. Whatever their shortcomings with regard to high policy issues, the members of the committee were relentless, thorough, and ingenious in their development of the alternatives involved in the financial trivia of the budget.[41]

How much information the subcommittee was denied on the grounds that it was classified, the record of the hearings does not indicate. It is certainly safe to assume that the committee did not learn all there was to know about the plans and capabilities of the services. During the floor debate Representative Chet Holifield, Democrat of California and a member of the Joint Committee on Atomic Energy, gently inquired whether the subcommittee had received any information regarding the number and power of the bombs in the atomic stockpile. Information of this order, he remarked, seemed "absolutely necessary" for an intelligent consideration of the kind of armed forces the budget should provide. Mahon replied that "it would not be appropriate for me to comment on the floor of the House in regard to what we know about atomic energy." The answer was as disingenuous as the question; they both knew that the subcommittee had not received the slightest information on this subject.[42]

[41] See *HCA, Hearings 1950 Budget,* IV, 217, 841–54, 1023–26, and *passim.* For a good description of the range and order of Congressional questions, see Huzar, *The Purse and the Sword,* pp. 93–104.

[42] *C.R.,* 95, pp. 4431–32. At this time not even the Joint Committee on Atomic Energy had been given stockpile information. See Brien McMahon, "Should We Reveal the Size of Our Atomic Stockpile," *Bulletin of the Atomic*

The point at issue here, however, is whether the committee learned as much as it could have about the plans and capabilities of the armed services. Did it push the Executive to the limits on the matter of sensitive information, or did it impose upon itself restrictions in excess of those which others would have insisted be observed? This question cannot be directly answered from the record. It can be demonstrated, however, that the committee took a very restrictive view of what the public needed to know. Mahon, as earlier noted, had a "strong conviction" that the appropriations hearings provided too much defense information to the public and, thereby, to the Russians. (Hundreds of millions of dollars was his estimate on the worth of the information they had made available in the last decade.) Thus, when Vinson appeared before the subcommittee Mahon declared that he had "gone to a very dangerous limit" in making available the composition of the 70-group Air Force. "I do not think the people of the country need to know exactly how many bombardment groups we have, fighter groups, reconnaissance, and so forth. I do not see that that necessarily helps."

Vinson protested that the Air Force had not objected to his making the information available.

Of course, there is no thought on my part at any time to divulge a single thing of a secret nature, but the House certainly has to know what we are going to buy when we make a lump-sum appropriation. I never in the 16 years that I was chairman of the Naval Affairs Committee brought in a bill appropriating $3,000,000,000 without saying that the $3,000,000,000 would turn out so many submarines, so many destroyers, and so many airplane carriers.

Now, the country is entitled to know it. The Congress is going to know, because the Congress wants to know what these things are for.

This was not Mahon's opinion. His view was the one he had earlier expressed to General Bradley.

Scientists, March 1949, p. 66. Moving to Mahon's defense, Representative James Van Zandt, Republican of Pennsylvania and a member of the Armed Services Committee, asked if it was not a fact that members of the armed forces "come fully prepared to give the committee the results of their years and years of experience involving the employment [sic] of the atom bomb in time of war." *C.R.*, 95, p. 4432.

I realize that you cannot come down here and say, "I want $15,000,-000,00 for the National Defense Establishment" and not justify it. I realize you have to give us some information, but there is no sense in putting a lot of these things in the printed record. There is no public demand from Congress, that I know of, that that be done. This committee always leaves it up to the military to decide what should or should not be on the record.[43]

Whether the committee took as restrictive a view of its *own* need for information as it did of the public's, these statements do not make clear. Perhaps the members of the committee left it to the military to decide what they should be told off the record, as well as what the public should be told on it. In any event, if the subcommittee was not limiting its own opportunities for information, it was certainly limiting the opportunity of Congress to perform the role of coordinate budget-maker. For if Congress was to exercise any effective direction over the President's budgetary policy, it had not only to decide what was wanting in that policy (for this the committee's judgment might be accepted), it had also to persuade other members of the policy elite and a substantial part of the attentive public as well that the President's policies were deficient. For this second purpose the closed hearings of the subcommittee and its recondite record hardly provided the best ammunition.

In sum, the handicaps inherent in the subcommittee's position with regard to ability, staff, time, and information are no more impressive than those which the committee voluntarily imposed on itself. The members of the committee may not have been in the best of positions to accomplish a rational review of the President's budget, but they obviously must not have seen much point in accomplishing what they could. Whatever the explanation for the committee's performance, it would appear, then, that it must be sought primarily in terms of the interests and motivation of its members rather than in terms of the analytical opportunities open to them.

---

[43] *HCA, Hearings 1950 Budget,* I, 218–20; IV, 580. Bradley believed that the appropriations hearings contained "all any nation would need to know" about the military establishment and that the basic "error" lay in publishing them in such detail.

IV *Congressional Choice and*

the Climate of Opinion

The discussion in Chapter III took as its point of departure Mahon's own description of Congress' role in the budgeting process: that of a coordinate budget-maker. If the actions of Congress are viewed in these terms, it is clear that neither the House nor the Senate actually performed this role and that their committees did not give the budget the kind of analysis necessary to equip them to do so. It is also evident that the absence of such an analysis cannot be explained simply through reference to the handicaps under which the committees would have labored if they had tried to undertake it.

This picture of events gives rise to three questions. First, why did the two subcommittees demonstrate so little interest in exploring alternatives to the President's budget? Second, since information of this sort did not guide Congress in its choices, what did? And, finally, does not the character of Congress' choices and the analysis of its committees suggest that the President could have secured practically any size budget he wished? Congress endorsed the $15-billion budget without question; why should it not have been equally acquiescent to a $7-billion budget or a $30-billion budget? Is not the measure of Congress' performance in the role of coordinate budget-maker the conclusion that it exercises basically little influence on the size and composition of the defense budget?

The answers to the first two questions will be clearer if discussion begins with the third, for the suggestion that Congress would have been equally receptive to any other size budget highlights the doubly deceptive nature of the role that Mahon and Vinson defined for Congress. Not only does Congress not, in fact, perform it; the role itself presupposes a conception of the budgeting process that distorts the real character of that process and obscures, as a result, the true areas of Congressional influence in it. The conception of Congress as a coordinate budget-maker suggests that the budget is developed in two independent and sequential stages. First, the Executive examines all the alternatives and determines what it thinks the budget should be, and then Congress reviews these alternatives through its committees and makes its own judgment about what to spend.

This conception of the budget's development is incorrect in two basic respects. In the first place, neither the Executive nor Congress approaches the defense budget as an ad hoc problem, intent on a free-ranging examination of all possible alternatives before making a choice. On the contrary, members of the Executive and Congress start their thinking about the budget with a common and very narrow range of figures in mind. The area of their choice is closely limited by the prevailing climate of opinion regarding desirable and possible defense budgets. All figures outside these limits, in either direction, are rejected out of hand as manifestly undesirable, infeasible, or just plain inconceivable.

Secondly, the particular choices made by members of the Executive and Congress within the limits set by the climate of opinion are not made in intellectual isolation and independence. They are, instead, strongly preconditioned by a sense for what other members want and will do. The $15-billion budget is a case in point. The general order of its size was set by the prevailing climate of opinion. Its particular dimensions were chosen by the Executive with an eye on what members of Congress wanted and would give, and the response of Congressmen to those particulars was influenced by a knowledge of what members of the Executive wanted and would spend.

If these two points are true—and their demonstration and illustration will follow—the nature of the Congressional performance in the fiscal 1950 budget must be comprehended in broader terms than those germane to the image of Congress as a coordinate budget-maker. The measure of Congressional influence on the budget cannot be taken solely through reference to committee action and floor votes. It must also be taken through reference to Congress' contribution to the climate of opinion and to the choices the Executive made in anticipation of Congressional wants and power. Similarly, the behavior of Congressmen in committee hearings and floor debates cannot be analyzed and appraised solely in terms of what would have constituted an effective rational review of the President's budget. An understanding and evaluation of this behavior must also be sought in terms of what would constitute appropriate action given Congress' perception of the climate of opinion and Executive wants and power.[1]

The "climate of opinion," as used here, is meant to refer to the prevailing image of the area of choice: what things it is conceivable to do, what things are generally wanted and what things can be practically accomplished. In terms of what was said in the Introduction about the conflict and consensus-building aspects of the policy process, the climate of opinion is the framework or context within which consensus-building occurs. It defines both the areas of agreement and the areas of possible agreement and therefore of fruitful conflict.

It is within the limits set by the prevailing climate of opinion regarding the possible and the desirable that the process of conflict

---

[1] No members of the appropriations committees or their staff were interviewed during the research for this study. This was not the result of the author's choice, but it will explain why certain points in the analysis are more hypothetical than one would wish.

The focus of the analysis has benefited greatly from the comments made on an earlier draft by Bernard C. Cohen and Roger Hilsman. See, in this instance, the latter's "Congressional-Executive Relations and the Foreign Policy Consensus," *The American Political Science Review*, September 1958, pp. 734–37. That Executive submissions to Congress are preconditioned by a sense for what Congress may accept has, of course, been long noted. See, for example, in the case of treaties, Royden J. Dangerfield, *In Defense of the Senate: A Study in Treaty Making* (Norman, University of Oklahoma Press, 1933), pp. 255–56. The references to the desirable and the possible are from William T. R. Fox, "The Reconciliation of the Desirable and the Possible," *The American Scholar*, Spring 1949, pp. 312–16.

and accommodation can effectively take place. It is here that the effort can be made to argue, fight, and bargain for particular goals and programs with some prospect of success. Outside of these limits lies the realm of what could be called the "opinion universe," the total range of views held by members of the policy elites about desirable or feasible courses of action. Here, too, voices may be raised in support of goals and programs. But these will be the voices in the policy wilderness. As in the case of the Alsop brothers with their December 1948 columns urging higher taxes and a larger defense budget, they will be advocating alternatives in support of which no effective political consensus is possible.

To state that the climate of opinion narrowly circumscribes the choices open to members of the Executive and Congress regarding the size of the defense budget is not to suggest that they should be conceived as captives of this opinion environment. Their own opinions constitute, after all, an integral part of this environment. Moreover, the climate is itself a product of the policy-making process, and members of Congress and the Executive—as key participants in that process—are active in changing the climate as well as in adapting to it.

The present study will not investigate the evolution of the climate of opinion prevailing at the time of the fiscal 1950 budget. As a result, the study will neglect one of the most important ways in which Congress exercised an influence on the content of the budget. (Another major means of influence, the choices the Executive made in anticipation of Congressional wants and power, will be considered in Chapter V.) The focus of investigation here will be, instead, on the relationship between the climate of opinion as it then existed and the kind of actions Congress took on the budget. Since this relationship was highly restrictive in its effect, it will be well to remember that Congressmen had earlier played no small part in shaping the opinions to which they were then reacting.

II

The content of the climate of opinion prevailing in 1948–1949 with regard to defense expenditures is not today a matter that can be directly researched. The relevant data, being by nature personal and subjective, are no longer available. Even at the time it would have been no easy matter to develop reliable empirical data for this concept. In its most extreme form the climate consisted of a composite of everybody's judgment about the substance, wisdom, and influence of everyone else's ideas on the subject. Obviously, for present purposes, only crude and indirect measures can be used to approximate the content of the actual opinion climate.

The following pages will rely on three major sources for such an approximation: the content of the elite press; the opinions expressed by Congressmen during floor debates; and the relevant publications of the Hoover Commission. This last was a nonpartisan group authorized by Congress in July 1947 to investigate the organization of the Executive branch of the government. The commission's investigation of the National Military Establishment took place during May–November 1948 and was conducted primarily by means of a subsidiary group, The Committee on the National Security Organization (the Eberstadt Committee). The committee and the commission proper published their reports, respectively, in January and February 1949.

The assumption made here is that the membership of the commission and its subsidiary committee (and therefore their conclusions) can be taken as broadly representative of the interested, informed, and experienced elites concerned with national defense matters. The assumption is further made that their reports, together with the opinions expressed in the press and in Congress, will mirror with reasonable accuracy the salient characteristics of any widespread consensus regarding desirable and possible defense expenditures and also Congressional perceptions of such a consensus.[2]

[2] Criteria of convenience guided the selection of the press content reviewed for this study: the clippings on file at the Council on Foreign Relations in New York.

For the membership of the Hoover Commission and the Eberstadt Committee, see *The National Security Organization*, A Report to the Congress by the Commission on Organization of the Executive Branch of the Government, February 1949 (Washington, 1949) [hereafter cited as *Hoover Commission Report*], pp. i, 23. The work of the two groups is generally described in Walter Millis, Harvey Mansfield, and Harold Stein, *Arms and the State* (New York, The Twentieth Century Fund, 1958), pp. 232–34.

Actually, the existence of a consensus regarding the gross size of the budget can be fairly easily demonstrated, and its content helps explain what—judged by the criteria for an effective rational review—was one of the more curious of the House subcommittee's actions on the budget: its failure to look into the alternative of spending significantly more money than that requested by the President. Seen in the context of the opinions prevailing at the time, the committee's lack of interest in a larger budget is not hard to comprehend. There was probably no more widely shared or firmly held belief regarding defense matters than the idea that $15 billion was all that the country could afford to spend.

President Truman had declared as much himself at a news conference in October 1948. It was his hope, he told reporters, that the international situation would soon permit the military budget to be reduced to $5 or $7 billion, for "the country could not go on spending $14,000,000,000 to $15,000,000,000 a year for defense." Expenditures for all defense purposes in the fiscal 1950 budget, it will be recalled, totaled $14.2 billion, and those for State Department activities, foreign aid, and atomic energy were about $7.4 billion more. Listing these sums in the New York *Times* in January 1949, Hanson Baldwin announced that "such expenditures, if long continued, might be fatal to the national economy." Similarly, the report of the Eberstadt Committee proclaimed the current costs of the military establishment "unduly high" in terms of "the ability of the economy to sustain them." They were, the report alleged, "already imposing strains on the civilian economy and on the underlying human, material, and financial resources on which effective military strength depends." [3]

The idea that military security rested ultimately on the state of the economy was voiced repeatedly during the House debate on the budget in April 1949. In peacetime, Mahon declared in reporting his bill, "we cannot afford to bankrupt the country or squander our dwindling resources; that would be the road to national inse-

[3] New York *Times*, October 17, 1948, and January 16, 1949, and *National Security Organization*, A Report with Recommendations Prepared for The Commission on Organization of the Executive Branch of the Government by The Committee on the National Security Organization (Washington, 1949) [hereafter cited as *Eberstadt Committee Report*], pp. 3, 45.

curity and the possible loss of the next war if one should come." The question, as Engel put it, was: "How much can we spend, yes, on airships and on ships that sail the seas before our Ship of State strikes and perhaps founders on the rocks of economic disaster?"

The answers advanced by members of the subcommittee and other Representatives varied in their phrasing, but not in their content. The consensus was that the economy was already at the limit, if not over it, of what it could spend on defense. Sikes warned that "the economy of the country could not stand much more than we are putting into arms at the present time." Plumley thought the budget was even now such "that it threatens our very economy." Short saw a desperate dilemma. "These astronomical sums will destroy us," but since they were also necessary, "What else can we do?" Twenty-one members of the House, led by Representative Frederick Coudert, Republican of New York and a member of the parent Appropriations Committee, attempted to answer this question through a proposal to cut the Air Force budget back to the level originally requested by the President. These votes were not moved by a significantly different conception of the nation's political-military needs than that held by Mahon or Cannon. The issue, as Coudert explained it, was rather that "The economic life of the United States is at stake." [4]

The Senate debate in August was characterized by even stronger expressions of concern for the state of the economy. A tax study completed in May had indicated that the revenues for fiscal 1950 might be $2 billion short of the January estimate. To offset this loss, Senator John McClellan (Democrat of Arkansas and a member of the Senate Subcommittee on Military Appropriations) proposed that all departmental budgets be cut from 5 to 10 percent. A majority of the Senators were in favor of this measure, and it was defeated only through a point of order. It was McClellan's contention that "Economic instability caused by deficit spending constitutes a much greater threat from within to both the security and survival of our liberties than does the military threat of communism from without." [5]

[4] *C.R.*, 95, pp. 4429, 4504, 4433, 4435, 4500, 4508.
[5] *Ibid.*, pp. 12389, 12391–92, and Stephen K. Bailey and Howard D. Samuel, *Congress at Work* (New York, Henry Holt and Co., 1952), pp. 378–79.

Although the syntax of McClellan's statement would suggest that he had reached this conclusion only after a careful weighing of the threat abroad against the threat within, the issue of how much to spend was not really seen as a matter of choice. Consider, for example, an editorial from the New York *Herald Tribune* of June 24, which McClellan cited in support of his amendment. Entitled "Economy's Last Stand," the editorial declared it imperative that President Truman "be jolted out of his complacent assumption that the Nation's taxing and borrowing power can be adapted to any budget requirements which he may put forward." There was no suggestion in these words or elsewhere in the Congressional debate that the adaptive power of the nation might vary with its perception of the security problem, that the people might be willing to pay more taxes and still retain their incentive to work or invest if they were persuaded that the gains to security were worth foregoing the alternative uses to which they or the government could have put the money.

On the contrary, most of the discussion was cast in simplistic terms: there was a fixed limit to what could be spent, and if this were exceeded economic ruin would result. At times, these statements almost seemed to suggest that it would be a physical impossibility to spend more. There were, to be sure, Congressmen who at least took note of the possibility that taxes could be higher or the deficit larger, but the burden of their comment was merely to spell out the nature of the ruin that would follow. Thus, Representative Olin Teague, Democrat of Texas, declared that higher taxes would "destroy that unique American enthusiasm and incentive which has made this country . . . the greatest country the world has ever known," and Senator Harry Byrd, Democrat of Virginia, announced that a larger deficit would mean "national bankruptcy to be accompanied by the kind of horrors not yet comprehended. . . ." For others, like Senator Robert Taft, Republican of Ohio, the day of ruin was already at hand. "There is a point," he warned, "at which free enterprise must go on a downward path." "If we insist upon these expenses, we must turn to a socialist form of government."

The determinate form in which the economy issue was cast is

well illustrated by the budgetary reform that Senator Henry Cabot Lodge, Republican of Massachusetts, had suggested in May 1948 to Arthur Krock of the New York *Times.*

There should be a thoroughly scientific determination of what the point of public expenditures is at which we shall have to militarize our economy and go to allocation, priorities, rationing and other controls. . . . We cannot legislate wisely without having a sure and definite idea of exactly what straw it is that breaks the camel's back. We know there is one, but which one is it? [6]

III

The climate of opinion did not admit much choice concerning the gross size of the President's budget, except the choice of spending less or incurring economic disaster. As previously noted, Congress ultimately took neither option and accepted the budget. There was, however, considerable sentiment in favor of spending less, and the explanation for this pressure is to be found in three other elements in the climate of opinion: the idea that the Russians were trying to spend the nation to death; the idea that the military had no regard for the state of the economy; and the idea that their requests had been needlessly inflated as a result of interservice rivalry.

In Chapter III it was observed that the subcommittees made no effort to explore the relationship between the international situation and the budget. They avoided even the obvious starting point for such an inquiry: the question of whether the situation had so improved since the crises in the spring of 1948 that the administration was justified in cutting back the programs started then. The failure to explore this matter was hardly rational in terms of the criteria for an effective review of the President's budget. It made sense, however, for those who believed the economy could not afford more than $15 billion anyway, for in this event there was really no point to be served by such an inquiry.

Another explanation for the failure to follow up the matter is

[6] *C.R.,* 95, pp. 4442, 5227, 12394, 12410, and New York *Times,* May 14, 1948.

to be found in the belief that the object of Russian foreign policy was to seduce the nation into spending more for defense. The point to this expectation was that it robbed a deterioration in the international situation of its "persuasive value" so far as increasing defense expenditures was concerned. Paradoxically enough, the logic of it was that the more truculent the Russians became, the more cause there was to look to the state of the economy rather than to the state of the defense budget. As Senator Lodge put it to Krock in May 1948: it was to be hoped that history would not record that the Russians "merely sat back and angered" the United States into spending so much that we "bled our economy to death."

In October 1948 a news story in the New York *Times* had labeled as "wild speculation" the idea that the Russians aimed "to produce such a constant and growing threat to the United States that the defense budget here will grow to such a size as to bring the national economy down crumbling." However deserving the idea may have been of such a judgment, the *Times* account was not quite a fair description of prevailing opinion on the subject. Mark Sullivan had assured readers of the New York *Herald Tribune* a few weeks earlier that it had "long been the judgment of thoughtful persons" that the "underlying purpose of Russia's conduct since the war has been to make the United States spend more and more." Among Sullivan's thoughtful people was General Bradley, who told the Economic Club of Chicago on October 29, so the *Times* reported, "that he doubted if the United States would ever put combat troops in any considerable quantity in Europe unless war actually broke out. To do so in peacetime might make this country go broke, as the Russians hope we will. . . ."

Readers of the *Times* were brought more in tune with reality at the end of October, when Hanson Baldwin reported that "Washington observers" in increasing number, in and out of uniform, "credit Russia with the Machiavellian aim of victory by bankruptcy. They believe the rulers in the Kremlin are deliberately trying to force the United States to greater and greater expenditures." At the time Baldwin wrote this column he was serving as a member of the Eberstadt Committee. Later, in January 1949, this description of

Russia's Machiavellian aim was duplicated almost verbatim in the report of that committee to the Hoover Commission, except that Washington observers became "responsible officials of Government." [7]

The idea that the Russians were trying to bleed the economy to death made a double contribution to the climate of opinion in which the fiscal 1950 budget was considered. In the first place it served to take the curse off the idea that the nation could not spend more that $15 billion for defense. The existence of this limit inhibited any consideration of a higher budget. But if the purpose of Russian power and hostility was to undermine the economy rather than to overrun American and allied military forces, there was really no need for a higher budget. To maintain military forces larger than those possible for $15 billion would serve Russian purposes, not American. "Nothing would please a potential enemy better," Mahon told the House when explaining why his committee had not considered the Joint Chiefs' $23.6-billion estimate, "than to have us bankrupt our country and destroy our economy by maintaining over a period of years complete readiness for armed conflict." [8]

The same dialectic pointed to a second conclusion. If spending more than $15 billion would help Russia and hurt America, perhaps spending less would help America and hurt Russia. If the Russian objective was the economic ruin of the United States, then the true measure of "security" was the state of the American economy, not the state of American armed power. Accordingly, a cut in the $15-billion budget, while reducing the strength of the armed services, would at the same time reduce the strain their maintenance imposed on the economy and thereby lead, conceivably, to a net gain in security.

This would seem the substance of the reasoning applied by the Senate subcommittee when it recommended a $1.1-billion cut in the House appropriation bill. It was the committee's "firm conviction," its report declared, that a "niggardly approach" to the defense budget would "encourage a belligerent attitude on the part of a possible aggressor."

[7] New York *Herald Tribune*, October 5, 1948; New York *Times*, October 24, 29, and 31, 1948; and *Eberstadt Committee Report*, p. 45.
[8] *C.R.*, 95, p. 4428.

However, in considering these appropriations the committee fully realized that second only to national security was the consideration of our internal economic security. A nation which exhausts itself in enervating overpreparation for defense against aggression may well fall prey to a cunning and patient enemy who fully realizes the debilitating influences of a war-geared economy over a long period of time.[9]

The Russians, then, were seen as cunningly aware of the fact that (as the Hoover Commission expressed it) "True national security depends more upon economic stability and political strength than upon military power." In contrast, the American military were generally believed to be oblivious of that fact. One of the "most important things that needs to be done in this country," Mahon told the House, "is to hammer into the heads of the military people the necessity for economy." The Hoover Commission was of the same mind. The preparation of the fiscal 1950 budget, it reported in February 1949, revealed that the services had a "serious lack of understanding of the effect of military costs and spending upon the total economy."

The Hoover Commission documented its conclusion with two examples, the most important of which was the fact that the services had even so much as considered a $30-billion budget. Additionally, the commission cited two budget "horribles": a misplaced figure that had added $30,000,000 to one estimate, and an Army request for funds to modernize a larger number of tanks of a certain type than it actually had. The remedy urged by the commission was more power to the Secretary of Defense and a reform of service accounting practices. Far more consequential was the recommendation of the Eberstadt Committee. It urged that the services be indoctrinated "through education and by every other means" to recognize "the fact that the strength of the Nation's economy is directly related to the Nation's defense strength. . . ." As will be shown in the Conclusion, there is perhaps no more effective way to hobble military estimates than to persuade the services that the "state of the economy" is a "military factor" and therefore entitled

[9] *Senate Report, 1950 Budget,* p. 5.

to be incorporated into their professional calculations regarding what is needed for national defense.[10]

The idea that the military were, as Mahon described them, "notoriously lacking in economy-mindedness," provided a favorable climate for those who were anxious to cut the budget in order to stave off economic ruin or to avoid playing Russia's game. So, too, did the belief that the size of the budget had been inflated by unnecessary interservice rivalries. This belief had its corrollary in the expectation that if only the National Military Establishment were properly organized, these rivalries could be eliminated, with a consequent reduction in the cost of maintaining that establishment. Unlike a cut imposed for the sake of the economy—which, however necessary for overall security, would still involve some cost in military strength—the savings possible through proper organization could be considered "cost free." Since the expenses produced by interservice rivalry were unnecessary, their elimination would involve no loss in effective military power.

Illustrative of the press comment on this matter are two selections from the New York *Times* in the fall of 1948. The "best chance of keeping the budget in balance," James Reston wrote in November, "lies in a well-administrated and carefully coordinated Department of Defense." At the moment, he reported, the services were "still competing actively for the big cut of the over-all defense appropriations," and unless Forrestal was able "to settle this competition, Mr. Truman's chances of keeping his budget in balance will not be good."

The chances looked no better early in December when the *Times* decided to address itself to the problem with an editorial. The Army had just announced that because of the $15-billion ceiling it would have to cut its January and February draft quotas, and the *Times* interpreted this as the first shot in a battle among the services to try to get from Congress the dollars that would not be available under the President's budget. This was the sort of activity,

[10] *C.R.*, 95, pp. 4428–29; *Hoover Commission Report*, pp. 5, 11–13; and *Eberstadt Committee Report*, pp. 5, 18.

the *Times* observed, that was supposed to have been stopped by the unification act of 1947. Congress did not have "the training or the time" to answer such questions as whether money should be spent on carriers or land-based bombers or how many soldiers would be required to support a given size Air Force. But Congress did "have the right to ask of our military leaders . . . that they agree upon the answers themselves."

There should be no vested interests, inside the services or among the industries that supply them, in any special weapons or in methods of warfare. . . . If there is a real "unified thinking" in the National Military Establishment we believe a pretty good defense apparatus can be built at the cost of $15,000,000,000 a year.[11]

Congressional opinion was more liberal in its judgment of that body's ability to choose between bombers and carriers, but it was no less impressed than the *Times* with the desirability of "unified thinking" in the Pentagon and the costs of interservice rivalry. Thus Mahon explained to the House that for the moment, unfortunately, it was necessary to take the recommendations of the Joint Chiefs of Staff with a "grain of salt." Each service was "angling for prestige, a place in the sun, a larger slice of the national defense dollar," and since the Chiefs operated on the basis of unanimity they had a tendency to logroll each other's requests and to keep the budget artificially divided into "three equal pieces." Mahon thought it would be "hard to prove" that unification had "thus far saved much money," but he expected that "as we go along the savings can be tremendous."[12]

How soon the benefits from true unification could be achieved was a matter on which Congressmen divided. Some, like Representative Francis Case, Republican of South Dakota who had served for years on the old subcommittee for Army appropriations, were far from sanguine. He doubted if the nation would ever "get rid of [interservice] rivalries and jealousies that bid for these various

[11] New York *Times*, November 20 and December 2, 1948.
[12] *C.R.*, 95, pp. 4428–30. Mahon's reference to logrolling was actually made in reference to Sheppard's effort to increase the Navy budget, but his remarks were all of a piece, and it is safe to infer he had the Chiefs in mind as well.

appropriations" until the services were so unified that commissions and ratings were completely interchangeable among them. Others, like Representative Overton Brooks, Democrat of Louisiana and a member of the Armed Services Committee, were more optimistic. He thought "a great deal of money could be saved," if Congress would merely support the unification measures recommended by the Hoover Commission.[13]

The recommendations of the Hoover Commission were designed to remedy a number of conditions reported by the Eberstadt Committee, among them that the Joint Chiefs had yet to formulate "integrated strategic plans" and that "intense interservice rivalry" was one of the major causes for the high cost of defense. The measures proposed were for the most part the same measures which Congress shortly did, in fact, authorize with the August 1949 amendment to the 1947 National Security Act. Under the terms of this amendment, the National Military Establishment was reorganized as the Department of Defense with a variety of provisions designed to increase the power of the Secretary of Defense. The language of the law was rewritten to make his authority over the department appear less qualified; he was provided with a Deputy Secretary, three Assistant Secretaries, and a Comptroller; the service Secretaries were removed from statutory membership on the National Security Council; and a non-voting Chairman was added to the Joint Chiefs to preside over them in the name of the Secretary.[14]

It was the hope of the Hoover Commission that these organizational changes, together with various reforms in accounting procedure, would put an end to the "continued disharmony and lack of unified planning" among the military and "assure budgeting and spending from the standpoint of national welfare, rather than from the standpoint of service rivalries." The only point at issue was that a minority of the commission, led by its Vice Chairman, Dean Acheson, believed that "one step more" was needed. They

[13] *Ibid.*, pp. 4502, 4510.
[14] *Eberstadt Committee Report*, pp. 3, 37; *Hoover Commission Report*, pp. 16–17; and Millis, Mansfield, and Stein, *Arms and the State*, p. 234.

proposed that the Department of Defense be given a single Chief of Staff with the power to initiate and terminate discussions among the Joint Chiefs and to whom the Joint Staff would be responsible. A single Chief of Staff would give the President and the Secretary of Defense advice "from an *over-all* strategic point of view," instead of advice "on the basis of a compromise of desires of three separate services." Moreover, the single Chief of Staff, by virtue of his high position, would become familiar with "national economic considerations" and transmit these down through the services "so they will become more economy-minded than they now are." [15]

Congress was quickly dazzled by the prospect of the savings to be effected through reorganization. Senator Millard Tydings, Democrat of Maryland and Chairman of the Armed Services Committee, opened his hearings on the unification bill in May 1949 with the announcement that former President Hoover had told him that the new measures would reduce the costs of the defense establishment by $1.5 billion. In June, Franz Schneider, who had headed the Eberstadt Committee's inquiry into the fiscal 1950 budget, assured Senator Thomas' Subcommittee on Military Appropriations that the savings might ultimately run as high as $2 billion. He also urged the subcommittee to consider making a cut in the fiscal 1950 budget in anticipation of such savings. Similarly, Robert L. Johnson, President of Temple University and Chairman of the Citizen's Committee for the Reorganization of the Executive Branch of the Government, released a statement early in August that reorganization would immediately pave the way for at least a $1-billion reduction in the defense budget. "This will be bad news in Moscow," he declared, "where, as the Hoover Commission task force warned, the Kremlin's Machiavellian aim is victory by bankruptcy." [16]

[15] *Hoover Commission Report*, pp. 5, 12, 25–29. Acheson was here endorsing the views and proposals filed by John J. McCloy (a former Assistant Secretary of War) in a minority report to the Eberstadt Committee Report. The nation could not afford, he wrote, the "wasteful character" of the "damaging rivalries and even controversies" among the services, and it "needs and deserves to have something other than plans based on the desires of any particular service or a compromise of the desires of all the services." See *Eberstadt Committee Report*, p. 58n.

[16] New York *Times*, May 24 and August 2, 1949, and *SCA, Hearings 1950 Budget*, pp. 16, 19.

Other points of view existed about interservice rivalry and the savings that could be expected from reorganization. In the Eberstadt Report itself one could read the assertion that a "reduction of the military budget by major amounts can be effected only by a reduction in the size of the military establishment, which is a matter of high policy and not organization or administration." There, one could also find the statement that "the sincere and deeply held differences over strategic theory and tactical method that divide the services . . . cannot and should not be removed by fiat."

To a great extent the underlying cause of . . . service controversies resides in the confusion and uncertainties of present-day military technology. Until the form and character of another war can be predicted with more exactness than is now possible, it will be unsafe to "put all our eggs in one basket." [17]

Hanson Baldwin endeavored to stem the rising expectations about the results of reorganization by repeating these ideas in the New York *Times.* Referring to the assertion that $1 billion or more could be saved in the cost of the armed forces, Baldwin cautioned that such sums could be saved only by "cutting down the size of those forces, not by reorganizational measures." With regard to the need for "unified thinking" and the hopes for an end to interservice rivalry, he wrote:

. . . no organizational changes can "solve" soundly basic strategical differences between the services . . . ultimately the decision on such grave policy matters as to whether or not we can win a war against Russia by atomic bombardment alone must go for decision to the President . . . and in the last analysis to Congress and the people . . . [It would be a mistake to] focus this power—now widely and properly diffused—in one man, particularly in one military man. [18]

These words, while wise, were of no avail. Congress remained seized by the evil of interservice rivalry and the promise of saving through reorganization. Nor did the Executive offer any reason not to be. Hoover had not been the only one to tell Tydings in May that the unification bill could cut $1.5 billion from the cost of the

[17] *Eberstadt Committee Report,* pp. 46–47, 53.
[18] New York *Times,* June 29 and March 31, 1949.

defense budget. The very same assurance had been given by President Truman's new Secretary of Defense, Louis Johnson, who also so testified on June 16 before Senator Thomas' committee.

If you give us the bill covering amendments to the National Security Act, I think we can say that without reducing the strength of the Army, Navy, and Air Force, I think we can save about a billion dollars by cutting out wastage, duplication, and by cutting down unnecessary civilian employment.[19]

How much of the billion could be saved from the fiscal 1950 budget, Johnson had been careful not to say, only that the "rate of saving" would be at $1 billion by the end of the fiscal year. A week later, however, he appeared before Thomas' committee in a closed session to discuss, so the *Times* reported, the committee's interest in cutting the fiscal 1950 budget itself by $1 billion. It was at this time that Johnson lent his agreement to the provision in the committee's report which recommended a $434-million cut in the House bill to be made at the discretion of the Secretary of Defense. During the Senate debate, Thomas quoted Johnson's statement of June 16 with obvious anticipation and enjoined the services to support fully the Secretary's endeavor "to bring about a truly unified military establishment which will, at one time, both weld the national defenses into an impregnable whole and bring about needed savings through proper unifying action." [20]

The idea that the $434-million cut should be applied at his discretion was Johnson's. Discussing the $1-billion saving on June 16, Johnson had told the committee: ". . . you cannot do the cutting here without destroying the fighting qualities of the services." As Senator A. Willis Robertson, Democrat of Virginia and a member of the committee, later explained to the Senate: Congress could not cut the budget safely because of the way the National Military Establishment was "now constituted"; but if Johnson were left to "institute reforms" under the reorganization bill, he could then make such cuts without cost to the fighting ability of the services.[21]

[19] *Ibid.*, May 24, 1949, and *SCA, Hearings 1950 Budget*, p. 32.
[20] New York *Times*, June 29, 1949; Bailey and Samuel, *Congress at Work*, p. 373; and *C.R.*, 95, p. 12249.
[21] *SCA, Hearings 1950 Budget*, p. 32, and *C.R.*, 95, p. 12313.

Johnson apparently expected much from reorganization. "Unification," he claimed in his first Annual Report, "provides a means of obtaining greater national security at less expense." Certainly, he was concerned about the state of the economy. He had told the House Armed Services Committee in June that he wanted the reorganization bill so he could "quarrel with wastage, duplication, and extravagance in peacetime that would do what the Russians want: wreck the economy of America, if not properly curbed." Even later, during the Korean War, Johnson was insistent that the major danger America faced was economic ruin, not war with Russia. The nation had made a serious mistake, he explained during the MacArthur hearings, in failing to take *Mein Kampf* seriously. In a classic example of "political learning" (although not scholarship), he warned the committee not to make the same error with regard to Stalin's writings. "You would conclude, if you read Stalin's books, and what Stalin said, that he doesn't look to a clash of arms, that he expects America to spend itself into bankruptcy." [22]

The proposal to cut the budget $434 million, a figure which Johnson himself described as "almost arbitrary," was in part at the initiative of Johnson and the President. Their interest in reducing the fiscal 1950 budget was the consequence of their plans for fiscal 1951. In July 1949 the ceiling for the fiscal 1951 budget was set at $13 billion, $1.2 billion lower than the President's submission for fiscal 1950. Accordingly, just as Truman had told Forrestal in May 1948 that the funds provided under the fiscal 1949 supplement could

[22] For Johnson's statements, see, respectively, United States Government, Department of Defense, *Second Report of the Secretary of Defense* (Washington, 1950), p. 9; *To Convert the National Military Establishment into an Executive Department of the Government* . . . , Hearings before the Committee on Armed Services, House of Representatives, 81st Cong., 1st Sess. (Washington, 1949), p. 2710; and *The Military Situation in the Far East*, Hearings before the Committees on Armed Services and Foreign Relations, United States Senate, 82d Cong., 1st Sess. (Washington, 1951) [hereafter cited as *MacArthur Hearings*], IV, 2626–27.

As for the Kremlin's Machiavellian aim of "victory by bankruptcy," exhaustive searches have failed to locate any such statement by Lenin, Stalin, or any other Bolshevik. See *Organizing for National Security*, Hearings before the Subcommittee on National Policy Machinery, Committee on Government Operations, United States Senate, 86th Cong., 2d Sess. (Washington, 1960) [hereafter cited as *Organizing for National Security Hearings*], pp. 60–61.

not all be spent, in order to avoid a "demoralizing demobilization" at the beginning of fiscal 1950, so now the President was intent on cutting back his fiscal 1950 budget so that the services could fit under the force levels that were to be maintained during fiscal 1951.

In equal part, however, Truman and Johnson were "leading by following in front." Johnson's expedient—"let me do it"—was clearly preemptive in character. Beset with worry for the safety of the economy, fearful of being mousetrapped by the Russians, suspicious of military extravagance, persuaded that the services had budgeted against each other as well as the enemy, and tantalized by the promise of billions to be saved through pending reorganization—the Senate was in no mood to be denied a budget cut. Nor was it a matter of practical moment that the provision for the $434-million cut was sacrificed during the October bargaining between the Senate and the House. Johnson's prestige was nonetheless bound to a budget reduction, and both he and Congress knew it.[23]

The Senate cut was, then, as "real" as the House Air Force increase was "unreal." The effecting of this reduction—the consequence of which neither Congress nor the Executive was really certain—was a typical example of the "radar approach" to policymaking discussed in the Introduction. Responsibility for the cut cannot be isolated; Congress and the Executive were each as much led as leading on the matter. In neither case, moreover, was this choice preceded by a careful analysis of the particular alternatives involved (foreign policy, military, or fiscal). The choice was rather a crude reflection of a variety of general considerations that constituted the prevailing climate of opinion.

IV

With these observations in mind regarding the content of the climate of opinion and the influence it exercised on both the gross size of the budget and some of the marginal changes made in it,

---

[23] Johnson's description of the process through which the $434-million figure was chosen is in *HCA, Hearings 1950 Budget,* V, 29. The ceiling for fiscal 1951 and Johnson's subsequent reductions in the fiscal 1950 budget are discussed in Chapter V.

attention may now be turned to the question which started this chapter. Why did the subcommittees demonstrate so little interest in exploring alternatives to the President's budget? One answer has already been given. The climate of opinion normally restricts the number of budgets judged desirable and feasible to a very narrow range. Since the same climate prevails down the Hill as on it, members of Congress and the Executive are unlikely to differ greatly in their sense for what constitutes a conceivable budget. Moreover, should the President take into consideration his estimate of what Congress will give when he calculates what he will ask, the opportuntiy for a difference in judgment may be even further reduced. Under such circumstances as these, Congress has no incentive to explore the possibility of departing widely, in one direction or another, from the President's budget. It is their budget, too.

The failure of Congress to explore major alternatives to the fiscal 1950 budget is a case in point. The content of the opinions then prevailing about defense expenditures ruled out such alternatives as beyond consideration. The services' $30-billion estimate was seen as an object of horror rather than a subject for intelligent inquiry. The fact that this figure was later reduced to $23.6 billion did not make any difference. The climate of opinion put even a modest increase like the Chiefs' $16.9-billion budget beyond the pale of reason and therefore of Congressional consideration.

On the other hand, it is to be noted that the subcommittees did not explore such alternatives as a $11.5-billion budget or a $5.4-billion budget either. Here, too, the climate of opinion was restrictive. If the international situation, for example, was not seen as a compelling reason to make a major increase in the budget, neither did anyone see anything in it to justify a major decrease. In sum, while the net effect of the climate of opinion was to facilitate the efforts of those who wanted to spend a little less than $14.2 billion, rather than a little more, it was as exclusive of large or modest cuts as it was of modest or large increases.

Even if the climate of opinion had been less restrictive and had permitted, for example, any Presidential budget from $11 billion to $17 billion to appear equally plausible, there were good reasons why the committees might still have forborne to play the part of coordinate budget-maker. Despite their formal protestations about Congress' rights and obligations, Congressmen would appear to have little incentive to play such a role. To begin with, it is a fair presumption that there will always be at least some Congressmen who will be far from eager to grasp responsibility for such a grave and complex matter as the nation's defense policy. The major cause for Congress' lack of incentive, however, would appear to lie not so much in the desire to avoid responsibility as in the expectation that there is little to be gained from trying to exercise it. The role of coordinate budget-maker can be justified Constitutionally, and it is feasible enough intellectually (provided the committees would limit themselves to a review of the high-policy choices involved), but politically the part is not very remunerative. Political conditions are normally such that Congress is little motivated and poorly set up to second-guess the President and make its own judgments stick.

Congress is certainly under no spur to do so from the electorate. So far as defense is concerned, the people are consumers, not producers, and the "consumer lobby" is even more markedly absent in defense policy than it is in farm policy. A Congressman may on occasion find himself subject to pressure from constituents who happen to be engaged in the "production" of defense (the Navy Yard, the aircraft factory), but even here constituent interests are more likely to be concerned with the nut-and-bolt aspects of defense than with high-policy alternatives. At election time little reward will await the Congressmen who chose to become expert critics of the defense budget, and no punishment will befall their colleagues who did not.[24]

[24] Much the same point is made in Elias Huzar, *The Purse and the Sword* (Ithaca, Cornell University Press, 1950), pp. 385–86.

In conversations with the present author (August 1961), the staff of one Senator nationally prominent in the field of defense policy (but not for work on an appropriations committee) stated that the Senator did pick up votes in counties otherwise unsympathetic to his party because of his "statesman" reputation (a general image of nonpartisan interest in national security). The staff also stated that the Senator was subject to very little pressure from the largest defense contractor in his state even on issues of military hardware. They also stated their suspicion that this company's practice was probably not typical of the practice of certain other companies in other states.

Nor do Congressmen have much incentive to subject the President's budget to a searching analysis in the service of their own interests. The problem here is not apathy, as in the case of the electorate, but rather power. They are simply not in a very good position to do much about the findings of such an analysis once it is made. So long as the President can mobilize the prestige of the military behind his budget, the Congressmen who choose to question it face an uphill battle, for neither their own colleagues nor the attentive public will be inclined to dismiss "expert military opinion" lightly.

The difficulty in securing a large increase in the President's budget may be taken as an example. Those who advocate it must perforce advocate either an increase in taxes, deficit financing, or a drastic cut somewhere else in the budget. None of these alternatives will be normally seen by others as especially attractive consequences. Thus, even when Vinson urged his rather moderate $1.6-billion increase to Mahon's committee, Plumley was quick to ask:

Will the gentleman permit an interruption?
Yes.
Where do you think you are going to get the money?
Well, I think the Government's first obligation is its defense. I think nothing comes ahead of insuring the people of the Nation that they can be protected as far as possible by an Army, a Navy, and an Air Force at adequate strength, which strength has in turn a stabilizing effect in maintaining peace throughout the world.
That is very fine, Mr. Vinson, but I want to tell you this: You have suggested a program which involves a very large increase in taxes, and I am not fooling.[25]

Should the advocates of a large increase succeed in persuading their colleagues that it is desirable—and this must be done in face of expert testimony that it is not necessary—and should Congress duly appropriate the sum, there still remains the problem of getting the President to spend it. Congress has no formal power to secure his compliance. It can only hope to build such a powerful consensus in support of the increase that the President will not dare incur the political costs of frustrating it. The opportunities of building such a consensus are limited, especially among the electorate. All

[25] *HCA, Hearings 1950 Budget*, I, 215–16.

they want is "adequate defense" and "low taxes," and with the support of his experts the President is in a position to assure them of both.[26]

Even more formidable obstacles confront those who would advocate a large decrease in the President's budget. The formal powers of Congress are more suited to this task, since the President cannot spend money Congress does not appropriate or maintain forces that body does not authorize. But the political task of persuasion is all but impossible in the context of the "permanent crisis" of the second half of the century. Who is going to vote for a large decrease in the budget in the face of an announcement from the Joint Chiefs that it would jeopardize the national defense?

Either way, then, if the President has the support of a united Executive, he can force the Congressional advocates of change to assume the losing end of the argument: they must inevitably appear to be either proposing taxes and deficits which are not needed or to be undermining national security. Under these circumstances, Congress has little prospect of effecting major changes in the President's budget, and its committees, therefore, have little incentive to undertake the task of developing major alternatives to that budget.

These conditions—the restrictive effect of the climate of opinion, the latent desire to avoid responsibility, and the political advantages of the Executive—constitute at least a hypothetical explanation for why the committees did not undertake a systematic exploration of the alternatives to the President's budget. At the same time, just as they served to preclude such an analysis, so the weight of tradition served to impel the appropriations committees along the course of action they did take: an intensive examination of the financial details of the budget.

But these conditions cannot completely explain the performance of Congress on the fiscal 1950 budget. The climate of opinion, while restrictive of choice, did not fix the size and composition of that

[26] The prestige of President Eisenhower was such that he could withstand even a consensus that included his own experts. See Roger Hilsman, "Congressional-Executive Relations and the Foreign Policy Consensus," *The American Political Science Review*, September 1958, pp. 732–33.

budget with absolute precision. Similarly, whatever their desire to avoid responsibility or their preoccupation with their watchdog function, the appropriations committees did try to make some policy changes in the President's budget. Finally, the President was by no means completely successful, especially in the case of the Air Force, in persuading the services to close ranks behind the particular sums he had decided to request. Congress was not confronted by a monolithic Executive. The actual lines of conflict were multiple, and many of the divisions were transinstitutional. Thus, the Senate and the President were aligned against the House in the case of the Air Force increase, and the conflict over the Navy increase was between one group of Congressmen and Navy officials and another group of Congressmen and Air Force officials.

The question must therefore be asked: what of the opportunities that the climate of opinion and the division of the Executive did permit, what of the alternatives Congress did see to the President's budget and the changes it did make? Why did the subcommittees fail to develop the kind of information from which more rational choices could have been made on these issues: the extra $300 million for the Navy, or the 48 versus 58-group Air Force? [27]

Part of the answer lies in the fact that the committee hearing is not a seminar in budget policy. It is a political arena. The alternatives involved in the budget may be open to rational analysis, but choice among them is made through the medium of politics, and the hearing is by no means politically neutral ground. It is, rather, an occasion for the manufacture and expenditure of political ammunition. The testimony of administration witnesses, as was shown in Chapter III, is generally designed to portray the President's budget in the best possible light and to fog the alternatives to it. So, too, with the interrogation of Congressmen. They are interested in building as persuasive a case as they can for the alternatives which they favor. Nor are these always different alternatives. Affirmations of the budget's "adequacy" are solicited by Congressmen as well as volunteered by the President's representatives. But

[27] The $434-million Senate cut can perhaps be excluded from this list because of the expectation that "no costs" were involved.

whether the object be agreement or conflict, the hearing is a political as well as an analytical exercise. Its content, the questions asked and the answers given, is therefore shaped by the participants' sense for necessary and desirable political action, as well as by their sense for useful and meaningful information.

The criteria for rational political behavior can explain much in the record of the subcommittees that the criteria for a rational review of the budget cannot. The Congressman who is rational in his expenditure of political energy will not, for example, bother to explore alternatives for which he believes there is no real political support.[28] In all probability, it was for this reason that Mahon's committee gave Vinson's proposal to add $1.6 billion to the budget such a superficial examination. Vinson, it will be recalled, had been unable to muster even his own committee behind it. Nor did Vinson pursue the matter any further himself; even the naval increase that he and Sheppard urged on the House floor provided less than half the funds the Navy would have received under his $1.6-billion proposal.

A sense for rational political action may also account for some of the questions Congressmen failed to ask about the issues to which they *did* give serious attention. When the Senate debated Thomas' bill, Senator Joseph O'Mahoney, Democrat of Wyoming, led the floor fight to restore the additional $800 million the House had voted the Air Force. Yet, as a member of the Subcommittee on Appropriations, he had not put a single question to the Air Force witnesses who appeared before it, much less had he interrogated Symington and Vandenberg about what they could do with a 58-group Air Force that they could not do with one of 48 groups.

If the hearing is conceived as an opportunity for a serious inquiry into the issues at hand, this was hardly rational. But if O'Mahoney's choice of questions was guided by a sense for whether the answers

[28] The distinction between "rational politics" and "rational analysis" is not meant to imply that analysis is not employed in both cases. The difference is between the goals for which analysis is employed: an effect on policy in the first instance, and an increase in knowledge in the second. Although these goals are not necessarily mutually exclusive, a Congressman intent on influencing policy may well spend his intellectual energy differently from one intent on gaining information.

would help or hurt politically an alternative on which he was already intent, his silence was a very rational option. By August the pressure to support the President's budget was such that the Air Force was in no position to make sounds about the need for more groups. All that O'Mahoney would have secured for his efforts would have been a record that his opponents could later cite against him. As it was, Senator Robertson, a member of the committee who was against the increase, was able to tell the Senate that when the committee asked the representatives of the Air Force if 48 groups were enough, "They said, 'A 48-group Air Force is enough for our security.'" O'Mahoney and his supporters were obliged to dismiss Symington's testimony as "the statement of a good soldier" who was following "orders" and base their case on the more outspoken testimony he had given the Senate Armed Services Committee in April 1948.[29]

An interest in avoiding questions which are politically fruitless or embarrassing may also explain, at least in part, why Mahon's committee developed so little information about the military alternatives involved in the Air Force increase. The committee recommended it without much attention to the additional operations it would permit the Air Force to accomplish and with no analysis at all of the possibility that an even greater military return might be had by spending the $800 million on the Army.

The key to this otherwise irrational choice is to be found in the committee's report. This announced that the committee's decision had been made after a "full and complete" consideration of the President's budget and after it "also took into account" the extra funds the House had provided for the Air Force in 1948 and the "practically unanimous" vote with which the House had just authorized the 70-group program. Engel made the point even clearer in his statement to the House. "Last year . . . this House by an overwhelming vote increased the Air Force far above the budget figures. That action of the House was a mandate to me which I felt compelled to obey."[30]

Politically, then, Mahon's committee had no need to secure de-

---

[29] *C.R.*, 95, pp. 12313–14, 12305–6.
[30] *House Report, 1950 Budget*, p. 31, and *C.R.*, 95, p. 4504.

tailed information about what the Air Force could do with 10 more groups. In recommending the increase to the House, they were reflecting a consensus, not trying to build one. Neither did the committee have a political incentive to explore the strategic consequences of spending the money on some other service. To have done so would have been to blunt the force of their recommendation and to provide ammunition for the "Couderts," the economy advocates who would have used it to argue the importance of keeping to the "balanced forces" provided by the President's budget.

Finally, the criteria for effective political conduct even governed the force of Congressional pronouncements about their responsibility as a coordinate budget-maker. It was no accident that Mahon, Vinson, and Short stressed Congress' obligation to reach an independent judgment about the defense budget. They were advocating appropriations that departed from the President's budget. Quite a different theme, however, was sounded by their opposite numbers in the Senate—Thomas, Tydings, and Gurney—when they argued in favor of eliminating the House's Air Force increase. The point they stressed was that the responsible course for Congress was to accept the recommendations of the President, since he had the very best expert advice.[31]

v

The imperatives of "rational politics," taken together with the effects of the climate of opinion and the political advantages of the Executive, can thus explain many of the instances in the committees' record where they seemed to develop far less information about the changes they were considering than a rational analysis of those issues would have required. There remain, however, actions which these conditions cannot explain, instances where the committees' failure to ask more penetrating questions is still puzzling.

[31] See *C.R.*, *95*, pp. 12300, 12306, 12314. Tydings' argument on this point was only indirect; he stressed that Symington was satisfied with the 48-group force and the administration's argument that to be really effective the additional groups would require the support of additional land and sea forces.

Take the case of Sheppard's $300-million Navy increase. This sum was clearly within the realm of "conceivable" spending, and if the Navy was not willing to make so sweeping a run around the end of the President's budget as the Air Force, it was nonetheless prepared to make some effort to carry its case to Congress. As for rational politics, the reasons why Mahon may not have seen any political need to make a detailed case for the Air Force increase hardly applied to Sheppard's amendment. His problem was to build a consensus, not reflect one. Nor was Sheppard's a politically hopeless cause. He had the support of a majority of the Subcommittee on Armed Services Appropriations (Plumley and Sikes joined him) and also that of the Chairman and ranking minority member of the Armed Services Committee, Vinson and Short. On the other hand, it seems fair to presume from the size of the final vote against him (125-65) that Sheppard could not have been overconfident. He had, in short, every incentive to make the most persuasive case that he could.

The purpose of Sheppard's amendment was to permit the Navy to procure 1,265 new airplanes during the fiscal year, instead of the 843 provided by the President's budget. During the subcommittee's hearing Sheppard and other members secured a great deal of "numerical" information about the meaning of the President's budget: for example, that it would procure 380 fewer planes than had the fiscal 1949 budget; and that if the rate of procurement in fiscal 1950 were continued the Navy would have only 3,000 operating aircraft by fiscal 1955 instead of the 6,000 it had currently. But the committee got nothing on record about the strategic consequences of these figures beyond the statement of the Deputy Chief of Naval Operations for Air that the President's budget was "dangerously low." [32]

As a result, the arguments advanced on the House floor by the advocates of the amendment were neither especially informative nor, as it turned out, the most persuasive in the world. They duly recited all the relevant numbers and pointed out that unless the

[32] *HCA, Hearings 1950 Budget*, III, 590, 600, 606–7, and Huzar, *The Purse and the Sword*, p. 193.

President's budget was amended the naval air arm would, as Sheppard phrased it, "begin a steady and inescapable decline." But to their colleagues who wondered if the current size of the naval air arm was not, perhaps, more reflective of World War II conditions than World War III needs, they had little to offer. Plumley and Short affirmed that all three services would be needed to win a future war, and Sikes spoke of the Navy's ability to move quickly to meet overseas emergencies. Vinson endeavored to prove that their proposal was more in accord with the recommendations of the Joint Chiefs than Mahon's bill (a point which Mahon immediately contested), and Sheppard pointed to the fall of the Philippines as an example of what could happen if the nation permitted the Navy's carrier strength to decline.

In the absence of any specific information about how the alternative numbers of airplanes involved could be related to the Navy's ability to perform particular operations in time of war, the House was obliged to set the issue in a strategic context of its own imagination. This proved to be the relative advantage of carrier- versus land-based bombers for the delivery of atomic bombs on Russia. Once the debate was cast in these terms, Sheppard's proposal was lost. The case for land-based bombers could be put much more persuasively: they could go farther, carry a heavier load, and appeared less vulnerable to counterattack. If the Navy did not have enough money for airplanes it was because, as Engel argued, they were spending too much on super-carriers designed to compete with the Air Force's strategic bombing mission instead of sticking to the job of antisubmarine warfare.

The House defeated the Navy increase in April 1949. Months later, in October, as a result of the "revolt of the Admirals" (a circumstance which will be described later), the Navy began to give Vinson's committee a coherent statement of its views about the use of carriers in a war against Russia. Looking back on the April defeat at that time, a member of Vinson's committee exclaimed that they had lost "Primarily because there had been no publicizing of what the Navy was doing . . . . the information had been marked as 'restricted,' 'confidential,' and so forth. The public didn't get the over-all picture." [33]

It would seem a fair conclusion that Sheppard might have been able to make a more persuasive case for his increase if he had asked more meaningful questions about the strategic consequences of the President's budget. There were, in fact, "better" reasons for the Navy increase than Sheppard got on the record. As will be seen in Chapter V, the Executive had information which would have permitted him to state his case in terms that would have been both analytically more rational *and* politically more persuasive. But the subcommittee's investigation never penetrated to these matters, and as a result its hearings fell as short of meeting Sheppard's political needs as they did the criteria for an effective rational review.

The same can also be said for the information the subcommittee developed about the Air Force increase, if Mahon's political target is defined in broader terms than the House. The Senate, after all, rejected his amendment (49-9) as decisively as the House endorsed it. The consensus to which Mahon's committee had responded actually had little more behind it than the weight of the past. Both the Senate and the House had provided an $822-million increase the year before, but the quality of the analysis that had accompanied the 1948 action was even lower than that to be found in the 1949 discussion described in Chapter III.

Mahon himself had been prepared to increase the Air Force's fiscal 1949 budget even before President Truman made his special address to Congress in March 1948. In anticipation of that speech, he told his colleagues:

I hope that he will say that we need a tremendous implementation in our Air Force. . . . I feel compelled to register my feeling to you that [re-

---

[33] For the arguments of the admendment's advocates and the turn of the debate to the strategic bombing issues, see *C.R.,* 95, pp. 4433, 4498–99, 4500–2, 4505, 4521–25, 4527–28. This debate is also summarized, with some differences, in Huzar, *The Purse and the Sword,* pp. 193–98. The October appraisal was made by Representative Lansdale Sasscer, Democrat of Maryland, in *HCAS, Unification and Strategy Hearings,* p. 92.

gardless of what the President says] . . . we ought to have a more adequate Air Force than we have. . . .

Similarly, in April 1948, Vinson inserted into the record of his committee, with obvious approval, the remarks of a Representative who had observed in the House that for three years the Air Force had been requesting a 70-group force and that such a force had now been endorsed by both the Finletter Commission and the Joint Congressional Aviation Board. "Why is the President waiting? The Congress should not wait." [34]

The Congress had not waited in 1948. Least of all had it waited, before adding the extra $822 million to Forrestal's $3-billion supplement, on a thorough review of the considerations which led the Finletter Commission and the Congressional Board to endorse the 70-group program. Although this was their first opportunity to do so, the various committees which held hearings bearing on the fiscal 1949 supplement paid only the scantiest of attention to the content of these reports, and they gave none at all to the question of whether a greater return to security might be had by allocating some or all the $822 million among the other services. Forrestal's initial argument that the Air Force increase would "unbalance" the services was received by many with open skepticism. Thus, Representative Carl Hinshaw, Democrat of California and Vice-Chairman of the Congressional Board, told the Senate Subcommittee on Military Appropriations:

. . . I say, although not without hesitation, because I am not perfectly sure I am right, but, nevertheless, I say that the so-called balance of forces is in the nature of an agreement among the members of the Joint Chiefs of Staff, arrived at by negotiation and not by the process of war-gaming the problems. [35]

[34] *HCA, Hearings 1949 Budget,* I, 28, and *House Selective Service Hearings, 1948,* p. 6152.

[35] Hinshaw's statement is in *SCA, Hearings 1948 Supplemental Budget,* p. 110. For a typical on-the-record discussion of the 70-group program, see *House Selective Service Hearings, 1948,* p. 6125–29. There were two obvious instances where an analysis of the program was conducted off the record, and in one case the context strongly suggests it was only for the purpose of enumerating groups. See *SCA, Hearings 1948 Supplemental Budget,* pp. 53, 67, and *House Selective Service Hearings, 1948,* p. 6154.

The fact that Forrestal himself, as a result of the circumstances described in Chapter II, shortly came forward with a $500-million increase to his original supplement, the main effect of which was to raise the Air Force from 55 to 66 groups, presumably did nothing to dissuade Congress of the wisdom of its own action or of the validity, for that matter, of Hinshaw's idea that bargaining, not war plans, determined the share each service received of the budget.

The 1948 increase appears to have been grounded on little more than the idea that the atomic bomb had made the Air Force the most important of the services, faith in the various "expert" assertions that a 70-group force was what the future would require, and, lurking in the background, the hope that atomic bombs and the planes to deliver them might be all that would be necessary to prevent war and even, perhaps, to win it if it came. So long as the programs of the other services appeared to have even less to recommend them, the case for the Air Force seemed sufficient, and in 1949 Mahon's committee obviously saw no need to add to it.

The House's action on the fiscal 1950 budget affords a good example of the "gyroscopic" tendency of the policy process. The policy set in motion in fiscal 1949 was continued without any real reexamination of its merits. As was discussed more fully in the Introduction, both the intrinsic difficulty of the problems connected with the defense budget and the difficulty of making policy on them combine to incline the elites, once they have worked their way to an operational consensus on a given matter, to live with their choice until external events demonstrate it manifestly infeasible or no longer desirable. But what seems especially curious here in the case of the Air Force increase in that such an important course of action was "set" on the basis of so little information and analysis.

In explanation, one must again call attention to the Introduction and to the points made there about the inordinate intellectual difficulty of finding a rational answer to the question "How much for defense?" and about the costs, risks, and uncertainties that attend any given course of action. Under such circumstances one might well expect the policy elites to grasp eagerly for any "constants" that could be put into the calculus of choice. The idea that there was only so much the economy could stand provided such a constant. For those who accepted the idea, and there appear to be few who did not, the problem of defense budgeting, while not made easy, certainly became much simpler.

The compelling attraction that particular force goals can exercise on the participants in the budgeting process (the professional military not excluded) appears to be of the same order. The temptation to accept them as "givens," as fixed points from which other courses of action can be plotted, is hard to resist. It was to prevent just this that Forrestal had struggled so desperately in the spring of 1948 following the publication of the Finletter Report.

. . . I am trying now [he told the House Armed Services Committee] to avoid getting frozen, particularly in the public mind . . . any figure we put out—we called it in the war the numbers racket. . . . Those concepts are all dangerously erroneous if we give the impression that any one of them gives us complete national security. They do not.[36]

Forrestal's words were in vain. For the House, the 70-group Air Force had become a "constant," a fixed and welcomed point of reference from which it could orient itself toward the other variables in the budget problem. And so, too, it might have served for the Senate, if the economy had not taken a downward turn in the spring of 1949. Instead, the House's Air Force increase was placed in conflict with still another "given" in the Congressional budget equation, the ever precarious state of the economy. This was to prove an unequal contest, and one of the major reasons for its outcome was the fact that in neither 1948 nor 1949 had the support for the Air Force increase been built on really meaningful information about the military, foreign policy, and fiscal alternatives involved.

The record compiled by Mahon's subcommittee in February and

---

[36] *House Selective Service Hearings, 1948*, p. 6082. The "freezing" of such figures in the public (and military) mind is hardly restricted to the case of the 70-group Air Force and the fiscal 1950 budget. For a detailed analysis of the same phenomenon—the case of the fiscal 1915 naval budget and the Navy's goal of 48 battleships by 1920—see the present author's forthcoming study, "Admirals and Foreign Policy."

March provided little help to Senator O'Mahoney when he labored in August to persuade the Senate to keep the $800-million increase.

We do not need any details here [he told the Senate.] All we need to know here is that this reduction, which has been recommended by the committee, is a reduction from a 58-group air force to a 48-group air force. In my judgment a 58-group air force would be too little.

Details were exactly what O'Mahoney did need. Referring to the "clamor in the headlines and in the editorials for the reduction of Government spending," he warned that "we are running before the wind, as though we did not know what the needs of the country are." The trouble was that neither O'Mahoney nor the eight Senators who sided with him were in a position to explain just what difference it would make for the country's needs if it had a 48 instead of a 58-group Air Force. Thus, Senator William Knowland of California, a Republican member of the Armed Services Committee, could inform the Senate only that he based his support of the House increase on the Finletter Report, the Brewster Report, and a column in *Newsweek* by General Spaatz.

These were not very persuasive arguments with which to confront those who believed that the economy had taken over the Navy's traditional role as the nation's first line of defense. Illustrative of the opposition's point of view was the comment of Senator Leverett Saltonstall of Massachusetts, a Republican member of both the Armed Services Committee and the Subcommittee on Military Appropriations. He was supporting Thomas' bill, he told the Senate, for two reasons:

. . . we shall thus be carrying out the suggestions of the Commander in Chief and his subordinates; secondly, we shall thus be appropriating at least as much as—and perhaps more than—the economic condition of the country can stand. . . .[37]

The Senate did not reject the Air Force increase because of Truman's military prestige or because the Senators did not appreciate that Symington really agreed with Spaatz. It certainly was

[37] This and preceding quotations from *C.R.*, 95, pp. 12305, 12301-2, 12311.

not because Thomas and his supporters presented a more detailed and informative description of the economic consequences of spending the extra $800 million than had O'Mahoney and his supporters of the military consequences of not spending it, for in this respect there was no difference in the analytical quality of their arguments. The difference between the persuasive weight of the two sets of arguments was that O'Mahoney's case needed more meaningful information and Thomas' did not.

Thomas needed less informative arguments than O'Mahoney for two reasons. To begin with, it was O'Mahoney who was asking the Senate to overrule a committee report, and it was on him therefore that the burden of demonstration first fell. In the second place, it was O'Mahoney's, not Thomas', arguments which had to contend with the operation of the "principle of immediacy": that immediate and certain costs will generally be more heavily weighed than those distant and uncertain, even if the latter have the prospect of being, in the actual event, of greater consequence.

In this case, it was the costs of making the $800-million increase which were immediate and certain. They would unavoidably be incurred as soon as the Executive began to expend its fiscal 1950 funds. And if the extent of these costs was not known in detail to the Senate, at least their order was familiar: inflation and the other anticipated horrors of deficit financing. In contrast, the costs of not making the $800-million increase were distant and uncertain. If they came at all, it would be when the Air Force was actually put to the task of deterring or defeating Soviet nuclear power, and who was to say when this would be? Airplanes bought in the near future, it occurred to more than one Senator, might never even be needed. Moreover, there was no real knowledge of what the costs of not voting the $800 million would be, even if it were given that they would one day come, for there was nowhere on record any specific information about just what, if the Air Force did not receive the money, it would then be unable to do and what consequences would then result.[38]

[38] There was, of course, the statement before Mahon's committee that the 10 additional groups would primarily strengthen the Air Force's capability for

Clearly, Mahon's alternative, like Sheppard's, would have benefited politically from more informative arguments on its behalf. Again, there was information in the hands of the Executive which would have made possible more persuasive arguments than those used. But to have secured this information, or at least to have made the attempt, Mahon's committee would have had to question much more carefully than it did the manner in which the alternative numbers they were considering could be related to actual strategic plans and problems. In sum, if Mahon's committee had shown more interest in exploring the alternatives involved in the President's budget, it would not only have made more rational choices, it would also have made its choices politically more effective.

VI

To conclude that there were questions which Mahon's committee failed to ask about the President's budget, that its exploration of the alternatives to that budget was politically as well as analytically deficient, is not to turn full circle and raise again the question of why Congress did not do a better job in the role of coordinate budget-maker. This was a role which Congress never really tried to perform. The point involved here is not the failure of the committee to undertake a rational review of the whole budget, but rather its failure to do a better job with regard to those limited areas of the budget where it did see desirable and possible alternatives.

There is no single reason that can explain why the subcommittee did not get more information than it did about such issues. Some of the reasons that have been advanced to explain why the committee did not ask more questions in general were probably operative here as well, in particular the demands that their watchdog function put on the energy of the committee members, and the committee's inherent handicaps in ability, staff, time, and information. Nor

---

ground support, but this was ignored by both sides of the argument. Thus, the companion to Cannon's plea for long-range land-based bombers with which to fight the short atomic war was Gurney's assertion that, while he would "feel safer" if the nation had an additional 100 or 200 B-36's [sic], "our first defense is keeping our economy sound." *C.R.*, 95, p. 12314.

should one rule out the possibility that one or another of the members may not have been up to the intellectual task involved, although the attributes of intelligence, interest, and talent are probably less scarce in Congress than in most places.

Worthy of special attention, however, is the influence exercised by two perspectives with which the committee approached its task: one dealing with the way the members thought about information, and the other with the way they viewed the problems about which they wanted information. With regard to information, the committee appears to have equated secrecy with security. As previously illustrated, Mahon viewed the public development and dissemination of information about the plans and capabilities of the armed forces primarily as a help to Russian policy rather than as a useful and necessary contribution to the formulation of American goals and programs. The quality of Congress' choices on the Navy and Air Force increases was no little affected, however, by the absence of more detailed information about the number and kind of planes involved and the strategies which they were intended to implement. The prospects for uninformed choice were even more dramatically evident in the case of nuclear weapons. Here, the position of Congress was forcefully described by Senator McMahon in March 1949.

Today we are like a general who must train his troops without knowing how many rounds of ammunition they will be issued. When we debate the necessity of a 65,000-ton aircraft carrier or a 70-group air force or universal military training, I fear that we quite literally do not know what we are talking about. We do not know how many atomic weapons we possess, and, therefore, I fear that we lack perspective to pass on any major defense issue.[39]

The second perspective which affected the committee's performance concerned their view of the nature of the problem they were confronting. At least some members seem to have believed that there was a determinate answer to the question of how much to spend for defense. They simply did not see the budget as unavoidably a problem in choice: choice among the values to be served,

[39] Brien McMahon, "Should We Reveal the Size of Our Atomic Stockpile," *Bulletin of the Atomic Scientists,* March 1949, p. 67.

and choice among the divergent expectations of what would happen if one or another course of action was followed.

Consider, for example, Engel's conception of the budgeting process, as he described it during the House debate. First, the Executive decided "just what nation is most likely to attack us." Next the Joint Chiefs determined what missions each of the services would have in the event of war. Then the Chiefs determined what each service would need to carry out its mission, for instance, "just how large an air force, number of groups, the type of equipment, and so forth, will be required to carry out that mission." Finally, all this having been accomplished, the Chiefs

. . . send the amount required for these purposes to the President, the budget figures are then revised and reduced . . . being dependent upon first, our ability to carry on a peacetime national budget without endangering or wrecking our financial or economic structure, and second, the length of time we have to build up our force in the light of the facts and circumstances as they exist at the time.

This, Engel assured his colleagues on the basis of his 12 years of service on military appropriations committees, "is in effect the way this budget should be and undoubtedly was made up." [40]

With a perspective of this sort, Engel had no incentive to approach the hearings as an occasion for developing a number of alternatives from which he and his colleagues might choose, depending on their individual preferences as to where the balance should be struck between the allocation of resources to welfare purposes as compared to security purposes, and on their individual guesses as to which service's theories about the kind of weapons and strategies it would take to win wars might, in the event, turn out to be the

[40] *C.R.*, 95, pp. 4504–5. The same perspective was reflected in an editorial of the New York *Times* on December 2, 1948. This described the $15-billion ceiling as a "limit that presumably was set with the advice of the National Security Council and that was based on an evaluation of the intentions and capabilities of other nations and on an evaluation of our economy." The overtones of objective precision were even more evident in the editorial's statement of the problem that would soon confront Congress: "just how much money is needed to give this country a reasonable guarantee of military security and, as a corollary to that, at what point will military expenditures so strain the national economy that they will defeat their purpose?"

more realistic. On the contrary, he approached the hearings intent on discovering the "right" budget. Thus, he assured Symington: "We either need a 48-, 50-, or 70-group air force to defend this country in the light of everything that is going on internationally. I am willing to give whatever we need." [41]

It is the existence of this perspective which constitutes the final explanation for the quality of the subcommittees' action on the President's budget. The questions of Engel and those who thought like him were not designed to explore the consequences of alternative budgets, but to ascertain whether the administration's budget was the "right" budget, the one the nation needed. Since they failed to see how large an element of choice was involved in the budgeting process, they did not think to ask the kind of questions that would have prepared Congress to take a more effective part in that choice. Paradoxically enough, their major error was a failure to recognize that the character of the Executive's choice was unavoidably political. Without an appreciation for the fact that it had necessarily been the interplay of power and interest within the Executive that had put the budget together in the first place, they lacked the incentive to secure the kind of information with which Congress might have more rationally exercised its power and more effectively served its interests.

[41] *HCA, Hearings 1950 Budget,* II, 25.

v   *The Executive Choice: Rationality*

and Politics

The history of the defense budget on the Executive side had its formal beginning on May 6, 1948. This was the date on which the Director of the Bureau of the Budget, James Webb, first proposed to Forrestal that the fiscal 1950 budget should not be permitted to exceed the level of $15 billion. In reality, of course, one can speak of "beginnings and ends" only as a matter of analytical convenience. Politically, the budgeting process is continuous. Thus, the interplay of power and interest associated with the fiscal 1950 budget developed out of the conflicts attendant to the determination of the supplement for fiscal 1949 and merged, ultimately, into the issues connected with the origins of the fiscal 1951 budget. In order to understand the considerations responsible for the $15-billion ceiling, it will be necessary, therefore, to return to the events discussed in Chapter II and supplement the description presented there of the problems associated with the fiscal 1949 budget.

The rearmament that Truman had heralded in his special address to Congress on March 17, 1948, had posed from the start a serious threat to the administration's fiscal policy. Since the end of World War II, Truman had been intent on a "hard money" policy. With the enthusiastic support of Webb and Secretary of the Treasury Snyder, he had endeavored to produce not just balanced budgets, but budgets with surpluses that could be used to reduce the national debt and halt the postwar inflation. This effort had met with some success, and the budgets for fiscal 1947 and fiscal 1948 had provided, respectively, surpluses of $754 million and $8.4 billion. In keeping with this policy, the fiscal 1949 budget that Truman had submitted to Congress in January 1948 had anticipated a surplus of $4.8 billion.[1]

As indicated by the decrease from the $8.4-billion surplus produced in fiscal 1948, the budget presented in January had already been subjected to the pressure of providing the new billions that would be required for Marshall Plan aid to Europe. By March, pressure from still another direction raised the prospect that there would be no surplus at all. The Republican 80th Congress, which had passed two tax reduction bills in 1947, both of which Truman had successfully vetoed, promptly undertook to pass another in the 1948 session. The House bill passed on February 2, and the Senate voted its version on March 19, two days after Truman had announced his intention to raise the defense budget. Under the provisions of the Senate bill the administration would lose $5 billion of the revenues on which the January budget had counted, and the number of Democrats supporting the measure indicated that Congress would this time be able to override the President's veto.[2]

In these circumstances, a large supplemental appropriation for the armed services could easily produce a deficit. The apprehension with which this possibility was viewed in the Bureau of the Budget and the Treasury Department was probably much the same as that expressed by the President's Council of Economic Advisers. Truman had not sought the advice of the council before making his March 17 address, and Edwin Nourse, the council's chairman, alarmed at the "vigorous" response to the speech and "concerned as to its inflationary consequences," decided that the council had better volunteer its views. These were communicated to the President in a letter on March 24.

The inflationary dangers which we emphasized in the materials presented for use in your Economic Report last January have by no means been

[1] Harry S. Truman, *Memoirs* (2 vols., Garden City, N.Y., Doubleday and Company, Inc., 1956), II, 33, 37–38; *U.S. Budget, FY 1952*, p. 1008; and *U.S. Budget, FY 1949*, p. M6.

[2] Richard E. Neustadt, "Congress and the Fair Deal: A Legislative Balance Sheet," *Public Policy*, Volume 5, 1954, p. 362, and *C.R., 94*, pp. 4019, D59, D190.

overcome. The additional pressures coming from the expenditure, the appropriation, or even the consideration of some additional billions of government money [for defense] must inevitably aggravate this danger. We feel we must face the question whether, at the very outset of this new spending program, we should not need to set aside the free market practices that we have been trying to guide toward stabilized peacetime operation and substitute a rather comprehensive set of controls of materials, plant operation, prices, wages, and business credit.[3]

The alarm with which the council viewed the prospect of inflation can be seen from the lengths to which it thought the administration would have to go to combat it. At the time the council wrote this letter, the size of the defense supplement had not yet been determined, but the council's fear that it might be so large as to require across-the-board controls on the economy was not unfounded. As it happened, Truman received the letter the same day the House approved the Senate's version of the tax reduction bill and Forrestal submitted the services' first proposal for the fiscal 1949 supplement: the program that had totaled $9 billion.

Both the House's action and the council's letter provide clues as to the considerations which led the President to tell Forrestal the next day (March 25) that he had decided to permit the services only a $3-billion supplement. The President's frame of mind is further indicated in the reply he sent on that date to the council.

I read your letter of the twenty-fourth with a great deal of interest and I think you are working in the right direction.

We must be very careful that the military does not overstep the bounds from an economic standpoint domestically. Most of them would like to go back to a war footing—that is not what we want.[4]

Subsequent events did little to shake Truman's conviction that the services were making more of his March address than he had meant. As was described in Chapter II, first the Air Force and then the Army failed to support the $3-billion supplement, and the only

[3] Nourse Diary, May 10, 1948, and letter, Council to Truman, March 24, 1948, Edwin G. Nourse Papers.
[4] Edwin G. Nourse, *Economics in the Public Service* (New York, Harcourt, Brace and Company, 1953), p. 223. The $9 and $3-billion figures, which represent new obligational authority (NOA), are not directly comparable to the $4.8-billion surplus or the $5-billion tax cut, which pertain to revenues and expenditures for fiscal 1949 only.

way Forrestal was able to bring them to close ranks was by promising to raise the supplement to $3.5 billion and by giving the Chiefs permission to tell Congress that they really wanted $9 billion. A $3.5-billion supplement, when added to the $10 billion originally requested for fiscal 1949, would have meant a total of $13.5 billion for the armed services and a total for all defense purposes (counting the funds for universal military training and stockpiling) of $14.7 billion. Moreover, the forces the services had programmed under this budget would lead, according to Forrestal's projection, to a budget of $16 billion in fiscal 1950 and one of $17.5 billion in fiscal 1951.

These were the figures on which the Budget Bureau had stuck. Its own analysis projected the cost of the fiscal 1949 build-up to a defense budget of $18.2 billion in fiscal 1952 and possibly to one as high as $20 billion, if prices continued to rise.[5] So far as the Budget Bureau was concerned, budgets of this size were out of the question. Accordingly, on May 6 Webb proposed to Forrestal that the supplement for fiscal 1949 be reduced to $2.5 billion. His purposes were twofold. First, since Congress on April 2 had overridden the President's veto of the tax reduction bill, a deficit was now expected for fiscal 1949, and a reduction in the money the services would spend during the year would help decrease its size.[6] More important, however, was Webb's interest in reducing the contract authority available to the services. This would insure that the programs they started in fiscal 1949 could be maintained without ex-

[5] Millis, ed., *The Forrestal Diaries*, p. 430. The bureau's projections do not appear to have been in terms of NOA, which is puzzling because its $15-billion ceiling was. The bureau's projections were made from a $15.5-billion base, a figure which presumably represented the $14.7-billion in NOA plus the appropriations the fiscal 1949 budget would provide to liquidate prior contract authority. In contrast, Forrestal's projections were in terms of NOA and appear to have been made from the $13.5-billion base, although it is possible he used the $14.7-billion base (see *SCA, Hearings 1948 Supplemental Budget*, p. 12).

[6] By April 1948, the administration had revised its January estimate of expected revenue ($44.5 billion) to $47.3 billion. In contrast, its expected expenditures had increased from $39.7 billion to $43.2 billion. (Of the $3.5-billion increase, $2 billion was the result of the President's $3-billion [NOA] defense supplement.) Accordingly, the deficit then expected to result from the $5-billion tax cut was $900 million. The actual deficit for fiscal 1949 was $1.8 billion. See *C.R.*, 94, p. 4024, and *U.S. Budget, FY 1951*, p. M5.

ceeding the $15-billion ceiling, which he now advanced as the limit to which the defense budget should be kept for fiscal 1950 and the years immediately following.

Forrestal's reaction to the idea of a $15-billion ceiling was prompt. "Is the world situation such," he asked, "as to warrant appropriations of this order at the present time?" He told Webb that in his judgment it was not. A larger program was "essential" because the next two years would be "a critical period in our relations with Russia." Webb did not attempt to refute this argument. Instead, he asked a question of his own, thereby revealing the considerations behind *his* judgment. "Can we," he queried, "carry out such a military program [that is, one beyond the $15-billion level], support ERP, provide a merchant marine program and implement the atomic energy plans without having available the controls and sanctions [over the civilian economy] which it seems very doubtful that we will get in this election year?" [7]

Here, in essence, were joined the issues over which the budget debate was to turn for the next seven months. There was to be no agreement between Forrestal and Webb on the answers to these two questions. Nor was there a basis for such an agreement. They approached the size of the defense budget with quite different responsibilities. Forrestal's proper concern was for the costs to security that would result from lower budgets; Webb's was for the costs to other administration purposes and programs that would result from higher budgets. In consequence, their judgments about the size of the budget were bound to conflict. Since neither could compel the other to accept his judgment and the stakes were too high for either to yield, their conflict had but one political course to follow. The two questions had to be taken to the President for an answer.

The heart of Webb's position was the expectation that if the defense budget were permitted to rise to $20 billion by fiscal 1952 the nation would end up with a total budget of $50 billion. The difficulty with a budget of this size, in Webb's opinion, was that it

[7] For the statements made at the May 6 meeting, see Millis, ed., *The Forrestal Diaries,* p. 430–31.

would be "several billion dollars more than the estimated [Federal] income at present tax rates. We would be in a position where even with full employment, business good, and the tax rates still at a very high level, we would be required to resort to large-scale deficit financing." [8] Deficit financing, either on a large scale in 1952 or a smaller scale in 1950, was about the last thing Webb wanted to see. Ever since he had assumed direction of the Budget Bureau in the summer of 1946, Webb had been one of the major spokesmen for Truman's "hard money" policy, as well as its instrument. Nor did Webb have cause in the spring of 1948 to think any better of deficit financing than he had in the past. The national debt was still far above the level to which Truman hoped to reduce it, and the postwar inflation had by no means abated.

Inflation and deficits were not, of course, the inevitable consequence of a defense budget in excess of $15 billion. Deficit financing could, as the Council of Economic Advisers had pointed out, be accompanied by wage and price controls designed to offset the resulting inflationary pressure. There was also the possibility of raising taxes to meet the new expenditures, thereby avoiding a deficit in the first place and most of the inflationary pressure. But, as Webb indicated in his conference with Forrestal on May 6, wage and price controls were not considered an alternative open to the administration. Webb's expectation that Congress and the people would not support them appeared well grounded. Congress had rejected the President's request for such controls in the fall of 1947, and it was to do so again in the special session that Truman called in the summer of 1948. Similarly, given Congress' action on the tax reduction bill, there was little reason to believe that it would support the fiscal 1950 budget with higher taxes, a conclusion which gained additional weight from the expectation that the Republicans would win the November elections.[9]

The case that Webb could put to the President on behalf of the ceiling was, then, a persuasive one. It seemed economically

[8] *Ibid.*, pp. 436–37. The quotation is from a paper written on May 13 at Webb's direction.

[9] Truman, *Memoirs*, II, 27–28, 37, and Nourse, *Economics in the Public Service*, pp. 213–15.

sound and politically realistic. It was, however, a case that rested on nonmilitary considerations. It was based on the desirability of avoiding deficits and inflation and on the infeasibility of securing controls and higher taxes. The specific sum earmarked for fiscal 1950, $15 billion, represented nothing more than an arbitrary guess at the amount of money that would be available for defense given the revenues to be expected, the goal of a balanced budget, and the absence of change in any of the other major items in the Federal budget.[10]

Webb's case was for this reason not necessarily a winning one. Truman's responsibilities were total. He was at once more concerned about the military consequences of the $15-billion ceiling than Webb, and more concerned about the costs that a higher budget would entail than Forrestal. The range of the President's responsibilities meant that, unlike Forrestal, he was at least open to the idea that a $15-billion budget might, on the balance, represent the optimum service to his purposes and programs. But if Truman was susceptible to the answer Webb gave to the question of whether more could be spent, his responsibilities also obliged him to heed the answer Forrestal would give to the question of whether more was not needed. The President was bound to consider the possibility (if only because Forrestal was bound to urge it upon him) that the need for a larger defense budget might be such as to justify the economic and social costs of inflation or the political costs and risks that he would incur in the effort to go once again to Congress and the people for controls or higher taxes.

It was to find out where Truman stood on these matters that Forrestal, immediately following his conference with Webb, requested one with the President. Forrestal was not himself unmoved by the argument Webb had made. He, too, shared the prevailing opinions about what the nation could afford to spend for defense. Writing in January 1947 with regard to the $10.5 billion that had been requested for the services in fiscal 1948, he predicted that

[10] Assuming the Budget Bureau expected the gross national product to rise in the years following fiscal 1950, the idea of keeping to the $15-billion ceiling presumably reflected the goal of accumulating a mounting surplus.

"the country simply cannot stand continuance of the heavy budget which is ahead of us next year. . . ." Similarly, in April 1948, summing up the funds requested for the armed services, the Marshall Plan, the Maritime Commission, and the Atomic Energy Commission, he declared:

You add onto that what they are talking about now, the lend-lease for Western Union in Europe of 5 or 6 millions, billions, and you have a barrel that is completely full now, and one blow of the hammer is going to burst the bungs on it. . . .

Some of Forrestal's comments the previous year provide a fair inkling of the consequences he anticipated should the bungs burst. At a lunch with members of the House Appropriations Committee in March 1947, he had affirmed: ". . . even naval officers were not economic fools and recognized the fact that by forfeiting a sound economy at home we could stumble into state socialism just as successfully as if we had marked our course for that harbor." And in a private talk with Secretary of the Treasury Snyder, he had argued:

. . . if we are going to have a run for our side in the competition between the Soviet system and our own, we shall have to harness all the talent and brains in this country just as we had to do during the war. I said I felt very strongly that the world could only be brought back to order by a restoration of commerce, trade and business, and that would have to be done by business men. . . . Domestically, we shall have to do all we can to encourage and not discourage business. That would have to take the form of wise taxation, freedom from unnecessary persecution, etc.[11]

These were sentiments worthy of a Taft or Byrd. But against his concern for the morale of businessmen and his fear of state socialism, he had to balance his belief that armed power was the most vital ingredient in the conduct of a successful foreign policy. Among the early Cold War statesmen in the United States, Forrestal was perhaps foremost in his appreciation for this fact. In the end, and not unnaturally considering his responsibilities, it was this last

[11] For these statements, see Millis, ed., *The Forrestal Diaries*, pp. 239, 439, 250, 247–48.

consideration that emerged the more dominant in his mind. Thus in 1947 he wrote:

God knows I am fully aware of the terrific task which this country faces if it is to keep a free economy and a free society. But to . . . deny Marshall the cards to play, when the stakes are as high as they are, would be a grave decision.[12]

By May of 1948 Forrestal was convinced that Marshall needed more and stronger cards. As was explained in Chapter II, the events of the spring—the Czech coup, the harbinger of the Berlin blockade, the situation in the Far East, and the preliminary commitments to the Atlantic alliance—had persuaded him that it was time to add significantly to the forces then at hand. If calculated risks were to be taken, Forrestal apparently wanted to see them taken for a change with the state of the economy instead of the armed services. Webb told Nourse that Ferdinand Eberstadt, a close friend and adviser of Forrestal, was exercising a "bad influence [on him], tending to act on the premise that we were now or shortly to go on a war footing and to be advocating a rather comprehensive system of wartime controls." [13]

Whether Forrestal was really prepared to go this far, it is difficult to say. In his conversation with Webb on May 6, he admitted that the larger budget he was proposing would require some controls on the economy, but he suggested that they might not have to be very extensive. In any event, Forrestal's position still left begging the question of how Truman would be able to secure controls from Congress, and in this respect his case was as one-sided as Webb's. Forrestal had no more answered Webb's "economy" argument for the lower budget than Webb had confronted Forrestal's "defense" argument for a higher budget.

II

The meeting Forrestal had requested with the President took place on May 7. Also present were Webb, Marshall, Snyder, Steel-

[12] *Ibid.*, p. 240. For examples of Forrestal's conceptual sensitivity to the role of power in international relations, see *ibid.*, pp. 6, 14, 25, 53, 57, 157.
[13] Nourse Diary, May 10, 1948.

man, and Sidney Souers (Truman's assistant for National Security Council affairs). Forrestal's need to find out where the President stood with regard to the $15-billion ceiling was urgent, since it affected the supplement then before Congress as well as the plans to be made for fiscal 1950. But in rushing so quickly to the President with the issue, he appears to have made a major error. His notes strongly suggest that he came to a meeting where everyone else had already caucused and had done so on the basis of an effective presentation of Webb's considerations, not his.[14]

If his timing was bad, Forrestal's style was not. He had asked for the meeting, he announced, so that they could all have an opportunity to hear why the President had decided to increase the fiscal 1949 budget. Forrestal's hope, obviously, was to turn the discussion so that Webb confronted Truman's "defense face" and he could avoid the President's "economy face." Truman promptly asked Marshall to comment on the matter. The words of Marshall —the Secretary of State, the Chief of Staff who had fashioned victory in World War II, and in Truman's judgment "the greatest living American"—were to be of critical importance, for it was Marshall who was likely to hold, so far as the President's interests were concerned, "the balance of persuasion" between Webb and Forrestal.

Marshall proceeded to make three points, none of which was the slightest help to Forrestal. The first was the statement that his foreign policy was based on "the assumption that there would be no war." The effect of this comment was to align Marshall with Webb and Truman in the judgment that Forrestal and the services were intent on putting the nation on a "war footing." The point was driven home by Marshall's second observation, which was an injunction "that we should not plunge into war preparations which would bring about the very thing we were taking steps to prevent." Taken together, the two statements added up to an argument that Forrestal's budget was not only not needed but might be positively harmful.

[14] For the statements made at the May 7 meeting, see Millis, ed., *The Forrestal Diaries*, pp. 431–32.

Marshall's third point was the assertion that he had "always" considered universal military training (UMT) to be the best way to demonstrate to the Europeans and to the Russians "our determination to continue our position in European matters." This was perhaps the most telling of the three blows Marshall delivered to Forrestal's rearmament program, for Forrestal, as was indicated in Chapter II, had seen as its primary justification the need to provide Marshall with troops that could back up his policies in the various trouble spots around the globe without the necessity of partial mobilization. By stressing instead the need for UMT, Marshall implied that he assigned a lower priority than Forrestal to the need to increase the size of the regular armed forces and that the events of the spring had not persuaded him that it was necessary to undertake a basic reversal of the nation's pre-March military posture. In addition to not helping Forrestal, Marshall's position was also one that avoided conflict with Webb. The dollar cost of UMT was not insignificant, but there was little prospect, despite Marshall's hopes, that Congress would pass the program, and it posed, therefore, no real threat to Webb's ceiling or the considerations that lay behind it.[15]

Although his words hurt Forrestal's cause, Marshall was not here serving as a handmaiden to Webb's interests or even the President's. The position of the Secretary of State was one which was responsive, as he saw them, to *his* interests. The difference between Marshall's and Forrestal's approach to the defense budget reflected basic dissimilarities in the interests and perspectives with which they approached the problem, dissimilarities which were, in turn, the consequence of their different institutional responsibilities. Thus, while Marshall, as Secretary of State, was ultimately responsible for national security, he had also the responsibility to secure the

[15] Forrestal had already concluded that universal military training (UMT) did not have the "slightest chance" of passage. See *ibid.*, p. 426–27. Neither Forrestal nor the Budget Bureau appear to have counted the future cost of UMT in their projections of the fiscal 1949 rearmament program, although the bureau included the initial $500-million request in its $15.5-billion base. Forrestal estimated that if UMT was enacted the total investment by fiscal 1953 would be $2 billion and the annual operating cost about $1.6 billion. See *HCA, Hearings 1949 Budget*, I, 25.

nation's objectives as cheaply as possible. The interest of the Secretary of State will always be to discharge his responsibilities, whenever possible, without the expense of blood and treasure that a war would entail. To base policy on the assumption that there will be a war has, therefore, somewhat the character of admitting defeat before the final returns are in, and it is an assumption that determined Secretaries of State are likely to avoid.

But while the premise that there will be no war—that nonmilitary means or the threat of violence alone can prevail—may be a useful spur to the plans and operations of the Department of State, it does not follow that it is an equally meaningful guide for the plans and operations of the military. Their responsibilities compel them to prepare for the possibility that more expensive and less desirable means may be required to secure national objectives. The difference in their responsibilities is not such as to make the Secretary of State necessarily indifferent to the need for force or even to the desirability of preparing for war. It does, however, tend to make the Secretary of State a less than wholly reliable ally in the cause of higher defense budgets. For, as Marshall's words indicate, if others identify such budgets as "going on a war footing," the Secretary of State may find it difficult to argue that this is what his foreign policy really requires.

Marshall's other statements were also related to his institutional responsibilities. National security is a function of both the intentions and the capabilities of other Powers, but it is the Department of State, not Defense, which has the primary responsibility for evaluating and influencing the intentions of others. Similarly, the responsibilities of the Department of Defense are mainly confined to military capabilities, whereas the Department of State has at least nominal responsibility for the range of foreign policy means. In consequence, the Secretary of State is likely to be more sensitive to the opportunities for achieving security through acts designed to influence the intentions of others or through the use of nonviolent means, while the major interests of those who speak for the defense establishment are likely to be restricted to programs which will enhance the nation's military capabilities vis-à-vis those of other states.

Marshall's concern for the provocative effect of Forrestal's program is a case in point. It is normally so difficult to predict whether a given defense budget will have a provocative or a deterrent effect that one or the other consequence can be easily cited in the budget debate to defend positions which were initially arrived at through other considerations.[16] In this instance, however, Marshall was not citing "good reasons for real reasons." The Department of State was genuinely worried that American rearmament might exercise an adverse effect on Russian intentions. The immediate cause for this concern was the discussion then under way with regard to the formation of a North Atlantic defense pact, and it was exemplified in a telegram the British sent on April 23 warning that "the Russians might be so provoked by the formation of [such a] defense organization that they would resort to rash measures and plunge the world into war."

When the Under Secretary of State, Robert Lovett, brought the telegram to President Truman, he affirmed that American experts shared this view. On the other hand, they also believed that once the alliance had been established and armed, it would exercise a deterrent effect on the Soviets and might, hopefully, even lead them to recast their objectives in a less aggressive mold. While the British and the American diplomats were willing to risk the provocation in order to reach the deterrent, they were determined to move cautiously. The most important step, the British telegram had concluded, was that the United States make a clear commitment to come to the defense of the nations of western Europe in the event of a Russian attack.[17]

Both the British warning and its conclusion jibed with the impressions Lovett had received from a series of private conversations with the Russian Ambassador in Washington. In a Cabinet meeting,

[16] Cf. Secretary of Defense Wilson's statement in reference to his plans to keep the fiscal 1956 budget at the same level as that for fiscal 1955: "[even] if our people would be willing to stand for twice as big a budget, which I don't think they would, I still don't think that's the solution." The problem, Wilson continued, was that "It might tempt us to rattle the atomic bomb too much, and I know it scares a lot of people over the world who think we are liable to precipitate another World War. No, I think the present policy and the budget are about right." New York *Times*, November 29, 1954.

[17] The account of the British telegram is from Truman, *Memoirs*, II, 244–45. The quotation is Truman's paraphrase.

also on April 23, Lovett reported on these conversations and summarized his view of Russian policy as follows:

. . . the position of Russia in his opinion . . . [was] of a dual nature at the moment: (1) constant probing to find out the solidity of our intent; and (2) a reflection of their own fear of a preventive or aggressive war on our part.

The logic of Lovett's analysis for Forrestal's rearmament program was obvious. What was needed was a clarification of American intentions, not a marked increase in American capabilities. Hence Marshall's injunction against plunging into provocative "war preparations."

Needless to say, Marshall, of all people, had reason to know that an increase in the Air Force from 55 to 66 groups or an increase in the size of the Army from 552,000 men to 790,000 men hardly constituted putting the services in a position to fight World War III. But he had to calculate the conclusions the Russians might draw from such measures in light of the fact that the State Department was itself planning to launch the Atlantic alliance with at least $3 billion in American arms aid to Europe.[18] In any event, whatever the merits of the State Department's analysis, its effect was to deny Forrestal the opportunity to cite the formation of NATO as an argument for raising the defense budget above Webb's ceiling.

Given his interests and perspectives, Marshall's willingness to see UMT emerge as America's major military response to the events of the spring made perfect sense. In its immediate effect, UMT would be less likely to seem a provocative preparation for war than an increase in the regular armed forces, but it would serve equally well to demonstrate America's intention to defend western Europe, and it would even, in time, make a significant contribution to the deterrent capability of the alliance. Marshall's reasoning on these points can be seen in the testimony he gave in March before the Senate Armed Services Committee in support of the program. When asked if, as the Secretary of State, "the psychological factor . . . [was not] the paramount thing with which you have to deal,"

[18] Lovett quotation and figures from Millis, ed., *The Forrestal Diaries,* pp. 424, 375, 419, 425.

Marshall had replied that it was, and he had gone on to agree with the questioner's interpretation that UMT "was not an effort to get ready for a possible immediate war, but [to show] that our people are wholeheartedly behind a complete change of attitude in our foreign policy. . . ." As Marshall put it himself, UMT would be of great effect "because it would register a decision of the American people in a very important matter, it would make plain to the world that we are going to be strong in a military way and that we are determined to back our course."

For Marshall to believe that UMT would make a significant contribution to the nation's military strength, his image of World War III could hardly have been one in which the A-bomb and strategic bombing figured as the decisive elements. Nor was it. "I think that however much any future war starts in the air," he told the committee, "as in the past it will end up in the mud and on the ground." Accordingly, Marshall considered it a point of some consequence that UMT might advance by a year the time it would take to ship the National Guard overseas.[19] Marshall recognized, of course, that until the forces at hand in western Europe reached the point where they could stand off a Russian attack until large American reinforcements arrived, the mobilization base provided by UMT would add little to the military capabilities of either the burgeoning alliance or the United States. In the meantime, however, UMT would demonstrate the strength of American intentions, and this he obviously considered the more immediately important objective.

As the preceding pages have endeavored to show, the difference between Marshall's approach to the defense budget and Forrestal's can be attributed in part to the interest of Secretaries of State in intent-oriented, as compared to capability-oriented, policy. But while the difference in their institutional responsibilities can help explain what Marshall said at the May 7 meeting, it is difficult to account, in these terms, for some of the things he left unsaid at that meeting. Marshall, after all, was not insensitive to the contribution that force could make to his policies; it had been he, not Forrestal,

[19] Marshall's statements are quoted from *Senate UMT Hearings, 1948*, pp. 24–25.

who had exclaimed at the February National Security Council meeting that "we are playing with fire while we have nothing with which to put it out." Similarly, in March he had publicly described the nation's defenses as "only a hollow shell." [20] Whatever his immediate fears about provoking the Russians, these were surely conditions which he hoped in time to see remedied. Why, then, had he not made this clear at the May meeting and at least protested the idea that the $15-billion ceiling was to hold not just for fiscal 1950 but for the years to follow thereafter?

The answer is that there was still another reason why Marshall did not take Forrestal's side in the argument against Webb's ceiling. The hard fact was that Marshall, for somewhat different reasons than Webb's, had similarly concluded that larger budgets would be politically neither desirable nor feasible. This conclusion had nothing to do with the nature of his institutional responsibilities; it was rather the product of Marshall's experience as an Army officer in the 1920's and 1930's. The famine budgets the Army had received during those years had left him with very little faith in the capacity of the American people to sustain a large military establishment on any long-term basis. So low was his confidence that at the end of the war, when the services were planning the size of their postwar forces, Marshall had found himself "in disagreement with almost everything that was being proposed." Marshall left the office of Chief of Staff in the fall of 1945 persuaded that the force levels then under consideration (which were about the same size as those the services were requesting in the spring of 1948) were "entirely too high and that the country just couldn't stand it."

Now, my associates who differed with me [he told Vinson's committee in October 1949, when he was no longer Secretary of State] did so, I felt, largely on the ground that they thought America had learned its lesson. When it comes to appropriations in piping times of peace, I don't think America will ever learn its lesson, because the political pressures are tremendous. In the next place, my associates haven't lived through the education I had had in the 1920's and the immediate problems I had inherited in 1938, 1939, and 1940, when our degree of poverty was very trying. I could well understand that. They just thought I underestimated public opinion in the United States.

[20] *Ibid.*, p. 7.

Well, I am a great respecter of public opinion, but, on the other hand, I am also a great respecter of the tremendous political influence of the budget and the fact that it almost gets beyond control when it relates to things that do not produce immediate results like good roads, agriculture matters, and such.[21]

The passage of two and a half years had had little effect on Marshall's views. The fear that the nation might slip back into the old "feast or famine" budgeting cycle was one of his recurrent themes in conversation with Truman, and it undoubtedly underlay Marshall's willingness to go along with Webb's ceiling. Indeed, in the spring of 1948, given the size of the appropriations that had just been requested for the European Recovery Program, Marshall may have been especially worried about the public reaction to a mounting defense budget. Marshall did not, therefore, really see UMT and larger regular forces as true alternatives; whatever its other policy merits, UMT was the only course of action he thought the nation would support over the long pull. It is important to note that, although Marshall was not insensitive to the climate of opinion regarding what the economy "could stand," the limit that loomed largest in his mind was clearly political. Thus, he told the Senate Armed Services Committee in March 1948:

I have felt it was absolutely necessary to find a system that did not involve national bankruptcy if you continued it, and universal military training was the only method that I could see that offered any solution except a large standing force, which I am convinced that we cannot possibly afford to maintain year after year.

. . . no one has been able to explain to me how it [maintaining a large standing force] could be done without tremendous expenditure year after year for the taxpayer. I do not think the funds would be provided, considering the fact that the annual budget is one of the principal issues of a political campaign.[22]

To return to the events at the meeting of May 7, Forrestal's diary does not record what reply he made to the three points that Mar-

---

[21] See *HCAS, Unification and Strategy Hearings*, p. 601. For the force levels the services had in mind at the war's end, see Walter Millis, Harvey Mansfield, and Harold Stein, *Arms and the State* (New York, The Twentieth Century Fund, 1958), pp. 147–48.

[22] *Senate UMT Hearings, 1948*, pp. 7–8.

shall had advanced: the assumption that there would be no war, the desirability of avoiding provocative preparations, and the need for UMT. Forrestal's entry concluded with an account of Truman's own remarks. These must have removed any remaining doubts on Forrestal's part that Webb had successfully cleared his ceiling with both the Secretary of State and the President. Truman announced his complete approval of Marshall's statements, and in answer to the question Forrestal had posed for the meeting (why had the President decided to increase the fiscal 1949 budget), Truman responded that in agreeing to supplement the fiscal 1949 budget, he had not meant to give "the green light" to preparation for war. Truman made his point even clearer to Forrestal a week later when he declared that the increase in the fiscal 1949 budget was to be "for the purpose of demonstrating a continuing firmness in world affairs, with the thought that we were preparing for peace and not for war." [23]

Truman and Webb, as their earlier remarks to Nourse indicated, were persuaded that the military were trying to turn the President's interest in a budget that would demonstrate the nation's intention to stabilize the postwar world into an opportunity to move to something approaching a war footing. They were, moreover, most suspicious of the services' motives. It was their belief, and it was substantially shared by Marshall and Lovett, that what lay behind Forrestal's $3.5-billion supplement and the Chiefs' $9-billion figure was not so much a considered plan for essential military operations, but rather the starkest kind of interservice rivalry.

Seen from their perspective, the services appeared to be at war with each other and in mutiny against their Secretary. As one of them later put it, the Air Force (which was the only service that could deliver the A-bomb at the time) seemed intent on parlaying its monopoly on the nation's new and obviously important weapon into an occasion for reducing the Army and the Navy to the status of police forces. On their part, the Army and the Navy seemed to be reacting to the advent of the A-bomb with all the attributes of

[23] Millis, ed., *The Forrestal Diaries*, p. 435. The occasion was the May 13 meeting shortly to be described.

labor unions intent on preserving their previously existing job, pay, and promotion opportunities in the face of a major technological change. Both in the Office of the President and the State Department, the feeling was that Forrestal could have done more than he had to settle some of these disputes and to keep the services in hand when they testified in connection with the $3-billion supplement that Truman had initially agreed to on March 25.

Given this perspective on the military's budget-making, Truman must have viewed the case for a budget in excess of $15 billion with some skepticism. He refrained, however, from making any of these points at the May 7 meeting. Instead, he presented Forrestal with an argument (Marshall's) which made the case for Webb's ceiling in strictly military terms.

He [Truman] . . . pointed out that the very people in Congress who would now vote for heavy Air appropriations are those who a year from now would deny anything to the Armed Forces, and that *if we permit the military budget to rise in proportions that will cut too deeply into the civilian economy, the ones that will suffer in the long run will be the Armed Services*. That, he said, is precisely what he is trying to avoid, and he is sure the advice he is giving . . . is sound.[24]

With these words Truman endeavored to show Forrestal only his "defense face" and to persuade him that the $15-billion ceiling needed no further justification than an examination of the best interests of the National Military Establishment. This effort was in keeping with the best strategy for successful political persuasion. In fact, however, Truman was far from indifferent to the fiscal and political interests that had been responsible for Webb's proposal in the first place. In contrast to the $43-billion budget then expected for fiscal 1949 (and the $50-billion budget to which Webb expected Forrestal's program would lead), it was Truman's conviction that the budget should be reduced to the neighborhood of $30 billion. Of this total, he hoped to bring that available to the services down to the vicinity of $5–7 billion. The precise reasoning behind these figures is not clear, but in general they were no doubt reflective of the same belief noted in the case of the Congressional climate of

[24] *Ibid.*, p. 432, italics added.

opinion: the idea that the economy could not continue to support defense expenditures of the order then current.[25]

Truman's long-run objectives thus anticipated an even greater restriction of military spending than that involved in Webb's ceiling. The President's short-run interests in the ceiling were equally strong. As previously noted, Truman was intent on budgets which would avoid deficit financing and would compile, whenever possible, budget surpluses. The tax reduction bill passed in April 1948 had removed the possibility of a surplus in fiscal 1949 and had assured a deficit. If Truman now endorsed Forrestal's $3.5-billion supplement, he would only add to that deficit and insure an even larger one in fiscal 1950. Given the power and prestige he commanded in the 80th Congress and what then seemed to be the likely political complexion of its successor, Truman presumably had no difficulty in accepting Webb's judgment that he would be unable to secure the wage and price controls necessary to cope with the inflationary pressures that those deficits would produce. Truman's interest in avoiding deficits and inflation would have been great in any year. In 1948, a Presidential election year, he was surely no less interested in demonstrating that the Democratic Party, and his leadership in particular, stood for the solidest kind of fiscal responsibility.

The weight of these long- and short-run considerations, together with Truman's suspicions about what lay behind the services' requests, was so heavily in the direction of Webb's rather than Forrestal's budget, that one may wonder if Truman would not have endorsed the ceiling even if Forrestal had received Marshall's support. Without it, Forrestal's defeat was a foregone conclusion.

The President formally announced his decision on May 13. Assembled at the White House for this occasion were the Joint Chiefs

[25] On the strategy of political persuasion, see Richard E. Neustadt, *Presidential Power* (New York, John Wiley and Sons, 1960), Chap. 3, especially p. 46. For Truman's views on total size of the budget, see Millis, ed., *The Forrestal Diaries*, pp. 245–46, and Truman, *Memoirs*, II, 40. It was Truman's practice to hold an annual "budget seminar" with the press (see Truman, *Memoirs*, II, 36), and he cited the $5 to $7 billion figure on these occasions in 1945, 1946, and 1947. He advanced this goal again during the 1948 campaign; see Chapter IV, p. 100, above.

and the service Secretaries as well as Webb and Forrestal. After recapitulating the arguments that Webb had advanced on behalf of the $15-billion ceiling, Truman declared his determination to adhere to it "unless world conditions deteriorate much further." To this end, as explained in Chapter II, he told Forrestal that, while he might ask Congress for a $3.1-billion supplement for fiscal 1949, the services were not to be permitted to spend all of it, and that the force levels planned for fiscal 1950 should be no higher than those which could be supported within the Budget Bureau's ceiling. (This, it will be recalled, was actually $14.4 billion in so far as the National Military Establishment was concerned.) In conclusion, the President declared:

. . . as Commander-in-Chief I expect these orders to be carried out wholeheartedly, in good spirit and without mental reservation. If anyone present has any questions or misgivings concerning the program I have outlined, make your views known now—for once this program goes forward officially, it will be the administration program, and I expect every member of the administration to support it fully, both in public and in private.

The invitation to object was only a formality. Truman was reading from a memorandum which he had already announced would be filed as the minutes of the meeting.[26]

III

Forrestal's reaction to Truman's decision and his interpretation of the motives that produced it are not a matter of record. His general perspective on the turn events had taken can be inferred, however, from the remarks he made later in May about the difficulties that had overtaken the selective service bill. There was, he reported to the Cabinet on May 21, serious doubt that the bill now would pass. In contrast, at the time Truman first asked for the renewal of the draft, they could have got it through Congress in three days. The explanation, Forrestal told the Cabinet, lay in the

[26] For the events on May 13, see Millis, ed., *The Forrestal Diaries*, pp. 435–38.

"swiftly changing moods" of Congress and the American public.

In a letter to Marshall on May 29, Forrestal elaborated on this theme. When the selective service bill had been introduced in March, the "critical" situation in Europe, which had been "highlighted" by the Communist coup in Czechoslovakia, had "served to focus public attention" on the need to increase America's armed forces. This need had been "vital," both in order to enhance the nation's military security and to provide a stronger backing for Marshall's diplomatic negotiations. But "In recent weeks we have witnessed what some people have interpreted as a slackening of the tensions between Russia and this country." The result was the absence of a visible crisis to focus attention on the need to strengthen the armed forces, and this, along "with the political stresses of an election year," had combined "to produce a dangerous complacency on the part of certain elements in the country." [27]

There is nothing in these remarks to suggest that Forrestal himself believed that there was any less need for rearmament in May than there had been in March, or that he had been persuaded of the wisdom of the considerations that had led to the ceiling. His words would imply that he saw Truman's decision as primarily a response to a change in what the President thought Congress and the electorate could be expected to support. The difficulty with making policy in this fashion was that policy was then vulnerable to the "swiftly changing moods" of those bodies. This appears to have been the lesson that Forrestal thought he had learned. He told the Cabinet on May 21 that, if the nation was to avoid a foreign policy that advanced "on a jagged and spasmodic line," the country "needed a constant restatement of our objectives and of the magnitude of our task. . . ." [28]

In making this point, Forrestal was presumably thinking mainly of the President and the importance of his constantly reminding Congress and the public of the need for the national security programs on which he was embarked. (His reference to the "stresses

[27] *Ibid.*, p. 444, and letter, Forrestal to Marshall, May 29, 1948, Forrestal Collection, Princeton University Library.
[28] Millis, ed., *The Forrestal Diaries*, pp. 443–44.

of an election year" suggests that he thought it was for fear of jeopardizing his own and his party's fortunes at the polls that Truman had failed to reiterate in May the need for the program he had begun in March.) But while it was Presidential repetition that was required on the national scene, Forrestal was prepared to do his part within the more circumscribed area of the Executive branch. Specifically, he was to spend the next seven months in the reiteration and restatement of the need for a defense budget in excess of the $14.4-billion ceiling and in a sustained political effort to reverse the decision responsible for it.

When Truman announced his decision on May 13, he had wrapped himself in the mantle of the Commander in Chief and ordered that it be carried out "without mental reservation" and that it be supported "in public and in private" by every member of the administration. How, then, could Forrestal responsibly undertake to contest it? And why did the President permit him to do so?

Forrestal's behavior was due to his choice of roles as well as his choice of policy. He could have cast himself in the role of the President's representative and bent his will toward the goal of seeing that the services came up with a fiscal 1950 budget within the President's ceiling. Alternatively, he could have assumed the role of spokesman for the interests of his department and spent his time trying to get the President to accept the budget figures proposed by the services. Finally, there was the possibility of assuming a quasi-independent position and attempting to mediate between the two. This was Forrestal's actual course, and, while the most difficult of the three, it corresponded best to the political realities of his position. He had responsibilities to himself as well as to his "constituents" and his chief.

There was another political "reality" which may have encouraged Forrestal to take this course. Forrestal, along with practically everyone else at this time, believed that Truman would be defeated in the November election. The expectation that this would be his last Truman budget probably made Forrestal more willing to contest the President's decision than would have been the case if he had expected (and wanted) to continue to work with the President after the budget battle was over. The expectation of Truman's defeat did not, however, rob Forrestal of the incentive to take the ceiling seriously. Given his conviction that the nation needed to increase its armed forces, it was to Forrestal's interest to peg Truman's budget to as high a level as possible no matter who won the election. If the new President were a Republican, Forrestal would at least have confronted him with the political handicap of having to cut a higher rather than a lower defense budget.

If Forrestal's behavior was a response to his multiple responsibilities and the impending election, Truman's was the result of his limited power complicated by that same election. The President could and no doubt did expect that his order would be met with compliance in so far as the fiscal 1949 supplement was concerned. That program was already before Congress, and a final, coordinated position on it was both needed and overdue in the Executive branch of the government. But with regard to the fiscal 1950 budget, the President could only hope. The presentation of that budget was many months away, and knowing Forrestal's own views and the kind of pressures that would be generated within his department, Truman was probably not surprised to discover that the order he had given as Commander in Chief turned out to be the first rather than the last round fired in the battle of the budget. Nor did he have any option but to let Forrestal mount his counterattack. The President was far better situated to cope with the arguments of an acting Secretary in private than he was to risk hearing them from an ex-Secretary in public, especially in an election year.[29]

Forrestal's political goal required a strategy of double envelopment. He had not only to persuade the President to raise the ceiling; he had also to persuade the Chiefs to meet it. This second objective was essential if he was to achieve the first. Before Forrestal could do battle with others he had to appear the master in his own house. He could not afford a repetition of the debacle that had overtaken him in March and April, when the Army and the Air Force publicly

[29] On the limited ability of Presidents to issue "self-executing" orders, see Neustadt, *Presidential Power*, Chap. 2 and pp. 39–46.

departed from his own budget proposals and Hanson Baldwin had proclaimed unification (and by implication Forrestal's leadership) a "joke." If he was to have any chance of convincing the President that the ceiling should be raised, he had to be able, first, to demonstrate that the Chiefs had done their best to develop a meaningful budget within it.[30]

Although the Joint Chiefs had been present at the May 13 meeting and were, therefore, bound by the pledge that the President had exacted on that occasion, Forrestal had serious doubts that they would be willing to accept responsibility for a $14.4-billion budget. From their point of view they had little interest in giving their professional blessings to what was basically a fait accompli on the part of the Budget Bureau. To meet this problem, Forrestal drafted a memorandum on June 23 for the three service Secretaries. In it he noted that he had asked the Chiefs whether they wished "to accept the responsibility for advising me upon the division of funds within the [ceiling]," and they had indicated that they would. But "past history [Forrestal obviously had in mind their revolt against the $3-billion supplement] does not give any guarantee that they will," and in this event he would need "some source of advice from men, both with experience in the Services and sufficiently advanced in rank to be free from the normal subjectivity and prejudices of the individual Services." Forrestal concluded the memorandum by listing the officers he wanted to be detached for duty in his office to provide him with such advice.[31]

The effect of this memorandum was to threaten the Joint Chiefs with the possibility that, if they were unwilling to work with him on the budget, he would get some other officers who would. Should Forrestal carry out this plan, the individuals chosen would, at least for budgeting purposes, become de facto Joint Chiefs. Faced with this prospect, the Joint Chiefs were forced to do a little "political costing." Would the future and somewhat uncertain gains that might

---

[30] Cf. Millis, ed., *The Forrestal Diaries*, p. 499.

[31] *Ibid.*, p. 450. Millis does not indicate whether the memorandum was actually sent, but, if not, the mere rumor of it was sufficient for Forrestal's purposes.

result for military security if they disassociated themselves from the budget (for example, the President might set a higher budget next year in order to avoid the embarrassment of the Chiefs' abstention) be worth the immediate and rather certain costs this action would bring to the prestige of the Office of the Joint Chiefs and to the personal power of those particular Chiefs?

The Chiefs answered this question in the negative. A special board of lesser officers, the McNarney Board, was established in mid-August to help Forrestal on the budget, but they did so under the appointment and direction of the Joint Chiefs.[32] In the final analysis, providing Forrestal was insistent, the Chiefs could not abstain from the budgeting process. They had only two practical alternatives vis-à-vis the President's budget: either to work with it or resign. Some indication of the considerations which led them to the former alternative may be gained from General Bradley's explanation of why he chose to work with the $13-billion ceiling that was imposed a year later for the fiscal 1951 budget.

I had the alternative of resigning or of accepting the decision of our civilian superiors and loyally trying to do the best within the limits provided. . . . Some people think I should have resigned, made a dramatic protest and "carried the issue to the country." I do not think that is a proper role for a military adviser.

Bradley offered two reasons to support this conclusion. First, he argued that if men felt obliged to resign "everytime their superiors made a decision with which they did not wholly agree, there would be constant upheavals and resignations. . . ." The difficulty with this proposition is that it failed to discriminate among kinds of disagreeable decisions. Resignation at no time is not the only alternative to resignation "everytime." Bradley's second reason for not resigning was more to the point and showed that he had taken the political measure of the prevailing climate of opinion. "I do not think," he declared, "that such a pseudo-dramatic act would have had the

[32] The JCS decision is another example of the working of the "principle of immediacy" (see Chapter IV, p. 130, above).

The members of the board were General J. T. McNarney (USAF), Vice Admiral R. B. Carney (USN), and Major General G. J. Richards (USA). See Millis, ed., *The Forrestal Diaries*, p. 450.

slightest effect during the economy wave which was sweeping Congress and the people. . . ." [33]

The assignment Forrestal gave the three officers on the McNarney Board was a formidable one. The initial estimates of the services, which Forrestal had received on August 16, had been formulated independently of each other.[34] Their sum total, as previously noted, was $30 billion, twice the size of the ceiling. The task of the McNarney Board was to give these estimates a joint review, to reduce their total to $14.4 billion, and to determine on a division of that sum agreeable to all three services. The board members were somewhat handicapped in their negotiations by the fact that there was considerable difference in the amount of authority each had been delegated, but they all, needless to say, drew upon the resources of their respective services. The organization at the disposal of the Navy member was typical. He set up an "offensive" and a "defensive" budget staff. The mission of the first group was to find flaws in the budget requirements of the other services; the purpose of the second was to develop persuasive arguments for the Navy's own requirements.

It was not difficult for the board to make a start at reducing the $30-billion figure. It will be recalled from Chapter III, for example, that for bargaining purposes Symington had arbitrarily increased the Air Force submission from $8 billion to $11 billion. "Additives" such as this soon fell before the work of the other services' "offensive" budget groups. Further reductions were made through the time-honored process of logrolling. (As Bradley was to put it later in October, when the Chiefs were canvassing the prospects for additional cuts, "Maybe Louie [Denfield, the Chief of Naval Operations] can get along without a better destroyer and I can get along without a better gun." [35]) The incentive to make such accommodations was provided by (a) the expectation that sooner or later there would *have* to be some division of the $14.4 billion; (b) the belief that if they did not determine the division,

[33] Bradley, "A Soldier's Farewell," *The Saturday Evening Post*, August 22, 1953, p. 63.
[34] SCA, *Hearings 1950 Budget*, p. 17.
[35] Millis, ed., *The Forrestal Diaries*, p. 504.

Forrestal would bring in some fourth party who would; and (c) the fear that the division fixed by a fourth party might be even less desirable than one which could be reached through the bargaining of the board.

The McNarney Board struggled manfully with the $30-billion figure, and by October they had reduced it to $23.6 billion. At this point, however, the board—and the Chiefs with them—had stalled. When, on October 6, Forrestal wrote the Joint Chiefs to remind them that he was "expecting a definitive recommendation from you, as an entity . . . as to allocations to the respective Services under a ceiling of $14.4 billion," the reply was prompt and negative. The next day the Chiefs sent him the $23.6-billion figure and announced that they were unable to agree on the division of funds under a $14.4-billion budget.[36]

The cause of the difficulty was twofold: dollars and doctrine. The services had not been without a common yardstick with which to measure their own and each other's requirements. They had as a point of departure what appears to have been the Joint Chiefs' minimum war plan. This plan anticipated two major actions: a strategic air offensive from British bases, and combined operations designed to hold open and exploit a line of communications into the Mediterranean. The virtue of this war plan was that it made a start toward satisfying everybody's idea of how to fight the Russians. The Air Force would be in a position to deliver atomic retaliation; the Navy's carriers would be in the Mediterranean where they could mount their own air strikes; and the Army would have at least some kind of toehold on the Continent where it could begin to build up the large land force it believed necessary for final victory.[37]

The trouble was that the cost of the forces the services considered necessary to implement this plan, along with their other missions, totaled $23.6 billion, not $14.4 billion. Out of whose requirements,

[36] *Ibid.*, pp. 499–500, 503.
[37] For references to the plan, see *ibid.*, pp. 504–5, 510. The British bases had been acquired in July when, as a result of the Berlin blockade, Britain had agreed to an American request to station two B-29 groups on British soil. For these negotiations, see *ibid.*, pp. 454–57, 498, 510.

then, should the $9.2-billion difference be taken? This was the question on which the Chiefs had been unable to reach a common answer. Nor did they have any rational basis for agreement. They had no common doctrine to guide them. Each service had instead a different theory about the relative importance of the activities they had envisioned jointly undertaking in pursuance of the war plan.

The Air Force, which had little faith in the utility of carrier operations in the Mediterranean, did not want to see funds allocated toward that purpose until the Air Force's own requirements had been met in full. The Navy, reasoning from a higher evaluation of carrier operations, approached the budget with a different set of priorities in mind. The Army's position, in turn, was that if their requirements were cut, there would be little point to the Navy being in the Mediterranean, since they would be there all by themselves. Ideally, of course, the Army wanted its toehold in northern Europe, not the Mediterranean, but this was dependent on the restoration of French and German land power. Similar differences underlay the bomb-from-Britain part of the plan. The Air Force was concerned about the security of the British bases and was looking forward to the development of a greater intercontinental capability, while the Army and the Navy were united in arguing the ability of land and sea power to defend overseas bases and the Air Force's need for them if strategic bombing was to be effective.

Since doctrinal differences such as these shaped much of the subsequent politics of the fiscal 1950 budget, it will be useful to halt for the moment the narrative of the budget's development and summarize the major theoretical points at issue. Given the absence of most of the relevant documents, the summary must be considered suggestive rather than circumstantial. It should also be clear that reference to the "Army," "Navy," or "Air Force" position is meant only as a shorthand for the more realistic but cumbersome expression: "what appears to have been the dominant view among officers influencing the determination of high policy." More complete evidence would probably show that there were a wide variety of views held on these matters within each service, and that simplistic, assertive positions were much more characteristic of what each service thought the other had than of the true state of opinion prevailing in any one.

IV

The differences between the Air Force and the Navy over the value of carrier operations turned primarily on the issue of how useful the naval air arm would be in destroying inland targets on the Eurasian Continent. Vandenberg did not question the Navy's need for carriers designed to help it secure command of the seas and to combat, in particular, the Russian submarine force. He did question, however, whether this mission would require the kind of carrier task forces the Navy had employed in World War II. The Air Force was persuaded that, since Russia did not have a large surface fleet and had no carriers of its own, the Navy's problem would be quite dissimilar to what it had confronted in securing command of the Pacific against Japan. Vandenberg also questioned whether, in conducting land and air operations against the Soviet Union, there would be any need for the large attack carriers that had proved so essential in fighting the land war in the Pacific and in delivering air strikes against the Japanese homeland. In Vandenberg's view, the war in Europe against Germany was much the more relevant experience, and there the contribution that naval air power had made to the ground and air war had been minimal.[38]

The issue of the utility of carrier air strikes against the Soviet Union was drawn to a point by the Navy's plan to build a carrier big enough to accommodate the large planes then required to lift atomic weapons. Forrestal had tried to resolve this matter at a meeting with the Joint Chiefs in March 1948. The agreement reached there, as Forrestal phrased it, had been that the Navy was "not to be denied use of A-bomb" and was to proceed with the construction of its super-carrier. The Air Force recognized the Navy's need to bomb

---

[38] *HCAS, Unification and Strategy Hearings,* pp. 471–72. These views were expressed in the fall of 1949, but it is a fair presumption that Vandenberg held them in the fall of 1948 as well.

inland targets in order to advance its mission to control the seas, and it also recognized "the right and need for the Navy to participate in an all-out air campaign." However, all this was on the understanding that the Navy would "not develop a separate strategic air force, this function being reserved to the Air Force."

The Air Force was far from content with this arrangement, as Vandenberg made clear to Forrestal in a conversation on July 28. Carefully tying his argument to the President's and Congress' concern over the size of the budget, Vandenberg declared that the nation "obviously . . . could not afford to spend $15 or $20 billion a year continuously on its military establishment." The solution was to stop "spending money for two duplicating programs, particularly when one involved the use of obsolescing weapons." The obsolescent weapons he had in mind were attack carriers, and the duplication was the Navy's interest in participating in strategic bombing and delivering A-bombs. The Air Force did not deny that there were targets the Navy might need to hit with an A-bomb in order to further its effort to secure command of the seas, but the Air Force wanted to have the sole authority to decide who got to use the A-bomb and for what targets.[39]

Not empire-building but patriotism lay behind the demand for a monopoly on the bomb. According to Air Force doctrine, the kinds of targets on which the Navy would use the weapon and the means it would use to deliver it would not be those which would best advance the goal of military victory. Hence, if the war was to be won at the least cost in blood and treasure or, perhaps, won at all, it was vital that the Air Force gain control of the weapon. Precisely the same considerations had moved the Army Air Force during World War II to keep airplanes out of the hands of the Army Ground Forces. The generals responsible for air and ground combat had different theories about the proper use of airplanes, the difference being essentially over the relative allocation of resources to be expended in providing air support for the battlefield and the interdiction of supplies to it as compared to strategic bombing. There was, then, good ground for the Navy's suspicion that the logical conclu-

[39] Millis, ed., *The Forrestal Diaries,* pp. 392–93, 466–67, 476.

sion of Air Force doctrine would lead it to demand control not just over the A-bomb but over all aviation, and Forrestal, remarking on this fear, noted that Vandenberg's predecessor, Spaatz, had admitted as much to him.[40]

What Vandenberg argued in private, Symington had as much as said publicly a week earlier. The speech had sent Forrestal to the President to discuss the possibility of asking for Symington's resignation, for in it the Air Secretary had assailed both those "dedicated to obsolete methods of warfare" and those who opposed larger Air Force appropriations on the grounds that they would "unbalance" the three services.[41] If the first was the Navy, the second most certainly was Forrestal himself. Whether the Air Force also included the Army among those dedicated to obsolete methods of war its spokesmen were careful not to say. For the moment, the Army was a valued ally in the struggle to reduce the Navy's share of the budget.

It was an uneasy alliance. During World War II it had been the tactical use of air power (in support of ground and sea operations) that proved of decisive importance, not the use of bombs and bombers against enemy cities and factories. But with the advent of the atomic bomb, the idea that the enemy's will to fight could be crushed solely through the use of air power against his homeland had been dramatically rehabilitated. The image of a short, atomic war had gained more than a little acceptance in Congress, and the measure of General Bradley's concern can be inferred from his repeated assertions that it would be "folly" to believe that an atomic strike alone could win a war with Russia.

Bradley was willing to grant that the atomic bomb was "the strongest single deterrent against war" and that the strategic air force should have "first priority" in the nation's defense posture. But he did not believe the nation could rely solely on the atomic

[40] For the Navy's fears in 1948, see *ibid.*, p. 466. The World War II issues are described in James A. Huston, "Tactical Use of Air Power in World War II: The Army Experience," *Military Affairs*, Winter 1950, pp. 165–85.

The idea that an air force interested in strategic bombing should secure control of *all* airplanes, in order to insure that they were not wasted on other missions, was advanced by Douhet. See Bernard Brodie, *Strategy in the Missile Age* (Princeton, Princeton University Press, 1959), pp. 93–94.

[41] Millis, ed., *The Forrestal Diaries*, pp. 462–63.

bomb even in the first phase of the war. To do so would be to permit the Red Army to occupy the whole of Europe, and the bomb could hardly be used to drive it from friendly cities. In Bradley's view (which was basically the same doctrine the Russians were to advance a decade later) the A-bomb could not in itself be decisive. Victory would depend on the combined operations of all arms. World War III would be "extended, bloody and horrible" and would turn on the course of the land battle in Europe. For this reason, he wanted at a minimum the capability of maintaining a toehold on the Continent from which a counterattack could be mounted. Ideally, his strategy called for a standing force in Europe strong enough to prevent the Russians from overrunning it in the first place. The "hard core" of this force would have to be European, but he believed that the United States should make as large a contribution as budgetary considerations would permit.[42]

The position of the Air Force on these matters was, in public at least, somewhat more equivocal. Its spokesmen did not claim that strategic bombing could win the war, but neither did they deny it with anywhere near Bradley's vigor. Thus Symington told Vinson's committee in August 1949: "We can hope, but no one can promise, that if war comes the impact of our bombing offensive with atomic weapons can bring it about that no surface forces ever have to become engaged." In October 1949, when the Air Force's conception of strategic bombing was under attack from the Navy, Vandenberg declared that the Air Force's ability to conduct a strategic offensive with atomic weapons was the only "equalizing factor" between the Western democracies and Russia's "masses of ground troops." There was, first, its "deterrent value"; the threat of strategic bombardment had been and was then preventing the Russians from overrunning

[42] For the development of strategic bombing doctrine and the World War II experience, see Brodie, *Strategy in the Missile Age*, Chaps. 3–4. The Bradley quotations are from his "This Way Lies Peace," *Saturday Evening Post*, October 15, 1949, pp. 168–70, but they can be taken as representative of his views in the fall of 1948. See, for example Chapter III, p. 67, and his speech before the Chicago Economic Club as reported in the New York *Times*, October 29, 1948). For later and comparable Soviet doctrine, see Raymond L. Garthoff, *Soviet Strategy in the Nuclear Age* (New York, Frederick A. Praeger, Inc., 1958), Chap. 4.

western Europe. Secondly, should war come, while it would "ultimately . . . be concluded on the ground, like most wars of the
past," the effect of strategic bombing would be "so to weaken the
sustaining sources of enemy troops that they can be defeated in
less time at less cost." How extensive a ground effort he thought
it would take to terminate the war, Vandenberg did not say. His
testimony also left uncertain whether he believed the Air Force's
inability to convert Symington's hope into a promise was due to
inherent limitations in the doctrine of strategic bombardment or
because of temporary shortcomings in the size of the atomic stockpile.[43]

What truly united the Army and the Air Force was their determination to cut the Navy's share of the budget. In May 1948 Bradley
was thinking in terms of as much as a 40 percent reduction in naval
appropriations, and he turned down an offer to become Forrestal's
principal military adviser because (so Army Secretary Royall explained) it would not be desirable for the Army "to incur the Navy's
displeasure" by being too closely identified with such cuts when and
if they were made. Throughout his tenure Forrestal resisted this
pressure. As a former Secretary of the Navy, he was more disposed
than Bradley or Vandenberg to believe that carriers might prove as
useful in European waters during World War III as they had been
in Pacific waters during World War II. Moreover, while he was
opposed to the Navy's building a fleet of super-carriers, he thought
it "most important" that the Navy be permitted to build at least one
carrier capable of delivering the atomic bomb.[44]

Forrestal's successor, Louis Johnson, was of a different persuasion,
and in April 1949, on the advice of two of the three Joint Chiefs, he
halted construction of the Navy's super-carrier. Johnson's plans for
fiscal 1951 went even further. In August 1949 it was alleged that he
intended to cut the Navy from the 8 large carriers budgeted in fiscal

[43] For Symington's and Vandenberg's testimony, see *HCAS, B-36 Hearings,*
p. 217, and *HCAS, Unification and Strategy Hearings,* pp. 454–56.

[44] Millis, ed., *The Forrestal Diaries,* pp. 434, 467. The Navy's existing carriers
could have launched a plane large enough to carry an A-bomb, but they were
not big enough for such a plane to land on them. See *HCAS, B-36 Hearings,*
pp. 198–99.

1950 to 4 carriers and to reduce from 14 to 6 the number of carrier air groups. The Navy's protest was recorded before Vinson's committee in October 1949 in the so-called "revolt of the Admirals." There Admiral Arthur Radford, the Commander in Chief of the Pacific Fleet, avowed that the Air Force was not trying to take over the naval air arm, "they are trying to eliminate it." The point was documented by Admiral Denfield, who revealed that in the confines of the Joint Chiefs of Staff the Air Force was now recommending that *no* heavy carriers be maintained.[45]

The divergence between Navy and Air Force doctrine was most clearly stated in the testimony of Rear Admiral Ralph Ofstie, a member of the Military Liaison Committee to the Atomic Energy Commission. His conception of World War III closely paralleled Bradley's in its emphasis on the importance of the land battle in Europe and the need, in particular, to develop enough strength in western Europe to keep it from being overrun by the Red Army. For this purpose, Ofstie argued, the strategic bombing of the Soviet Union would be of little help; if the Russians moved, they would do so with armies already mobilized. What was needed were superior tactical air forces which could hit the enemy in the field and interdict his lines of communication. It was here, in addition to securing the seas across which the men and material necessary to win the land battle would have to be moved, that carrier aircraft could make a significant contribution to the fighting of the war.

Ofstie denied that the Navy's interest in the super-carrier was based on a desire to participate in the strategic bombing of the Soviet Union. "We consider that strategic air warfare, as practiced in the past and as proposed in the future, is militarily unsound and of limited effect, is morally wrong, and is decidedly harmful to the stability of a postwar world." Ofstie denounced the bombing of cities as a "ruthless and barbaric policy." As contemplated by the Air Force, strategic bombing would lead to the "random mass slaughter of men, women, and children in the enemy country." This, he de-

---

[45] See the Washington *Post*, August 9, 1949, as quoted in Hammond MS., "The Missions of the Services" (see Chapter III, footnote 15, above), and *HCAS, Unification and Strategy Hearings*, pp. 96, 355, 360.

clared, was "contrary to our fundamental ideals. It is time that strategic bombing be squarely faced in this light; that it be examined in relation to the decent opinions of mankind." [46]

Vandenberg was equally quick to call the Navy's arguments "militarily unsound." If the United States were to renounce the atomic bombardment of the Soviet Union, it would destroy the deterrent that was then protecting the western Europeans, an action which they could only view with "contempt or despair." The Navy's alternative, a large standing army in Europe supported by tactical air, would commit the West either to a "wholly defensive war" or to the "fairly unattractive example of Napoleon and Hitler." On his part, Bradley observed that "war itself is immoral." Americans could find their justification for the use of the A-bomb in the fact that if war came it would be the Soviet Union, not the United States, that would start it. He also pointed out that it had been the Navy's "continuous argument" before the Joint Chiefs of Staff that "they should be permitted to use the atomic bomb, both strategically and tactically." This information, together with the Navy's interest in building the super-carrier, put the Navy under a moral cloud of its own. As one concerned Air Force General later quipped: "An immoral weapon is one too big for your service to deliver." [47]

Actually, naval doctrine seems to have been not so much hypocritical as complex and not entirely thought through. Admiral Radford, who had been the Vice Chief of Naval Operations during the preparation of the fiscal 1950 budget, tried to make a distinction between strategic bombing and the "indiscriminate bombing of cities." It was the latter to which he was opposed, and it was only this which he thought the Air Force could accomplish with the B-36. In contrast, the faster and more accurate carrier aircraft would be able to hit precise "military targets," such as oil refineries and transportation facilities. He did not advocate the "complete abandonment" of the atomic bomb. The nation should continue to be prepared to use it "with precision on military objectives." He did think, how-

[46] *HCAS, Unification and Strategy Hearings*, pp. 183–89.

[47] *Ibid.*, pp. 454, 456, 522, 525. The comment was made to the present author in an interview on May 27, 1957.

ever, that, since the Russians had now acquired the bomb themselves, "we may have a sort of stalemate as we did on poison gas in this last war. Each of us will be reluctant to use it." [48]

There were those in 1949, chiefly some members of the Atomic Energy Commission and the scientists on its General Advisory Committee, who tried to turn the explosion of Russia's first A-bomb and the consequent debate about accelerating the American effort to make an H-bomb into an occasion for facing the moral and political implications of strategic bombing, but they failed. They did so in part because of lack of support in the Pentagon, for Radford and Ofstie went further in their challenge of strategic bombing doctrine than their superiors were later prepared to follow.

The Navy views of World War III, strategic bombing excepted, would appear to have had more in common with those of the Army than did those of the Air Force. There was Ofstie's emphasis on the ground defense of western Europe and Radford's insistence that "the threat of instant atomic retaliation" could not prevent a war, and an "atom blitz of annihilation" would not win it if it came. Why, then, was the Army not allied with the Navy instead of the Air Force? The answer was that the Admirals had failed to persuade the Army that carriers could make an important contribution to the Army's tactical support in northern Europe or even in the Mediterranean. As the commander of the Twelfth Army Group in World War II, Bradley had received his tactical air support from Vandenberg's Ninth Air Force, and he was quite prepared to continue the relationship now that they were both Chiefs of Staff. In political terms, the central fault in the Navy's doctrine was that it had not been sold to the Army before it was forced to compete with the doctrine of the Air Force, and this was as true in the fall of 1948 as it was in 1949.[49]

The issues which divided the services were clearly deep and basic. Moreover, while they may have had the form of a conflict among vested interests in weapons systems (carriers, bombers,

[48] *Ibid.*, pp. 64–65, 74–75. Cf. Radford's views in 1953 as described in Glenn Snyder, *The "New Look" of 1953*, below.
[49] HCAS, *Unification and Strategy Hearings*, pp. 52, 528–30.

divisions), they were fundamentally an expression of complicated and serious problems to which no one knew the answer. Could the Air Force bombers get through to their targets in the face of radar and jet fighters? And if they did, what would be the military and political result for Russia's war effort? In October 1948 Forrestal referred both questions to the Joint Chiefs for special study. Symington hastened to assure him that Vandenberg was "absolutely certain" that the Air Force would be able to drop the A-bomb when and where it wanted. But Forrestal was well aware that the Navy thought differently. "No one knows the form and character of any war of the future," he observed in his diary, and he listed the matter as an "unresolved question." [50]

The intractable nature of the problems involved is well illustrated by the subsequent history of the two reports Forrestal had requested. Neither was ready by the time he left office, and the first—the question of how many bombers could get through to their targets—was still under preparation a year later, in October 1949. The second—that dealing with the results of strategic bombing—was completed in May 1949. But even with the simplifying assumption of 100 percent success in the delivery of bombs on target, the question had not yielded easily to expert analysis. As a result, during the October 1949 hearings both the Navy and the Air Force claimed that the report supported their views about the efficacy of strategic bombing.[51] It should be noted that this was before the era of nuclear plenty and that the total megatonnage in the stockpile at this time was probably of the same order as the amount of TNT the United States had dropped in World War II.

The same difficulties were to be met in Navy and Army doctrine. Could carriers survive against land-based planes in a narrow sea like the Mediterranean? The Navy was confident that they could, and Vandenberg that they could not. Forrestal himself thought they would be able to do so until the advent of operational guided missiles, and the British Chiefs (so Forrestal learned in November 1948) believed that carrier operations would be possible at the beginning

---

[50] Millis, ed., *The Forrestal Diaries*, pp. 493–94, 513–14.

[51] See the New York *Times*, October 14, 1949, and *HCAS, Unification and Strategy Hearings*, pp. 352, 362–64, 403–4.

of hostilities provided the ships got there fast enough. All of these opinions were informed, and none of them agreed. Similarly, the number of divisions necessary to hold on the Rhine was set at 20 by General Clay in Germany, while the French were considering 30 and the Joint Chiefs, reportedly, believed 45 would be required. An equivalent range of uncertainty was no doubt associated with whatever estimate the Army had made about the forces required to keep a foothold in the Mediterranean.[52]

If these problems and issues in military doctrine were not enough, there was overhanging all of them the possibility that, in the actual event of war, the President might decide for political reasons not to let the A-bomb be used at all. The services, it must be remembered, did not even have physical possession of the weapon that bulked so large in their disputes. It was in the hands of a civilian agency subject to the authority of the President, but not the military, and the only clear national policy with regard to the bomb was that, under proper conditions, it would be given up.

Illustrative of the doubts the services may have had about the certainty of the weapon's use were the remarks Marshall had made in March 1948 before the Senate Armed Services Committee. Strategic bombing, the Secretary of State pointed out, meant the killing of children and other nonmilitary personnel. "That is almost unavoidable, and yet that is very very terrible." The former Chief of Staff thought that the United States had been willing to engage in strategic bombing in World War II because the prior actions of Germany and Japan had infuriated the American people.

. . . but it was a terrible thing to have to use that type of power. If you are confronted with the use of that type of power in the beginning of the war you are also confronted with a very certain reaction of the American people. They have to be driven very hard before they will agree to such a drastic use of force.[53]

In July 1948, Forrestal told Marshall that in view of the crisis caused by the Berlin blockade he wished a "resolution of the question of whether or not we are to use the A-bomb in war." Forrestal ap-

[52] See Millis, ed., *The Forrestal Diaries*, pp. 467, 525, 460, 521, and Chapter II, p. 49, above.
[53] *Senate UMT Hearings, 1948*, p. 21.

parently had in mind that the services would continue to make plans on the assumption that the bomb would not be used, but first priority would be assigned to plans assuming the use of the weapon. When this matter finally reached the President in September, Truman declared that if he had to use the bomb he would not shrink from it. Despite the conditional clause, this answer apparently satisfied Forrestal with regard to the President's intent. He next undertook in the fall of 1948 to sound out various members of the American elites on the subject. The results of his survey would indicate that Marshall's and Ofstie's views of their countrymen's moral inhibitions were somewhat inaccurate. Typical of the opinions Forrestal collected was that of John Foster Dulles: "the American people would execute you if you did not use the bomb in the event of war." A modest spectre of uncertainty continued, however, to haunt the plans of a succession of Joint Chiefs, and it was apparently not until October 1953 that that body received a formal statement from the President authorizing them to count on the use of nuclear weapons in the event of general war.[54]

v

To return to October 1948 and the inability of the Chiefs to agree on how to go from a $23.6-billion budget to one of $14.4 billion, it is clear that those who suspected an absence of "unified thinking" in the Pentagon were absolutely correct. The Joint Chiefs of Staff were enveloped in a fog of concept, fact, and conjecture about World War III. It should also be clear that the presence of a single Chief of Staff or "principal military adviser" would in no way have changed this condition. A single Chief of Staff could, to be sure, have turned his power to the task of stamping American military policy into the mold of his own guesses about the shape of World War III. This would have had the virtue of producing more "integrated" plans, but there would have been nothing to recommend *his* plans against those of anyone else except the accident of his position.

[54] Millis, ed., *The Forrestal Diaries,* pp. 461–62, 486–88, and Glenn Snyder, pp. 427, 433–47, below.

It was all very well to call—as the Hoover Commission did in the spring of 1949—for an end to "continued disharmony and lack of unified planning." But to whose tune should the services harmonize? Around whose concepts should plans be unified? Certainly, so far as Forrestal could see, the answers to the questions which divided the Chiefs were not just lying around in wait for someone with an "over-all strategic point of view" to express them. The truth of the matter, as Forrestal seemed to recognize, was that there were no definitive answers to the problems the Joint Chiefs faced. Information, analysis, and discussion could take them far—but not far enough. In the end, if there was to be a resolution of these doctrinal differences, it would require a large element of guess and a determined exercise of power.

The budget was an excellent device for cutting the Gordian knot of these issues, but Forrestal was reluctant to so use it. His judgment, and his inclination, was to postpone the choices—and the conflicts— that Johnson was later to force. "The difficulty [between the services] stems mainly from money," he had sympathetically observed in August.

Each Service knows the magnitude of its own responsibilities. The simple fact is, however, that the economy simply cannot stand fulfillment of all the requirements without the nation accepting very substantial deficit financing.[55]

Although this analysis slid past the way in which the services had defined their responsibilities—overlapping or challenging each other's—it was to the point. The fewer the dollars the harder they found it to live with each other's doctrine. And it was from this analysis that Forrestal drew his remedy. Rather than force a foreclosure on some doctrinal alternatives, he would secure more money.

It was time for Forrestal to close with the Joint Chiefs and instruct them in his strategy. They met at his office on October 15. Forrestal began by expressing his understanding of their problem. "Of course," he said, they had not been able to reach an agreement on how to

[55] Millis, ed., *The Forrestal Diaries*, p. 478. Millis repeatedly calls attention to Forrestal's qualities of "patience, tolerance, and gradualism." See, for example, *ibid.*, pp. 420, 433, 464–65.

allocate the $14.4-billion sum. "You cannot have a satisfactory and usable military power under that ceiling." But nonetheless he wanted a unanimous decision on how to divide that figure. ". . . I am most anxious to say we have made a terrific effort to come under the 15 billion." [56]

After the Chiefs had agreed on a budget within the President's ceiling, Forrestal continued, he wanted them to go to work on their $23.6-billion estimate. In particular, he wanted them to see if they could find some "intermediate" figure that "would give you a possible force that could jump off if war came." Forrestal suggested that they might find that with a budget of $17.5 or $18 billion, while they would not "have the competence to make an effective and immediate reprisal if the Russians move," they would still be able to make a "healthy response," one which would "enable us to make reprisals and at the same time have the tables of organization and cadres to fill out promptly."

Forrestal now made his plan clear. The Joint Chiefs would make a "terrific effort" to agree on a $14.4-billion budget. This would show the President that they had not taken his decision lightly. ("My job," Forrestal pointed out, "is going to have to be to convince the President and his successor [sic], if there is one, that we have gone into this thing from the ground up and prefer to go at it from the top down.") At the same time, they would also develop a budget in the neighborhood of $18 billion that would represent the bare minimum to put into operation the two aspects of the war plan: the air offensive from Britain and the combined operations to hold open the Mediterranean. Then, as Forrestal explained, "I should like to present these two, if I could, together." The hope was that the President, when confronted with the alternatives, would prefer a

[56] The factual account of the October 15 conference that follows is from *ibid.*, pp. 502–6. The interpretation is more extensive and sometimes different.

In referring to the ceiling as $15 billion, Forrestal was including the $600 million that was expected to be allocated for stockpiling. However, neither the Chiefs' $23.6 billion nor Forrestal's suggested $17 to $18 billion figure (see below) included this sum, and these figures are therefore directly comparable to the $14.4 billion that the services themselves would receive under the ceiling.

capacity for a "healthy response" to a "non-usable" military power, and they could "go to the Congress and back this one [the $18-billion budget]."

The lure with which Forrestal was trying to get the Chiefs down to $14.4 billion was the prospect of their being able to raise it to $17–$18 billion. He had also to persuade them to come down to this intermediate figure from the only sum on which they had so far been able to agree: the $23.6-billion estimate. The necessity for this he explained to them in terms of the best interests of "the concept of the JCS." If they met the President's ceiling in the fashion he had outlined, it would bring them "a tremendous gain in stature." On the other hand, if they were unable to achieve unanimity on budget policy, they would "lose face with the country," for it would be interpreted as a "confession of inability to get away from Service interests and look at the whole business in the light of what the national interest is."

Forrestal obviously believed that there was still "give" left in the $23.6-billion estimate. To begin with, the McNarney Board had apparently intimated its belief that they could reduce the figure to $21 billion (as in fact they were to do by the end of the month). Beyond this, Forrestal undoubtedly recognized that a large degree of imprecision necessarily attended any estimate of the number and quality of men and weapons required to perform a service mission. The multiplicity of rather imponderable factors involved (including the guesses that had to be made about the enemy's actions) unavoidably gave such estimates a somewhat arbitrary character. In this respect the Chiefs' figures were no different from those which the Budget Bureau had used in reaching its conclusion in May that only $14.4 billion could be made available to the services. The origins of the third major figure involved—Forrestal's suggested "intermediate" budget in the neighborhood of $18 billion—were quite in keeping with the other two. He had apparently hit on this sum in a conversation with Lovett, and it had been reached by a process that at least had simplicity to recommend it. The $18-billion figure represented nothing more than the difference between what they took to be the Chiefs' top figure, $21 billion, and the $3 billion the State Department was considering for arms aid to Europe (itself another arbitrary figure).

The combination of Forrestal's plan and his appeal to "the concept of the JCS" was successful. The Chiefs readily fell behind the idea of the intermediate budget and began to discuss the ways and means of paring down their shares of the $23.6-billion estimate. (It was obviously from this conference that the bulk of the news leaks summarized in Chapter II were inspired, for there were those in the military establishment who appreciated the utility of flanking the President in the public as well as in the intra-Executive arena.) The Chiefs were also willing to reach an agreement on the division of funds under the $14.4-billion budget, except that they could not agree on how to do so.

Forrestal had pointed out that there were really only "two possible approaches to this problem." One was to take their $23.6-billion estimate and simply pare each service's share down proportionately until they reached the President's level. This approach was "easier," he admitted, but he announced that it was "not satisfactory to me. Sixty-six per cent complements on board your ships in the Navy. That is breathing, but not moting [sic]."

The other approach was functional. They could restrict their war plan "only to the mounting of the atomic offensive from Britain." This would mean giving up any effort to hold open the Mediterranean and would confine Army and Navy requirements to those necessary to support the Air Force mission at home and in England. Vandenberg was not present at this meeting; his Vice Chief was there in his place. He apparently made no comment, but this idea was to have a decided impact on the Air Force's subsequent approach to the budget.

General Bradley's response was vocal and negative. This would be to "put all your eggs in one basket." Bradley was not forgetting that the $14.4-billion budget was to be only a bargaining device to secure one of $18 billion; he was prudently remembering that they might fail in the effort, and he would then be stuck with the "unbalanced" budget. General Gruenther moved to mollify Bradley. The idea of concentrating on the air offensive from Britain had never "for one moment" been considered "an acceptable concept." Forrestal hastened to explain himself. He had advanced this alternative "simply to bring out the absurdity" of the President's ceiling.

Forrestal was sincere on this point. He had no more faith in the "atomic blitz" theory of victory than Bradley. But of the two alternative ways of dividing the $14.4 billion (which appear to have been his own idea), he much preferred this one. As he explained to the Chiefs, it was necessary for them to translate the budget into functional terms in order to provide him with a convincing argument against the ceiling. (Interestingly enough, it was Webb, in 1946, who first suggested to Forrestal that he consider submitting alternative budgets with a description of the security consequences of each.) If they could show that with $14.4 billion they could mount an air offensive from Britain but that was all, that the rest of the military establishment would be rendered useless, the President's budget would appear an absurdity. Unless, Gruenther added, "you are willing to gamble . . . that [the air offensive] will bring the end of the war." [57]

The conference adjourned without any sign that the Army and the Navy were prepared to accept the "unbalanced" approach to the division of the $14.4 billion. It is not clear how Machiavellian Forrestal's plan was, but there could have been an additional consideration in his mind. If he could get the Army and Navy to agree to a $14.4 budget that was grossly out of balance in favor of the Air Force, he would confront Truman with more than an "absurdity." Truman would then be obliged to choose between this version of his ceiling and the higher *but balanced* intermediate figure. A choice of this sort (as compared to one between two balanced budgets) would have compelled him to weigh more carefully the costs of rejecting the higher budget. For if he chose the lower budget, it would then be *Truman* who would be making the large guess about the future course of warfare, and it would be Truman's exercise of power that would foreclose on some major doctrinal alternatives.

[57] For Forrestal's views on the need for balanced forces and Webb's 1946 suggestion, see *ibid.*, pp. 235, 514.

This was a choice before which the President might well hesitate, for it would be certain to raise a storm of opposition, not only within two of the three services, but among their partisans in Congress as well. Moreover, when the circumstances became known, as they almost certainly would, it would be transparently his choice, and he would be obliged to defend it without the shield of his Secretary and two-thirds of his leading "experts."

Whether or not Forrestal had plotted quite this carefully, the choices he was trying to create afford a good example of how a President's subordinate might design alternatives which, in rational terms, have the appearance of free choice but which, politically, are decidedly rigged in advance. Certainly, Forrestal had need for every point of vantage he could find. His task was formidable: to persuade the President to accept a military budget which the Director of the Bureau of the Budget and the Secretary of the Treasury believed to be fiscally undesirable and for which the Secretary of State had indicated there was no foreign policy need.

Moreover, in asking Truman to return to the spirit of the March crisis, he was asking the President to espouse the politically unpopular cause of controls, higher taxes, or larger deficits before a public which had long since lost its own sense of crisis. This was in part a condition of Truman's own making, since he had contributed to the damping of the public mood by his action on the fiscal 1949 supplement. Still, when he had announced the ceiling, Truman had said that it would be contingent on "world conditions" not deteriorating. Since then, the Russians had placed Berlin under blockade, and the movement toward the Atlantic Pact had in consequence gained considerable momentum. It was here that Forrestal thought he saw the companion argument to the military absurdity of a $14.4-billion budget. "We are looking at a situation which is not war," he told the Chiefs at the October 15 conference, "but it certainly is a lot grayer than it was last May."

Forrestal had not taken the Joint Chiefs fully into his confidence, for he failed to indicate that with these arguments in hand he had already scouted the President's position. Possibly he did not refer to the occasion because the results had not been very promising.

He had seen the President on October 5. After first briefing him on the content of the minimum war plan, Forrestal told Truman that with a $14.4-billion budget the services would have only the capacity to conduct an air offensive from Britain. "The Mediterranean would be ruled out." (Note that Forrestal presented Truman with only one of the two possible approaches to the $14.4 figure: the unbalanced, functional approach he was later to urge the Chiefs to take.) He also apprised the President of his intention to submit two budgets, one within the ceiling and the other in the vicinity of $18.5 billion. This second budget, he explained, "would be predicated on the attainment of a capability of exploiting the holding of the Mediterranean LOC [line of communications]."

The President's reaction to this exposition must have been most disappointing. Unlike Forrestal, he did not appear struck by the "absurdity" of his ceiling when seen in the light of these alternatives, and unlike General Bradley he showed no alarm at the idea of putting all the nation's eggs in the Air Force's basket. (If Truman sensed any political squeeze in the way these alternative budgets had been cast, he did not show it.) Finally, unlike Webb, Truman did not appear receptive to the idea of receiving alternative budgets. He told Forrestal that he wanted the higher budget "held in reserve" because "the fact of its presentation [to him?] would be interpreted as a step toward preparation for war. . . ." The higher budget could be kept in the form of a supplemental "to be presented if and when the situation became more dangerous." [58]

The difficulty with waiting until the actual perception of danger was that it took time before money could be translated into trained men and fabricated weapons. This Truman knew as well as Forrestal. Earlier, in July, they had both heard Marshall request at a Cabinet meeting that the services cease being "quite so explicit [in public] as to the substantial times that must elapse before the recent decision to augment our military position would become effective." Such statements, the Secretary of State complained, would

---

[58] *Ibid.*, p. 498. The text of Forrestal's entry would also permit the interpretation that Truman was referring to the "presentation" of the higher budget to Congress.

only "emphasize our present weakness and add to the difficulty of negotiations with Russia." [59]

The promise of a supplemental budget was no answer to the problem posed by the uncertainty of the future. Who could tell how swiftly danger would come or what form it would take? But if there were risks to Truman's course, there were also those to Forrestal's. How could he tell whether there would be any need at all for an $18-billion budget? The only elements of certainty in the picture were the considerations that had moved Truman to endorse the ceiling in the first place: the knowledge that a higher budget would bring either inflation or a politically exhausting (and probably losing) battle for controls or higher taxes.

To counterbalance the weight of these immediate and certain costs on Truman's judgment, Forrestal had no doubt advanced on October 5 his argument that the international situation had turned for the worse since May and that the ceiling should therefore be reconsidered. But Truman—as his "if and when" phrase indicated—was by no means persuaded that the visible course of international politics had rendered unacceptable the risks inherent in the $14.4-billion budget. Indeed, he was shortly to tell the press that the outlook for peace had improved since the start of the Berlin blockade and to reiterate his belief that the country could not go on spending $14–$15 billion a year for defense.[60]

Nevertheless, given that blockade, the imminent possibility of military intervention by the United Nations in Palestine, and the mounting victories of the Chinese Communists, there was a case to be made for Forrestal's point of view, and at the end of their talk the President had left the door slightly open. Marshall, who was then in Paris attending a General Assembly meeting, was due to fly back for the week end. When Marshall came, Truman said, he would "explore the international situation directly with him." [61]

As Truman's words clearly indicated, in the fall as in the spring, the balance between Webb's considerations and Forrestal's lay with

[59] *Ibid.*, p. 457.   [60] New York *Times*, October 17, 1948.
[61] For the cast of the Berlin, Near East, and China situation at this time, see Millis, ed., *The Forrestal Diaries*, pp. 455, 459, 470, 481, 496–97, 507, 517–18.

Marshall's. If the President was to be convinced that the international situation was gray enough to necessitate a higher budget, the picture of his risk with a lower one would have to be painted by the Secretary of State, not the Secretary of Defense. Forrestal's next political task was, then, obvious: he must enlist the support of the nation's greatest wartime Chief of Staff behind the cause of a higher defense budget.

VI

In order to reconnoiter the prospects of Marshall's becoming an active ally in the assault on the ceiling, Forrestal had arranged for him to be briefed by McNarney and the Joint Chiefs on the results the ceiling would have for capabilities of the services. The meeting took place on October 10. According to the notes kept by General Gruenther, Marshall sat silently through the briefing, asked a few questions, and then proceeded to give Forrestal and the Chiefs an hour-long description of the state of *Europe's* military defenses. Marshall, who had just returned from Paris, referred "repeatedly" to his "strong conviction of the tremendous importance of furnishing equipment—particularly ground equipment—to the Western European nations." The Europeans, he reported, were "completely out of their skin, and sitting on their nerves."

At one point General Bradley asked if the United States, in addition to arming the Europeans, did not also need to maintain more than "token forces" itself, so that it would be able to give the Europeans "tangible evidence that we would be able to come to their assistance in the event of war." Marshall replied that this would of course be desirable, but from the briefing he had just heard "it was clear that we would have nothing but token forces to supply. . . ." Having thus shown that he saw the bait in the question, Marshall next demonstrated that he had no intention of taking it. He concluded his answer not with an affirmation of the necessity of increasing the budget but with another assertion of how important it was to start arming the Europeans.

A British military delegation was due to arrive in Washington in

November to discuss joint plans for the defense of Europe, and Forrestal indicated that if the ceiling was not raised they might have "to cool their heels" for several weeks while the Americans decided on a "new strategic concept" more in keeping with the reduced forces they would have at their disposal. Marshall did not rise to this bait either. He suggested that if the Joint Chiefs felt "embarrassed" by the meager forces the ceiling would provide, they could "explain [to the British] that we were considering the budget at a time when considerations other than those of national security were occupying the limelight; and that the situation would probably be better for supplementary funds after the election." On the other hand, Marshall added, if the Russians were to make any acts indicating peaceful intentions on their part, it would then "be extremely difficult to secure additional appropriations."

Marshall's behavior at the conference made it obvious that he was not going to enlist in Forrestal's cause. When the meeting was over, Gruenther summarized the intelligence they had gained as follows:

It is my distinct impression that General Marshall, although sympathetic with the Chiefs because of the budget ceilings which have been imposed, was not particularly disturbed over the implications in the field of foreign relations. He certainly uttered no caveats which could be used by the Secretary of Defense in an appeal for more funds. Mr. Forrestal referred obliquely on two occasions to the probability that the reduced capabilities of our Armed Forces might prove to be an embarrassment in executing our foreign policy but General Marshall made no comment. He appeared reasonably confident that Congress would give relief. His prime concern was the prospect of equipment for the French. . . .[62]

If Marshall was not going to volunteer his help, Forrestal had but one alternative, and that was to try to draft him. This he had already tried earlier without success. On July 10 he had addressed a letter to the National Security Council requesting guidance in the formulation of the fiscal 1950 budget. He obviously hoped to secure an admission (primarily from Marshall) that the ceiling had not been derived from national security considerations. Souers, the Executive Secretary of the National Security Council, had been present at the May

[62] For the October 10 meeting, see *ibid.*, pp. 500–502.

10 meeting when Truman had endorsed the ceiling, and he presumably checked with the President about placing the matter on the Council's agenda. In any event, nothing came of Forrestal's request, although he did receive a letter on July 16 from the Budget Bureau reaffirming the $15-billion ceiling.[63]

In December an editorial in the New York *Times* was to presume that the defense budget had been determined "with the advice of the National Security Council." Actually, that body never did act on Forrestal's request. This fact was discovered by the Eberstadt Committee during its fall investigation of the Military Establishment, and the Committee's report in February 1949 cited it as an example of how the NSC had failed to perform "the very essence of the Council's basic function." This was superficial criticism: it confused procedure with policy. Bargaining, not information, was Forrestal's intent, and Truman knew it.[64]

Having thus failed to pin Marshall down indirectly, through the NSC, Forrestal determined in October on a frontal assault. He decided to write a letter directly to the Secretary of State on the subject of the budget. In considering the form in which to cast his letter, Forrestal pulled from his files a memorandum he had received from the State Department on June 23, the day before the Berlin blockade had started. The paper had been prepared by the Policy Planning Staff, and its subject—how Soviet policy affected "the nature of U.S. defense arrangements"—showed that, NSC mechanics to the contrary, Forrestal had not been without some formal guidance from the Department of State since the May meeting.

It was Kennan's subsequent recollection that the memorandum had been Marshall's idea, and the assignment he gave the Planning Staff was to examine the question of whether the defense budget should be pointed toward any given peak of danger. Both the Finletter Report and the Air Force had, of course, advanced such a date—1953—and it had served effectively to rally Congressional support behind the 70-group program. The "peak of danger" ap-

[63] *Ibid.*, p. 509, and *HCA, Hearings 1950 Budget*, I, 16.
[64] New York *Times*, December 2, 1948, and *Eberstadt Committee Report*, pp. 75–76.

proach had also been used by Forrestal in May, when he was first confronted with Webb's ceiling. A larger budget was "essential," he had declared, because the next two years would be "a critical period in our relations with Russia."

On his part, Marshall had been convinced since 1945 that the proper budgeting course was to strive "to see a system and organization develop which would endure for years rather than be organized against a certain date for war." Marshall's opposition against building toward military peaks followed naturally from his fear that the American public would prove all too willing to descend into military valleys. In addition, Marshall also believed that the alleged military advantage of preparing for peaks of danger was based on a "misunderstanding" of the strategic problem involved. An aggressor nation, like Germany in the 1930's, could gain much by building toward war on a certain date because it had the option of starting it, but there was no comparable advantage in such a course for a nation intent on avoiding war.

Marshall's analysis showed some evidence of the American military's tendency to dismiss, perhaps too quickly, the possibilities for designing security policies which reflect an appreciation for the enemy's intentions, as well as his capabilities, but in this area he was to be well served by his Planning Staff. The analysis of Kennan and his colleagues was addressed directly to the question of Soviet intentions, and they ended up, at least, in the same place as the Secretary. The memorandum forwarded to Forrestal announced that "war is not a probability but is always a possibility," and concluded that a defense policy based "on the maintenance of a permanent state of adequate military preparation is better than an effort pointed toward a given peak of danger." [65]

There was nothing in this statement that could help Forrestal in his argument against the ceiling. The Planning Staff, moreover, did not face the hard problem. It said nothing about the criteria with which "adequacy" could be measured. The paper did, however, list

[65] The quotations from the State Department memorandum are from Millis, ed., *The Forrestal Diaries*, p. 508. Marshall's views are stated in *HCAS, Unification and Strategy Hearings*, p. 601, and Kennan's recollections in *Organizing for National Security Hearings*, p. 849.

the purposes for which the armed forces were to be maintained. These were to serve as "support for our political position; as a deterrent; as encouragement to nations endeavoring to resist Soviet political aggression . . . [and to] wage war successfully in case war should develop." It would impose too much rigor on the analysis to infer that the Planning Staff meant the order of this listing to indicate their degree of priority, but the progression was suggestive. Certainly, the use Truman and Marshall had made in May of the argument that they were "preparing for peace and not for war" indicated that they were relatively unmoved by the need to prepare to wage war successfully in case it should develop.

It was from this listing that Forrestal took his cue in October. If he was to tie his cause to Marshall's, he would do better to make the case for the $18-billion budget in terms of "peace needs" rather than "war needs," and this was the tactic he decided to employ in his letter to Marshall. The time seemed propitious. On October 21 the State Department had alerted the National Security Council to the possibility that 6,000 American troops might be required to help the United Nations enforce peace in Palestine. The ability of the military establishment to provide forces of this size had changed but little since February 1948, when Truman had been told that any local emergency requiring more than a division would necessitate partial mobilization.[66]

The letter to Marshall was sent on October 31. In it, Forrestal observed that there were "two basic problems" involved in determining upon the size of the budget. The first was to estimate the forces required "to combat possible acts of aggression." This was what the Joint Chiefs were currently doing. At the moment, he informed Marshall, they had three alternatives before them: (a) a $21-billion budget which was based on a war plan which would give them "a capability of effective reaction immediately at the outset of war"; (b) a $17.5-billion budget which, "while involving some risks," would in his judgment still provide "forces capable of taking effective action in the event of trouble"; and (c) the $14.4-billion budget. Forrestal did not describe what could be done with

[66] For the Palestine request, see Millis, ed., *The Forrestal Diaries*, p. 507.

a budget of this last size. He stated only that it was his intention to submit both the $14.4 and the $17.5-billion budgets to the President and to recommend the latter.

It was, however, with regard to the second basic problem connected with the budget that Forrestal wanted Marshall's advice. "Over and above" the problem of estimating the forces required for war, Forrestal declared, "and of greater importance in my opinion—is the problem with which you are concerned—namely, that we maintain sufficient strength to assist you in your difficult negotiations, in order that peace may be maintained." As a result of the President's ceiling, he pointed out, the services would be obliged to cut back the forces that they had been scheduled to have on hand at the end of fiscal 1949. It was because of this fact, Forrestal explained, that he desired Marshall's judgment on the following matters:

(a) Has there been an improvement in the international picture which would warrant a substantial reduction in the military forces we had planned to have in being by the end of the current fiscal year?

(b) Has the situation worsened since last Spring and should we, therefore, be considering an augmentation of the forces that we were planning at that time?

(c) Is the situation about the same—that is, neither better nor worse?

Forrestal granted that these questions involved "many imponderables" and that an answering letter might not be "an easy one to draft." Nevertheless, he needed as "much guidance as possible" from Marshall in order to determine "the degree of vigor" with which he should support the proposed $17.5-billion budget.[67]

Marshall had by this time returned to Europe, but Lovett telephoned the next day to find out how soon Forrestal wanted an answer. Forrestal replied that he would need it by November 15. In an "effort to be helpful," Lovett indicated that he would himself say "no" to the first and third questions, but he would "make no comment on the second." Lovett recognized, of course, what Forrestal was up to, and he was not unsympathetic with his objective. He had, however, no authority to commit his Secretary on the matter, hence his avoidance of what he obviously considered the operational question.

[67] *Ibid.*, pp. 508–10.

Marshall's answer, which arrived a week later, was much worse. The Secretary of State answered the third question in the affirmative and went on to insist again on the importance of arming the Europeans. So far as help from Marshall was concerned, this effectively put Forrestal back where he had started in May.[68]

The reasons why Marshall was so unwilling to lend his support to the cause of a higher defense budget deserve an explanation. Obviously, Forrestal had hoped for better. Did Marshall really believe, in face of the Berlin blockade, that the international situation had not deteriorated since May? The blockade might rather have been interpreted to mean he had failed in his effort not "to provoke" the Russians, and that there was, accordingly, no longer cause to forebear doing something about the "hollow shell" of American defenses. Moreover, given Congress' rejection of UMT, was not Forrestal correct in believing that an increase in the regular forces was now the only realistic approach to the problem?

In accounting for Marshall's action, it is important to recognize that he had no ready criteria by which to measure *his* need, as Secretary of State, for armed force. The question Forrestal and the Joint Chiefs faced—what kind of force and how much of it did they need to fight a war?—was an extremely difficult one to answer. The question Forrestal had put to Marshall—what did he need to maintain the peace?—was even more so. In March, when Marshall told the Senate Armed Services Committee that an increase in the armed forces would help back up his foreign policies, a Senator had seized on the statement and had asked him directly just how many more men in uniform his foreign policy required. Marshall had answered that the current situation, in which the United States had only one division available for emergency use overseas, was obvi-

[68] *Ibid.*, p. 511. Whether by design or error, the phrasing of Forrestal's questions was ambiguous. What was meant by the forces "we had planned to have in being by the end of the fiscal year?"—the forces that had been planned under the $3.5-billion supplement, the forces that had been planned under the budget passed by Congress, or the forces that had been planned in order to meet the President's ceiling? The point to these differences is that, in the event of the first two interpretations, the only way Marshall could have endorsed the force levels imposed by the ceiling would have been by answering the first question in the affirmative.

ously inadequate. But as to how many more divisions were needed, he had offered only the rather weak and inappropriate suggestion that the committee consult "the military authorities." [69]

The fact was that with the best of intent and analysis the State Department could not possibly specify with any certainty what the relationship would be between this or that size budget and the outcome of the political negotiations on which it was then engaged or those which it might conceivably confront one or two years in the future. The diplomatic difference between a $14.4-billion budget and a $17.5-billion budget was a highly indeterminate problem. Marshall might well feel that the larger budget would be helpful, but how much harm could he ascribe to the smaller?

If Marshall's diplomatic responsibilities did not point clearly to the need for a $17.5-billion budget, his interest in rearming the Europeans gave him considerable incentive to favor one of $14.4 billion. This was an issue which, in so far as the fiscal 1950 budget was concerned, made State and Defense not allies but enemies. The potential conflict had been shaping ever since April 1948 when Lovett told Forrestal that the State Department was planning a $3-billion program for European arms aid. At an NSC meeting on May 20, Forrestal took note of the French desire to receive aid in reequipping 25 of their divisions and announced that the Joint Chiefs believed that American military strength should be built up first. If the Chiefs had their way, he admitted, "it would be some time before the French could get what they wanted." [70]

The State Department had by then decided against action on the program in fiscal 1949. Lovett told the NSC that it would be "virtually impossible" to get Congressional approval for a revival of lend-lease except in an "emergency" and that, if Congress got wind of what they were considering, there would be "drastic cuts in domestic military appropriations." In late June the Berlin blockade

[69] *Senate UMT Hearings, 1948,* pp. 17–19.

[70] French and American rearmament were primarily in competition for budget dollars, but there was some possibility of conflict because of the limited military surplus available. In Bradley's judgment, the United States had enough World War II surplus to equip only 20 divisions. See *House Selective Service Hearings, 1948,* p. 6217.

providentially produced the "crisis" which the State Department thought the public and Congress needed, and within ten days the NSC had recommended and the President had approved the basic outline of a European arms aid program. The size and timing of the request were to be contingent on further military conferences with the European nations and the completion of the negotiations which were to result in the North Atlantic Treaty. Accordingly, in his budget message for fiscal 1950 Truman announced only that he expected to submit a request for arms aid later in the year. This he did in August 1949, immediately following the ratification of the Treaty, when he asked Congress for $1.4 billion to start the Mutual Defense Assistance Program.[71]

In the fall of 1948, Marshall's knowledge that he would later want to recommend to the President that some such sum be added to the budget could not help but color his response to Forrestal's invitations to help the Joint Chiefs increase their share of the budget. Forrestal was not, of course, asking Marshall to give up military aid to Europe in return for a larger defense appropriation. His point was that the total budget should be raised to cover the costs of both programs. But Marshall, knowing the dimensions of Truman's budget problems, had to consider the possibility that it might prove a case of either-or rather than both and that, in this event, any additional funds for the military establishment would be at the expense of his later request for foreign military aid. Under these circumstances (and so long as he believed that his program deserved priority) the prudent course for Marshall was to save the leverage he possessed on the President's budget policy for the protection and advancement of his own claims on the Federal revenue.

That Marshall was, in fact, prepared to place the arming of the Europeans above an increase in America's own forces was perfectly

---

[71] For the above events see Truman, *Memoirs*, II, 245–47, 251, and *U.S. Budget, FY 1950*, pp. M7, M16. The NSC quotations are from Truman's paraphrase. In October, Congress returned a bill for $1.3 billion (New York *Times*, October 19, 1949). This sum did not include the cost of the surplus equipment involved. See the *Joint Hearings before the Committee on Foreign Relations and the Committee on Armed Services on S.2388*, United States Senate, 81st Cong., 1st Sess. (Washington, 1949), p. 16.

clear from his remarks to Forrestal and the Chiefs at the October 10 conference. He was still intent on his basic foreign policy strategy: to restore the European balance of power. Forrestal, as pointed out in Chapter II, was in complete agreement with this objective. The difference between them lay in the priority European rearmament was to have over American. In part this difference reflected their different institutional responsibilities. If the Joint Chiefs of Staff were Forrestal's "constituents," the Europeans were Marshall's. It was, moreover, the responsibility of the Secretary of State, not that of the Secretary of Defense, to weigh the relative gains to American security from the variety of means available, and this difference in their approach to the problem could not help but bend their judgment in divergent directions.

A second reason for the difference in their priorities was that they had drawn somewhat different conclusions from the Berlin blockade. So far as Forrestal was concerned, the Russian action seemed to italicize the imprudence of the ceiling that had been set in May. On his part, Marshall admitted to the worry that the blockade might mean that the Russians were much more belligerent than he had thought them in May, but the effect of this conclusion was offset in his mind by another. This was his conviction that "the Soviets are beginning to realize for the first time that the United States would really use the atomic bomb against them in the event of war." [72] The evidence which led Marshall to conclude that the Russians were now taking the A-bomb more seriously is not available, but its result was to balance out his alarm at the blockade. It was, perhaps, in this sense that he had meant the answer he gave Forrestal's letter: the statement that the international situation was about the same as it had been in the spring.

Still a third reason for the difference in their approach was that Marshall was willing, psychologically, to run a greater risk with the size of America's forces than was Forrestal. The explanation, ironically enough, lay in Marshall's own military experience. As Chief of Staff in 1941 he had seen the nation take essentially the same risk with the original lend-lease program under what, militarily,

[72] The quotation is from Marshall's statement at the October 10 conference; see Millis, ed., *The Forrestal Diaries*, p. 502.

seemed much more threatening circumstances. The parallel had not escaped Marshall's mind. In July, when Forrestal pointed out that if war developed out of the Berlin blockade the United States had all of one division that it could commit with any speed, Marshall had observed that "we were much better off than in 1940. . . ." [73]

These considerations—his difficulty in estimating how much force his diplomacy would need, his interest in European arms aid, his heightened confidence in the deterrent effect of the A-bomb, and his World War II experience—all constituted policy reasons why Marshall was less concerned about consequences of the ceiling than Forrestal. They do not, however, completely explain the position he took on the budget. His stand, after all, was not one of less vigorous support for a larger defense budget, but one of no support. In further explanation, it is necessary to turn to certain political considerations which weighed in Marshall's calculus.

The first of these was that Truman's May decision in favor of the ceiling had been in the form of a flat order from the Commander in Chief. It is likely that Marshall's military background gave him some cause to doubt the propriety of collaborating in Forrestal's effort to circumvent that order. Even more certain is that, given that background, Marshall had been leaning over backwards in an effort to avoid seeming to take, as Secretary of State, a "military" point of view with regard to national security policy. This, too, served to inhibit him from taking issue with the President's choice of defense budgets. This was, moreover, a consideration that would have been fresh in his mind when Forrestal solicited his help at the October 10 conference. The day before, Truman had told Marshall that he was disturbed to find in his campaigning that many people were critical of what they believed to be the influence of a "military clique" in his administration.[74] Finally, Marshall had also to reckon the cost to his own prestige should he fight Forrestal's battle and lose. It was the later judgment of one of Forrestal's aides that Marshall "had had his brains beat out on China and the Pearl Harbor hearings, and he just wasn't willing to get into any more battles than he had to."

In contrast to this last observation, a recollection more privy to

[73] *Ibid.*, p. 459.   [74] *Ibid.*, p. 502.

Marshall's views at the time is that he would have been willing to go to Truman on behalf of a larger budget if there had been any real consensus among the services as to what they needed. What Marshall did not want to do was to put himself at the spearhead of an effort to increase the budget without good military arguments to back up his position. Marshall was well aware that there was no such consensus among the Chiefs, and he was very much disturbed by the scope and intensity of the interservice conflict.

Marshall's concern, like so many of his other perspectives, was rooted in his fear of the resurrection of feast or famine budgeting. If the blatant competition and conflict among the services were to continue, they might drive the budget to a size which would trigger the public reaction he so dreaded. The other possible outcome was equally to be avoided. For if the budget were kept within the bounds the public would tolerate, the divisions among the services could then result in such extensive compromises among them that the services would have, in effect, sabotaged each other's programs and left the country with none.

For these reasons, Marshall considered "unity" among the services to be "absolutely mandatory." He had, of course, seen his own share of service (and theater) conflict, and he knew that on issues of great weight and uncertainty the routes of persuasion and compromise were often the only ones available. But he was convinced that somehow, "out of the cleverness of somebody's mind or the vision of somebody's mind," an approach had to be found to the peacetime budget which would evidence a greater regard for economy and "the security of the country." Measured against these expectations, Marshall found the military establishment wanting. He believed that if the Chiefs had taken their responsibilities more seriously and Forrestal had exercised more determined leadership, they could have reached an agreement on the strategic issues that divided them.[75]

As it was, Forrestal's appeals for help did not strike him so much as a request to lend his support to a program which the Chiefs were united in believing the country needed, as they seemed a plea to

[75] For Marshall's views, see, in part, *HCAS, Unification and Strategy Hearings,* pp. 600–2.

help persuade the President that all was well in the Pentagon and an invitation to substitute his blessings on the budget for those of the Joint Chiefs. This was tantamount to being asked to be Secretary of Defense as well as Secretary of State, and this Marshall was not about to do.

VII

While Forrestal had been negotiating with Marshall, the Joint Chiefs had been struggling to carry out their end of the strategy whereby the President's ceiling was to be raised. On the matter of the $14.4-billion budget—which was to be presented to the President as evidence of their good intent—the Chiefs decided against the approach that Forrestal had urged. Instead of developing an "unbalanced" budget, which by allocating the bulk of the money to the Air Force would permit them to implement at least the bomb-from-Britain part of the war plan, they had determined to take the "easier" path and to pare down proportionately from their top figure—which had by now been reduced to $21 billion.

The Air Force, it may be safely presumed, had acquiesced to this approach only after it became perfectly clear that the Army and the Navy would never agree to the other. The considerations which moved the Army and the Navy are equally apparent. Although they had not been privy to Forrestal's conference with the President on October 5, they had been present at the meeting with Marshall on October 10. The results had hardly been such as to lead them to believe that the strategy outlined by Forrestal on October 15 had a high probability of success. Neither could they have drawn much encouragement from Forrestal's performance the previous spring. On that occasion the Secretary had persuaded the Chiefs to abandon their claim for a $9-billion supplement on the promise that he could raise the supplement then before Congress from $3 to $3.5 billion. But the Budget Bureau had cut the $3.5 to $3.1 and had tried to reduce it to $2.5, and in the end the President had permitted them somewhat less than $3 billion—which left the services worse off than they had begun.

Under the circumstances, the Chiefs might well have suspected that the real purpose behind the plan Forrestal presented on October 15 was not to bargain the President up to $18 billion but to snare them down to $14.4 billion. Although the Secretary may have had this in mind as a minimum objective, the evidence leaves no doubt that he took his plan to raise the ceiling seriously. So, too, did the Chiefs, and throughout November the military establishment continued to feed the press stories emphasizing the desirability of raising the ceiling and the probability that the President would do so.

In private, however, Bradley and Denfield must have rated the likelihood of failure as high. Given such expectations, they had little incentive to gamble the future of their services on an unbalanced $14.4-billion budget. This might be the best budget to present to the President for the purpose of persuading him to choose one of $18 billion, but if it proved instead to be the budget the President actually chose, it might then start a pattern of defense spending which they could never reverse.

It seems a fair presumption that their concern for the share of the budget the Army and Navy might receive in the future was moved not by service interest but, as they saw it, by national interest. If war should come in the very near future, the capacity to do a thorough job of bombing from Britain might be a better defense posture than a capacity to do nothing very well about any part of the war plan. But who could say that war would come in the very near future? And if it did not, the "balanced" $14.4-billion budget would not only provide a better base from which to expand to the force levels actually needed, it would also avoid setting what (according to Army and Navy doctrine) would be a very dangerous precedent. For should future defense budgets continue to provide only for the strategic bombing effort, it would mean that when war did come the nation would be forced to fight it with the wrong weapons and the wrong doctrine.

The course of reducing proportionately from the $21 billion estimate was, then, the only approach to the President's ceiling that the Chiefs could take with any prospect of agreement. There had to be, as Denfield later told Mahon's committee, a "certain give and take in order to get agreement," and it was obviously more feasible for one service to give in to two, than for two to give in to one. Even under these terms, agreement was not easily reached. The Navy and the Army had combined to insure that all the eggs were not placed in the Air Force's basket, but the Army was equally reluctant to place very many in the Navy's basket. Accordingly, once it had been agreed that each would scale down from its share of the $21-billion estimate rather than concentrate on the bomb-from-Britain part of the war plan, the Army promptly realigned itself with the Air Force against the Navy in so far as the Navy's share of the scale-down was concerned. The result was that Forrestal received early in November not a unanimous agreement on the division of the $14.4 billion, but a split recommendation. The Navy's conception of the division was $4.9 billion for the Army; $4.9 for the Navy; and $4.6 for the Air Force. The Army and the Air Force, on the other hand, both recommended $4.9 billion for the Army; $4.4 for the Navy; and $5.1 for the Air Force.

Forrestal had wanted the Chiefs to take the unbalanced approach to the $14.4 billion. He had also wanted unanimity with regard to the division of funds under that ceiling. Although he had explained to the Chiefs why he needed both in order to argue effectively against the President's decision, he had received neither. Of the two objectives, Forrestal's need for unanimity was the greater, and to achieve it he recognized that he would have to sacrifice the other. He said no more about the desirability of budgeting exclusively for the atomic offensive part of the war plan. On November 9 he suggested that the $14.4 billion be divided: $4.8 billion for the Army; $4.6 for the Navy; and $5 for the Air Force. That same day he left for Europe, where he remained until November 16. In his absence, the Chiefs continued to work on both the $14.4 and the $18-billion budgets, and the final product of their labor was sent to Forrestal's office on November 15.

With regard to the $14.4-billion budget, the Chiefs had accepted the division of funds advanced by Forrestal on November 9. They were, however, still divided over the number of large carriers that the Navy should maintain on active duty with its $4.6-billion share. The Navy wanted to operate 9 carriers, the Army thought it should operate only 6, and the Air Force recommended 4. Forrestal had to decide this one himself, and he settled on 8. Forrestal submitted this budget to the President on December 1. Between December 15 and December 22 these figures were worked over by the Budget Bureau, and it was there that the budget was reduced to $14.2 billion and the specific allocations set forth at the end of Chapter II were finally determined.[76]

The Chiefs had much less difficulty with the "intermediate" budget. There were no split recommendations, and the figure on which they finally agreed—$16.9 billion—was even lower than the $17.5 to $18 billion that Forrestal had suggested in October. The intermediate budget was designed to give the services a total of 1,980,000 men and to provide a 59-group Air Force. (In contrast, the $14.2-billion budget that was finally submitted to Congress provided 1,617,000 men and a 48-group Air Force, and the forces scheduled under the $3.5-billion supplement that had led to the setting of the ceiling in the first place had been 1,795,000 men and a 66-group Air Force.) The main point to the $16.9-billion budget was, of course, that it would permit the services to take effective action on both the Mediterranean and the bomb-from-Britain parts of the war plan, whereas under the division of funds they had submitted for the $14.4-billion budget they could do neither.

Forrestal sent this budget to the President on December 1 along with the one for $14.4 billion. He also enclosed a letter noting that Marshall had authorized him to say that he would find the higher budget most helpful.[77] There was, however, nothing especially helpful about Marshall's statement. He did not say that the lower budget would be most harmful or dangerous, and this was the only kind of assertion that was likely to carry any weight in Forrestal's argument against the ceiling.

[76] For the dates and figures in the preceding pages, see SCA, *Hearings 1950 Budget*, p. 17; and HCA, *Hearings 1950 Budget*, I, 12; II, 42, 99–111; III, 43, 51. It is typical of the Congressional performance that, of all the alternatives considered by the Executive, the committees secured the most information about these—the least different.

[77] For the figures on the intermediate budget and Marshall's letter, see Millis, ed., *The Forrestal Diaries*, pp. 419, 536, 538.

VIII

Finally, the day for which Forrestal had been seven months in preparation arrived. On December 9 he and Webb met with the President at the White House, together with the Chiefs, the service Secretaries, Gruenther, Webb, and Souers. With maps and charts the military briefed Truman on the difference between what they could accomplish with a $14.4-billion budget and a $16.9-billion budget. The President listened. When the presentation was over, he thanked them and announced that the ceiling still stood. After a few minutes of informal conversation, the meeting, which had lasted less than an hour, was over.[78]

Forrestal's defeat on December 9 was complete and final. "In the person of Harry Truman," he concluded, "I have seen the most rocklike example of civilian control that the world has ever witnessed." [79] Truman had indeed been firm in his decision. Not once since May had he given Forrestal any reason to believe that he could be moved from the ceiling.

Truman obviously saw no cause to change his mind at the December meeting. His fiscal problem was basically no different from what it had been in May, and his interest in avoiding inflation and deficit financing had not in the least abated. The Council of Economic Advisers had warned him on December 7 that new taxes would probably be required to balance the fiscal 1950 budget, and they had urged that these taxes be high enough to produce a surplus. This advice fell on ready ears. In his budget message Truman asked for $4 billion in new taxes, arguing that it was "not sound public policy" to operate at a deficit during a period of high prosperity (his budget anticipated a $873-million deficit given existing taxes) and asserting the need for a surplus to reduce the national debt and counteract inflation.[80]

[78] *Ibid.*, p. 536.
[79] Forrestal made this statement in reference to budget before the National Press Club. New York *Times*, February 2, 1949.
[80] Memorandum, Council of Economic Advisers to President, December 7, 1948; Nourse Papers; and *U.S. Budget, FY 1950*, p. M5.

There was, however, no real prospect that a higher defense budget could have been financed through such taxes. His victory at the polls in November had not significantly enhanced Truman's opportunity to get new taxes, nor was he in fact to secure them. If anything the election had made his fiscal problems worse, for he had now to contend with more vigorous claims for Fair Deal expenditures. (Webb had been quick to appreciate this, and four days after the election he had sought and gained Truman's assurance that he would stick by the ceiling.) Truman's final budget did contain $790 million for new programs of this character, but the argument that had been advanced in the December 1948 *Fortune* article—that he could finance an $18-billion defense budget by reducing spending on farm supports, housing, and other welfare programs—was not a real alternative either. Truman's total expenditures for *all* housing and agricultural programs in the fiscal 1950 budget amounted, for example, to only $2 billion.[81]

If Truman saw no change in the dimensions of his fiscal problem, what of his national security responsibilities and the demonstration that a $16.9-billion budget would put the services in a postion to implement their war plan, while a $14.4-billion budget would not? One may wonder how seriously Truman took the services' description of what could be accomplished with the additional $2.5 billion, especially since he knew the services were not really agreed on how the war should be fought. In any event, the knowledge that his ceiling would not leave the services in a very good position to fight a war was not really news. This was the risk he had decided to take in May. Once determined on his course, Truman was not one to agonize over the imponderables involved, and he had heard nothing from his Secretary of State to lead him to believe that it had to be recalculated. The attention Truman gave on December 9 to the $16.9-billion versus $14.4-billion choice was, in all probability, as perfunctory as the record suggests.[82]

[81] *U.S. Budget, FY 1950*, p. M13. For Webb's action, see Stephen K. Bailey and Howard D. Samuel, *Congress at Work* (New York, Henry Holt and Co., 1952), p. 362.
[82] For Truman's style of decision on national security matters, see Neustadt, *Presidential Power*, pp. 172–73, 176.

There were two major reasons for Forrestal's failure. One was the position taken by Marshall. The other was the fact that Forrestal never developed an *economic* argument against the ceiling. The advocates of the ceiling, it will be recalled, had been able to justify it on military as well as economic grounds: the argument that if the ceiling were exceeded Congress would only appropriate less money at some future date and thereby introduce such an element of instability into defense budgeting that the services would be net losers. This line of reasoning may not have convinced Forrestal, but it did help the proponents of the ceiling to persuade themselves of its merits. In contrast, Forrestal's case for a higher budget was never more than half made. He offered military reasons for it but no economic reasons. He made no effort to argue that if the ceiling were exceeded the consequences for the economy might be positively beneficial, or, at least, not as harmful as the ceiling's advocates made out.

Such an argument might have been made. Forrestal surely could have found economists who would have taken issue with some of the premises on which the Budget Bureau had based its case or with some of the more calamitous views of what would happen to the economy if the defense budget rose above $15 billion. Such arguments, even if not totally persuasive, would at least have flanked and weakened his opposition. But Forrestal never sought to develop them. The trouble was that Forrestal was himself more than half persuaded of the validity of Webb's reasoning. Thus a few days after the December 9 meeting, he wrote:

. . . I have the greatest sympathy with [Truman] because he is determined not to spend more than we take in in taxes. He is a hard-money man if I ever saw one, and believing as I do that we can't afford to wreck our economy in the process of trying to fight the "cold war," there is much to be said for his thesis of holding down spending to the absolute minimum of necessity. . . .[83]

Although these two factors would appear sufficient in themselves to explain the fate of the $16.9-billion budget, Forrestal's attempt to secure more funds was additionally handicapped by two other con-

[83] Millis, ed., *The Forrestal Diaries*, pp. 536–37.

ditions worthy of note. One was the fact that the Chiefs had refused to give him the "absurd" version of the $14.4-billion budget. Forrestal was probably correct in believing that if they had allocated the bulk of the ceiling's funds to the Air Force it would have presented Truman with a more difficult choice. The second was that by December Forrestal's personal relationship with the President was definitely strained. The press was full of rumors that Forrestal had not exactly viewed the prospect of a Dewey victory with alarm and that he would not be kept on in the new Cabinet.

Forrestal was not at all certain what the President thought of these allegations, and on his return from Europe he had flown to see Truman at Key West in the hope that he could clarify their relationship and secure Truman's assurance of his continued confidence. He failed to do so, and to his other burdens he now added that of continued anxiety regarding his relationship to the President. While there were at this time no signs of the unbalance that was shortly to overcome him, he appeared mentally exhausted and incapable of decision. What Truman made of all this is not known. One might infer from his short treatment of the case for the $16.9-billion budget on December 9 that the President was not going out of his way to encourage Forrestal, the Joint Chiefs, or anyone else to spend seven months in a plot to reverse one of his decisions. In all events, there was no element of personal rapport to ease the way for Forrestal's final effort to persuade the President to abandon the $15-billion ceiling.[84]

IX

It is pertinent at this point to recall Forrestal's description of the budget he presented to Mahon's committee some six weeks after the conference of December 9.

. . . the military forces provided under this budget are for a national defense position of relative military readiness, coupled with a higher degree of mobilization preparedness with proper balance between man-

[84] On Forrestal's post-November relations with Truman, see *ibid.*, pp. 518–19, 529–31.

power and material, consistent with our traditional concept of military strength for purposes of defense.

The conclusion seems inescapable that the Congressional committees might have learned more than they did about what lay behind these words. The budget presented to Congress in January was one which Forrestal and the Joint Chiefs had agreed in October could not provide the nation "'a satisfactory and usable military power." What Congress was asked to appropriate and what the Executive witnesses described as adequate was a budget that had been primarily designed as a bargaining device to impress the President with the good intentions of the Joint Chiefs. It was a budget which allegedly left the services incapable of undertaking either one of the two major operations required by their minimum war plan.

It is also evident that those who tried to increase the funds for naval air power—Sheppard, Plumley, Sikes, and Vinson—could have made their case more persuasively if they had been in a position to argue it in terms of the contribution that carriers could make to one of the major objectives of that plan: the holding open of the Mediterranean line of communications. In the absence of this point of reference, they were obliged instead to fight on grounds of their opposition's choosing: the question of whether carriers or land-based bombers were the better vehicles for conducting an atomic strike against the Soviet Union.

The cost of inadequate information to the advocates of an increase in Air Force funds is even more apparent. Although Forrestal had urged the Chiefs to bring forward a budget that concentrated on implementing the bomb-from-Britain part of the war plan primarily because he hoped it would highlight the absurdity of the President's ceiling, he had nonetheless proclaimed it in October a more "satisfactory" approach to the $14.4-billion figure than the one the Chiefs finally took. The Air Force certainly was of this opinion. This was what Symington and Vandenberg had had in mind when they assured Mahon's committee "that adequate national defense can be obtained for money in the vicinity of $15,000,000,000." Yet without an appreciation of the basic premises of the war plan and a knowledge of the two alternative ways in which forces could have been budgeted in relation to the operations anticipated in that plan, the Air Force testimony could only seem either a defense of the President's budget or an instance of "beggar thy neighbor" service politics.

Given Forrestal's October statement, his failure to pressure the Army and Navy into taking the unbalanced approach to the President's ceiling must have rankled the Air Force—especially after it became evident that the Chiefs were not going to get the $16.9-billion budget. It also seems a fair supposition that Forrestal's October position permitted the Air Force to make its end run to Congress with less of a sense of disloyalty than might otherwise have been the case. Indeed, as the months went by, Forrestal's "absurdity" alternative appears to have been elevated in Symington's memory to the status of an agreed plan. On October 18, 1949—the day Congress finally passed the fiscal 1950 appropriation bill—he told Vinson's committee that the budget would have been "more than enough, if properly allocated on the basis of a strategic plan" that had been made by the Joint Chiefs of Staff.[85]

The Air Force must have been further encouraged to solicit additional money from Congress by Forrestal's own action following the December 9 conference. On December 20 he met with the President in an attempt to persuade him to increase the Air Force budget by nearly $700 million. Forrestal was not reopening the question of the ceiling. His idea was that the government would get back $200 million in the form of income tax from the pay increases the budget would provide and that to this sum could be added $525 million, if only the stockpile appropriation were treated as a capital investment instead of an expenditure.

Truman rejected these expedients, but Forrestal's supporting argument marks an historic turning point in the ascendency of Air Force doctrine. A year ago, he told the President, he had had "substantial misgivings" about the ability of long-range bombers to get through to their targets in the Russian homeland. He now believed that they could. Moreover, his trip to Europe had led him to con-

[85] New York *Times*, October 19, 1949. Cf. the version in HCAS, *Unification and Strategy Hearings*, p. 418.

clude that the United States had perhaps underestimated the psychological importance of its nuclear weapon.

Throughout my recent trip in Europe [he wrote the President] I was increasingly impressed by the fact that the only balance that we have against the overwhelming manpower of the Russians, and therefore the chief deterrent to war, is the threat of immediate retaliation with the atomic bomb. I have substantial misgivings that reduction in the potential of the Air Force in the long-range bombing field might be misunderstood both by the world at large and particularly by our only enemy.[86]

Forrestal had recommended that the additional $700 million be used to add 6 more strategic bombing groups to the 48 groups the Air Force would possess under the President's final budget of $14.2 billion. In this, his action seems quite parallel to that later taken by Mahon's committee and would suggest that, whatever the deficiencies of the committee's public investigation, its policy conclusion corresponded closely to the privately held views of the Secretary of Defense. The appearance of similarity is most deceiving. Forrestal's memorandum in support of the 6-group increase continued as follows: "The Air Force *will have* the heavy bombers necessary for *carrying the atomic bomb,* but these atomic carriers will need support by *conventional* bomb groups. . . ." [87]

Here is the final commentary on the rationality of the Congressional choice with regard to the Air Force increase. One and all, the proponents of that increase had made their case in terms of the critical importance of delivering the nuclear weapon. Atomic bombardment, as Cannon had put it, might end the war in three weeks; they should put their money "in the only place that counts . . . on long-range, land-based bombers." Yet, what the House would have actually purchased with its 10-group increase, in so far as strategic

---

[86] Millis, ed., *The Forrestal Diaries,* pp. 537–38. A small part of the $700 million was to be made available to the Army and the Navy.

[87] *Ibid.,* p. 538, italics added. Forrestal's 6 groups were probably all medium-bombardment groups, although at this time the Air Force had not yet changed from the 2-12 division between the heavy and medium bombardment groups to be maintained in the 48-group force to the 4-10 division.

bombing was concerned, were 4 medium bombardment groups that would have had the mission of conducting sorties for the delivery of TNT bombs and the diversion of Russian defenses. This far was the Congress led astray in the absence of information regarding the size of the nuclear stockpile.

The difference between what Forrestal knew to be involved in an increase in the number of bombardment groups and that anticipated by Congress is startling. Revealing, too, is what the Air Force itself expected to buy with additional money. The increase recommended by Forrestal had amounted to something less than $700 million, and he had wanted it all to go for 6 more bombardment groups. But when the Air Force came to allocate a larger sum of money—the $800 million voted by the House—it planned to add only 4 more bombardment groups. With the other 5 groups, as was explained to the disconcerted members of Mahon's committee, the Air Force had "balanced off as far as we can the ground support, and so forth, we are providing the Army." The choice of the Air Force no doubt had its basis in doctrine, but it was also politic. The Air Force had far more cause to be sensitive to Army interests than Congress and, perhaps, even Forrestal—so long as it wished to keep the Army as an ally against the Navy.

The final view on the Air Force increase was, of course, Truman's. In his statement on October 29, 1949, announcing that he would not spend the additional $800 million, Truman described the budget he had presented to Congress as one that had represented a careful "balance between security needs in the light of our foreign policy and the economic and fiscal problems facing us domestically." The additional funds, if spent, would be but the first step "in an expanding program which would have to be supported by greatly increased appropriations in future years."

Furthermore, the programs provided in the budget were based on national defense plans in which our air, naval, and land forces were planned and operated under a unified strategic concept. To build up the strength of the other services so that they could complement and support an expanded Air Force would require additional very large appropriations.[88]

[88] New York *Times*, October 29, 1949.

Truman's effort to ground his decision on the importance of preserving the "unified strategic concept" behind his budget was so much camouflage. In the first place, he knew very well that no one's strategic concept had envisioned that the Russians would explode an A-bomb in August 1949.[89] Similarly, while Truman may not have known the exact political circumstances under which Forrestal had persuaded the Chiefs in October 1948 to agree unanimously to a budget within his ceiling, by October 1949 he and everyone else in the country were witness to the "war" that had broken out between the Navy and the Air Force. Finally, as for the necessity of preserving the budgetary balance among the services, there was the fact that it had been known since August that Johnson planned to carry out the long-held hope of the Army and the Air Force and cut back the naval air arm by 50 percent.

More to the point were the President's references to the consequences for future appropriations if the Air Force were to receive the increase. To maintain 58 groups the Air Force, according to its estimate, would require a $6-billion budget in fiscal 1951. But the ceiling that had been set for fiscal 1951 was only $13 billion. The problem was therefore obvious. In fact, to make certain that the force levels scheduled by the services would fit under this ceiling, Johnson had already reconstituted the McNarney Board and put it to work reducing the funds the services were to receive under the fiscal 1950 budget—even as Congress was still deliberating on the original bill.[90] Thus the fiscal 1950 budget ended as it had begun. It had had its policy beginnings in the final stages of the budget for fiscal 1949, and its policies were now to terminate in the development of the budget for fiscal 1951.

x

The reasoning behind the fiscal 1951 ceiling was a case of Webb's fiscal 1950 argument only more so. As a result of the 1949 recession,

[89] Cf. Johnson's statement that there was no cause to increase the defense budget because of the Russian explosion, since the budget had been prepared with "all contingencies" in mind. *Ibid.*, October 4, 1949.

[90] *HCA, Hearings 1950 Budget*, I, 243, and New York *Times*, October 9 and 12, 1949.

the prospect for revenues was lower, the size of the deficit loomed larger (one of $5.5 billion was now expected for fiscal 1950), and the opportunity for new taxation remained the same. Both as a result of these conditions and, it may be presumed, because he had taken his predecessor's experience to heart, Johnson's bargaining was conducted on an appreciably lower level than Forrestal's the year before. According to Johnson's later testimony, Forrestal had been thinking in terms of a $17-billion budget, while the Bureau of the Budget had $12.5 billion in mind. After he took office, Johnson decided to split the difference and advanced $14.6 as his estimate. Frank Pace, who had succeeded Webb as the Bureau's Director, refused the compromise and offered $13 billion. The final bargain, in July, was struck at $13.5 billion, which included, as did the other figures, $500 million for stockpiling. In announcing this figure to the National Security Council, Truman declared:

The budget policy on which my ceiling determinations for 1951 are based is that of (a) holding governmental expenditures as closely as possible to present levels and, in particular, (b) preventing the prospective large rise in the military area by adjustments in present plans.[91]

Early in October Vinson established that Johnson was planning to reduce the appropriations requested in the fiscal 1950 budget by $800 million. Of this amount the Navy was to lose $350 million, the Army $300 million, and the Air Force $150 million. Both Vinson and Baldwin in the New York *Times* claimed that Johnson was trying to make good his assertion the previous spring that he could save a billion dollars in the budget if Congress would pass the bill reorganizing the military establishment. They also charged that reductions of this order could only be made at the expense of the actual fighting performance of the armed forces.[92] Johnson's prestige was undoubtedly committed to the idea that large, "cost-free" savings could come from reorganizing the Pentagon, but the pressure imposed by the fiscal 1951 ceiling provided the more compelling motive for his cuts.

The budget presented to Congress in January 1950 proved even

[91] See *U.S. Budget, FY 1951*, p. M5, *MacArthur Hearings*, IV, 2597–2602, and Nourse, *Economics in the Public Service*, p. 250
[92] New York *Times*, October 9 and 12, 1949

lower than the ceiling. Of the $13 billion earmarked for the armed services, $873 million was in the form of new obligational authority that Johnson had cut out of the fiscal 1950 budget in October. New obligational authority for fiscal 1951 therefore totaled only $12.2 billion, in contrast to the $14.2 billion that had been requested the year before. In anticipation of this reduction, by June 1950 Johnson had reduced the services from the 1.6-million men originally scheduled for fiscal 1950 to 1.4-million men, a figure slightly lower than even the 1.5-million men the services were scheduled to maintain under the fiscal 1951 budget.[93]

Congress never had a chance to complete its action on the fiscal 1951 budget. Six days before the fiscal year 1950 ended, the North Korean armies crossed the 38th parallel. With American entry into the war, the ruin of Truman's budget policy was complete. One by one, the major assumptions that had shaped the fiscal 1950 budget— strategic, scientific, military, diplomatic, and economic—had been shown false.

The first to fall had been the keystone to Marshall's whole postwar strategy: the expectation that it would prove feasible to restore the balance of power on the Continent. It was to this end that he had set European armament above American, and for this goal that he had been willing to risk a budget that would not permit the services to undertake their minimum war plan. But in the spring of 1949 a joint State-Defense mission to Europe discovered that the Europeans were either unable or unwilling to spend the money necessary to develop the power to contain the Russians. While Marshall, to be sure, had probably never conceived of his goal as one which would permit American power to be completely withdrawn from the defense of Europe, the news did basically alter the strategic and budgetary problem. For one thing, if the American strategic bombing effort were to be complemented by any sort of holding action on the

[93] HCA, *Hearings 1951 Budget*, pp. 45, 84, 91, 1734; *U.S. Budget, FY 1951*, p. M28; and Millis, ed., *The Forrestal Diaries*, p. 538.

Of the $12.2 billion, the Navy was to receive $3.8 billion, the Army $4 billion, and the Air Force $4.4 billion. With these sums the services were to maintain 1.5 million men and to try to field basically the same operating units scheduled under the fiscal 1950 budget: a 48-group Air Force, a 10-division Army, and a Navy with 7 heavy carriers.

Continent, the American contribution to that holding force would now have to be much greater than it otherwise might have been. Secondly, in the absence of a truly effective holding force, the defense of Europe would now have to rest more heavily on the threat of strategic bombing, and this, once the Russians developed their own intercontinental striking power, would prove to be a wasting asset.

The next assumption behind the fiscal 1950 budget to be violated by reality was its major scientific and technological premise. The Russians broke the American nuclear monopoly in August 1949, not some time in 1952 or later as nearly all had expected. What Forrestal had called the "years of opportunity" seemed abruptly and prematurely closed. With this event American politicians, diplomats, soldiers, and scientists were thrust, plans unprepared, into the beginning of the second revolution in the American security position. Whether as a result of this handicap or not, their concepts and theories were never to catch up with and sort out (much less anticipate), at least to their mutual satisfaction, the meaning of the successive technological developments that followed in the decade thereafter.

The revolt of the Admirals in October 1949, as a result of unilateral cuts in the Navy's budget, marked the demise of still another assumption that had conditioned the composition of the budget for fiscal 1950 and those before it. This was the idea that the conflicts in military doctrine that had developed since World War II could be met through the expedient of dividing the budget equally among the three services. The viability of a military policy that substituted dollars for choice depended on there being more rather than fewer dollars. Instead, the increasing disparity in fiscal 1950 and fiscal 1951 between service estimates and the funds believed available for defense generated so much pressure for choice, both within and outside the Pentagon, that it proved the policy's undoing.[94]

[94] As the figures in footnote 93 indicate, the Navy did not fare quite so badly in the fiscal 1951 budget as Johnson's August plans had promised. But whereas the number of large carriers dropped only from 8 to 7, the number of carrier air groups was reduced from 14 to 9, and aircraft procurement (817 planes) was even lower than that (843) which had evoked such a protest in fiscal 1950. See *HCA, Hearings 1951 Budget,* pp. 1727, 1734–35.

The Korean War was to ease the pressure for doctrinal choice, but the issues were only postponed. When they were rejoined in the post-Korean years, the Air Force was to capitalize rather successfully on the advantage that its doctrine had been shown to have in the fiscal 1950 budget debate. Air Force doctrine permitted its advocates to point, in good conscience, to where the budget could be cut: the Navy's carriers and the Army's divisions. The Army and Navy, in contrast, were inevitably obliged to argue the necessity for a larger budget. Their doctrine did not so much question the need for bombs, bombers, and bombing (hence, Air Force needs) as it contended that this activity by itself was not enough, that the kind of operations they planned to undertake would be necessary too. This, as Congressional action in the fiscal 1950 budget foreshadowed, was to prove politically a losing argument.

The major foreign policy premise of the fiscal 1950 budget—that the nation was "preparing for peace and not for war"—was shattered by the events of June 1950. The "possible explosive points in the world" to which Truman's attention had been called in February 1948—Greece, Italy, Korea, and Palestine—had not been forgotten, but neither had they been the focus for budgetary plans and preparations. It had been precisely in this general area, the nation's "short of all-out war" needs, that Forrestal had so vainly invited Marshall to advance a statement in the fall of 1948. Marshall, if anyone, had had the power to secure a budget that discriminated among the things that the Russians *could* do through reference to what they were *likely* to do. It was his department that had the responsibility to analyze and evaluate the intentions of foreign Powers. Left to their own responsibilities, the Chiefs were bound to act as they did and follow the time-honored maxim of putting worst things first. Accordingly, neither of the two approaches the Chiefs had considered taking to the $14.4-billion budget had been weighed in reference to their utility in the event a local "explosive point" actually took fire. They chose the right approach, given the war they were to fight, but it was for the wrong or at least irrelevant reasons.

The difficulty, of course, had been primarily conceptual. The war which the State Department (and everyone else) had not expected the Russians to start, at least until they achieved a nuclear capability, had been World War III, not a satellite attack in Asia. As will be seen in Professor Hammond's study, in July 1949, by which time Dean Acheson had succeeded Marshall as Secretary of State, George Kennan urged the Joint Strategic Survey Committee of the Joint Chiefs of Staff to consider establishing two specialized divisions that could be used for limited wars along the Soviet periphery. Given the character of Soviet foreign policy (as he saw it) and the American commitment to containment, Kennan considered the possibility of such wars a more likely contingency than that of all-out war. As an instance of forward planning, Kennan's recommendation was outstanding. But it hardly provided a point of leverage from which the Department of State could immediately reverse the direction of the whole budgeting process. For their part, the representatives of the Joint Chiefs did not contest the need for the divisions Kennan recommended. They merely observed that the size of the budget was not large enough to provide the forces required to fight World War III, much less the kind of wars Kennan had envisioned.[95]

By the time of the Korean War the fiscal 1950 budget had been found wanting in nearly every category of major assumption: strategic, scientific, military, and diplomatic. It remained for the war itself to contradict the fundamental economic premise behind the budget: the idea that $15 billion was all the nation could stand to spend for defense. On this point, the figures later assembled by Gerhard Colm speak eloquently. In the first half of calendar 1950, national security expenditures were at the rate of about $19 billion a year (all figures in 1952 prices) and consumed about 6 percent of the gross national product. In the first half of 1953, national security expenditures were on the order of $51 billion and constituted some 14 percent of the gross national product. The impact of the war had been such that security expenditures had almost tripled, and their percent of the gross national product had more than doubled. But at the same time the size of the gross national product itself had increased from $307 to $363 billion, an increment nearly twice as large

[95] See Paul Y. Hammond, *NSC-68: Prologue to Rearmament,* pp. 287–88, below.

as the increase in security expenditures. As a result, the nation was able to carry the greatly enlarged defense burden and still enjoy both an increasing rate of investment and a rising standard of living.[96]

Investment, to be sure, would have been greater and per capita consumption higher if the resources allocated to national security programs had been available for other purposes. But this is beside the point. The pertinent fact is that the economy did not collapse under the impact of these programs. The barrel did not burst. Workers still worked and investors continued to invest. The limitations which the nation faced in fiscal 1950 with regard to the size of the defense budget were political, not economic. The problem was not the capacity of the economy to carry larger expenditures, but rather the ability and desire of the administration to undertake the task of persuading the taxpayers and their representatives that the gains from larger expenditures would be worth the costs.

[96] Gerhard Colm and Marilyn Young, *Can We Afford Additional Programs for National Security*, Planning Pamphlet No. 84, The National Planning Association, October 1953, pp. 6, 17.

VI *Conclusions*

The central fact about the defense budget is that it is a political problem. The issue is enveloped in the aura of "national security" and made up of complex and technical military and foreign policy considerations. The effect is to generate among many the impression that it is and certainly ought to be far removed from "politics." But the defense budget is the very stuff of which politics is made. The size and composition of the armed forces are issues on which the blood, treasure, and freedom of society turn in increasing and fateful degree. Yet the determination of these forces is inescapably tied to questions of value and questions of fact for which there are no definitive answers. These questions involve matters on which the judgments of experts and politicians alike are bound to conflict. Issues of great public consequences about which intelligent, informed, and dedicated men disagree can have but one destiny and one destination. They must be resolved through the exercise of power in a political arena.

These points and the reasoning to support them were set forth at length in the Introduction. The purpose of the intervening chapters has been their illustration. The examples afforded by the fiscal 1950 budget of the element of conflict involved in its determination are legion. There were conflicts among the services; between the services and the Secretary of Defense; between the Department of Defense and the Bureau of the Budget and the Department of State; between the President and his Secretary of Defense; between the President and Congress; and conflicts both between the House and the Senate and within them. The matters at issue in these conflicts were not peripheral but central to the budget. They involved both the total resources to be made available for defense and the manner in which these resources were to be allocated. They reflected differences in judgment regarding such basic questions as the likelihood of war, the best means of fighting it if it came, and the degree of sacrifice the nation should make in support of its armed forces.

The causes for these conflicts were not to be found in the foibles and faults of the men who were making the decisions, but in the nature of the problems they faced. Was it the policy of the government to use the A-bomb in future war under any circumstances? What kind of military force would best back up Marshall's foreign policies? Would security be better advanced by arming the Europeans or the Americans? the Navy or the Air Force? Would war come in the near future? Had the international situation deteriorated since the spring of 1948? If the United States accompanied the formation of an Atlantic pact with an increase in armament would the Soviet Union be stirred to greater belligerence or would it be additionally deterred? How much inflation was the capacity to implement the minimum war plan worth?

Differences and uncertainty with regard to the answers to such questions as these were unavoidable. Conflict was built into these problems by the fact that more than one value was at stake, and by the fact that it was impossible to establish with certainty what the consequences would be for those values from any given course of action.

The alignment of the Executive participants with regard to these conflicts was, in turn, largely fixed by the nature of their responsibilities. The issue of the priority to be assigned to European as compared to American rearmament, for example, was given by the political-military situation of the United States vis-à-vis the Soviet Union and the goal of restoring the European balance of power. What was not given by the problem, however, were the organizational lines on which this issue was ultimately fought: State versus Defense. These were set by the responsibilities (hence, the interests) of the two institutions. So, too, with the divergent perspectives with which Marshall and Forrestal approached the problem of rearmament; they were derived from the interest of the one in intent-oriented and the other in capability-oriented strategy. Similarly, Webb, who was obliged to balance the needs of the whole range of the administration's purposes and programs, could not help but evaluate the costs of defense differently than Forrestal, whose responsibilities were formally confined to but one purpose and one program.

The conflicts between government needs and private wants, between welfare programs and security programs, and between one security program and another were thrust upon members of Congress as well as members of the Executive. But in the former body the organization of responsibility was more generalized, and the alignment of Congressmen with respect to these issues appears to have been more the result of the coincidence of individual preferences and common factual premises than the result of committee structure. It is plausible, however, that a closer examination of Congressional views and votes than that undertaken in the present study would reveal that the character of committee jurisdiction exercises a discernible influence on the character of the preferences and premises of its members.

The means used to resolve these conflicts—whether between institutions or ad hoc coalitions of individuals—were necessarily political. Power alone could decide the order in which conflicting values were to be served (as in the case between the desire to avoid inflation and the desire to be able to fight a war effectively if it came) or decide which among conflicting factual premises would be used to guide the allocation of resources (as in the case of the dispute between the Navy and the Air Force regarding the best means of using aircraft). Most of these choices, in their final form, were the result of the application of formal authority. Thus the votes and bills of Congress fixed the money that would be available, and the orders of the President determined the amounts requested and later spent. Antecedent to these actions, however, and largely conditioning their outcome, were the informal political negotiations among the contending groups, and it was primarily at this stage that the crucial battles over the content of the budget were fought.

The political necessity for the persuasion and bargaining that made up these preliminary negotiations lay in the fact that none of the contending parties could secure their interests without the action and support of others. The strategy of persuasion was to convince those sharing direct authority to choose the course favored by the advocate ("do what I want")—as in the case with Vinson's testimony before Mahon's committee or Forrestal's conversations with Truman —and to induce "third parties" to lend the weight of their prestige to such a choice ("help me to get others to do what I want")—as in the case with Forrestal's arguments to Marshall. But "doing" and "helping" were not acts which could be undertaken in the normal course of events without costs to the interests of the doer or the helper. (Marshall, Forrestal, and Truman each had something to lose, as well as gain, through the policies of the others.) Accordingly, the key political tactic in persuasion was the design of arguments which would cast the need for the action and support of others in terms of their interests rather than those of the advocate: "this is what *you* should want"; "help *yourself* by helping me." This was the rationale behind Truman's effort to explain how a budget within the ceiling would net the services more force than one which exceeded it, or Forrestal's effort to get the Chiefs to agree to a $14.4-billion budget (an agreement which *he* needed if he was to appear an effective Secretary) by an appeal to the "concept of the JCS."

Where persuasion failed and authority was absent, bargaining was the prescribed strategy. Within the House or the Senate, the residue of difference that remained after persuasive debate could be settled through the vote. Between the House and the Senate there was only the conference table. As in the case with persuasion, the incentive to compromise and to accommodate to the interests of others lay in the fact that the goals of all required the cooperation of each. Thus, given the agreement to scale down their estimates from $23.6 to $14.4 billion (an agreement which was itself the product of a bargain: Forrestal's promise to get them $18 billion), there was no other tactic for the Chiefs to follow except to bargain away the difference.

The determinants of bargaining power varied with the occasion, but among the quasi-sovereign units of the Executive the prime determinant was the expectation of what would happen if one side decided to incur the political costs of taking the issue to higher authority. The failure of the Air Force, for example, to insist that the Chiefs take the "unbalanced" approach to the $14.4-billion budget undoubtedly reflected their belief that Forrestal would not himself persist in this preference in the face of Army and Navy opposition. Similarly, in the bargaining between the Department of Defense and the Bureau of the Budget with regard to the fiscal 1951 ceiling, the fact that the final figure of $13.5 billion was closer to the $12.5 originally put forward by the bureau than the $17 advanced by the department can be considered a measure of the kind of support that each expected to find at the White House.

The policy consequence of the factors here summarized—the conditions that made the budget a political problem and its resolution a product of the political process—was that the content of the fiscal 1950 budget demonstrated in one degree or another every one of the policy "symptoms" that make up the "foreign policy syndrome" outlined in the Introduction. The conflict among the autonomous and competing elites concerned with the budget did not, to be sure, lead to "no policy at all." With regard to a matter like the determination of the budget, the "strain toward agreement" is irresistible, since a complete stalemate would mean the collapse of government itself. But the potential of the policy-making process for such stalemate is well illustrated by the temporary inability of the Chiefs to agree to any budget within the President's ceiling or by the months at the start of the fiscal year during which the Executive was obliged to live off emergency appropriations while the Senate and the House struggled to compose their differences with regard to the content of the budget.

It is hard to conceive of a better example of "compromised policy" than the budget that finally went to Congress. So many different accommodations had been made to reach it that the direction of its choice could hardly have been described in any other than the general and vacuous terms that Forrestal used upon its presentation. The fluctuating fortunes of the naval air arm under the fiscal 1949, fiscal 1950, and the preliminary and final fiscal 1951 budgets testify to the capacity of the political process to produce "unstable policy" as a result of changes in the ad hoc groupings of the elites and the distribution of power among them. The fact that the services were acquiring men and material to follow not one but three divergent and conflicting roads to victory is but an instance of "contradictory policy," a possibility forever inherent in the quasi-sovereign structure of the Executive. For an example of "paper policy" one need go no farther than President Truman's order in May commanding public and private support of the $15-billion ceiling. The words were those of the Commander in Chief, but the consensus necessary to insure obedience was notably absent. As for how the policy process can result in "blind policy" under conditions where sight is restricted to the few, the inability of Kennan in the summer of 1949 to muster the attention and support of the elites to the possibility of limited war affords an adequate and dramatic demonstration.

In its fashioning, the fiscal 1950 budget was similarly marked by the symptoms of the policy process. The process is unavoidably "slow"; conflict and consensus-building are time-consuming activities, and the greater the conflict or the scope of the consensus the more time they are likely to require. In many areas of policy the price of time may be the prolonging of choice beyond the opportunity for action. In the case of the budget, where the deadline is clear and the penalties for exceeding it great, the toll of time is exacted in the opposite direction. Rather than running past the point for action, the process is started earlier. Choices are not made "too late"; they are made "too early." Not all of the lead time required by the budget can be charged to the difficulty of reaching a consensus, nor does the shape of the future always come closer into focus the nearer one is to it. Nevertheless, to attempt to decide in May 1948 what kind of forces the nation will need in June 1950 is to contribute to the want of foresight in order to meet the necessity for agreement.

The tendency of the policy process to be "leaderless," to lack a central point of coordination as a result of the diffusion of power and responsibility among elites, is exemplified in the final budget. So many hands and considerations had shaped its content—the services', Forrestal's, Webb's, Marshall's, and all those who contributed to the climate of opinion—that only a formalist could label it Truman's. No one, and he least of all, had set out to present to Congress a bargain that the Chiefs had reached in order to reach a bargain with him. The program for which the Chiefs had been bargaining, the minimum war plan, was itself a manifestation of the "indecisive" propensity of the policy process. The Chiefs were able to agree to its content only because it avoided choice with regard to the doctrine that divided them. None of the central strategic issues involved in the preparation of the fiscal 1950 budget were decided by it. Such matters as the role of the naval air arm in the nuclear bombardment of the Soviet Union, the need for and character of a land battle in Europe, and the size of the Air Force and the kind of doctrine that should guide it survived to return in successively and only moderately altered forms for the budget debates of fiscal 1951 and those of many years thereafter.

The "gyroscopic" effect that the policy process exercises on the content of foreign policy appears to be especially marked in the case of the defense budget. Congress and Executive alike have tended to spin along at the same general level of expenditure year after year in spite of rather startling developments elsewhere in the nation's security position. In the years immediately preceeding the Korean War, the Truman administration led the nation through a series of dramatic and far-reaching changes in the nation's foreign policy commitments that marked the first of the two major revolutions in the American security position following World War II. Yet expenditures on the armed services for these years remained relatively uniform—$11.8 billion in fiscal 1947; $10.5 billion in fiscal 1948; $11.3 billion in fiscal 1949; and $11.6 billion in fiscal 1950—as did the proportions in which these sums were divided among the services, an approximately even split. Similarly, in the years immediately following the Korean War, the Eisenhower administration led the nation through the equally dramatic and far-reaching changes in military technology that have ushered in the second major revolution while maintaining an equivalent uniformity in expenditures on the armed services. Expenditures were at a higher level than that of the pre-Korean years, but the order of these expenditures did not appreciably vary. Between fiscal 1954 and fiscal 1959 they ranged from $35.5 billion to $40.8 billion. The proportions in which these sums were divided among the services also remained relatively constant, although the terms of the division had changed to 46-28-23 for the Air Force, Navy, and Army, respectively.[1]

Once formed, the climate of opinion with regard to desirable and possible defense spending has been remarkably impervious to change. The result has been "outmoded policy." Whatever the merits of the strategic rationale behind the fiscal 1950 budget, it hardly provided a justification for that of fiscal 1951. And what the Soviet A-bomb and the knowledge that the Europeans would not raise enough force to balance the Russians failed to do to Truman's last pre-Korean budget, the advent of Soviet space and missile superiority and the rise of Red China failed to do to the later budgets of Eisenhower.

The most notable change that did take place in the Truman budgets, the fiscal 1949 supplement, was a clear case of "crisis-oriented policy." The deficiencies in American military power had been well marked before the events of March 1948, but it took the concentrated sum of those events to produce the beginnings of a budgetary change. Even so the policy process soon evidenced its "short-reaction" symptom, and the subsidence of public and elite concern dissipated a significant part of the momentum previously generated. The Berlin crisis in June provided the spark to revive the military aid program, but this disturbance proved insufficient to raise the budget ceiling too.

The structure of the policy process was not, of course, totally responsible for these gyroscopic tendencies. The results are attributable to the want of ideas as well as to the consequences of conflict and consensus-building. Both administrations, for example, were burdened by the belief that the budget level at which they were operating was pushing at the limit of what the economy could bear.

---

[1] *U.S. Budget, FY 1954,* p. 1136, and *U.S. Budget, FY 1960,* p. 1013. The division among the services during the fiscal 1955–1959 budgets is given in General Maxwell P. Taylor, *The Uncertain Trumpet* (New York, Harper and Brothers, 1960), pp. 65–66. The remaining 3 percent has been budgeted to the department as a whole.

Still, even with the best of ideas, the problems associated with the defense budget are among the most complex that the policy elites confront, and they are problems which involve the interest and power of many and disparate groupings among these elites. Under these circumstances, ideas once established are not easily challenged and agreements once reached not easily disturbed. It would appear to be the combination of the two factors, as noted in the Introduction, that accounts for the stability of the budget consensus and why it is so difficult to change except through successive, prolonged, and modest adjustments or under a condition of extreme trauma, such as the Korean War.

The fiscal 1950 budget was, in sum, a political problem resolved in the political arena. Conflict and choice were unavoidable: with regard to the values to be served, and with regard to the divergent conceptions of how to secure them. Institutional responsibilities shaped the alignment of officials with respect to these conflicts, and power the terms of their settlement. The distribution of power and responsibility necessitated the negotiation of these terms through persuasion and bargaining as often as it permitted their specification through the exercise of formal authority, and in consequence the choices that made up the content of the budget evidenced all the characteristic symptoms of a product of the foreign-policy process: no policy at all; compromised, unstable, and contradictory policy; paper policy and blind policy; slow, leaderless, and indecisive policy; gyroscopic, crisis-oriented, short-reacting, and outmoded policy.

THE BUDGET AND RATIONALITY

The opportunities for perfectly rational choice with regard to the content of the defense budget are limited. They are limited first of all by the complex and contingent character of the problems involved. The foreign policy purposes to be served by the budget, the relative utility of the means available to implement those purposes, the likely shapes of the future, the influence alternative budgets might have on that future, and the costs it is desirable to incur for defense—these are matters about which, after the best of information and analysis, the judgment of any one individual is likely to remain confused and uncertain. Multiply the number of individuals and the result will be judgments which are divergent and conflicting. Rational choice for the individual will involve a large element of guess. Coordinated choice among individuals will require a large exercise of power. The end product of guesses and power, of the inherent difficulty of the problem and the need to accommodate its resolution to a diversity of views and interests, is quite likely to be a budget which will not seem very rational to anyone.

Granted these limits, the fact remains that the choices made in the case of the fiscal 1950 budget, both individual and group, could have been more rational than they were. That they were not can be attributed in large part to the influence of four ideas in the prevailing climate of opinion: (a) the idea that the budget was open to determinate solution; (b) the idea that, by reorganizing the Department of Defense, unified planning could be secured and billions of dollars saved through the elimination of interservice rivalry; (c) the idea that there was a fixed limit to what the economy could stand to spend on defense; and (d) the idea that secrecy was synonymous with security. The error and influence of these ideas are doubly worth description, for they not only handicapped the rationality of the choices made in fiscal 1950, they have continued to do so in the budgets of later years as well.

The idea of the one right budget is propagated annually in the budget presentations given Congress and the public by administration witnesses. In the effort to persuade others to endorse his choice, the President has little incentive to accent the fact that he had made one, or to lay bare the political struggle behind it. Instead, with varying degrees of success, the effort is made to portray the budget as just right. It may, at times, be admitted that there are areas where it might be desirable to spend more, but even so the amount provided is always "adequate." [2]

The reasons why the size and composition of the budget are not

[2] In this respect the case of the fiscal 1950 budget is hardly unique. See Edward L. Katzenbach, Jr., "Information as a Limitation on Military Legislation: A Problem in National Security," *Journal of International Affairs* (VIII, 2, 1954), p. 200.

matters open to a determinate solution have been discussed at length. But if the budget is not perceived as a problem in choice, one is not likely to be very conscious or rational about the choices that any action on the budget necessarily involves. Thus, the belief on the part of many Congressmen that the Executive had been engaged in the development of the "one right budget" was in part responsible for their failure to solicit information about the alternatives that had been considered and rejected during the course of the Executive's deliberations. Lacking such information, they were in no position to see the character of the choice that the Executive had made, much less reach any judgment on their own about the relative utility of the particular package of men and material before them.

The second major handicap to rational choice on the fiscal 1950 budget was the idea that, if only the Department of Defense were properly organized, an end could be put to interservice rivalry, thereby insuring unified strategic thinking and the saving of the billions wasted through duplication. This search for the "one right organization" is but a variant of the belief in the "one right budget." Both concepts assume that the disputes which divide the services are undesirable and avoidable. Each restricts the rationality of political choice through the presumption that such choice is not necessary.

The passage of a decade since fiscal 1950 has done little to loosen the place of these ideas in the climate of opinion or to change the terminology with which they are expressed. Thus, in 1957 Mahon, still chairman of the House subcommittee, charged that "inordinate jealousy and rivalry" among the services was responsible for the rising military budget. Billions could be saved, Mahon declared, but only if "real unification" took place. In 1958, when President Eisenhower informed Congress of his plans for a reorganization of the Department of Defense, his second, he announced that its most important result would be that "Strategic planning will be unified." The Secretary of Defense, Neil McElroy, advanced only the relatively modest claim that the reorganization might save "hundreds of millions." The savings through reorganization were raised again to billions, however, by the now Senator Symington in a report submitted to President-Elect Kennedy in December 1960. Returning to

Dean Acheson's 1949 solution of a single Chief of Staff, Symington proposed a reorganization of the Department of Defense designed to secure, among other goals, clear, unified war plans determined by "defense interest rather than particular service interest." [3]

The root causes for interservice rivalry, at the level of high budget policy, are the services' "sincere and deeply held differences" in strategic and tactical theory, as the Eberstadt Committee Report correctly noted in the case of the fiscal 1950 budget. The resolution of these differences is not, as Forrestal recognized, simply a matter that awaits the application of an "over-all" strategic point of view. Similarly, while there are a hundred ways that money can be saved by administrative reforms, substantial reductions in the budget, as Johnson discovered when he tried to find $800 million to cut from the fiscal 1950 budget, can be achieved only by changes in strategic programs. However significant the savings that can be effected through such innovations as the "unified" procurement of peanut butter or missile parts, they will necessarily be a fraction of what could be accomplished by eliminating the men or the missiles.

This is not to say that the disputes among the services may not be sharpened and exaggerated by specialized responsibilities for weapons or missions and thereby rendered less amenable to dispassionate discussion and analysis. The subject matter of military doctrine is, moreover, much more likely to breed impassioned zealots than detached theorists, for the choices are those for which the participants must prepare themselves or others to die. Finally, the services, like most human organizations, are not unmoved by a concern for institutional aggrandizement, survival, and stability. The members of a service who are dependent upon it for their pay, promotion, and prestige are bound to identify with the fortunes of their organization, just as its leaders, if they have an interest in the morale and effectiveness of the service, must be alert to the prestige, pay, and promotion it affords its members.

[3] For the Mahon, Eisenhower, and McElroy statements, see, respectively, the New York *Times* for April 27, 1947; April 4, 1948; and June 18, 1958. The text of Symington's report, and his prediction that as much as $8 billion out of a $40-billion budget might be saved, is printed in the New York *Times*, December 6, 1960. See also the account in *ibid.*, February 1, 1960.

Conditions, ramifications, and manifestations such as these may blur, compound, and confuse the matter, but they do not alter it. The origin of the doctrinal disputes among the services lies in the difficulty of the problems to which they are addressed and in the fact that the available tools of analysis cannot yield determinate solutions to them. These differences are intense because they are important, and they exist because no one can demonstrate to the satisfaction of all concerned that *his* theories about how present and future weapons can be used to prevent and win wars are the predictions that reality could or will prove correct.

Given these circumstances, the development and clash of divergent doctrine is unavoidable. This does not mean that analysis and reason are pointless; they must be continually developed and employed. Nor is it to say that choice among doctrines is therefore impossible or undesirable. The point is rather the importance of recognizing that, when choices are made (and dollars "saved" through the decision not to buy the weapons necessary to implement this or that doctrine), the choices will necessarily have a contingent and uncertain character and that, as a result, if they are at all consequential in their policy import, their making will require the exercise of power as well as reason.

What is involved, then, in the question of the organization of the Department of Defense is not a choice between "rivalry" and "unification," but rather a choice among different kinds of political procedures for the making of political choices among conflicting doctrines. The point can be illustrated by reference to one of the more currently popular plans for reorganization, that advanced in 1958 in the report of the Rockefeller Brothers Fund Panel on military security.

The distinguished experts and public servants who served on the Rockefeller Panel found, as did the members of the 1949 Hoover Commission before them, that the development of "an integrated national strategic plan has been beset by interservice rivalry" and that as a result military plans tended "to be a patchwork of compromise . . . or simply the uncoordinated war plans of the several services." The panel declared the cause of interservice rivalry to be the "competitive rather than complementary" character of the roles and missions assigned to the services. These led each to duplicate in part the efforts of others. Both the Navy and the Air Force, for example, had the responsibility of developing tactical air support, and the Army and the Air Force shared responsibility for continental air defense. The panel therefore recommended that all the operational military forces—whether land, sea, or air—be reorganized into unified, "functional" commands: for example, one for the conduct of limited war; one for the conduct of all-out war; and one for the conduct of continental defense.[4]

The panel explained the failure of the Joint Chiefs and the Joint Staff to produce integrated strategic plans on the grounds that they tended "to represent the point of view of a service rather than an over-all approach." The solution proposed was to remove the Joint Chiefs entirely from the planning process and put the Joint Staff on a "unified" basis by reorganizing it along the same functional lines as the operational military forces.[5] The unified Joint Staff and the commanders of the functional forces would be placed under the control of a single officer, the old Chairman of the Joint Chiefs, who would now become the Principal Military Adviser to the Secretary of Defense and the President. These reforms, the panel concluded, would provide the "unity and coherence now absent from our defense organization" and "achieve economies" through the elimination of the duplicating missions of the old services. It would also free

[4] *International Security, The Military Aspect,* Report of Panel II of the Special Studies Project, The Rockefeller Brothers Fund (New York, Doubleday and Company, Inc., 1958), pp. 27–31. Cf. the proposals in Taylor, *The Uncertain Trumpet,* pp. 176–78, and Symington's plan in the New York *Times,* December 6, 1960.

It is worth noting that most such listings of "functional" commands and forces avoid reference to NATO, perhaps because of some uncertainty as to just how its forces would be related to the All-Out War and Limited War Commands.

[5] The Joint Chiefs would retain advisory responsibility with regard to logistics, training, and procurement—the only tasks left to the services. Their analogues under the reorganization, the Commanders of the functional forces, were not, however, to constitute a "Joint Chiefs of Forces."

the Secretary of Defense to play "his full part" in the determination of high military policy, instead of being "burdened with the negative task of trying to arbitrate and control interservice disputes." [6]

The effect of such a reorganization would be quite different from what was apparently expected. Not unity and coherence but dispute and conflict would be the distinguishing characteristics of such a defense establishment. The same doctrinal issues would remain. The rearrangement of power and responsibility would not, for example, do away with the choice between a first and a second strike strategy. What reorganization would change, and it would be a consequential change, would be the political conditions under which these issues would be argued and resolved.

Some of the issues which had formerly been subject to interservice argument and determination would become matters for intracommand argument and determination (for example, the Air Force–Navy dispute over the relative merits of sea as compared to land-launched vehicles for the delivery of a nuclear strike would now take place within the confines of the All-Out War Command). Conversely, other issues formerly subjects of intraservice conflict would now become matters of intercommand dispute (for example, the argument within the Air Force over the allocation of resources between tactical and strategic air forces would now be joined between the All-Out War Command and the Limited War Command). Similarly, some issues that had formerly been matters for intraservice dispute would become matters for intracommand dispute (the bomber versus missile mix in the strategic striking force). Finally, some issues would merely move from the status of interservice dispute to that of intercommand dispute (thus, the Army–Air Force argument over the likelihood of general as compared to limited war and the means for conducting the latter would be taken over by the All-Out War and Limited War Commands).

The change, in short, would be from interservice rivalry to inter-command rivalry, from a Joint Staff and war plans accommodating service points of view to Staff and plans accommodating command points of view, and from budgetary struggles between services to

[6] See *ibid.*, pp. 27, 29, 32–33, 35.

budgetary struggles between commands.[7] This is not to say that the change might not be desirable. There is much to be said, for example, in favor of accentuating the present dispute over the relative priority of strategic and tactical air forces by endowing the disputants with an independent institutional base. But the good that is to be said for it is primarily not in the name of doing away with competition and conflict, but in the name of its desirability as a means of developing, clarifying, and accenting the opportunities for choice. In this sense, the proposed reorganization would be "right for the wrong reasons." On the other hand, those persuaded of the advantages of submarine-launched missiles relative to land-launched missiles might well pause before a reorganization that would deprive the former of its present institutional champion, at least long enough to inquire into the doctrinal views of those who would command the All-Out War Command.

This last point is meant to illustrate the fact that the pros and cons of this or any other reorganization touching on high policy should be discussed not in terms of whether it would bring the Department of Defense closer to the mirage of unification, but in terms of the desirability of having doctrinal conflicts develop and be resolved under one set of political conditions as compared to some other. The design of organization thus turns on the question of which problems one wants to have highlighted by conflict and the question of by whom one wants the critical choices to be made.

By whom should the power of choice be exercised? By a single Chief of Staff? This is an organizational design which may well insure unity of plan and purpose, but whose plans and whose purposes? The possibility of compromise can always be avoided by eliminating all but one party to the dispute. Interestingly enough, both Army and Air Force officials in recent years have proclaimed the virtues of an organization with a single Chief of Staff. No doubt some, like Major General J. B. Medaris, the Commanding General of the

---

[7] Malcolm Hoag, "Some Complexities in Military Planning," *World Politics,* July 1959, pp. 573–78, has made the same point regarding the change from interservice to intercommand conflict and discusses at length the reasons why the proposed reorganization would not ease the complexities of resource allocation.

Army Ballistic Missile Agency during 1956–1960, are persuaded that any one of the services' doctrinal positions would be preferable to the policies that result from the efforts of the Joint Chiefs to compromise among all three. Others, however, are clearly casting the single Chief of Staff in the image of their own doctrine. In this they show the same optimism that Spaatz displayed in the summer of 1949, when he argued the need for a single Chief of Staff in order to keep the nation from the expense of supporting "two air forces with duplicate establishments." Apparently he took it for granted that the single Chief of Staff would not be an Ofstie, Radford, or Denfield.[8]

Should the critical choices be made by the Secretary of Defense? If so, then the analysis of the Rockefeller Panel was topsy-turvy. The so-called "negative task" of arbitrating interservice disputes is the very essence of power. As Paul Appleby pointed out in 1948, a Secretary of Defense interested in enhancing *his* control over policy will see to it that the branches of his organization are roughly equal in power, that they have conflicting and competitive responsibilities, and that he has a civilian staff to aid him in choosing among the alternatives thus thrown up—not a military Chief of Staff to stand between him and the choices to be made.[9]

The choice of organization is a political choice. The "best" organization is that which distributes power and responsibility in such a fashion as to facilitate the policies you favor and make difficult the policies you oppose. To the extent that the organization of the Department of Defense is seen in terms of its relationship to the politics of choice, as a means of selecting among conflicting goals and ideas, a concern with organizational alternatives is hardly a handicap to rational action. It becomes so only when reorganization is seen as a means of somehow avoiding conflict in the first place or as a means that will somehow generate new ideas all by itself.

[8] See Major General J. B. Medaris, *Countdown for Decision* (New York, Paperback Library, Inc., 1961), pp. 49, 231, and Carl Spaatz, "Our Diminishing Air Power," *Newsweek*, August 8, 1949, as quoted in *C.R.*, 95, p. 12302. For expressions from Army and Air Force quarters on the desirability of a single Chief, see Taylor, *The Uncertain Trumpet*, p. 176, and the New York *Times*, May 25, 1957.

[9] Paul N. Appleby, "Civilian Control of a Department of National Defense," in Jerome G. Kerwin, ed., *Civil-Military Relationships in American Life* (Chicago, The University of Chicago Press, 1948), pp. 72–75.

If the idea that there was a determinate answer to the size and composition of the defense budget constituted the fallacy of the "one right figure," and the idea that the disputes among the services could be eliminated was the fallacy of the "one right organization," the idea that $15 billion was all the economy could stand can be considered the fallacy of the "one fixed limit." No perspective was more crippling of rational choice on the fiscal 1950 budget than the belief that it was necessary to keep the budget from rising above the the $15-billion level if the barrel of the economy was not to be burst. The preoccupation with the question of whether the economy was not already at the limit of what it could afford helped to give the budget the shape of a determinate problem, and the size of the limit assumed had the effect of foreclosing automatically on a number of alternatives which might otherwise have seemed rather desirable.

The point was made at the conclusion of Chapter V that the experience of the Korean War effectively demonstrated the fallacy of the idea of a fixed limit. So it did, but the lesson has been little appreciated. The size of the post-Korean budgets was larger, but the terms in which their relation to the economy was discussed changed hardly at all. "Defeat through economic ruin can be as disastrous as defeat through failure at arms." These were the words of an Assistant Secretary of Defense in January 1955, but they could just as easily have been those of a Senator in 1949. Eisenhower's first Secretary of the Treasury, George Humphrey, is reported to have said that "two more years of Truman budgets [Korean War period] would have meant communism in America." Eisenhower, like Forrestal, was concerned lest defense expenditures "become such an intolerable burden as to occasion loss of civilian morale or the individual initiative on which, in a free country, depends the dynamic industrial effort which is the continuing foundation of our nation's security." Finally, it should be noted that the post-Korean climate of opinion continued to hold the "Kremlin's Machiavellian aim" in healthy respect. In June 1960, commenting on the seeming turn for the worse in Soviet-American relations following the collapse of the Paris Summit Conference and the mounting suggestions that the defense budget be increased, the Comptroller of the Defense Department hastened to warn: "To yield to such a temptation could, in effect, play into the Russians' hands for they would like to stampede us into insolvency." [10]

In the years since World War II considerable comment and study have been devoted to the question of how the professional skills and knowledge of the soldier and, more recently, those of the scientist can be best related to and utilized in the making of national security policy. A good case can be made for the proposition that there has been as great a need for an examination of the ways in which the skills and knowledge of that more familiar expert, the economist, have been brought to bear on security policies. One is entitled to wonder if the Truman and Eisenhower administrations could have based their budgets on military or scientific assumptions as far out of line from the generally accepted body of knowledge of those two professions as they were able to do in the case of the economists. It is hard, for example, to conceive of a policy that could have been based for long on the assumption that the nuclear weapon was *not* a revolutionary military development or on the premise that other Powers would *never* achieve it. On these matters the weight of professional military and scientific analysis was agreed and insistent, whatever the differences regarding the military doctrine which should govern the use of the weapon or the rate and ease with which the American monopoly would be broken. In contrast, although they probably had little to recommend them in the judgment of most economists, the expectations of automatic ruin and bankruptcy, and the images of bursting barrels and a totalitarian America, have constituted an integral part of the climate of opinion conditioning both the Truman and the Eisenhower budgets.

The economists, to be sure, have not been completely silent on the subject. Since the end of the Korean War, professional analyses of the economic consequences to be expected from higher defense

[10] Quotations, in order of use, from Assistant Secretary R. W. Lewis, New York *Times,* January 25, 1955; Joseph and Stewart Alsop, *The Reporter's Trade* (New York, Reynal and Company, 1958), p. 93; letter, Eisenhower to Secretary of Defense Wilson, January 5, 1955, New York *Times,* January 6, 1955; and Assistant Secretary F. D. Lincoln, *ibid.,* June 3, 1960. See also Glenn Snyder, pp. 389–90, 477, below.

budgets have been increasingly available. The general burden of this comment can be illustrated by the pioneering work (in the public domain, at least) of Gerhard Colm. Assuming the desirability of providing for the steady growth of the economy and some rise in the standard of living, he has concluded that, starting in any year since 1953, the defense budget could have been increased over a three-year period by a factor of 50 percent without imposing a tax rate much different from that carried in the Korean War and that, under these conditions, the standard of living would have continued to rise at about the same rate as it did during that war.

There is obviously nothing objectively ruinous about these conditions. Indeed, Colm's analysis indicates that an annual increase in the standard of living would have been possible even if the defense budget had been almost doubled during these years. What would have actually happened to production, innovation, management, and investment incentives under such circumstances is not, of course, a matter that can be directly deduced from an estimate of how much higher taxes would have gone or how much lower the rate of increase in per capita consumption would have been. Motivation will turn on people's sense of need, purpose, and accomplishment, and of all the simplifying assumptions behind Colm's analysis, the most vital was his first: that the country had been politically persuaded that higher defense expenditures were worth the costs involved.[11]

The major limit on the size of the defense budget is not how much the economy can "stand" but how much the people can be persuaded to support. To recognize that the limit is political in character, that

---

[11] Gerhard Colm and Marilyn Young, *Can We Afford Additional Programs for National Security,* Planning Pamphlet No. 84, National Planning Association, October 1953, pp. 4, 21–22, 29, 33, 41, and also Colm and Manuel Helzer, "General Economic Feasibility of National Security Programs," mimeographed, March 20, 1957, National Planning Association, pp. 1, 8–9, 16–17.

Since the first draft of this present study was written, there have been a number of notable statements by other economists to this same and related points. See, especially, Arthur Smithies, *The Budgetary Process in the United States* (New York, McGraw-Hill Book Company, Inc., 1955), Chapter 18; Klaus Knorr, "Is the American Defense Effort Enough?" Memorandum Number 14, Center of International Studies, Princeton University, December 23, 1957, pp. 20–29; and Charles J. Hitch and Roland N. McKean, *The Economics of Defense in the Nuclear Age* (Cambridge, The Harvard University Press, 1960), Part L.

it turns on the desire and ability of the administration and Congress to undertake the necessary tasks of persuasion, is to accent the element of choice and to change a seemingly determinate problem into an open one. But such a perspective, while it would enhance both the realism of analysis and the rationality of choice, carries no guarantee that because of it defense budgets would be higher. An administration cannot conduct even a winning campaign to increase the level of expenditures, much less a losing one, without incurring costs to its power and its other purposes. Take the case of the fiscal 1950 budget. A President in Truman's political position in 1948 would have found it hard, in considering the advisability of a higher defense budget, not to halt before Webb's analysis of his chances of persuading Congress to increase taxes or grant him economic controls even if he were not, as Truman was, already convinced that if the economy had to carry for long a budget in excess of $15 billion it would somehow be overtaken by involuntary and inevitable collapse.[12]

The three elements in the climate of opinion previously discussed —the fallacies of the one right budget, the one right organization, and the one fixed limit—prevented more rational decisions by obscuring the extent and necessity of choice. The last to be considered, the tendency to equate secrecy with security, served to handicap the participants' ability to make a rational analysis of the choices they did see.

Rational decisions regarding the size and composition of the armed forces can hardly be made without information about the purposes such forces are to serve and about how variations in those forces can be expected to affect the ability of the military establishment to achieve those purposes. But this is precisely the kind of information that the Soviet Union would like to have in order to

---

[12] Cf. General Ridgway's experience with Eisenhower's first budget. In view of the administration's own expectations about the growth of the gross national product, he "was not greatly impressed with the argument that $2 billion more in the Defense Department budget was going to bankrupt the economy." "The real situation then dawned on me. This military budget was not based so much on military requirements, or on what the economy of the country could stand, as on political considerations." General Matthew B. Ridgway, *Soldier* (New York, Harper and Brothers, 1956), p. 272.

facilitate the rationality of *its* programs and the achievement of *its* purposes. It is true that in the case of the fiscal 1950 budget, and it is probably typical in this respect, a fair amount of the relevant information found its way into the press anyway, but the difference between confronting Soviet intelligence with an anonymous and somewhat inaccurate article in *Fortune* and the sworn testimony of the Joint Chiefs is not insignificant.

The customary resolution of this problem has been to restrict, in the name of security, the availability of such information to those who "need to know." In practice, this has meant that information bearing on the plans and capabilities of the armed services is given limited circulation even within the Department of Defense; still less is available to other Executive Departments and the concerned committees of Congress; and least of all is provided to Congress as a whole and the general public.

There is a value problem here. To the extent that importance is attached to making decisions and the decision-making process matters of public property (on the presumption that they are matters of public consequence), then some sacrifice in security will not only be necessary, it will also be desirable. One cannot simultaneously enjoy both the secrecy characteristic of a Presidium debate and the substance of a government that is supposed to be characterized by autonomous elites competing before an attentive public on all matters of public consequence. There is also a policy problem involved. It is obviously not true that the less the Russians know of American plans and capabilities the better it will be for national security. There are some things which the enemy himself "needs to know" if security policy is to be successful, especially if the object of that policy should be to convince him that he cannot attack you successfully and that you, in turn, do not intend to attack him. But even assuming some resolution of the value problem and the policy problem, there remains still a third, and that is to evaluate the costs and gains of secrecy in terms of the performance of the policy-making process.

The professional military have long been accustomed to assign information on the basis of the "need to know," especially in the planning and conduct of combat operations. At one point during their mutual lament over the "millions of dollars worth of information" that the subcommittee's hearing was making available to the Russians, Bradley explained to Mahon that "I do not want to know a lot of things myself, until the time I need to know them for certain planning." [13] Within an administrative hierarchy, such as one of the armed services, where power and responsibility are relatively fixed and ordered, there are visible criteria for a determination of who needs to know what in order that the goals and programs of the organization can be rationally planned and executed. The assignment of information can be matched with the assignment of power and responsibility. But in a situation where power and responsibility are diffused and overlapping, a condition that prevails whenever military policy is determined in whole or in part through the working of the political process, the criteria for predicting who will need to know what and when are by no means so evident. The guide line easiest to apply, and therefore the most operative, is the criterion of keeping information from the enemy. Thus, information is kept from Congress and the public not so much on the grounds that it is not relevant on occasion to their choices, as it is for the reason that it would then be most easily available to the Russians.

The difficulty with the application of this criterion is that it leads to the weakness rather than the strength of the American political process. There is no way, among autonomous and competing elites, to insure that the exercise of power will be commensurate with knowledge. On the contrary, as the action of Congress on the Air Force increase during fiscal 1950 amply illustrates, when the political process involves the less informed groups in the determination of military policy they will simply exercise their power from ignorance rather than information.

But the price of secrecy is not only to be measured in terms of the irrationality of the policy product. One of the advantages to be gained from a condition in which policy is determined through the interaction of autonomous and competing elites is the opportunity to have rejected alternatives brought up again and again for renewed consideration. That the presence or absence of such opportunities can

[13] *HCA, Hearings 1950 Budget,* IV, 580.

on occasion have great consequence for national security can be
easily illustrated from two incidents in World War II. Hitler's decision to give a low priority to the use of the ME-262 as a jet fighter
was both swift and unsound. In the absence of any independent
power base from which his judgment could be challenged, the
decision stood until it was far too late for a reversal to retrieve the
fortunes of the German Air Force. In contrast, when the scientists
advocating the development of a uranium bomb in the United States
became dissatisfied with the effort the problem appeared to be
receiving in the Navy Dpartment, they took their case to the President, and one can easily imagine what would have happened if
Franklin Roosevelt had proved unresponsive. It would not have been
long before the scientists would have reached the ears of Congressmen and, if necessary, leaked the prospects to commentators, and
thereby have forced the issue back to the President's desk.[14]

The potential of the political process for second-guessing itself can
only be capitalized upon under conditions in which information on
policy alternatives is freely and widely available. In the case of the
fiscal 1950 budget, one of the major causes for the irrationality of the
House's Air Force increase was that it did not know the size of the
atomic stockpile. Had it been made available, the Russians would
have gained some very useful intelligence. But so, too, would the
Congress, and instead of pushing for more bombers, the Mahons and
Cannons might well have prodded the Executive to produce more
bombs. This was, in fact, what the Joint Committee on Atomic
Energy was to do a few years later, when it received access to stockpile data. It appeared (to the committee at least) that, because of the
secrecy in which the Executive had surrounded itself on this matter,
a situation had developed in which the Department of Defense
thought the Atomic Energy Commission was producing all the
bombs it could, and the commission thought it was producing all the
bombs the military wanted, whereas in fact the military did want

[14] See Eugene Emme, *Hitler's Blitz Bomber,* Air University Documentary
Research Study, Maxwell Air Force Base, December 1951, especially pp. 25–
30; Adolf Galland, *The First and The Last* (New York, Ballantine Books,
1954), Chaps. 27–28, especially pp. 257–62; and Arthur H. Compton, *Atomic
Quest* (New York, Oxford University Press, 1956), pp. 25–28, 37.

more bombs and the commission could have produced them. It is unlikely that these conditions would have survived the light of publicity, and whether security was better served by having the Russians guess at the size of a smaller stockpile than it would have been by having them know the size of a larger one would seem at least an arguable point.[15]

THE CHOICE OF POLITICS

The preceding section was meant to show how a change in four of the key perspectives that made up the climate of opinion could have had considerable consequence for the kind of choices made in the fiscal 1950 budget. The question to be discussed in this section—whether and how changes in the policy process could have affected those choices—is more difficult to answer. Certainly, as seen in the first section of these conclusions, the structure of the policy process (how power and responsibility were distributed among the participants) was responsible for much that might, from hindsight, be found objectionable in the character of the budget's choices. But to describe the extent to which the policy process shaped those choices is not necessarily tantamount to identifying the opportunities that existed for changing them.

The opportunities for affecting budget policy by changes in the budgeting process are, in fact, quite limited. Changes in the distribution of power and responsibility among the participants in the budgeting process can modify the kinds of interests and skills they will bring to the budget problem or alter the influence exercised by

[15] The same point can be made in reference to the pre-sputnik decisions of the Eisenhower administration to assign a low priority to the American effort to put a satellite into orbit. It is doubtful if these decisions would have stood if their content and reasoning had been a matter of public record at the time.

The considerations responsible for the size of the stockpile at this time were actually more complex than the Joint Committee's perspective would suggest, especially as to the factors behind the military requirements. The point, however, remains the same: as soon as the committee secured information about these matters, it began to press with energy and success for a greatly expanded stockpile. These and other consequences of the secrecy surrounding early atomic energy policy will be developed in the present author's forthcoming study of the decision in 1950 to accelerate the effort to make an H-bomb.

those interests and skills, but they cannot in themselves generate a whole new set of ideas about foreign and military policy. Neither can such changes revolutionize the American political process or transform the nature of the budget problem. There is no possibility of changing the basic structure of the policy elites; they will remain autonomous and competing. Similarly, there is no way in which those engaged in the determination of the budget can escape from conflicts of interest and premise and use of political power to resolve them. It would, therefore, be unrealistic to expect that the fiscal 1950 budget or any other could have avoided having its content marked by the policy symptoms that result from these conditions.

The effects that can be produced by rearranging the distribution of power and responsibility among the participants in the budgeting process are, then, almost inevitably modest. They are also likely to be uncertain in consequence and normative in character. Uncertainty is insured by the fact that power and responsibility are usually assigned not just to individuals for the moment, but to offices and institutions over time, and, as the actions of Forrestal and Johnson illustrate, there can be considerable difference in the way officials choose to interpret the responsibilities or exercise the powers of their office. As for the desirability of any given change in the policy process, the point made earlier in connection with the organization of the Department of Defense holds true for all variations in political structure. The prescription of what constitutes a "good change" cannot be divorced from a conception of what constitutes "good policy."

These general points can best be illustrated by turning to the choices Congress made on the fiscal 1950 budget and the question of how they might have been affected by changes in the budgeting process. Perhaps the most obvious that comes to mind is the possibility of a change in character of the budget presentation that was made to the appropriations committees. The potential influence of Congressmen on high budget policy and the rationality of their choices would have been greatly enhanced if the administration witnesses had identified the alternative budgets they had earlier considered and spelled out their conception of the welfare and security consequences of each. Had such a procedure been followed in the case of fiscal 1950, the kind of information that would have been made available would at least have altered significantly the actions Congress took on the Air Force and the Navy increases. Needless to say, as these instances make clear, the immediate consequences of such a change would not have been equally welcomed by all the parties concerned.

There is historical precedent for a budgeting procedure of this order. At the onset of the Wilson administration, the Secretary of the Navy, Josephus Daniels, instituted the practice of permitting the officers of the Navy to go before Congress and state, without restraint or reprisal, both the extent and urgency of their budgetary requirements and the particulars wherein they found the budget submissions of the President wanting. On his own part, Daniels presented the budget he and Wilson had determined the Navy should receive (which before 1915 was usually about half as much as the Admirals requested) and endeavored to explain the reasons for the President's decision. This procedure, obviously, was one which did more than optimize the opportunity for rational choices on the part of Congress. It also provided Congressmen with the professional arguments and experts with which to try to build a consensus powerful enough to challenge the President's choices.

Daniels initiated this procedure for two major reasons. First, his theory of the political process was one which assigned great importance to the coordinate power of Congress with regard to the budget. Second, by encouraging the Admirals to testify freely as to *past* as well as present demands, he was able to deflate the image of the preceding Republican administrations as having been more zealous in their concern for American naval power than the Democratic Congressmen of those years. Daniels was able to follow this procedure without incurring serious challenge to Wilson's own budgets because, even with the open support of the Admirals, there was at first no prospect of an effective consensus being formed in favor of higher budgets. After the war started in Europe, and before Wilson determined on rearmament himself, the possibility of challenge did arise. To meet it, Daniels prohibited certain statements of naval need which he thought might be especially politically embarrassing. The Admirals consented to this selective restriction out of fear that, if they refused to comply, Daniels would revert to the practice of preceding administrations and not permit them to speak out at all about the need for programs larger than those endorsed by the President.[16]

As Daniels' actions illustrate, the desirability of presenting alternative budgets to Congress and permitting military witnesses to testify freely about their consequences is hardly a politically neutral issue. While such a procedure would advance the power and interests of some politicians (especially in Congress), it would come at considerable cost to that of others (especially in the administration). Congress houses a number of men whose daily preoccupation is the search for means to undermine the prestige and programs of the President. The sensitivity of Presidents on this score is well exemplified by the remarks Forrestal recorded from a Cabinet meeting in December 1946.

> The President expressed the hope that all members of the Cabinet would support the budget as submitted, because otherwise, he said, we would expose ourselves to sniping from the Republicans, particularly in the House.[17]

If a President were to submit alternative budgets to the Congress, along with the reasons for rejecting as well as choosing each, he would arm his critics with the ammunition to use against his own choices.

The rationale behind the effort to secure the silence of the military with regard to their differences with the President's budget is compounded of the same considerations. As the "experts" on national defense, the words of the military carry great weight in the budget debate. The objections and reservations of military experts, if available to Congress and the public, would make more difficult the task of the President and his representatives to persuade them to

[16] See "Civil-Naval Politics in World War I," *World Politics,* July 1955, pp. 581–89.

[17] Millis, ed., *The Forrestal Diaries,* p. 237.

support the budget, and, conversely, they would make easier the task of those who would seek to persuade Congress and the public that the budget should not be supported. Thus, when Truman made his May decision in favor of the $15-billion ceiling, he told the Chiefs that he expected "every member of the administration to support it fully, both in public and in private." Similarly, in 1959, the armed services received a memorandum from the Budget Bureau enjoining them to "carefully avoid volunteering views different from the budget, either on or off the record." [18]

In addition to the difficulties this procedure causes the members of Congress interested in reviewing or changing items in the President's budget, it also creates rather complex problems for the military witnesses. They are pulled in three directions, as the testimony in 1957 of Lieutenant General James Gavin, Chief of Army Research and Development, illustrates.

We have seen our Army deteriorate steadily . . . program after program denied support, and then you see we come before a committee on the Hill and we try to defend a budget we don't believe in, and yet we try to be honest with you about it and serve our masters across the river and it is entirely untenable.
One can't continue to do this sort of thing, and I am sincere in saying I did not want to come before Congress one more year.

Gavin, as a result of this and other frustrations, resigned. Few officers take this route. Their conditioning with regard to organization and command runs against it. As General Nathan Twining, Chairman of the Joint Chiefs of Staff in 1958, explained to the committee that had heard Gavin:

If you are a military man, you can say it [the budget] is inadequate and turn in your suit. We do not play in the military that way. . . .
In the military terminology, a commander [the President] has made a decision [the budget]. If everybody starts bucking it, it is just no good, you have no military system left.

On the other hand, Twining saw no more merit than Gavin in affirming that the budget was adequate: ". . . if [the military man] says it is adequate, he has more or less perjured himself." Twining's

[18] New York *Times*, January 14, 1959.

solution was that the Congressional committees should stop asking the military if the President's budget was adequate: ". . . you know the rules just as well as I do. I think it is a hell of a note."

The reaction of Senator Symington to Twining's suggestion was negative.

If the idea is that when you come up before this committee, once the Commander in Chief says "This is it," we have no right to ask you, as a military man, what your opinion is. On that basis I think it is only a question of time before the Soviets will have us in their clutches.

The people cannot act unless they and their representatives have the right to know.[19]

The conclusion that the military should be free to speak out before Congress has also been advanced by Generals Matthew Ridgway and Maxwell Taylor, who served respectively as Chief of Staff of the Army during 1953–55 and 1955–59. Ridgway, in his "farewell" letter to the Secretary of Defense in 1955, argued that a military adviser should never be asked, as he had been, to support in public policies which he had previously argued against in private. Taylor, noting the military adviser's dilemma between the "position of either appearing to oppose his civilian superiors or of withholding facts from the Congress," announced that he had "found no way of coping with the situation other than by replying frankly to [Congressional] questions and letting the chips fall where they may." Taylor also suggested that form could be brought more in line with reality if the Joint Chiefs were designated the legal military advisers to the Congress as well as to the President.[20]

Of the answers to the problem suggested by these officers, Gavin's meets the dilemma of the witness by suggesting that he leave Washington. Twining's and Ridgway's solve the dilemma by removing a horn. If Congress did not ask, or if the President did not demand, there would be no problem—for the military. But these solutions come at the price of adding greatly to the problems of one of the

[19] For this and the preceding statements, see *Inquiry Into Satellite and Missile Programs*, Hearings before the Preparedness Investigating Subcommittee of the Committee on Armed Services, United States Senate, 85th Cong., 1st and 2d Sess. (Washington, 1958), pp. 1499, 1844–45, 1849.

[20] Ridgway, *Soldier*, p. 331, and Taylor, *The Uncertain Trumpet*, pp. 113–14.

other parties: either Congress must accept a severe handicap in its effort to reach independent judgments about the budget, or the President a severe handicap in his effort to secure the adoption of his budget. The one description of how to live with the dilemma, that of Taylor—answer the question and let the chips fall where they may—belittles somewhat the force of the pressures involved. Much depends on the kind of answers given and the size of the chips that fall.

As Symington's own testimony during fiscal 1950 indicates, the answers of even the bold may not always be the most forthright. The techniques available to Secretaries and Chiefs for harassing and inhibiting the junior officers who on occasion speak out are many and effective.[21] As for Chiefs of Staff themselves, the circumstances under which both Ridgway and Taylor ended their tours of duty (coupled with their failure to improve the Army's situation) would indicate that at a minimum an administration can make object lessons of them. The Forrestals may not always be followed by the Johnsons, but the dynamics of the situation point in that direction.

On balance, a change to the procedure of World War I seems an unlikely prospect. The conditions under which Daniels decided to "free" his Admirals are not readily comparable to those which have prevailed since the end of World War II.[22] The arguments advanced for such a change, as noted, focus only on the gains for the military and Congress. They do not confront the question of what kind of considerations could be advanced to persuade a President to incur the costs such a course would involve for his interests.

In all probability, if an administration did decide to free its military, the consequences would not be revolutionary. Congress would be unlikely to alter greatly the gross size of the military budget in any given year—if only out of recognition that too great an alteration would require a rearrangement of the whole budget, a task which Congress is by no means equipped to undertake. The impact of the procedure would more likely take two forms. There would be

[21] See *Inquiry Into Satellite and Missile Programs*, pp. 1470, 1502.
[22] For an argument to the contrary, see Katzenbach, "Should Our Military Leaders Speak Up?" New York *Times* Magazine, April 15, 1956, p. 36.

much more of what Congress already does in part: the rearranging of sums among and within the services. (At least some of the military would find a state of "freedom" to be not without its costs.) The second consequence would be to weaken the gyroscopic tendencies of the defense budget. The free testimony taken one year would register its maximum impact in the form of pressure for changes in the budget for the next and following years, for either more or less money as the case might be.

There would appear to be little in these consequences that would strike a President as advancing his purposes. He is unlikely to see much virtue in jeopardizing the rationality of his decisions in order to enhance those of Congressmen, and if he is determined on changes in the size or composition of the defense budget he is likely to want to see them occur at times and for reasons of his own choosing. Whatever his general beliefs about the desirability of having a Congress to second-guess his policies, a President's immediate interests will be in his programs of the moment, and these will lead him to demand that they be supported and defended by his subordinates. The interests of the President, however, are not the same as the interests of Chiefs or Secretaries, and, as was seen in the case of fiscal 1950, Presidential demands are not always met with compliance. An end to semi-open campaigns or revolts against Presidential budget policy is therefore as unlikely a prospect as an end to all restraints on testimony. In sum, there would seem to be no clear and easy way for the military to escape Gavin's three-way pull. The "politics of testimony" are built into the system.

Although political considerations thus point against the probability of a change in the manner of the budget's presentation, most of the consequences that might be expected from such a change could be approximated if the committees were to change the way in which they respond to the presentation they do receive. The salient features of the Congressional choice in fiscal 1950—the passive acceptance of the major provisions of the budget and the irrational and ineffectual character of the decisions that were made on the few items which were questioned—were in no little part the result of the kind of analysis its committees gave the budget. They made no effort to explore the central diplomatic, military, and fiscal issues involved, to establish a meaningful relation between the force levels provided and war plans, or to develop the consequences which might be expected from alternative expenditures. There was instead an elaborate discussion of the policy trivia of the budget.

The available evidence would indicate that the analytical character of the fiscal 1950 performance was by no means untypical. The same characteristics—the lack of attention to high policy and the preoccupation with details—have been observed in such otherwise disparate examples as the naval budget for fiscal 1915 and the defense budget for fiscal 1955. Nor can much change be detected in the hearings held on the fiscal 1961 budget by Mahon's committee (expanded by then from 5 to 16 members and aided by 8 instead of 2 full-time staff assistants). Relative to fiscal 1950, the committee was perhaps more alert to the strategic issues of the budget, but it was no more rigorous or extensive in its analysis of those issues, and its time was even more thinly spread because of a marked increase in the amount of attention given to the performance characteristics of various weapons, vehicles, and other devices under development by the armed services.[23]

The persistence of this pattern is not hard to understand. Although by declaration of intent, demonstrated effort, and the mere fact of their action or inaction on the budget, the appropriations committees have become central participants in the determination of military policy, the opportunities open to them to influence the high policy of

[23] For the fiscal 1915 and fiscal 1955 budgets, see, respectively, "Civil-Naval Politics in World War I," *World Politics*, July 1955, p. 585, and Katzenbach, "How Congress Strains at Gnats, Then Swallows Military Budgets," *Reporter*, July 20, 1954, pp. 31–35.

The points made about the fiscal 1961 budget are based on the present author's reading of *Department of Defense Appropriations for 1961*, Hearings before the Subcommittee of the Committee on Appropriations, House of Representatives, 86th Cong., 2d Sess., 7 vols. (Washington, 1960). The fact that the committee's report endorsed a preemptive strike strategy, while its hearings contained practically no discussion of such a strategy or its alternatives, is reminiscent of the treatment given to the Air Force increase in fiscal 1950. For examples of the "discussion," see *ibid.*, II, 233, 238, 240, 283, and VII, 71–73, 85–86, 104, 115–16, 127. For the endorsement, see House Report No. 1561, *Department of Defense Appropriation Bill, 1961*, 86th Cong., 2d Sess. (Washington, 1960), p. 8. See also the New York *Times*, April 25, 1960.

the budget are not great. The electorate neither spurs Congress on to act on the strategic issues of the budget nor provides, as a result, a point of leverage for use against the President on such issues. So long as the President can keep his experts in line, the committees may find it difficult to discover the alternatives hidden in the budget and find it even more difficult to persuade anyone that choices other than those expressed in it would have been better. And even if a majority of Congressmen should be so persuaded, their immediate power is only the negative one of denial.

Add to these circumstances the other factors previously discussed (the limitations in ability, staff, time, and information; the restrictive effect of the climate of opinion; and the political character of the hearings), and it is easy to see how the committees are led to forgo a comprehensive review of the major budget issues and (aside from the attention given to one or two particulars where they may see both some need and some chance for change) to let their curiosities be captured by the increasingly fascinating gadgets to be found in the nation's armories and to concentrate their energies on discharging their traditional watchdog function with regard to the prices in budget programs. The end result, however, has tended to be the collection of information more useful to weapons specialists than statesmen and a compulsive auditing of the Executive's accounts which is penny-wise and policy foolish and more suited to clerks than politicians.

The budgeting change that might be made here involves not so much a change in the responsibilities of the appropriations committees as a reconsideration of the manner in which those responsibilities can be met. The committees can hardly be expected to ignore their time-honored responsibility for appraising the costs of military programs, but it would seem feasible for them to be much more selective in their inquiries to this end. The returns from plodding through the price of overcoats, *and* the price of oats, *and* the price of .22 calibre ammunition, *and* hundreds of similar items are surely meager and diminishing. An alternative would be to break completely with the traditional program-by-program and item-by-item scrutiny of the budget. Instead of endeavoring to review the whole of the budget for instances of waste, mismanagement, and the like, the committees could restrict their search to a limited number of budget areas, selected secretly each year on the basis of both random techniques and prior staff investigations. This procedure might not turn up as many budget "horribles" or keep the Executive quite as "honest" as the present approach, but it would serve to remove most of the tempting details of the budget from the committees' attention and thereby make available the time required for a more careful consideration of the policy issues at stake.

In so far as the high policy of the budget is concerned, the committees may conceivably be taking too short a view of their political opportunities. In acting as a watchdog over budget accounts, they have necessarily focused their attention on the budget immediately before them. Waste and mismanagement that go "uncorrected" in any given budget are, for all practical purposes, Executive actions about which nothing more can be done. It is possible that because of the force of this precedent the committees have also tended to cast their policy concerns and options in terms of the budget at hand. Certainly, so long as their attention is restricted to the budget before them, their opportunity to influence its content will seem minimal, and their incentive to review that content will be accordingly small. Such a focus, however, would be a significant error. For unlike the dollars at issue in the budget, which once appropriated are then spent, the policy issues involved will return again and again to the committees' purview. The opportunity to influence the outcome of these issues must be measured, therefore, by what can be accomplished in not one but several sessions of Congress.

The committees might do well, then, to change their policy target from the budget to the climate of opinion that shaped it. As was pointed out earlier, the influence Congress exercises on the budget cannot be gauged solely by reference to committee recommendations or floor debates and votes. Far more consequential is the influence Congressmen exercise by virtue of their contribution to the general climate of opinion regarding desirable and possible defense expenditures. This climate heavily conditions Executive and Congressional choices alike. The relevance of the point for the committees' approach to the budget is that it is today's hearing which contributes to tomorrow's climate of opinion. Seen in these terms, a committee intent on influencing the high policy of the budget could undertake a serious review of the alternatives involved, not in the expectation that there would be any opportunity thereby to effect major changes in that budget, but in the knowledge that the effort would make possible some change in and control over the opinions which would otherwise prevail at the time of the determination of the next budget and the ones thereafter.

The obstacles in the path of such a change are many. Congressmen who see the budget as a determinate problem would not see the point of the effort, and those who equate security with secrecy would be unable to undertake it. There will also be Congressmen who will be no more willing to assume a greater responsibility for high budget policy than Presidents will be willing to help them get it. Finally, even if Congressmen were to conclude that they had been underestimating their potential influence on high budget policy, they might still hesitate to exchange the immediate and relatively certain gains to be had from their traditional scrutiny of the budget's details for the prospect of exercising an uncertain and indirect influence on the high policy of some future budget. Given these circumstances, a radical change in the committees' approach to the budget is probably as unlikely a development as a change in the manner of the budget's presentation.

In the case of the Executive choices on the fiscal 1950 budget, analysis must proceed somewhat differently than was the case with Congress. It is possible at least to conceive of changes in the budgeting process which would have altered some of the choices that Congress made. But it is difficult to see equivalent possibilities for change in the choices made by the Executive. In the case of the Executive's action on the budget, the limits on the extent to which policy can be affected by changes in the policy process become all too evident.

The outstanding characteristic of the budget Truman sent to Congress was that it provided too little money for the wrong kind of world. From hindsight, it is clear that this was the result of four major fallacies: the idea that the Russians would not get the A-bomb until 1952; the idea that it would be feasible in the immediate future to restore the European balance of power; the idea that World War III was the only major military contingency for which the services needed to budget; and the idea that $15 billion was all the economy could afford to spend on defense. These were the premises that shaped most of the content of the budget, and they were responsible for most of what was "wrong" with it.

The point to be made about these ideas is important and simple. There was no way in which the budget could have been rescued from these errors as a result of changes in the Executive's budgeting process. There were no key offices or departments possessing skills and information relevant to these issues which were shut out of the decision-making process, nor, so far as the available evidence would indicate, were there any key officials in such offices and departments who were bursting with different ideas and frustrated in an effort to voice them. The policy deficiencies of the fiscal 1950 budget were, in short, the result of failures in political conception not the product of peculiarities in political structure.

Paradoxically enough, if the procedures employed by the Executive in fashioning the budget are viewed in terms of their potential contribution to rational decision-making, it is hard to see how they could have been improved. In essence, the development of the fiscal 1950 budget involved four major actions. First, the President, in conjunction with the Bureau of the Budget and the Department of the Treasury, developed an estimate of what he thought he could provide for defense given the other programs for which he was responsible and his general fiscal and political policies. Secondly, the services developed an estimate of what they thought they would require given the programs and policies they believed necessary to meet their responsibilities. The difference between these two estimates ($14.4 billion and $23.6 billion) was much too great to provide a meaningful basis for further analysis and negotiation, as was only to be expected in view of the divergent criteria through which the figures had been reached. The potential rationality of the President's choice was therefore greatly enhanced by the third step: the development by the Joint Chiefs of alternative budgets ($16.9 billion and $14.4 billion) and the effort that was made to describe the consequences of these alternative budgets in terms of the services' ability to carry out their war plans. Finally, the Secretary of State was also alerted to these alternatives, and he in turn provided the President with a judgment as to how they would affect the problems and opportunities that confronted the nation's foreign policy.

So far as they went, and seen thus in outline, the fiscal 1950 procedures were quite sophisticated. That is to say, they had a very high potential for enabling the participants to be aware of what they were doing: to know the problems they faced, the purposes they wished to serve, the alternatives open to them, and the character of the process through which their choices were being made.

This potential, however, was never realized. The procedures through which the Executive fashioned the fiscal 1950 budget may have been sophisticated, but the ideas the participants had about the point and value of those actions were not. The perspectives with which they viewed those procedures limited their insight into their own actions and severely restricted the contribution that the procedures actually made to the sophistication of their choices. It is here in the content of these perspectives that the analogue can be found to Congress' action on the budget. For if the choices of Congress could have been changed by different procedures (either in the manner of the budget's presentation or in their approach to it), those of the Executive could have been affected by different ideas about the procedures they had. This statement is not meant to contradict the previous conclusion that the Executive's action on the budget was the result of errors in political conception which could not have been altered by changes in the policy process. As will be seen, some of the same ideas that conditioned the major choices of the budget were also responsible for shaping the perspectives the participants had about the procedures through which it was developed.

The development of the $23.6-billion estimate is a case in point. This could have been an act of considerable analytical value. It not only provided the military with a sense for what their plans and policies might actually entail in men and material, it could also have served as a means of flagging the attention of the President and Congress to the possible costs of a $14.4-billion budget. But instead of being welcomed as useful contributions to rational analysis, the $30 and $23.6-billion estimates were viewed as alarming indications of the insensitivity of the military to the state of the economy, Presidential policy, and the Kremlin's objective of victory by bankruptcy. The effect of the estimates was not to stimulate a close look at the President's ceiling but to kindle demands for new procedures which would make military planners more appreciative of the costs of their programs. Thus, the Eberstadt Committee Report urged the need to indoctrinate the services into recognizing "the fact that the strength of the Nation's economy is directly related to the Nation's defense strength. . . ." Similarly, in discussing the advantages of a single Chief of Staff, the Minority Report of the Hoover Commission observed that among them was the prospect that he would become familiar with "national economic considerations" and make the services "more economy-minded than they now are."

As these words suggest, from the idea that the state of the economy is as great if not a greater factor in determining national security as the state of the armed forces, it is but a short step to the idea that the state of the economy is a military factor and ought, therefore, to be incorporated into the thinking of the military when they draft their budget. As can be seen in Professor Snyder's study, in the Eisenhower administration a determined effort was made to make the Joint Chiefs take this step, and as the Minority Report anticipated, the Chairman proved to be a ready and willing instrument to this end.[24] Thus, in 1954 the Chairman of the Joint Chiefs of Staff, the then Admiral Radford, described the difference between his own and his colleagues' approach to the budget as follows:

. . . the difference comes as to whether we agreed to accept the fact that the national economy over the long pull is a military factor, and

[24] Those among the military who stand closest to the Secretary are the most likely to become vulnerable to his regard for costs. See the difference in the perspectives among Daniels' Admirals noted in "Civil-Naval Politics in World War I," *World Politics,* July 1955, pp. 586–87.

therefore the Chiefs would get estimates of the national income and make an assumption as to the amount that might be allocated for defense, or whether in so doing we were in fact accepting a directive to follow that procedure. . . .

Without any reservation, I subscribe to the theory that as military men, in trying to work out plans for the long pull . . . we must take economic factors into consideration. I did not feel in this case that we were operating under a ceiling or directive. We were merely taking notice of what we thought could be made available without any assurance, of course, that we could get it.

From figures we obtained on prospective national income over the long pull, we eliminated the more or less fixed expenses, and within the remaining estimated amount, we did feel—at least I did, and I thought the others did—that we came up with a military program which was adequate for the security of the United States. The question as to whether we did that voluntarily or under a directive I think is the real point at issue.[25]

Radford's reasoning can be contrasted with that of Bradley on the same point. When he testified, as Chairman of the Joint Chiefs of Staff, in support of the budget for fiscal 1951, Bradley declared that the Chiefs hoped that succeeding budgets would plug up its vulnerable parts. If it were not for this hope, he declared, "the appropriation request which we would have to recommend would be all out of proportion to that which we believe this country could afford at this time." Several years later, Bradley announced that he could no longer agree with the position he had taken. His testimony, he declared, was

. . . outside the responsibility of the nation's military advisers. We have no way of knowing what this country *will* afford or its economy *can* afford. Only the economic advisers and the civilian advisers, including Congress, can make that estimate and that decision, and certainly our military recommendations on forces we need should not be curbed in any way by economic assumptions.[26]

The two procedures provide a good illustration of the normative element to be found in most alterations in the budgeting process.

[25] *Department of Defense Appropriations for 1955*, Hearings before the Subcommittee of the Committee on Appropriations, United States Senate, 83d Cong., 2d Sess. (Washington, 1954), p. 83.
[26] Bradley, "A Soldier's Farewell," *Saturday Evening Post*, August 22, 1953, pp. 63–64.

Measured against the value of rational analysis, there is much to be said for Bradley's later view. All aside from the fact that the military have no mandate to speak for public wants or other government needs, their professional skills and knowledge are hardly such as to prepare them for the task of predicting the consequences for such wants and needs that would result from this or that size military budget. (On this point Radford's description of the intellectual process followed in fiscal 1955 speaks eloquently.) For his part, a President risks much in denying himself an unrestricted estimate of his possible military needs and analytically he gains little, for an administration is well equipped with alternative agencies to perform, and perform more effectively, the "costing" operations that Radford's procedure asks of the military.

Seen in terms of the politics of the defense budget, however, the choice between the two procedures may be something else again. The military do not develop their estimates in a political vacuum (the $30-billion estimate contained Symington's interservice "additive," and the size of the $16.9-billion alternative was chosen with an eye to what the President might possibly accept). Neither are the other participants likely to be blind to the policy implications of military budgeting procedures. If the military assume the responsibility of incorporating costs, their worst enemy, into their initial budgetary calculations, they will obviously end up with smaller estimates than if they did not. Accordingly, just as an administration intent on reducing the level of defense expenditures may find persuasive value (if not sense) in the concept of a limited and vulnerable economy, so too it may find political utility in a military budgeting procedure that will expose the policy elites to professional arguments for lower rather than higher budgets and to choices among fewer rather than more alternatives.

The interrelationship among perspective, procedure, and policy is similarly evident in the case of the State Department's action on the fiscal 1950 budget. Analytically, the relevance of foreign policy considerations for the choices that confront the Department of Defense is matched only by the relevance of military considerations for the problems and policies of the Department of State. The determination of the fiscal 1950 budget was certainly reflective of this condition, for Marshall was far from uninvolved in the major policy issues of the budget. The attitude of detached neutrality that characterized the State Department's approach to the budget choices of the late 1950's can be seen foreshadowed, however, in Kennan's rather ambiguous memorandum on the relationship between the defense budget and foreign policy and in Forrestal's desperate pursuit of Marshall with regard to the choice between the $14.4-billion and the $16.9-billion budgets.[27]

The major question which Forrestal wanted the State Department to answer was, to be sure, unanswerable. Marshall had no reliable way of specifying what kind of armed forces his foreign policy would require. About problems of this order, only informed guesses can be made. Nevertheless, the budget does represent an operational answer, and since the basic rationale of the armed forces is to serve the nation's foreign policy, the logic whereby the burden for making those guesses is placed upon the Department of Defense is by no means immediately apparent. This is not to say that Marshall did not in the end put his judgment on the line, for he did. In the mere fact of his action, the determination of the fiscal 1950 budget was more sophisticated than were apparently some that came after it. But it is to be noted that Marshall expressed his judgment on alternatives which he had no part in shaping and through an ad hoc procedure which was not at his initiative. The reasons for this action were many, but not the least among them was his belief that the doctrinal issues which divided the services were not matters on which the Department of State should responsibly intervene. This was a perspective of no little consequence, for the procedures of State-Defense collaboration it entailed were such as to rule out the strategic heart of the budget as a subject for State Department influence.

As the three studies in this volume illustrate, the attention with which the State Department has followed the development of the

[27] Taylor described the State Department's attitude toward the budget debates in 1956 and 1957 as one of "curious detachment"; they looked upon it as a "fire across the river." *The Uncertain Trumpet*, p. 55. See also Glenn Snyder, p. 435, below.

defense budget since World War II and the actions it has taken on that budget have varied greatly, depending on the personal interests, experiences, and enthusiasms of the Secretaries involved. The participation of the department in budget policy has been at best, however, intermittent and selective. Somewhat symbolic of the relationship is the fact that since 1945 not one Secretary of State has appeared before a military appropriations committee to discuss the relationship between the budget and the nation's foreign policy. Marshall was once asked to do so, but he declined on the grounds that it might be "misinterpreted as an effort by him to introduce immediately a military factor into his work." [28]

The dissatisfaction with the character of this relationship has been both analytical and normative in its source. So long as the Secretary of State is given the responsibility of being the President's chief agent in national security policy, rational policy would seem to require that he and his department take an active and influential part in the determination of military policy. The need to make certain that military preparations are consistent with the State Department's conception of the security problems that confront the nation cannot be met solely by procedures for review and communication. The process of "coordination" will also require the exercise of power and choice, as can be seen from such instances as Marshall's belief in the spring of 1948 that the rearmament desired by the Joint Chiefs would provoke rather than deter the Russians, and Kennan's concern in the summer of 1949 that in concentrating on general war preparations the defense budget was neglecting what he considered the more likely Russian strategy of limited aggressions.

The normative interest in seeing the State Department assume a larger role in the determination of military policy has been the result of dissatisfaction with particular policy decisions and the expectation that they might have been made differently if the State Department had been more involved. (Those who were pleased with the decisions are less likely to be dissatisfied with the degree of the State Department's involvement.) Needless to say, the two considerations are easily mixed. Thus, Forrestal's letter to Marshall reflected

[28] Millis, ed., *The Forrestal Diaries*, pp. 238–39.

a genuine conviction that the armed forces were properly conceived as instruments for Marshall's foreign policy. In the writing of the letter, however, he was obviously spurred by the hope that the nature of Marshall's interests would provide him with the ally he needed to turn the tide of battle against the military's natural enemies, the Bureau of the Budget and the Department of the Treasury.[29]

However strong the interest in having the State Department assume more responsibility for military policy and exercise more power in its formulation, it is not a change that will be easily made. This the history of the last 15 years makes clear. As in the case of the appropriations committees, if a change is to occur it must first take place in the manner in which department officials define their responsibilities and identify their opportunities for meeting them. In the effecting of such transformations, if not in personnel of the department at least in their ideas, there is little that changes in the mechanisms of the policy process can contribute. The best that procedural mechanisms can do is to facilitate the efforts of Secretaries already inclined to take a more active part in defense policy and impose obligations on those who are not.

Within these limits, there would appear to be merit in the suggestion that the President be required to deliver a separate annual report to the Congress on the subject of long-range security policy. The Secretary of State could be assigned the responsibility for assisting the President in preparing the report and the responsibility for testifying on its behalf before Congress. If the report obliged the President to survey the likely political, military, economic, and scientific developments of the future, to indicate the changes in current policies and programs that might be required to meet those developments, and to assess the resources the government would require to implement such new policies and programs in terms of

[29] Taylor, for example, clearly hoped for more help from the State Department in his disputes with Air Force doctrine. See *The Uncertain Trumpet*, pp. 55–60, 82–83, 87. For an exposition of the doctrine of the Secretary of State as the chief agent in national security policy and the consequent importance of his concerning himself actively with military policy, see the testimony of Paul Nitze, *Organizing for National Security Hearings*, pp. 859–60, 863, 883.

those both currently and potentially available to it, the Department of State might conceivably be led into a wide variety of policy areas where it is now only sporadically or superficially involved.[30]

There is something to be said for such a report simply for the pressures it might create for more systematic forward planning and for the more flexible views it might stimulate about the resources available for government programs. The fiscal 1950 budget was not the last to be based on a false picture of the future and a rigid conception of what the economy could afford. A report of this order could also weaken the gyroscopic tendencies of the budgeting process, especially if it were delivered in June, for it would then be prepared when programs and budget estimates are most fluid and the opportunity to turn the report into a justification of current budget policy would be at its minimum. Finally, while the obligation to draft a report of this order would not automatically turn the Department of State into an advocate of higher defense budgets, it could involve the department so intimately in the plans and programs of the military that the department would find it difficult to avoid taking some stand on budget issues, and the character of its own responsibilities would tend to make that stand more favorable than that to be expected from any other government agency.

These are impressive possibilities, but they are no more than that. The assignment of responsibility will not determine the manner in which it is exercised, nor can the allocation of power insure its use. Furthermore, they have nothing at all to do with the kind of ideas officials may have about the world in which they live or what may happen in it. The full measure of these limits can be seen in the case of the fiscal 1950 budget, for if such a report had been in effect preceding its determination, the central choices of that budget would probably have been affected little if at all.

The last Executive procedure to be examined is the development of alternative budgets by the Joint Chiefs. On the face of it, this was an act of great analytical utility. By listening to the presentation of

[30] For the need for an annual "requirements" report, see Senator Henry M. Jackson, "Organizing for Survival," *Foreign Affairs*, April 1960, pp. 455–56. The form and content of the report suggested above represents a substantial variation on Senator Jackson's suggestion.

the security consequences of both a $14.4-billion budget and a $16.9-billion budget, the President could get a far better idea of the military import of his ceiling than if he had received only the first. Then, depending upon his evaluation of the consequences of spending $2.5 billion more, he could either abide by the ceiling or reconsider it and, in this event, take a second look at the costs he would incur by reducing his other programs or increasing the size of his total budget.

This face was false. The presentation of the alternatives at the December 9 conference was not a procedure of substantive importance, only a formality. It was expedient for Truman to grant Forrestal and the Chiefs their day in court, but the date of the meeting alone (three weeks before the budget was to go to Congress) would indicate how little regard he had for the possibility that it might lead him to rearrange his budget. While the lateness of the date was largely the result of the time it took Forrestal and the Chiefs to negotiate the terms of the alternatives, Truman had at no time expressed the desire that they be placed before him any earlier. On the contrary, when Forrestal previewed the alternatives at their October 5 meeting, Truman had not even expressed an interest in their further development.

There were several reasons for the President's attitude. Most of them turned on the fact that he had seen the ceiling from the beginning not as a guide line for further discussion but as the limit of what he was prepared to do in view of certain intractable economic and political conditions, and he had therefore advanced it as the last, not the first, word in the budget debate. Since the considerations responsible for this decision seemed as valid and compelling in the fall as they had in the spring, he saw the Chiefs' action not as facilitating his choice but challenging it. In part, however, both Truman's initial willingness to foreclose on discussion and his later lack of interest in an alternative budget were simply a reflection of his distrust of the military establishment's budgeting procedures. As previously noted, the President shared with many others the opinion that the military were lacking in "economy-mindedness" and the suspicion that their mounting estimates were not so much inspired by jointly considered appreciations of the Soviet threat as they were inflated by self-seeking interservice rivalries.

Impressed, then, with the desirability of greater service unity, Truman, along with Webb and Marshall, viewed the obvious conflict and division that had accompanied the development of the $14.4 and $16.9-billion budgets as evidence that once again Forrestal and the Chiefs had failed to come to grips with their responsibilities. Seen in this perspective, the analytical utility of the act was easily obscured. The submission of alternative budgets appeared to be not so much a clarification of the President's choice as a reflection of the Chiefs' inability to make their own.

The policy consequences from these expectations about what the Chiefs could and should accomplish through their own budgeting procedures were marked. Both Truman and Webb were able to ease their sense of risk with a $14.4-billion budget by the thought that the Chiefs were, anyway, not really agreed on the need for what they were requesting in the $16.9-billion budget. Similarly, one of the reasons why Marshall was unwilling to serve as a spearhead for Forrestal's effort to raise the ceiling was his belief that if the Chiefs had done their job properly they would have been united rather than divided on the kind of forces they required. Had these expectations been different, had they seen the issues involved more as matters for political guesses and less as problems for professional determination, Marshall might have been more willing to back the alternatives that made sense to him (for he reportedly did want more ground troops), and Truman would not have dulled his sense for the extent of his own choice.

The fallacy of these expectations has already been discussed. The conflicts which divided the services were, in fact, unavoidable. They were the result of basic differences about how to win World War III, and while they may have been nourished by specialized institutional responsibilities and exacerbated by the zeal that attends all patriotic causes, their origin lay in the uncertainty of any effort to predict the future. Changes in the structure of the military establishment cannot put an end to such differences; they can only alter the kind of power that can be mobilized on behalf of the issues involved.

These same general points also hold for the budgeting procedures of the military. A choice of politics exists with regard to the opportunity to affect the political outcome of their budget debate, but there is no equivalent choice with regard to the political characteristics of that debate. The durability of these characteristics can be illustrated through reference to the budget procedures recommended by General Taylor, which he developed in reaction to those he encountered during his tour of duty in 1955–59. According to Taylor's account, military planners during those years were actively discouraged from developing estimates of their requirements that were calculated without regard for the size of the President's ceilings ("Blue Sky planning"). The Joint Chiefs did not submit alternative budgets for the President's consideration. In fact, they were not even required to take collective responsibility for the formulation of the budget. The services budgeted separately from each other, and no effort was made to explain the consequences of the final product in terms of the military establishment's "functional" plans and forces (those to which more than one service contributed: for example, strategic retaliation or limited warfare).

Taylor's own proposals were designed to meet what he considered the deficiencies in these procedures and to secure "an analytical appraisal of our military requirements and . . . a scientific budget formulation directed at supporting those requirements." The first step in his proposal is that the Joint Chiefs should determine the "military requirements" necessary to fulfill each of the missions of the functional forces. "Having determined how much is enough," without consideration for any budget ceiling, the Chiefs would then be in a position to build a "defense budget in consistence with the requirements of these functional forces." The next step would be "the difficult task of compressing the desired force structure within a dollar ceiling. . . ." Finally, in addition to having a "reasonable" ceiling, it would "be most useful" if the Chiefs could present "two or more [compressed] force structures, corresponding to as many levels of fiscal availability. This device would permit the Secretary of Defense to see clearly the implications of fiscal limitations on the Armed Forces." [31]

The suggested procedures bear more than a little resemblance to those followed in fiscal 1950. As such, they would obviously provide a greater opportunity for rational budget choices than those with which Taylor had had to contend. But the point to be made here is that the change to budgeting in trans-service functional terms would in no way permit an escape from the political problems encountered in budgeting in transfunctional service terms. The problems of the defense budget will remain as indeterminate as ever, and while the emphasis on functional "requirements" might enhance analysis, there are fundamental difficulties involved in the approach which, in the end, would lead it to assume characteristics far more political than scientific.

There is, to begin with, a great deal of analytical "give" in the question of "how much is enough" to fulfill a mission, be it service or trans-service. The amount will depend on the kind of assumptions made about the problem and the degree of certainty one demands of the answers considered. In 1948, when the Chiefs reduced their "Blue Sky" requirements from $30 to $21 billion, they were cutting muscle as well as fat; it was a matter of deciding to revise expectations about the kind of jobs to be done or deciding to attempt them with fewer or older weapons. Similarly, the requirements for limited war forces could, as Taylor suggests, be calculated from studies of hypothetical limited wars, but what criteria will guide the choice of hypotheses? [32]

A second major difficulty with the "requirements" approach is that the size and purpose of the so-called functional forces are themselves matters of intense theoretical dispute. Taylor, like Forrestal before him, concluded that the fixed and low budget ceiling "has become the prime cause of the service rivalry which is undermining national confidence in our military programs." But as his own descriptions of the service "positions" during his tour of duty make

[31] Taylor, *The Uncertain Trumpet*, pp. 86–87, 92, 97, 127–28, 163.
[32] *Ibid.*, pp. 150, 159.

clear, the doctrinal differences that divided them were marked and consequential. Army doctrine measured the requirements of the strategic retaliatory force in terms of what it would take to launch a slow second strike against Soviet cities: one that can start after the Russian bombs have already landed on target but is still able to inflict such destruction on Soviet cities as to make them unwilling to strike in the first place. The Air Force, however, had a different doctrine of deterrence. It measured requirements in terms of what it would take to launch a preemptive first strike against Soviet delivery forces: one that, if alerted to the impending Russian attack, would be able to destroy most of their carriers on the ground and thereby not only confront the Russians with the prospect of unacceptable destruction to their cities, but also reduce greatly the destruction that could be visited on American cities and carriers. Failing this, the Air Force wanted the ability to launch at least a fast second strike: one that would start after the Russian carriers were on their way, but before the bombs were on target, thereby making "available" American carriers for strikes against possible second-wave Russian carriers and bases.

The point to these differences, which were the issues of the Finletter Report finally joined, was that they made impossible any joint determination of "requirements." The numbers and kinds of weapons involved in the execution of each strategy were too different. Nor were matters helped by the fact that the Air Force also believed that the capability to launch an initiating first strike and the threat of its use could serve to deter the Russians from attacking other areas of the globe and was thus led to take quite a different view than the Army of the requirements for limited-war forces.[33]

In outlining his proposed budgeting process, Taylor avoided a discussion of how these differences would be resolved by the happy assumption that the Joint Chiefs had embraced the particular doc-

---

[33] *Ibid.*, pp. 102–3, 105, 97–105, 132–33, 148–49. For the Air Force interest in a preemptive strike strategy, see especially the statement of the Commander of the Strategic Air Command, General T. S. Power, in the New York *Times*, September 4, 1959. For a critical analysis of these and related doctrines, see Bernard Brodie, *Strategy in the Missile Age* (Princeton, Princeton University Press, 1959), Chapters 7–9.

trines that he advocated.[34] Doctrinal unanimity among the professional military seems an unrealistic prospect. In reality, the only route likely to be available is that taken by the Chiefs in fiscal 1950. Agreement had been reached on the requirements that made up the minimum war plan only because each was willing to see the other develop competing capabilities, as in the case of the Air Force and the Navy with regard to strategic bombing, or contradictory capabilities, as in the case of the long, land war of the Army and the short, air war of the Air Force.

Once the functionally oriented Chiefs had met these problems and reached some consensus on "requirements," they would still confront a final intellectual difficulty when they undertook to compress the desired force structure. As the Chiefs discovered in fiscal 1950, when they tried to reduce the budget from $23.6 billion to $14.4 billion, the "mix" of forces that seems rational at the budget level where all requirements are considered fully met may no longer seem a rational mix, at least to some (as was the case with Symington and Vandenberg), when it is scaled down to fit under a Presidential ceiling.[35] Questions such as the extent to which the requirements for all-out war should be met ahead of those for limited war will not only be answered differently; they will also serve to reopen the disputes over the doctrinal assumptions on which those requirements were calculated in the first place. And it is at this point, if not long before, that the division and conflict among functionally oriented Chiefs will be politically indistinguishable from that observed in fiscal 1950.

The 1948 Chiefs met the compression problem by scaling down proportionately from their "requirements." There would appear to be little in the responsibilities of functionally oriented Chiefs which would serve to point them in a different direction. If the budget is to reflect strategic choices other than those reached through the bargaining of the Chiefs, the pressure for such choices must come from outside them—as was the case with Forrestal's proposal for an "unbalanced" approach to the $14.4-billion budget. Forrestal was

---

[34] Taylor, *The Uncertain Trumpet*, p. 162.

[35] The point about this last difficulty with the requirements approach is taken from Malcolm Hoag's discussion, "Some Complexities in Military Planning," *World Politics*, July 1959, pp. 555–56, 566.

unable to press his proposal because of the weakness of his political position. He had little reason to believe that he could pick a fight with two of the three services and win, especially in view of the President's indifference to the alternatives involved and his ebbing confidence in Forrestal himself. The power of "outsiders" will always be limited by their dependence on the cooperation of the Chiefs, but it is obvious that under other circumstances Forrestal's opportunity to impose the unbalanced (or "unbargained") budget on the Chiefs would have been much greater.

It is here that the significance of a change which would make the Chiefs' budgeting procedures more explicitly functional is to be found. The change would not make their budget debate any less political in character, but it would, as Taylor noted, make the point of that debate clearer to the civilian participants in the budgeting process. The presentation of the budget to Congress in functional terms would help to focus the committees' attention on the strategic choices of the budget, just as its development in those terms would help the President and his Secretaries for Defense and State to monitor the strategic implications of the Chiefs' budgeting process and would enhance their opportunity to intervene to influence the outcome of that process.

The case for more civilian attention to the doctrinal choices involved in the budget is easily made. The civilian participants are already halfway into the tent by virtue of the power that they exercise in pursuance of their formal responsibilities. The President does send the budget to Congress, Congressmen do vote on it, and the Secretary of State if he does not participate in its formulation is nonetheless dependent on its content. Their choices and policies are thus unavoidably tied to the issues of strategy which the budget reflects. Rationality alone would seem to demand closer attention to those issues than Mahon's committee evidenced in the case of the Air Force increase, or Marshall showed for the foreign policy aspects of the Navy–Air Force dispute over strategic bombing, or Truman gave to the question of which approach the Chiefs took to the $14.4-billion budget.

It would be rash to presume, however, that the civilian participants are especially moved to take part in such matters or that the military, for that matter, are intent on preventing them from doing so. Given the grave costs and risks involved and the uncertainty attendant to all courses of action, one might well presume some desire on the part of all parties to shift the burden of choice. It may not entirely be due to the "leaderless" and "radar-oriented" characteristics of the policy process that the dialogue on the defense budget so often seems to have the form of the Congress saying, "We gave all the President asked for," and the President declaring, "I asked for all that Congress would give," while the Secretary of State stands silent and the Joint Chiefs affirm that "It is not up to us to challenge the decisions of the politicians."

Still, in a formal sense at least, high military policy since the end of World War II has become increasingly a "political" matter. There are few governmental choices which carry greater public consequence than that, for example, between a second-strike doctrine and a preemptive strike doctrine or that among possible doctrines for the fighting of limited wars. Professional expertise can develop and clarify such issues, but it cannot resolve them. They will be determined in *some* political arena, and if the politicians are to continue to be concerned with politics, it would not be inappropriate if it should be an arena where politicians, not soldiers, lead the contending armies.

NSC-68: PROLOGUE TO

REARMAMENT

by Paul Y. Hammond

Contents

Introduction

The first of the three studies in this book was concerned with examining the fiscal 1950 defense budget and appraising the rationality of the process by which this budget was formulated and adopted. Professor Schilling found that there was little to recommend the budget when it was measured against standards of rationality, although many of the alternative processes usually recommended as improvements over it were equally nonrational. This second study deals with a policy—or rather, a plan, or a proposed policy—which meets many of the requirements of rationality. It was NSC-68, a document which was reputedly prepared in the National Security Council in the spring of 1950 and which, also by reputation, anticipated in some measure the military requirements of the Korean War. How justified that reputation is will be assessed in the course of what follows, although that is not our main concern.

The issue, let it be clear at the outset, is not so much whether NSC-68 was rational, but to what extent it was relevant. Allowing for a certain latitude in our standards of rationality, NSC-68 was a comprehensive and integrated general statement of the American position in the international political world, of its objectives and capabilities in that world, and of the means which were necessary to achieve those objectives. This is not to say that it was the most rational formulation possible, or even that in another such document very different conclusions might not have been reached. It was, however, rational in the sense that it did attempt to raise and to answer the major questions necessary to answer if the United States were to have a general foreign policy position—questions of a scope and fundamental character that Schilling, in the first part of this book, found so lacking.

In order to raise and cope with these questions, however, the authors of NSC-68 had to avoid the real administrative world of bargaining and negotiation both by arranging to have these questions dealt with in the never-never world of staff work, and, further, by keeping the discussion general enough so that official interests were not easily inferable. It is doubtful that even these devices would have proved sufficient if it had not been for rare circumstances which opened the way to a common viewpoint across several agencies in the government.

1 *The Problem of Coordinating*

National Security Policy

The National Security Council, established by statute in 1947, was intended as the means for developing fully coordinated policies in peacetime for the foreign and defense affairs of the United States. Many obstacles still stood in the way of achieving that objective after 1947, however. To begin with, there were inherent difficulties with the machinery of the NSC itself. The President, not the council, was responsible for national security matters in the Executive branch. The council could advise him, but it was no substitute for Presidential authority or Presidential leadership. Moreover, in the three years before the beginning of the Korean War, although coordination was an important objective, the overriding problems of policy-making in foreign affairs were those of Presidential leadership. Coordination involved the fine balancing of factors for optimum achievement. But the more urgent questions concerned how much the American commitment to its own defense and the fate of its allies ought to be, and how heavy a political burden the administration ought to assume in meeting that commitment.

To put it another way, the careful balancing of all facets of policy, which was implied by coordination, was possible only if adjustments could be marginal. Yet the questions of national security faced between 1945 and 1950 (not to speak, one way or the other, of other periods of time) involved grand alternatives rather than fine adjustments. For instance, when the Marshall-Acheson proposals for assistance to the collapsing economy of Europe were under consideration in late 1947 and early 1948, the issue was not one of balance, but of whether or not to embark on an ambitious scheme of reconstruction. Similarly, the first defense budgets under unification could not be balanced with other government costs by marginal adjustments in the military estimates. Relatively unguided budget estimates, such as the military made for the fiscal 1949 supplementary budget in the spring of 1948, had to be cut arbitrarily to a third of their original size; otherwise, budgets were prepared under an arbitrary ceiling imposed by the White House.

OBSTACLES TO AN INTEGRATED POLICY

The establishment in 1947 of the National Security Council, and of a single (though federally structured) Military Establishment, created a new situation in the machinery of American government. Some formal account was now to be taken of military judgments in peacetime. Both sides of the civil-military relationship had difficulties with the accomplishment of that objective. For the military, there were difficulties in deciding what kinds of judgments were relevant, particularly when they were expected to be interservice military judgments. The rhetoric of budget-making, both in the Executive branch and in the legislative process, held the military to a declaration of sufficiency: What size and configuration of military forces (force levels) and what budget magnitudes would provide military capabilities sufficient to insure the national security? If the assumption that a distinct line could be drawn between sufficiency and insufficiency had ever had any validity, after World War II it no longer did. Faced with such an awkward form in which to cast their judgments, the military chiefs during 1948 and 1949 sought protection in the "purely military" judgment: an estimate of military needs which assertedly had no relationship to economic or political feasibility. The effort was understandable and in some ways commendable: the Chiefs seemingly wanted the responsibility for force-level and budget-level decisions to rest unmistakably upon the shoulders of the politically responsible officials involved, the Secretary of Defense and the President. In the end, however, they were drawn into the endorsement of the administration's budget ceilings for defense. Yet, whether they stated a figure quite distinct from what the White House would allow (in the 1949 supplement it was three times what the President accepted), or produced a compromise which took into account in some degree what the administration would allow, as they did for the 1950 budget, or simply proceeded with the budget estimates in conformity with an imposed ceiling, as they did for the 1951 budget, the problem remained the same: their claim to a professional status for their judgments did not allow them to endorse without some reservation the force levels and budget magnitudes for the military establishment set more or less arbitrarily in the White House. Yet they were unable, without showing disloyalty, to avoid endorsement of the President's program in each of these cases.

The problem for responsible civilian officials was not much easier to handle. The administration simply could not spend the moneys the services thought they needed. The gap between what seemed politically feasible and what the military said was necessary was alarmingly wide. It yawned even wider when other urgent or seemingly urgent demands for public funds in the domestic sector of public affairs were considered: "If we are able to spend another $5 billion for defense, how much more ought we to spend on the Fair Deal?" was one way the problem could be put, especially after the 1948 election. The limit which the administration was willing to accept involved some notion about what the economy could stand. It was, to be sure, more of a political judgment than an economic one, although the economic justification for it was the one almost always presented.

Moreover, nowhere in the government, either within or outside of the Military Establishment, did anyone have much confidence in the soundness of the estimates of total military requirements. The methods of estimating were crude and cumbersome and, among the services, undoubtedly duplicatory of each other's capabilities. The conflicts over roles and missions and the evident lack of an integrated military strategy accepted by all services left each suspicious of the others' programs, and officials both within and outside of the services who were not service partisans themselves were doubtful about all of them. Since no one therefore had much confidence in what the gap between budget ceilings sponsored in the Bureau of the Budget and the budget estimates of the Military Establishment meant, there was little incentive to take the gap very seriously—certainly not seriously enough to justify the systematic and painstaking closing of it through the welding of a common viewpoint among the various elements of the administration concerned with shaping the President's program in military affairs. James Forrestal, the first Secretary of Defense, exemplified the divergent views which resulted. Greatly alarmed though he was both with the declining military capability of the United States and with, as he saw it, the threat of Soviet intentions and capabilities, in the end he was willing to join the President in cutting the Joint Chiefs' estimates drastically and—what is more significant—to support the cut with the argument that economic reasons made it necessary.[1]

Economic factors, of course, can never be ignored in the setting of defense budgets. But Forrestal's presentation of the economic limit argument aligned him with an approach to fiscal policy which had sound political, though not economic, grounds. It was the contention that a ceiling could be determined for Federal expenditures beyond which lay fiscal ruin, and that the ceiling was very close to current expenditures. In the language of Forrestal's endorsement of this notion one could observe that it did not rest easily with him. He emphasized the principle that economic considerations had to be taken into account—a point which no one could dispute. But in the end, he accepted the particular application of that principle by the Truman administration. Lacking a real integration of viewpoints, the issue had to be resolved arbitrarily. And the authority

[1] *Military Functions, National Military Establishment Appropriations Bill for 1949,* Hearings before the Committee on Appropriations, House of Representatives, 80th Cong., 2d Sess. (Washington, 1948), pp. 3, 13–14; *Supplemental National Defense Appropriations Bill, 1948,* Hearings before the Committee on Appropriations, United States Senate, 80th Cong., 2d Sess. (Washington, 1948), pp. 3–4, 8–9, 12–13. Excerpts from Forrestal's testimony are quoted in *Supplemental Appropriations for 1951,* Hearings before the Committee on Appropriations, United States Senate, 81st Cong., 2d Sess. (Washington, 1950), pp. 33–34. For a more extended and somewhat conflicting version of Forrestal's views see *supra* (Schilling, Chap. II, Part I).

of the President within the Executive branch to resolve it could not be questioned. Hence, it could be said that the idea of fiscal grounds for rigid budget ceilings was itself a sign of the lack of coordination in national policies, and a lack of confidence that, at least for the time being, national security policies could be integrated.

In sum, the achievement of integrated national security policies remained an unlikely prospect even after the establishment of the National Security Council. None of the four principal elements of such policies—diplomatic, foreign economic aid, military, and budgetary—could be put together with each other without great difficulty. The military spokesmen and those people in the Military Establishment, the White House, and the Bureau of the Budget whose particular frame of reference was budgetary considerations had little confidence in each other. The budget people, including the civilian Secretaries in the Military Establishment, further doubted the reliability of military budget processes. They had sufficient reason. Not until the winter of 1948 were the most elementary comparisons between forces and costs and relationships between costs, weapons, and strategy attempted on an interservice basis.[2] And this initial effort was more a landmark of intent than of any substantive achieve-

[2] This statement, and much of what follows, is based upon information obtained from interviews and/or correspondence conducted by the author with the following people, who are listed by their agency affiliation in 1950: Dean G. Acheson, Lucius D. Battle, Charles H. Bohlen, Dorothy Fosdick, George F. Kennan, Paul Nitze, Marshall Shulman, Walter S. Surrey, Robert Tufts, and James Webb of the State Department; Major General Charles L. Bolte, Jr., Major General Donald P. Booth, Major General James H. Burns, General J. Lawton Collins, Rear Admiral Arthur C. Davis, John T. Floberg, General Alonzo P. Fox, William B. Franke, Lyle S. Garlock, Najeeb Halaby, Vice Admiral Herbert G. Hopwood, Louis Johnson, Major General Truman H. Landon, W. Barton Leach, Robert LeBaron, Max Lehrer, Major General Lyman L. Lemnitzer, Robert A. Lovett, Major General J. V. Matijka, Frank Nash, Charles P. Noyes, John H. Ohly, General Matthew B. Ridgway, General Gordon P. Saville, and Vice Admiral Arthur D. Struble of the Defense Department; Richard Bissell, Walter S. Salant, and Theodore Tannenwald, Jr., of the Economic Cooperation Administration; William McChesney Martin of the Treasury Department; Daniel C. Fahey of the National Security Resources Board; Leon Keyserling of the Council of Economic Advisers; David Bell, George Elsey, Charles S. Murphy, and Sidney W. Souers of the White House Staff; and Phillip C. Holt, Frederick J. Lawton, Frank Pace, William Schaub, George Schwartzwalder, Elmer Staats, and Ellis Veatch of the Bureau of the Budget. Hereafter, as the source for a statement in the text, these interviews and letters will be cited simply as "Interviews" without further differentiation.

ment. The military spokesmen, on the other hand, fluctuated between an uncritical faith in the budget ceiling argument of their civilian superiors and a belief that these budgets were set on the basis of criteria which bore no relationship to the requirements of defense. Neither of these interpretations of budget-making, it should be noted, encouraged them to believe that a constructive accommodation with budgetary factors was possible.

The foreign economic aid program received its first Congressional endorsement in the shadow cast by the Communist coup in Czechoslovakia in February 1948. The program was large and costly in its drain not only on the American purse, but also on the political commitments of its supporters in the administration and on both sides of the aisle in Congress. To achieve its success, or so it appeared, other competing demands for resources had to be disavowed. Its supporters paid in neglect of Asia and the underdeveloped countries and in American military strength.

Military needs and diplomacy were difficult or impossible to consolidate into an integrated program for two reasons. State Department officials were fearful that too sympathetic a consideration of military needs might undermine the foreign economic aid program. The military, moreover, could not relate their strategic capabilities to foreign policy needs due to the gap between military capabilities and military requirements and to interservice disagreements over roles and missions. Even the foreign economic aid program and American diplomacy in general were not wholly compatible, although economic aid was supposed to be an instrument of diplomacy. They competed with each other for scarce resources, as did also military needs and economic aid. Moreover, the requirements for their respective administration were quite different. Foreign policy had never before in peacetime been tied to an operating program of such scope. Although normally it would be accepted without serious challenge that diplomacy ought to be kept flexible, American foreign policy was now committed to a large-scale administrative effort which would take several years to complete and which involved the rigidities of large-scale operations.

Some of these difficulties were more important than others. Together, however, they constituted a formidable obstacle to the development of integrated national security policies. Furthermore, these difficulties, or at least some of them, grew as time went on. By the time of the Soviet atomic bomb explosion in September 1949, four things in particular had forced their growth: the Presidential election of 1948, the air-power dispute, the developing military alliance of NATO, and the fall of China.

THE AMERICAN POLICY SETTING FOR THE
SOVIET ATOM BOMB EXPLOSION

Economy and the 1948 presidential election

The election of 1948 was a surprise victory for President Truman. He had made his Fair Deal program of domestic welfare the prominent campaign issue, for foreign policy remained a matter of bipartisan agreement, at least until the last week of the campaign. Quite naturally, considerable pressure built up after the election to carry out the President's domestic program. Its proponents were inclined to believe that the increased expenditures needed for its accomplishment could be provided by reducing expenditures in other sectors—in foreign aid and particularly the armed forces. On the other hand, some officials in the Military Establishment hoped that with a clearer electoral mandate President Truman would be willing to accept a higher ceiling on defense expenditures; and the most powerful voices in the administration of foreign economic aid, the highest ranking officials of the Economic Cooperation Administration, were either Republicans with no commitments to the administration's domestic welfare program or Democrats whose interest and public service had been predominantly in international affairs. In the State Department, similarly, it was to be expected that the agency outlook would give priority to the international responsibilities of the government.

The election of 1948 did not alter this orientation, although it was, by a peculiar combination of circumstances, to make the State Department leadership more "defense-minded" than it had been and Defense Department leadership less so. General George C.

Marshall, the Secretary of State from January 1947 until January 1949, had pinned his hopes for a rational postwar military policy on universal military training, unification, and a relatively modest defense budget. When he committed himself to European economic recovery, his belief in limited military expenditures was reinforced by a characteristic determination to avoid diversion from the large objective, as his failure to support Forrestal in breaking the long-range defense budget ceiling of $15 billion imposed in the spring of 1948 suggests.[3] Acheson, who replaced Marshall after the 1948 election, had no such rigid commitments. Since this was a period of accumulating evidence about the necessity for an increase in military expenditures, the difference between Acheson and Marshall was to be important. Meanwhile, President Truman replaced Forrestal in the Defense Department with Louis Johnson, a prominent Democrat who had handled the difficult chore of raising the funds to finance the Democratic Presidential campaign of 1948. A new Director of the Budget, Frank Pace, bolstered by the antimilitary attitudes of Edwin G. Nourse, Chairman of the Council of Economic Advisers,[4] had soon won the President's approval of a $13.5-billion defense budget for fiscal 1950, rather than the $15 billion anticipated the previous spring, and Johnson had gone on record in favor of greater economy in defense expenditures. The Military Establishment was once again headed into the economy trough.

The air-power dispute of 1949

The combined economy pressures which resulted were intense. Air Force officials could take some comfort from the popularity which their service enjoyed at the time in Congress. But top-ranking

[3] Walter Millis, ed., *The Forrestal Diaries* (New York, The Viking Press, 1951), pp. 431–32. For a somewhat different version of Marshall's views, see *supra* (Schilling, pp. 148–51, 189–95).

[4] Pace's sympathies for Nourse's views, and the nature of the latter, are indicated in Edwin G. Nourse, *Economics in the Public Service* (New York, Harcourt, Brace, 1953), pp. 249, 283, 485–95. The connection between Nourse and Pace is summarized in H. Bradford Westerfield, *Foreign Policy and Party Politics: Pearl Harbor to Korea* (New Haven, Yale University Press, 1955), p. 339. The fiscal 1950 budget is discussed in greater detail *supra* (Chap. II, Part V).

naval officers, in despair, forced a Congressional investigation of the B-36 and of the general issues of unification and strategy. Though almost equally alarmed over the severity of the administration's economy objectives, compounded by Congress' propensity to favor the Air Force in the economy pinch, the Army avoided joining the dispute only because of the caution of its new Chief of Staff, General J. Lawton Collins, and the prevalent belief in Army circles that the Navy needed cutting down to size anyway.[5]

The military and the administration (including the President and the Director of the Budget) had hung onto the vestiges of a balanced-force conception, while budget limitations dictated increasing reliance solely on the most "efficient" weapons system, strategic air atomic retaliation, which was a military capability designed for a showdown war with the Soviet Union. Whether as a cause or an effect of the identification of efficiency with air power, the armed services occupied themselves with large-scale war. A striking indication of this fact came in the House Armed Services Committee hearings on "Unification and Strategy," which were the last phase of the Navy-Air Force dispute over the B-36. There, Admiral Arthur W. Radford led a group of naval officers in a challenge of the prevailing reliance upon the nuclear air retaliatory capabilities of the Air Force as the basis for American military security. The Navy's case included the charge that such massive retaliation would be immoral. It is significant that, although the Navy could have drawn from its traditional strategic doctrines of sea power to suggest an alternative strategy of peripheral warfare, emphasizing its flexibility, selectivity, and restraint, Radford and his group chose to argue instead that the Navy could handle the massive air strikes at the heart of Russia better than could the Air Force.[6] The issue within the Military Establishment was thus put in terms of who could carry out best a strategy which equated threats to our national security interests with the necessity of inflicting maxi-

[5] Millis, ed., *The Forrestal Diaries*, p. 152; Paul Y. Hammond, "Supercarriers and B-36 Bombers: Appropriations, Strategy, and Politics," in Casebook, Twentieth Century Fund Study of Civil-Military Relations, in press.

[6] *Ibid.*; Robert E. Osgood, *Limited War, The Challenge to American Strategy* (Chicago, University of Chicago Press, 1957), p. 153.

mum devastation on the heart of the Soviet Union. The air-power dispute revealed at once how far from an integrated strategic viewpoint the armed services were and how large an obstacle to the achievement of such a viewpoint interservice politics and the suspicions it aroused were. It also added considerably to those suspicions.

NATO and MDAP

The third principal cause of the growing barriers to an integrated national security policy within the American government, the effects of which had been felt by the time of the first Soviet nuclear explosion, was the developing military alliance with NATO, the high costs of which were only now becoming evident, and only to a small number of officials in the Executive branch.

The Communist coup in Czechoslovakia in February 1948 had assured the passage by Congress of the foreign economic aid program, but it also encouraged interest in the next necessary step, a foreign military aid program. Western Europe was already moving toward a collective military effort comparable to the economic cooperation program being built upon Marshall aid. On March 17, 1948, France, Great Britain, and the Benelux Powers signed a collective security agreement at Brussels. On the same day President Truman, in a dramatic message to Congress on the March crisis, related American security arrangements to the Brussels Pact.

Congressional supporters of military aid attempted to associate the developing military security arrangements with the Economic Cooperation Act of 1948, but the administration declined to support the effort because of the adverse effects which such a linkage might have upon the economic aid program and the increased American defense appropriations.[7] Instead, the groundwork was carefully laid for bipartisan and joint Congressional-Executive cooperation in the development of support for a military alliance with western Europe. The Vandenberg Resolution, adopted in June 1948, which expressed the sense of the Senate in favor of such an alliance, was the first public step in that direction.

There were three phases in the development of the Mutual

[7] William Adams Brown, Jr., and Redvers Opie, *American Foreign Assistance* (Washington, The Brookings Institution, 1953), p. 450.

Defense Assistance Program (MDAP) which resulted: (1) the encouragement of European efforts at cooperation, (2) the negotiation of a military alliance between the United States and the western European countries, and (3) the underwriting of the whole effort with American material support. The administration adopted the tactic of keeping the three phases as separate as possible. For instance, in the hearings on the North Atlantic Treaty the administration continued to assert that ratifying the treaty would not commit the United States, or any Senator, to support of a foreign military aid program. And the administration did not submit the original MDAP bill to Congress until the Senate's consent had been obtained for the North Atlantic Treaty.[8]

This cautious proceeding, one step at a time, had evidently been necessary because of the difficulties encountered in gaining Congressional support for a foreign military assistance program. However, military attitudes dictated the caution as much as did anticipated difficulties in Congress. From the beginning of the development of the Atlantic military alliance, when the prospects of a military build-up in western Europe partially financed by the United States was first under consideration, prominent officers viewed it with suspicion. In May 1948, while the Vandenberg Resolution was pending in the Senate, Secretary Forrestal reported to the National Security Council the opinion of the Joint Chiefs of Staff that American military strength should be bolstered considerably before the expansion of western European forces was undertaken with American resources. In addition to seeing foreign military aid as a potential rival to appropriations for American forces, military officials apparently also feared that by disapproval of a foreign military aid program Congress might cut the Defense Department budget drastically.[9]

If MDAP were going to accomplish its objectives, considerably more American aid than had been anticipated would have to be

---

[8] *Ibid.*, pp. 454–55, 458.
[9] Harry S. Truman, *Memoirs, II, Years of Trial and Hope 1946–1952* (Garden City, Doubleday, 1956), pp. 245–46. Robert A. Lovett, then Under Secretary of State, expressed the concern over defense budget cuts. His long experience in the Military Establishment, however, makes it unwise to discount his point as an expression of military concern.

given. Yet, Congress had cut the original budget estimate by the administration from $1.45 billion to an even $1 billion. How much money the interagency planners of MDAP thought necessary and what sum they could get from the President and Congress were diverging figures. Two circumstances, however, delayed any showdown on the magnitude of the MDAP program until the next fiscal year—the late approval (on October 6, 1949) of the original authorization and unexpected slowness in initiating the procurement and shipment of arms.[10]

In 1947 the administration had set its foot upon the road to a major cooperative effort with western Europe. The new costs had initially been reconciled in the Executive budget-making process. By the fall of 1949, however, estimates within the Truman administration of what was needed for foreign aid and estimates of what could be made available were growing further and further apart, making the reconciliation of viewpoints about national security policy within the administration more and more difficult.

The fall of China

The fourth principal cause of the growing barriers to integrated national security policy was the fall of China. The development of American diplomacy which led to the Truman Doctrine, the Greek-Turkish Aid Program, the Marshall Plan, and the Mutual Defense Assistance Program had been built upon a base of carefully nurtured support in both political parties. Bipartisanship, however, had not included agreement about China. The administration, indeed, had passed up the opportunity to associate Congressional Republicans with its China policy by its apparent negligence in administering the China Aid Act of 1948, which they had supported.[11]

By April 1949 the Communists had crossed the Yangtze River on a broad front. Stopped by floods, they resumed their general advance

[10] Indicative of the viewpoint in MDAP planning was the fact that after the drafting of NSC-68, but before the outbreak of the Korean War, MDAP officials who saw that document regarded it as "putting into print what was actually going on," rather than as a radical departure from present policies. Interviews.

[11] Westerfield, *Foreign Policy and Party Politics,* pp. 266–68.

in July. By the end of September no one could doubt that continental China had fallen to the Reds. Even if such an enormous shift in the fortunes of the bipolar world at this time did not demand a revision in the American conception of the nature of the enemy, the new situation which brought Communist power to the borders of India and Indo-China should have. Yet, not only was the administration committed to its western European undertakings, but it could not easily acknowledge the new, or newly revealed, situation without making admissions which would be politically damaging to it.

Summary at time of Soviet atom bomb announcement

By September 23, 1949, when President Truman announced the detection of a Soviet atomic detonation, the economy pressures on defense and foreign aid expenditures had become intense. In a variety of ways it had become evident within the government that defense capabilities and commitments bore little relationship to each other. Secretary of Defense Johnson, who was now heavily committed to economizing, had built personal political support with that commitment. The developing program for economic and military assistance, on the other hand, had led Secretary of State Acheson, who was almost entirely dependent upon President Truman for his political support, to conclude that still greater expenditures were necessary. As important as the economic recovery and the military rearmament of Europe were, however, the fall of China had called into question the validity of the American emphasis on European problems, and, by implication, any methods which were adapted exclusively to their use. Finally, the air-power dispute, although it was not to be concluded until a month later, was to reveal the inadequacy of defense strategy, the absence of an integrated perspective within the Military Establishment on national security policy, and the shortcomings of an exclusive reliance on strategic air power for American defense.

The fact that the Russians had developed an atomic weapon was to have practically no immediate effect upon the air-power dispute raging between the Navy and the Air Force. However, it had important implications for most of the main features of American security policy: for strategic air power, so popular now in Congress, and evidently rapidly gaining Johnson's support, for the value of American atomic weapons as a deterrent to Soviet conventional forces, for the utility of NATO, and for the nature of the Soviet challenge.

The Origins of NSC-68

In the summer of 1949 the Director of the Policy Planning Staff of the State Department, George Kennan, with the encouragement of Secretary Acheson, assigned a new member of the staff, Paul Nitze, to establish better liaison with the strategic planners of the Defense Department. The Defense Department arranged briefings for Kennan and Nitze. At the first one, Kennan made clear his own view of the military implications of the containment policy for which he had been such a prominent spokesman. He indicated that he thought the military requirements of foreign policy could be met within current budget ceilings (of about $13.5 billion annually) by the development of small, unified task forces, highly qualified, highly mechanized, highly mobile, and well trained. These he regarded as sufficient to deal with the military threat posed within the policy of containment: localized, individual military tests of limited size. Nitze immediately found himself in disagreement with Kennan in a peculiar way which was, as we shall see, to plague them for the next year: It was a disagreement in which Kennan was more certain that they disagreed than was Nitze, and Nitze was not always certain of the basis for their disagreement.

At least initially, however, the point of difference was reasonably clear. Nitze was more concerned about the overall threat of Soviet arms, necessitating the achievement of superiority over them in an all-out war. He had been a member of the Joint Strategic Bombing Survey at the end of World War II, and had brought from that the airmen's conception of full-scale warfare. Kennan, he believed, failed to give proper weight to the importance of preparation for the contingency of a major aggressive move by the Russians. Kennan felt that Nitze's emphasis was too much in that direction. He doubted the value of the Strategic Air Command, and was impressed with what he considered to be the fact that the U.S.S.R. could not be occupied. His own views ruled out the large-scale war between the U.S.S.R. and the United States as too remote a possibility to deserve attention, particularly when that attention was bound, as he believed, to overweight military factors to the neglect of diplomatic ones in Soviet-American relations.

Besides these personal differences—important not for themselves as much as for clarifying other positions—the Defense Department briefings revealed differences between State and Defense thinking on strategic planning. General Richard C. Lindsay, Deputy Director for Strategic Plans of the Joint Staff, briefed Kennan and Nitze on Defense Department strategic planning. Lindsay indicated that the Defense Department was planning only for a big-war capability. When questioned about this assumption, he explained that while his committee agreed on the need for the capability of fighting small wars as well as big ones, budgetary limitations made it necessary for the Defense Department to prepare for only one. In order to be ready for the worst, they had given up special limited-war capabilities to concentrate on large-scale war capabilities, particularly the Strategic Air Command with its massive air atomic retaliatory capability.[1]

For different reasons, this information was alarming to Kennan and disconcerting to Nitze. Kennan was not disturbed by the budget ceiling. What would be necessary to meet strategic requirements as he saw them would be to reslice the defense dollar, giving the Army more and the Air Force, and possibly the Navy, less, so that his conception of a small, mobile, tri-service force could be carried out. Nitze was not as dissatisfied as Kennan was with the military planners' emphasis on big-war capabilities. On the other hand, he was disturbed that both the big-war and the limited-war capabilities were not big enough, for despite the emphasis given in military planning to strategic air retaliatory capacity, Lindsay had indicated

[1] Interviews.

that American air forces were not expected to control the air in a third world war—a requirement Nitze had learned from his work on the Joint Strategic Bombing Survey had been essential in World War II.[2]

These were initial reactions. Nitze took back to his work in the Policy Planning Staff of the State Department a deep concern over the budgetary limits imposed upon American defense policy, and over the relative importance of military and nonmilitary factors in foreign policy. During the latter part of the summer of 1949 the Policy Planning Staff interested itself in a comparative analysis of military costs between the Soviet Union and the United States, and the capability of the Soviet economy to depress consumption and carry a high rate of capital investment simultaneously with a high rate of military expenditure.[3] These were activities which Kennan would never have undertaken on his own initiative, for his own view of military requirements did not pose the question of economic capacity.

THREE SOURCES OF PREPARATION

It is a tribute to NSC-68 that so many people have claimed credit for it. Actually, three converging developments seem to have been the sources for its preparation. One was centered in the State Department, where programming for Mutual Defense Assistance had thrown officials into contact with strategic planning in the National Military Establishment. MDAP itself was, among other things, an acknowledgment that with lengthened lead times for military equipment, the prospect that another major war would be or might be short, and the breaking up of the atomic monopoly of the United States, coalition military planning and preparedness had to be kept in a high state of readiness. Coping with MDAP impressed upon State Department officials anew the necessity for correlating military and foreign policy as closely as possible.[4]

Thus sensitized to strategic planning problems, these officials

[2] Interviews.   [3] Interviews.
[4] William Adams Brown, Jr., and Redvers Opie, *American Foreign Assistance* (Washington, The Brookings Institution, 1953), pp. 455 ff.

viewed recent developments in the Soviet camp with growing concern. Since the Czech coup in February 1948, Soviet fortunes had seemed to be ebbing. In the middle of 1949 it began to appear that they had changed decisively and ominously, however. In the spring, Communist forces had crossed the Yangtze, marking the beginning of the end for the regime of Chiang Kai-shek on the mainland of China. Then, in September, the Soviet atomic explosion shattered American complacency about its technological and scientific lead. On November 6, 1949, on the thirty-second anniversary of the revolution, official speeches in Moscow showed a new confidence in the Soviet position, evidently based on the Soviet regime's own interpretation of these events. American officials reluctantly were inclined to agree, or at least to take the apparent Soviet interpretation itself with foreboding.

Correlative with the fall of China and the atomic explosion, State Department officials became anxious to press ahead with an examination of foreign policy and national strategy. In September 1949, when the members of the Policy Planning Staff undertook to examine the foreign policy implications of building the hydrogen bomb, they evidently had in mind also a more comprehensive reexamination of policy.[5] In so far as they could accomplish that reexamination, they did. Beyond this, they wanted the subject to be studied on an interdepartmental level, where, for instance, State and Defense Department policy planning could be integrated, with the benefit of information available in the Atomic Energy Commission.[6]

The second occurrence which contributed to the preparation of NSC-68 was the controversy over the decision to build a hydrogen bomb. The question whether to undertake the development of a fusion bomb had come up in 1946 and had been settled in the negative, in favor of developing the full potential of fission weapons. Following the explosion of the first Russian atom bomb in September 1949, approximately three years ahead of American intelligence estimates, the question was raised again with the proposal

[5] Interviews. Cf. testimony of George Kennan in United States Atomic Energy Commission, *In the Matter of J. Robert Oppenheimer,* Transcript of Hearing before Personnel Security Board (Washington, 1954), p. 360.
[6] Interviews.

of a crash program for its accomplishment as a possible means of keeping ahead of the Soviet Union's rapid development of nuclear technology. The answer was not easily forthcoming. The urgency was now greater, and so was the technological capability. The need to keep up the pace of development, and the importance of building the first hydrogen bomb, were obvious. But, in addition to the great costs that would be involved in undertaking the development of a fusion bomb, significant risks would have to be run if the bomb were to be produced on the crash basis then under consideration. In the belief of those most likely to know, a crash program would seriously reduce the rate of fission bomb development because men and resources would have to be shifted from that work to the crash program. It was also their judgment that there was no assurance that the crash program would yield any positive results.

For these, and for other reasons, the Advisory Committee of the Atomic Energy Commission recommended against the proposed crash attempt to produce a fusion bomb. The commission agreed with the committee. The Defense Department disagreed with both. The State Department took a position in favor of an urgent program for developing a fusion bomb which would not substantially interfere with improving the fission bombs. In discussing their differences, Acheson reportedly learned from David Lilienthal, the Chairman of the Atomic Energy Commission, that the latter's own objection to the fusion bomb program was due to his belief that the State and Defense Departments had not thought through the strategic implications of nuclear weapons. He indicated to Acheson that he intended to use his opposition to the proposed program as a means of forcing the strategic appraisal he thought was so needed. In effect, he wanted to postpone an undertaking of the "super" until American foreign policy had undergone a comprehensive reappraisal.[7]

While State Department officials could not agree with Lilienthal that an appraisal of the meaning to strategy of nuclear weapons had been neglected, they were anxious to clear the air of what they considered extraneous issues in the hydrogen bomb controversy,

[7] Interviews; Atomic Energy Commission, *In the Matter of J. Robert Oppenheimer*, pp. 401–10, 431–33, for example.

and, at the same time, they were delighted at the opportunity which might now be afforded them to follow through with the Defense Department to a greater integration between strategic and foreign policy planning. The result was that when, on January 30, 1950, President Truman signed a directive initiating the H-bomb program, appended to it was a letter drafted in the State Department which directed the Secretaries of State and Defense to make an overall review and reassessment of American foreign and defense policy in the light of the loss of China, the Soviet mastery of atomic energy, and the prospect of the fusion bomb.[8] The building of the "super" and the reappraisal of strategy were to proceed simultaneously.

The reassessment letter was the encouragement and reassurance necessary to win Lilienthal's approval of the H-bomb project, and by itself a desirable opportunity in the eyes of the Secretary of State, his policy planners, and other members of his staff. For strategic planners in the Defense Department, it was an opportunity to improve their contacts with the State Department, which had been under such restrictions since Secretary Johnson's directive that all communications with State had to be channeled through Johnson's deputy, Major General James H. Burns. But for Johnson it posed some real difficulties.

Louis Johnson, it will be recalled, had succeeded James Forrestal as Secretary of Defense in March 1949, at a time when the administration's outlook for the defense budget was becoming bearish again. By the summer of 1949 Johnson had become so fully committed in public to a far-reaching economy program in the Military Establishment that it was identified with him, rather than with the administration itself. He had encountered strong resistance to "his" economy program. His effort to choke off all Defense Department contacts with the State Department except through his office, although there were undoubtedly other commendable, if ill-conceived, reasons for it, was nevertheless part of his attempt to "keep the lid on" the Military Establishment. For Johnson, a Presidential request to have the State Department and the Defense Department cooperate in

[8] Interviews; Stewart Alsop in New York *Herald Tribune,* June 23, 1950.

the reassessment of defense and foreign policy was, it would appear, an invitation to cause trouble with the economy program in the Military Establishment. On the other hand, he favored the development of the H-bomb, and this seemed to be a small price for getting it. Johnson had approved the proposed program for a fusion weapon as a member of the National Security Council subcommittee concerned with that question. Not until later was it linked with the proposal for a reassessment of defense policy.

Furthermore, in his economy stand Johnson was faced with some deep personal dilemmas. He had been a founder of the American Legion, and, in the 1930's, its National President. From 1937 to 1940, as Assistant Secretary of War, he served under an isolationist Secretary, Harry H. Woodring, where he personally carried the burden of War Department preparedness with the not unfounded hope that, when Roosevelt could afford to do without Woodring, he would be promoted to Secretary. Let go when Stimson, a Republican, was made Secretary, Johnson remained out of the government until 1949, when he returned as Secretary of Defense. There was, thus, nothing in his background to suggest that he would become a wielder of the economy ax in the Defense Department. On the contrary, he had been a builder for the military up to 1940. But he was also a fighter. In 1940 he had fought for the beginnings of mobilization in the War Department; in 1949, he undertook a fight to impose a budget ceiling of $13.5 billion on the Defense Department. At first he opposed it. However, he evidently came to believe that it would force an increase in efficiency through a greater integration of the services. The press often claimed another reason for his demands for economy: that he nourished an ambition for the Democratic nomination for the Presidency in 1952.

The third development which contributed to the preparation of NSC-68 was the undertaking of a comprehensive survey of American strategic policy by the National Security Council itself. In response to discontent in the Senior Staff of the NSC over trends in American defense policy, Admiral Sidney Souers, the Secretary of the NSC, advised the council by memorandum on December 20, 1949, that at the first meeting of the NSC it had called for a general appraisal of the strategic situation of the United States, that NSC-20 was the first document on that subject, but that since it dealt only with the Soviet threat, it was not really general, and that no subsequent document had been either. What was needed, he indicated, was a statement of the situation which was world-wide in scope and thoroughly up to date.[9]

NSC-20, it should be noted, was a formulation of the containment policy. Prepared in late 1947 or early 1948, presumably it was little more than an elaboration of the State Department thinking, including its ambiguities, to which Kennan had given expression in his "Sources of Soviet Conduct," published in *Foreign Affairs* in the spring of 1947.[10] Since then, the completeness of the victory of the Communist regime in China over the Chinese Nationalists had become clear, necessitating, at the least, a reconsideration of the nature of the enemy to be contained. Moreover, NSC-20 had implied that in-being military superiority was a requisite of containment, yet whether that requirement was now being satisfied had been called into question. Since December 1948, when Forrestal had desperately appealed, at the last moment in the preparation of the President's fiscal 1950 budget, for funds to augment the strategic bombing capability of the United States, and although his appeal was rejected, the Military Establishment had steadily increased its reliance upon strategic bombing with nuclear weapons, both as its principal military capability and as its primary strategy. The strategy of nuclear retaliation as a way to match the Soviet Union's conventional armed forces rested on the assumption of an atomic monopoly. The detection of a Soviet nuclear explosion in September 1949 threw into doubt this reliance on the deterrent effect of nuclear retaliation, which was considered the primary military means for implementing NSC-20.

On January 5, 1950, the National Security Council decided to do a general strategic appraisal on the basis of present commitments and the existing strategic situation. Two weeks later, on January

[9] Interviews.
[10] George F. Kennan, "The Sources of Soviet Conduct," *Foreign Affairs*, July 1947, pp. 566–82.

18, the State Department set up a group to do its share of the appraisal. Thus, when the President signed the reappraisal letter connected with the hydrogen bomb directive, he approved a project already under consideration through NSC channels.[11]

The effect of the President's letter to the Secretaries of State and Defense requesting that they reappraise American foreign and defense policy was to take the proposed study of strategy out of NSC channels. The shift probably made little immediate difference, for in order to carry out the directions in the letter the two Secretaries established a joint ad hoc study group, which was not dissimilar to what would have been done for the NSC study. However, if State Department officials feared that otherwise Secretary Johnson would fail to assist in the reappraisal, the Presidential directive reassured them. A more substantial avoidance of NSC channels came later, when the completed paper went from the Secretaries of State and Defense directly to the President for approval, rather than through the NSC, where it might have been delayed or picked to pieces.

Yet, it is not likely that the project would initially have gone very far *within* the National Security Council, the deliberations of which, since Johnson had become Secretary of Defense, were impeded by deteriorating personal relations. The service Secretaries were statutory members until the National Security Act amendments put them off in the fall of 1949. But during this period one was ineffectual and another antagonistic. Suspicion and distrust isolated Francis P. Matthews, the Secretary of the Navy after May 1949, from his department, keeping him quite useless in the NSC. After Johnson impounded additional Air Force appropriations voted by Congress in the summer of 1949, his relations with W. Stuart Symington, the Secretary of the Air Force until April 1950, were greatly strained. The service Secretaries were dropped from NSC membership in the fall of 1949. From then until Symington returned the next April as the new Chairman of the National Security Resources Board, the National Security Council might have operated with few impedances had it not been for Johnson's deteriorating

[11] Interviews.

relations with the State Department, also. His relations with Acheson were bad enough to affect the operation of the NSC itself. Furthermore, his opposition to Defense Department contact with other agencies at the working level would have hobbled such an ambitious undertaking by the NSC staff as a general survey of national strategy because the staff was not large enough to carry out an assignment of that magnitude without help from the agencies involved.[12]

Acheson delegated the responsibility assigned him in the President's letter for reappraisal to the Policy Planning Staff. Johnson gave the responsibility to his Assistant for Foreign Military Affairs, Major General James H. Burns (Ret.), the only Defense Department official authorized to maintain contacts with the State Department. Burns was faced immediately with a procedural and organizational problem recurrent in the department: if the study were to have any real significance, the Joint Chiefs of Staff would have to be brought into it. But the Chairman of the JCS, General Omar N. Bradley, and the Director of the Joint Staff, Admiral Arthur W. Davis, consistent with long-standing JCS policy, ruled against having a JCS representative on the State-Defense study group.[13] They did, however, agree to associate the Joint Strategic Survey Committee (JSSC) with the work of the group. The JSSC was the unit within the JCS staff structure concerned with advising the Joint Chiefs on the overall national security implications of their strategic plans. The Joint Chiefs of Staff placed a high value on the independence of judgment and frankness of expression of the JSSC. Its views, however, were in no way authoritative. Major General Truman H. Landon, the Air Force member of the JSSC, who had worked with the NSC subcommittee concerned with the H-bomb problem, was assigned to represent the JSSC on the study group. The other members were Major General Ray T. Maddocks and Rear Admiral Thomas H. Robbins.[14]

[12] Interviews.

[13] For a lengthy account of the Joint Chiefs of Staff's determination not to allow anyone to represent them see Paul Y. Hammond, "Directives for the Occupation of Germany: The Washington Story," in casebook, Twentieth Century Fund Study of Civil-Military Relations, in press.

[14] Interviews.

Landon assumed the main burden of Defense Department representation and carried it throughout the work of the group. Since he formally represented only the views of an advisory staff, no commitment by the Defense Department prior to approval by JCS or the Office of the Secretary of Defense (OSD) could be inferred from his participation in and support of the group's work.

Although Landon carried most of the responsibility, besides Burns, who was limited by ill health to half-time work, two other officials participated for the Defense Department. Najeeb E. Halaby, Burns's subordinate as Director of the Office of Foreign Military Affairs, regularly attended the meetings. And Robert LeBaron, the Chairman of the Military Liaison Committee to the Atomic Energy Commission (hence, Johnson's chief adviser on atomic energy), attended occasionally or sent his assistant.[15]

In January 1950 Paul Nitze had replaced George Kennan as Director of the Policy Planning Staff (PPS), Kennan becoming State Department Counsellor. Nitze was head of the State Department contingent of the study group and chaired the study group itself. The Policy Planning Staff was too large for all of its members to participate. Besides Nitze, Robert Tufts, John Davies, and Robert Hooker were drawn into this work, and Carlton Savage, the Secretary of the Policy Planning Staff, acted as Secretary of the study group. James Lay, since January 1 the Executive Secretary of the National Security Council staff, and Everett Gleason, his assistant, attended meetings of the study group in order to maintain liaison with the NSC.[16]

[15] Interviews.   [16] Interviews.

III *Drafting* NSC-68

The drafting of the document which became the basis for NSC-68 occupied six weeks of intensive effort for the study group, beginning in mid-February and extending through March 1950. Nitze and his associates from the State Department came to the first meeting with a general, though definite, belief that the American response to the Soviet challenge was inadequate. The Policy Planning Staff had, it will be recalled, gone to the trouble of examining comparative defense costs between the United States and the Soviet Union in the autumn of 1949. From the beginning they could anticipate the direction in which the study would move.[1]

Landon may have arrived with similar preconceptions, but their practical effect was nullified by a recent experience with two State Department officials which had left him with little confidence in State Department skills in defense-related subjects. Furthermore, on its face, the State-Defense study proved less of an innovation in the Defense Department than it did in the State Department. Military planning is an incredibly complex process in which the particular view of a participant is so different from the overall view of officials with highest rank and responsibility that the relationship between the two often seems to defy rational explanation. As important as particular military requirements appear initially to be, as a matter of course they are reduced in the process of budget-making or military programming both within and beyond the department. Moreover, it is part of the American tradition of civil supremacy that in the final outcome the military accept the direction

[1] Interviews.

of civil authorities in such matters as budget ceilings. Finally, the Bureau of the Budget during this period had not been reluctant to relate the question of the level of Federal, and particularly defense, expenditures to the survival of American institutions in a way which precluded the possibility of the military challenging the overall budget ceilings imposed upon them. For instance, as desperate as the Navy partisans had been in their struggle to defend the air-power capabilities of their service during the B-36 investigation of 1949, they never suggested that budget ceilings were in error, only that the limited funds were being distributed among the services unwisely. Evidently Landon came to the State-Defense study group reacting somewhat the same way to the budget pressures under which the Defense Department had been laboring. At least initially, and for the apparent purposes of the study group, he came committed to existing budgets, programs, and plans, although his commitment was an uneasy one.

In an early meeting Landon agreed to produce a working draft of the joint study paper. He came back with a paper which he, General Maddocks, and Admiral Robbins had drafted in the Joint Strategic Survey Committee. Reflecting the tendency of the Military Establishment to be reconciled to current budget policies, it was optimistic regarding the relative military capabilities of the United States and the U.S.S.R. The Policy Planning Staff then tried its hand at drafting a paper. It was a broader paper than Landon's, but not so broad as the final product. Compared with the JSSC paper, it was pessimistic about relative military capabilities. With the two papers before it, the study group argued out the major differences between them, particularly the issue of comparative strengths. When the Policy Planning Staff people attacked the optimism of Landon's paper, they found that he was not really convinced with his own document. For Landon and for his associates in the JSSC, this experience served to show that the study group was really interested in a reappraisal which did not take for granted the validity of existing strategic assessments, assumptions, and plans. It was, that is to say, an invitation to break out of the straitjacket of Defense Department strategic thinking and to explore, unencumbered by the severe budgetary pressures of the Truman-Johnson administration, the strategic requirements of national security. Landon and his associates accepted that invitation.[2]

The procedure of the study group focused upon an open discussion of the merits of substantive issues. At the same time, however, the State Department spokesmen wanted an estimation of what could be cleared through the Joint Chiefs of Staff, based on the judgments of the Joint Strategic Survey Committee and informal clearances in the Joint Staff. Nitze's daily meetings with Acheson kept the study group assured of the relationship of what they were doing to authoritative opinion in the State Department. They had no such reassurance from the Defense Department, however. From the beginning, they were aware that in view of Secretary Johnson's widely publicized commitment to economy in the Defense Department, Landon and Burns were walking on eggs in their participation in the study group.[3] They did not hope for Johnson's support during the drafting of their paper; they hoped, however, and were inclined to think, that Landon spoke, if not for the Joint Chiefs of Staff, at least accurately about what the JCS would do when confronted with the results of the study. Their hope had little foundation, yet in the end it proved correct.

Once candor had been established in the study group, Nitze was evidently anxious to minimize the hypothetical character of the study group's work. He was, after all, in a relatively secure position. He was planning with the support of the Secretary of State and was fully in Acheson's confidence. He could afford to test the work of the committee against authoritative judgment in the State Department. Landon, on the other hand, would have faced a showdown prematurely had he done the same thing in the Defense Department, and he would probably have embarrassed the Joint Chiefs of Staff into yielding to Johnson's policies against their better judgment. Therefore, although he cleared all the study group's work with his own committee (the JSSC), his contacts beyond that in the Defense Department concerning his work were deliberately minimized, and

[2] Interviews.   [3] Interviews.

he fell back upon the independence of the JSSC as the authority for what he did.[4]

The fact that Johnson was known, or thought, to be hostile to the work of the joint State-Defense study group, while Acheson supported it, can be used to explain too much, however, for other factors contributed to the difference in perspective between Nitze and his associates and Landon and his associates. Three, in particular, are worth mentioning. Landon's lack of authority to speak for the JCS, even though he was in a particular sense their spokesman, was by no means unique. Almost without exception, the Joint Chiefs have refused to authorize representatives or spokesmen to act for them, even on a working level. Undoubtedly one reason for such meticulous concern over maintaining its freedom of action has been that the JCS is a committee, not a command. In addition, two other reasons seem plausible. Possibly the Chiefs have recognized that the practice of military organization to delegate responsibility out from the center would, if it were not resisted, rob them of the opportunity to make decisions. Furthermore, in order to prolong its wartime preeminence, the JCS avoided identification of itself or its staff with the Office of the Secretary of Defense as long as it could, which was until the 1949 amendments to the National Security Act began to be felt.[5]

The second reason why the State Department officials involved in drafting the study paper were less concerned with the problem of breaking away from official policies and more concerned with relating what they were doing to responsible opinion than were their counterparts in the Defense Department involves a subtle but profound distinction between the two Executive agencies involved. The Secretary of State can be more casual about the status of his advisers than can the Joint Chiefs of Staff. For instance, although Acheson maintained oversight of the study group's work through

---

[4] Interviews.

[5] See, for example, Paul Y. Hammond, "Directives for the Occupation of Germany: The Washington Story," in Casebook, Twentieth Century Fund Study of Civil-Military Relations, in press, for an account of a comparable problem in World War II.

daily conferences with Nitze, he could quite easily have said in the end that it was a good try, but the results were impractical. Such action would undoubtedly have undermined Nitze's position as Director of the Policy Planning Staff, but the repercussions from that would have been unimportant. However, had the Joint Chiefs of Staff remained silent, while the JSSC claimed to speak for it, and then repudiated the results of the JSSC's work, it would have risked starting hopeless interservice wrangles and reducing its own status as a body of military experts. Whether because the Secretary of State is avowedly more involved in policy-making and less of an expert than the Joint Chiefs of Staff, because he is likely to be closer to the President, because he is a civilian, or simply because he is one person, not four people, or for whatever reason, the search for authoritative judgment can follow more flexible channels in the State Department than it can in the Defense Department.

Finally, a special reason for Landon's independence of the Joint Chiefs should be noted. For the previous six months, the Joint Chiefs of Staff structure had been in turmoil. General Bradley had been appointed Chairman of the Joint Chiefs in August 1949, under the terms of the new legislation. At the end of October, Admiral Louis A. Denfeld was, in effect, dismissed and replaced by Admiral Forrest P. Sherman, who faced an enormous task of drawing the Navy together again after the so-called "revolt of the Admirals." The House Armed Services Committee report on the "Unification and Strategy" hearings of October, which could be, and was, an important judgment of interservice disputes and national strategic planning as it pertained to the Department of Defense, was awaited there with some concern. Its issuance on March 1, 1950, laid to rest fears long held in the Navy and the Air Force of its anticipated tone.[6] The JCS was not in a position in February 1950 to run the risk of incurring the wrath of the Secretary of Defense again. Under the circumstances, it was better that the study group work without close touch with the Joint Chiefs of Staff.

[6] *Unification and Strategy,* Report of Investigation made by the Committee on Armed Services, House of Representatives, 81st Cong., 2d Sess. (Washington, 1950).

Landon's view was by no means unique. Indeed, it was more common than Nitze's. The study group, rather than including all the agencies later represented on the National Security Council subcommittee established to formulate a program for NSC-68, had been limited to two departments in order to increase the prospects that it would break away from established policies and particular interests. Because of the limited membership of the group, the prominent role Landon played in it had particular significance. Of the three Defense Department members of the group, Burns had ruled himself and his assistant, Halaby, out as the representatives of a Defense Department viewpoint by his support of Landon as spokesman for the department. This was perhaps the most important decision made in connection with NSC-68. Burns was a career Army officer, but his position as a deputy to the Secretary of Defense meant that, if he were to represent any viewpoint, it would be that of Louis Johnson—the dominant civilian viewpoint in the Military Establishment. Had he done so, had he performed a role in the committee comparable to that played by Nitze in behalf of the Secretary of State, the whole project would have deadlocked, or would have been what Landon initially expected it to be, another exercise in justifying the current defense budget.

Bringing Landon into the group was in one respect simply a recognition that the JCS, as well as the Office of the Secretary of Defense, was involved in the kind of matters with which the group expected to deal. But encouraging Landon to take the leading role for Defense made it possible to by-pass the question-begging economy viewpoint of the administration, which Johnson represented, and to explore the problem afresh with the military professionals. Landon was the voice of these professionals, and the Joint Strategic Survey Committee, their major interpreter. The study group generated questions and concepts to be tried out in the JSSC through Landon. The group viewed this process as a way to obtain both competent professional military judgment and an estimate of JCS views—not as they were being expressed at the time in Congressional hearings, but as they would be expressed under different circumstances.

Indeed, military spokesmen in the defense budget hearings for fiscal 1951 were saying quite different things at the very time of the study group's deliberations. General Omar N. Bradley, the Chairman of the Joint Chiefs of Staff, in his opening statement to the House Appropriations Committee, had made no reference to the detonation the previous September of a Soviet atomic bomb and had assured the committee that $13 billion was adequate as the total defense budget figure.[7] Then, on March 15, before the Senate committee, he said:

. . . the eventual strength of our country depends upon its industrial capacity. We must not destroy that by spending too much from year to year. So if we came here and recommended to you a $30,000,000,000 or $40,000,000,000 budget for defense, I think we would be doing a disservice and that maybe you should get a new Chairman of the Joint Chiefs of Staff if I were the one who did it.[8]

Clearly, the economy issue was begging the question of military requirements for Bradley, as it was also for his colleagues on the Joint Chiefs of Staff.

THE CONTENTS OF NSC-68

As the document finally took shape, NSC-68 was relatively brief. Reportedly, it began with a statement of the nature of the world crisis and ended with a call to action by the United States. The world crisis it defined primarily in terms of long-range historical processes affected specifically by, first, the Russian revolution and the Communist movement since then and, second, the development of nuclear weapons, the significance of which it explored. It provided a general theory about what Russia was trying to do, which concluded that the Kremlin had no master plan and that it had three major objectives. In order of priority, these were: (1) to preserve the internal power position of the regime and develop the

[7] *Department of Defense Appropriations for 1951,* Hearings before the Committee on Appropriations, House of Representatives, 81st Cong., 2d Sess. (Washington, 1950), pp. 80–83.

[8] *Department of Defense Appropriations for 1951,* Hearings before the Committee on Appropriations, United States Senate, 81st Cong., 2d Sess. (Washington, 1950), p. 73.

U.S.S.R. as the base for that power; (2) to consolidate control over the Soviet satellites and add them as support for that base; and (3), to weaken any opposing centers of power and aspire to world hegemony.[9] Against these objectives of the Kremlin it set a definition of American purpose. As it has been paraphrased elsewhere,

> One way in which that purpose can be stated is found in the Constitution. It is ". . . to form a more perfect union, establish justice, insure domestic tranquility, provide for the common defense, promote the general welfare, and secure the blessings of liberty to ourselves and our posterity."
>
> Four corollaries flow from this purpose: (1) our resolve to establish and preserve a system based on the concept of human dignity; (2) our determination to promote and secure conditions at home and abroad under which this system can live and prosper; (3) our willingness to cooperate with others in any action, however costly or challenging, needed to achieve this purpose by peaceful means; and (4) our readiness to fight, if necessary, to defend this system for ourselves and for our children.[10]

Although, as will be described in greater detail below, NSC-68 intentionally avoided making the assertion that the Kremlin design was an ideological commitment to achieve world hegemony, it did picture an inherent conflict of interest between the United States and the Soviet Union because of ideological differences. The incompatibility of the concept of freedom with Soviet political institutions, it held, made the United States a threat to all three of the Kremlin's objectives, even the preservation of its own internal power.[11]

The document examined and compared Soviet capabilities with Western capabilities, including conventional military forces and nuclear weapons and a projection of future nuclear capabilities and economic strength. It asserted that the Soviet system had vulnerabilities, three of which were identified: agriculture as an economic problem, the brittleness of the relationship of the Soviet masses to the top Soviet leadership, and relations with the satellites. But on the whole, the result was disquieting. The Soviet Union was pictured

[9] Interviews.

[10] Paul H. Nitze, "U.S. Foreign Policy, 1945–1955," *Foreign Policy Association, Headline Series*, March–April 1956, p. 54.

[11] Interviews.

as capable of rapid economic growth at the same time that it maintained a large military establishment. The document estimated that within four years the Soviet Union would have enough atomic bombs and a sufficient capability of delivering them to offset substantially the deterrent capability of American nuclear weapons. In comparison, it emphasized the inadequacy of the Western capability to meet limited military challenges due to a lack of conventional forces, shortcomings in the Western alliance system, and the military and economic weaknesses of western Europe.[12]

The paper rejected the possibility of negotiation with the Soviet Union except on the basis of power political considerations. Similarly, it concluded that the prospects of achieving effective regulation of armaments were remote because the necessary methods were (or semed to be) incompatible with the Stalinist regime. Persistent efforts to achieve an effective agreement on arms regulation were considered necessary, particularly for nuclear weapons, although it was held that the success of these efforts depended upon the growth of free-world strength and cohesion.[13]

Since the end of World War II all national strategic planning had run up against the argument that the nation could not afford to spend more. The study paper concluded that even in peacetime up to 20 percent of the gross national product could be devoted to national security, if necessary, without economic bankruptcy.[14] (In 1959, 20 percent of the gross national product was about $60 billion, about three times the total annual expenditures of the United States on national security at that time.)

In conclusion, NSC-68 pictured four alternatives facing the United States: (1) continuing on the present course of limited budgets with no increase in capabilities and no decrease in commitments; (2) preventive war; (3) withdrawal to the Western Hemisphere—the Fortress America concept; and (4) the development of free-world cohesion through a program to increase free-world

[12] Interviews. The four-year figure can be inferred from the fact that NSC-68 first had a four-year schedule. See Joseph and Stewart Alsop column, New York *Herald Tribune,* December 3, 1950.

[13] Interviews.

[14] Interviews.

capabilities. The fourth alternative it examined in greater detail, analyzing the relationship between the strength of the United States, as the center of the free world, with the strength of the countries on its periphery, the relationship of economic and military programs to each other, and of both to psychological factors of strategy. It stressed the importance of allies to American security, the inadequate military preparedness of the free world, hence the need for improving it.[15]

Simultaneously with the preparation of this document, the Policy Planning Staff was working with the Director of Mutual Defense Assistance on estimates of the costs of the troops needed to defend Europe, and on what the scope and level of foreign aid activities should be for the next five years. Probably this part of the study paper was closely related to the MDAP staff work. Yet, although it stressed the importance of allies, it concluded that the best way to build free-world military strength would be to begin at the "center," with the building up of American military capabilities—no doubt a reassuring position for Defense Department personnel. The expansion of Allied capabilities should then proceed concurrently. The new capabilities were to be both for general war and for other things as well.[16]

The conclusion of the document was a real call to action, claiming that more, much more, was needed to be committed in effort and resources by the United States if the American strategic situation were not to deteriorate steadily.[17]

MAJOR CONTENTIONS INVOLVED: ISSUES, DIFFERENCES, FRAMES OF REFERENCE

The Policy Planning Staff members of the joint State–Defense study group were initially more willing than were their Defense Department counterparts to consider policies which implied greater annual expenditures on foreign affairs. They were also more committed to the establishment of a comprehensive policy than were Landon and his JSSC associates. Both views were due, among other

---

[15] Interviews.   [16] Interviews.   [17] Interviews.

things, to the concern of the State Department, and of the Policy Planning Staff in particular, with the Mutual Defense Assistance Program. But these were differences in perspective brought by the two groups to their first meetings and, as we have seen, soon overcome. Once a mutual understanding had been established, no important differences of opinion (with one exception) split the study group down departmental lines. The exception will be discussed later. It should be recalled, however, that there was a procedural difference between the two departments in the status each gave the study group. In the State Department, the group, working under the benevolent eye of the Secretary of State, was never in serious doubt that in the end he would endorse what it was doing. In the Defense Department, the sympathy of the Secretary of Defense with the purposes of the group was open to question and his final support in constant doubt.

A recurrent theme in the policy paper on which the joint State-Defense study group worked was the nature of the Soviet threat. In addition to the judgment of its own members, the State-Defense study group could draw upon the views of two foreign service officers in the State Department who were recognized as experts on the Soviet Union, and the American naval attaché in Moscow. The views of these officials, analyzed together with those of Nitze and Landon, reveal some striking differences in outlook and approach.

George Kennan, one of the experts on Russia, was away from the State Department on a tour of Latin America from February 18 until March 24, 1950, during which time most of the work on the study paper was completed. Charles E. Bohlen, the other expert, was stationed in Paris throughout this period. He visited Washington for a few days shortly after Kennan's return in order to advise the study group. Most of the differences between Kennan and Bohlen, on the one hand, and Nitze, on the other, over the nature of the Soviet threat are explainable by their backgrounds, by the fact that Kennan and Bohlen, unlike Nitze, were foreign service officers and Soviet experts. The backgrounds, of course, do not explain the differences between Kennan and Bohlen; and, in any case, such explanations are suggestive, not definitive.

The group's draft of the study had listed world domination as the primary objective of the Kremlin design. Bohlen objected to this assumption. He argued that the Kremlin had no grand design in view, that world hegemony was a tertiary goal, following the Soviet regime's primary interest in preserving and improving its internal power position and its secondary objective of consolidating control over the Soviet satellites. In his view, the Russians worried a great deal about overextending their commitments—for instance, because of the fact that they had troops stationed in Europe. This view was finally accepted by the study group. Before it was, Acheson, who was kept informed throughout, had become bored with the dispute, for he thought it of little practical consequence in which order the Soviet objectives were listed, so long as they were all there.[18] To Bohlen and Nitze, however, the order was not so insignificant.

Nitze had listed Soviet objectives in order of their importance to the United States, and in such a way as to emphasize the Soviet threat. Apparently, his was largely a rhetorical point. Obviously, he recognized that there was more to the motivations of the Soviet state than following Communist dogma. But since Soviet motivations (or those of any nation) are so much more complex than that, he apparently reasoned, one is entitled to select a dramatic and prominent theme such as world domination and emphasize it as the most important, or at least the most uniquely characteristic, of Soviet objectives. What Nitze did with his original ranking of Soviet objectives, it is evident, was to set them in an order which would make that portion of the study paper where they appeared carry as much of the burden of the argument as he could give it. His judgment of the ordering of Soviet objectives, therefore, was identical with that of Acheson. Neither of them thought it intrinsically important. Nitze, however, adopted and defended a particular order for its persuasive impact: If his argument could begin with a

[18] Interviews.

convincing statement which maximized the nature of the Soviet threat, the burden of proof of the rest of his case would be reduced.

But the order of Soviet objectives was not persuasive to Bohlen because he was more sensitive, both to the Soviet viewpoint and to the possibility of drawing false conclusions from inaccurate premises about that viewpoint. He insisted on ranking Soviet objectives by their priority to the Soviet Union so that how far down the list Russia would get—that is, how many of those objectives she would attempt to achieve—would depend upon her capabilities of achieving them. He wanted to emphasize the flexibility and opportunism in Soviet policy, but, somewhat ironically, his revision of the statement on the nature of the Soviet threat also had the effect of emphasizing and clarifying the study group's inclination to deduce Soviet intentions from Soviet capabilities. Kennan considered this equation of capabilities with intentions to be a crude oversimplification of the problem of predicting Soviet actions. Specifically, he argued that their actions would not be determined by their capabilities—for one reason, because of their caution. Bohlen, it should be noted, agreed with Kennan on this point and, indeed, about the general one regarding intentions. He had reordered the listing of Soviet objectives, not because he regarded capabilities and intentions to be equivalent, but only because he considered Soviet intentions to be proportional to her capabilities, rather than simply to dogma.[19]

Bohlen and Kennan agreed that the nature of the Soviet threat was too complex to serve as the starting point for planning either military strategy or foreign policy. Although Bohlen accepted as necessary an attempt, such as the study group effort, to define the problem and outline a response to it, such planning, he apparently thought, could not legitimately rest on any particular prediction about future Soviet behavior, for any prediction would be too arbitrary. Yet all planning must be arbitrary in some respects. The art of planning lies in the ability to select the points of arbitrary choice which will limit the relevance of the plan the least. Nitze evidently thought one of those points could be the nature of the

[19] Interviews.

Soviet threat. Bohlen thought quite the contrary. Kennan agreed with Bohlen, but went on to conclude that formal policy planning of this character is necessarily too simplified to be useful.

From the naval attaché at the American Embassy in Moscow, Rear Admiral Leslie C. Stevens, the study group received quite a different interpretation of the Soviet threat. Stevens, a naval aviator with wide experience in naval air staff work, was also a member of the National Advisory Committee for Aeronautics. In his estimate, Soviet capabilities were less than the American intelligence community (the estimates of which were coordinated by the Central Intelligence Agency) said it was; but her intentions were wholly bad. She was so bent on world domination that negotiation with her was impossible, for she had nothing to concede.

Whether world hegemony was first or last in Russia's aims, and whatever the relationship between her capabilities and her intentions, the important question remained whether she threatened full-scale war with the United States. Nitze's position on this point had been stated eight months earlier at the time he and Kennan had been briefed by Defense Department officials on their strategic plans. He believed that a general war capability deserved the first priority. If General Landon's service viewpoint affected his position on the Soviet threat, it was in the same direction, to emphasize the importance of strategic air power. If it did not, his position as a member of the Joint Strategic Survey Committee was nonetheless substantially the same. Military staff planning insisted that the worst contingency be provided for first, hence, that a general war capability have priority over any other possible military capabilities. Both Bohlen and Kennan disagreed with this emphasis on general war, for both believed that the Soviet Union did not pose a sufficient threat of general war for that contingency to be given first priority. The prime Soviet threat, Kennan argued, was political, diplomatic, and economic; and that which was military, he argued, was largely a threat of limited military challenges which would require the United States to be capable of fighting limited war with conventional forces.[20]

[20] Interviews.

The joint State-Defense study group did not disagree with Kennan that conventional military forces were needed for a limited-war capability. The group had reasoned that the atomic stalemate which was approaching would neutralize the American nuclear deterrent, leaving the United States exposed to the might of Soviet conventional forces. It concluded that in preparation for that day we ought to improve the capabilities of our conventional forces. In the summer of 1949, Kennan had, it will be remembered, advocated concentration on the development of a small, mobile task force, approximately the size of two divisions, to meet and to deter military challenges on the Soviet perimeter. The forces Kennan envisaged, however, were considerably smaller than the conventional military capability the study group had in mind for fighting something less than an all-out war with Russia.[21]

At the same time, Kennan and Bohlen seem to have had substantial reservations about the joint study group's concern with seeing that the United States be prepared to meet an all-out military challenge from the Soviet Union. Bohlen had not, after all, insisted that the aspiration for world hegemony be dropped from the list describing the power objectives of the Soviet regime, only that it be listed last in order to emphasize the opportunism of Soviet designs. Kennan's position was somewhat comparable to Bohlen's. Neither of them doubted that the Soviet Union would, if given sufficient opportunity, directly challenge American security. Neither was certain that the opportunity would not occur, although Kennan was certain enough to rule out the *prime* necessity for an all-out war capability for the American military establishment in favor of the smaller, more discriminating forces.[22]

But always, differences involved matters of degree and proportion. Kennan discounted large-scale war as a practical problem, not only because of his strong belief in Soviet caution, but also because of his concern lest preparation for it should close off possibilities of diplomatic settlement, because he feared the dominance of policy by military considerations, and because of his belief in the im-

[21] Interviews.   [22] Interviews.

portance of political and economic factors in the cold war.[23] When the proposal for an H-bomb program was under discussion a few months earlier, he had opposed it for the same reasons. Bohlen merely regarded the more limited probings as the more likely of the two: he did not exclude a showdown military challenge as a possibility worth anticipating.

In one way or another, therefore, all of these discussants saw a need for something besides a capability to meet a major Soviet military challenge; yet no one specifically anticipated the challenge posed in Korea within four months. The study group members would have considered it as premature—something not likely to occur until after 1954, when, it was estimated, the growing stockpile of Soviet fission bombs would have neutralized the deterrent force of American weapons.[24]

The study group, like the two State Department experts on Russia, wanted a conventional military force capable of fighting limited military engagements. Where, then, in practical terms, did they disagree with the experts on Russia? The answer to this question was never entirely clear to the Policy Planning Staff members. They were puzzled that Bohlen continued to object to their policy paper after they had changed it to suit him. At least two of them thought that Kennan exaggerated his differences with them, evidently because Kennan was not objecting to the substance of the policy paper itself, as he appeared to be, as much as to the effect he anticipated it would have at Cabinet and White House levels, and to the very wisdom of drafting it. Bohlen accepted the necessity for policy papers of this kind, but also doubted its anticipated effect, and remained unsatisfied with its statement on the nature of the Soviet threat.[25]

Evidently both experts on Russia feared that, at best, the document would scare the administration into making a large-scale increase in defense capabilities, that this increase would be accomplished in the "cheapest" way by a continued, or even increased, concentration on strategic air forces and nuclear weapons, and that

[23] See, for example, George F. Keenan, "Is War with Russia Inevitable?," *Readers' Digest,* March 1950, pp. 1–9.
[24] Interviews.   [25] Interviews.

armed forces with more discriminating capabilities would be more and more neglected. Kennan's concentration on the anticipated results of the paper, rather than on the merits of the points made, is more clearly demonstrated by another of his criticisms. He insisted that too much weight was given in the paper to military, and not enough to diplomatic, factors. Here again, when he tried to clarify his criticism to the Policy Planning Staff, its members could not see any specific points of difference between their paper and his own position. Evidently the difficulty was that for Kennan the main issue did not turn on the content or emphasis of the paper, but upon whether it ought to have been undertaken at all. He did not conceive of policy as something which could be set down in such a document.

The failure of Kennan's criticisms to jibe with the viewpoint of the joint study group might suggest that his viewpoint had never occurred to them, that they were working with a "let the chips fall where they may" attitude which left them oblivious to considerations of what the reactions and effects of their paper were likely to be. To a certain extent this was undoubtedly their attitude. It was intended to be. The object of the study was to take a new look at the general strategic picture, and to reappraise it. In order to do that, it was necessary to put aside current budget ceilings, and the political considerations which helped to set them, even to ignore to some extent what the Secretary of Defense would say about the reappraisal. It is clear that the work of the joint study group was carried on in what was at least a partial policy vacuum. It was an attempt, that is to say, at a rational projection of strategic policy requirements from the national strategic situation. It is true that both Acheson and the Joint Chiefs of Staff—or at least the Joint Staff—were, in some measure, mooring points to policy for the study group. But in both cases the working status of the study group was well understood. It was expected to produce a staff paper, a "think piece," which, without endorsement by the policy-makers, would have no official status.

Inevitably, however, the group anticipated the problems of clearance for the policy paper. The procedures followed in its drafting make it evident that the Defense Department side of the joint study group operated independently of the Joint Chiefs of Staff or the Office of the Secretary of Defense, and that the State Department side maintained the continuing support of the Secretary of State. To what extent was the study group paper a product of anticipations about clearance problems and to what extent was it a logical projection from the strategic situation as the group saw it? Of course, neither consideration was excluded, but the emphasis was certainly on the logic of their paper rather than on its palatability to the Truman administration. This was one reason for Kennan's criticism of it. In view of its unpalatability, he feared that it would be made actually harmful before it was swallowed by the government.

One might imply from this that Kennan was less confident than his former colleagues in the Policy Planning Staff, as well as Acheson or General Landon, of the possibility, or at least the advisability, of divorcing a major activity of government, even in its planning stage, from the day-to-day context of public affairs with its inhibiting suppositions and pressures. "You cannot," he seemed to be saying, "carry on an undertaking like this, isolated from the irrational pressures which bear upon public affairs, without rendering your effort useless." But these were not Kennan's objections at all. He objected to formal planning, not to isolation from the pressures of popular government. At the time, and consistently since then, he placed great reliance upon secret diplomatic negotiation of a general settlement with the Soviet Union as a means of reducing the prevailing tensions in international relations.[26]

What troubled Kennan about the study project was the very idea that the vast and complex problems of American foreign policy could be set down on a few sheets of paper without transforming them into crude and clumsy oversimplifications, or without making them less than candid in anticipation of opposition to them. He had been disturbed with what he considered to be a tendency to overemphasize military factors and methods in the conduct of American foreign policy, a tendency which he feared would grow if the recommendations of the study were implemented. Although he was fully

[26] See, for example, George F. Kennan, *Russia, the Atom and the West* (New York, Harper and Bros., 1958), Chap. II.

aware of its origins and anxious to see some changes in American policy, he saw this new appraisal of American policy developing characteristics which he had already learned to distrust: the systematization of policy-making by which a simplified, coordinated, and programmed general solution was adopted, but which submerged real issues and eliminated flexibility in policy-making and diplomacy. A general policy statement, he believed, could not cover the unique aspects of a particular time and place, nor embrace the real issue involved.

Kennan himself had once attempted a general formulation of American policy towards the Soviet Union, an imaginative summary of thinking in the Executive branch which had become the basis for NSC-20. This was the famous Mr. "X" article, published in *Foreign Affairs* in 1947, which had the effect of identifying Kennan with the policy of containment.[27] But apparently he had come to regret the article, or at least its publication. He had wanted a quiet development of American policy. The article had the effect of exacerbating the differences of viewpoint and judgment within the government upon which development would feed. He now felt that it would be better to leave the policy largely implicit, for that would provide optimum conditions for flexibility, freedom from popular pressures, and the constructive use of professional diplomatic judgment.[28]

Bohlen had had no experience with publication comparable to that of Kennan. Whether this was the point of departure in their views or not, the degree of congruence in them is worth noting. Bohlen evidently doubted that what could be known about Soviet behavior could be set down with sufficient precision to be circulated in the government without the statement suffering badly in the process. Kennan went further, to doubt in addition that policy could be set down, laid out in advance, and followed, without so crippling the practice of the diplomatic art that what could be gained thereby in consistency, coordination, and preparation would be more than

---

[27] Kennan, "The Sources of Soviet Conduct," *Foreign Affairs*, July 1947, pp. 566–82.

[28] Interviews.

lost in rigidity and oversimplification. Both men, that is to say, objected to what they considered an attempt to congeal and disseminate an esoteric skill, although Kennan's conception of the breadth of the esoteric skill involved was considerably greater than was Bohlen's.

Kennan's view, and to a lesser extent Bohlen's, it should be noted, rejected the need for the planning, programming, and making of prior commitments to policy on administrative grounds, a central requirement of large-scale organization, the primary mission of which is the performance of integrated operations, whether it be military or of any other, such as economic aid administration. The view of these two foreign service officers was shared only in part on the State Department side of the study group table. As a member of the Joint Staff, Landon was involved in the policy planning process of the Defense Department. The experiences of a military career had demonstrated the utility of planning objectives and long-range preparations for the successful completion of operations. Nitze, for his part, had worked in the economic mobilization agencies of the government during World War II, and was in close touch with the officials who coped with programming for foreign economic aid and, more recently, with military aid. He was concerned with a lack of cohesion in the operations of the American government in foreign affairs—not just in diplomacy, but also in the vast undertakings of the Mutual Defense Assistance Program and the European Recovery Program. He wanted a brief statement of American policy which could be accepted throughout the government as the basis for a common effort.[29] The discussions with Kennan and Bohlen may not have been of crucial importance to the outcome of the study document, and in any case they can be regarded as internal State Department relations. On the other hand, they are important because they represented a difference of viewpoint between the career foreign service officer and the administrator. At the extreme, the foreign service officer would, if this distinction is valid, rely emphatically upon the personal skills and noncommunicable wisdom of the experienced career official and would view the requirements of large-scale organizations

[29] Interviews.

(such as the armed forces with their demands for forward planning) as a direct threat to the practice of this diplomatic art. On the other hand, officials sympathetic to the problems of administration, such as those who dominated both sides of the study group table, accept the necessity in the administration of large-scale operations of forward planning with all its rigidities, simplifications, and artificialities.

Although these differences of viewpoint and assumption were possibly revealing of an important cleavage within the government between the foreign service officer and the administrator, or simply between the career and the noncareer appointee in the State Department, no side-taking general enough to prove anything occurred at the time in the State Department. Indeed, the discussion of the study paper in the State Department was limited in its drafting stage to a very few people. Perhaps it was limited even more in the Defense Department. Landon, it is true, went back to his colleagues in the Joint Strategic Survey Committee each day to report, to discuss, and to hammer out new drafts. But for the most part they worked without any formal guidance from their superiors. Indeed, their State Department associates were evidently more anxious for the Defense Department members to keep themselves cleared with the Joint Chiefs of Staff during the drafting stage than they were. Consequently, important disagreements did not develop in the Defense Department at this stage. Had the committee made some effort to define the character of the military expansion, disagreement over service roles and forces might have developed, but no such definition was attempted. Disagreement was therefore conspicuous by its absence.[30]

The one point on which a State-Defense division occurred on the joint study group was the question of overall cost estimates. The group did not attempt to work out cost estimates on any systematic basis; certainly it was incapable of doing so. Nevertheless, when its members discussed capabilities and increases, even in the most general way, it would have been difficult for them not to have in mind at least some orders of magnitude. The Policy Planning Staff members thought the military budget should be increased from

[30] Interviews.

the current annual rate of expenditure of about $13 billion to around $35 billion. An even higher figure, $50 billion, was considered a reasonable guess.

Landon and the JSSC, and the Army and Air Force planners, Generals Alfred M. Gruenther and Lauris Norstad,[31] with whom Nitze and Kennan, respectively, had discussed the matter directly, thought in terms of an increase of about $5 billion, to an annual budget for defense totaling about $17 or $18 billion.[32] Possible reasons for this difference in viewpoint over costs will be discussed below.

In the study group the difference in costs proved irreconcilable. It is not clear whether there had been any intention originally to include in the paper an estimate of costs for implementing its recommendations. Surely some members of the group thought there should be, notably Tufts from the Policy Planning Staff.[33] Evidently out of the deadlock grew the belief, perhaps sponsored by Nitze, that figures should be excluded because they would prejudice officials against the policy statement before they had read it. In any case, this view prevailed. The policy paper, as it came from the study group, gave no indication of what its program would cost. Some of the members of the group hoped that, as a result, the merits of their arguments would be considered before fiscal or political considerations intervened.[34]

Costs were the most striking and intentional omission, but there were others. Two in particular are noteworthy. The study group attempted no searching examination of military strategy and provided no schedule for rearmament beyond proposing the target date of 1954. Undoubtedly, any attempt to reach agreement on the elements of a common military strategy would have tangled the group hopelessly in interservice conflict. The Navy and the Air Force had been engaged in public dispute over military policy not four months before the study group began its work. If the group had probed very

---

[31] Norstad was Deputy Chief of Staff Operations, and then, after March 17, Acting Vice Chief of Staff, in United States Air Force Headquarters; Gruenther was Deputy Chief of Staff for Plans in the Office of the Chief of Staff, United States Army.

[32] Interviews.   [33] Interview with Robert Tufts.   [34] Interviews.

far into military strategy, it would have destroyed the prospect that the results of its work could be considered on their merits, for it could not have avoided touching sensitive nerves only recently frayed. What the group did do was to make the case that strategic air power was not enough—perhaps the most important single point needed in military strategy then and in the decade since then, although always it has verged on being undisputed and inanely obvious.

The group made no attempt to provide a schedule for rearmament because it had so little to go on. Costing techniques in the Defense Department, as we have seen, were crude and cumbersome. At the very time of their involvement in the study group, State Department officials were encountering the appalling problems of pricing the rearmament of America's allies. Without some kind of dollar figures with which to work, any attempt to suggest how fast rearmament should be accomplished and what economic policies should be adopted to cope with the stresses which would result was bound to be unproductive and diversionary.

The particular reasons for the omission of a thorough examination of strategy and of at least an outline of mobilization policy were plain enough. In addition, they were justified by the principle of putting first things first. NSC-68 was intended to be an analysis of the problem, not a program for its solution. It pointed in the direction in which the solution was thought to lie, and examined in a general way the feasibility of moving in that direction. It did not, nor was it intended to, specify the route. But as important as it is to have objectives clearly in mind before undertaking an enterprise, objectives, or ends, usually need to be adjusted to means. NSC-68 was preoccupied with the task of breaking out of a mode of thinking in which means had seemed to dictate ends. It emphasized, as a result, the importance of new and larger ends and the sufficiency of the means. No doubt it was right about the sufficiency of means within the scope of its inquiry and justified not to explore the means because of the opposition which it would arouse by doing so. Not doing so, however, had other consequences. Because rearmament was never defined, it was evidently never clear what anyone meant by his estimates of what the defense budget ought to cost. The State Department side of the study group took rather seriously the differences in estimates between themselves and, say, Norstad and Gruenther, while the military side of the group discounted them.

What, indeed, did these figures mean? Did the State Department's $35 to $50 billion and Norstad's and Gruenther's $17 or $18 billion mean the peak, or the first phase, or what? Obviously, the individuals involved had some idea of their own terms of reference, for all had some familiarity with the problems of mobilization. Nitze surely did not mean that the first-year expenditures could be $50 billion. On the other hand, he could not have intended that expansion to a level of $35 or $50 billion could be carried on at a leisurely pace, for the point of the study group paper was one of alarming urgency. The end magnitudes and time phases involved were, in combination, abstract and complex concepts. Because the study group did not examine them systematically, what any of its members meant them to be was not clarified.

A more important consequence of the omissions—of both omissions in this case—was that the assumption that the United States could match Soviet power went unexamined and unquestioned. Although accepting it without reservation at the time was understandable, a thorough inquiry would have subjected it to critical consideration, as the decade which followed was to make quite evident. Once again, the thrust of the argument for a greater effort was so strong that it by-passed an important question along the way. Judged by contemporary perspectives, these omissions concerned subsidiary questions. Nothing could guarantee, however, that they would not become primary ones.

SECRETARY JOHNSON'S REACTION TO THE DRAFTED DOCUMENT

As their work progressed, it was evident to the joint study group that, whether it meant $17 billion or $50 billion, their policy paper was going to be a radical departure, particularly from the economy policies with which Secretary Johnson had identified himself. Johnson had not been kept posted on the day-to-day work of the study group. But the group felt that Johnson should be made acquainted with the work before its completion so that he would not repudiate it on the grounds that he had not been informed about it until it was too late to change it.[35]

An additional reason for briefing Johnson before the group had completed its work may have been the fact that he was to preside over the Defense Ministers' Conference at The Hague at the end of March. While the Mutual Defense Assistance Program was not far enough along to make a discussion of the breadth undertaken by the joint study group an agenda item for the conference, some State and Defense Department officials thought that the change of outlook presaged by the work of the study group would be valuable baggage at The Hague.[36]

Whatever the reason, Nitze suggested to Acheson that Johnson be briefed on the work of the group before it was frozen into final form, and Acheson agreed. The strictest of protocol was followed in arranging the meeting. H. Freeman Matthews, who was Acheson's official liaison with the Defense Department in accordance with the Presidential directive Johnson had sponsored the year before, arranged through Burns, Johnson's liaison with the State Department, a meeting of the joint State-Defense study group with Johnson, Acheson, and General Omar N. Bradley, the Chairman of the Joint Chiefs of Staff, on about March 20.[37]

The study group suffered some anxiety over the prospects of this meeting. Johnson had two possible reasons for objecting to their work. He could object to the substance of policies proposed because they ran counter to existing Defense Department policies, which were based on given fiscal limitations imposed by the White House. And he could object to the procedures followed because they had not conformed strictly to the pattern set up the previous year that all contacts between the State Department and the Defense Department be handled directly by Burns and Matthews.

The study group prepared a two-page summary of the current draft of the policy paper. Burns and Halaby undertook to brief Johnson on the paper and have him read the summary. But Johnson

[35] Interviews.   [36] Interviews.   [37] Interviews.

was too busy, and in the end they prepared a one-page summary of the two-page summary and hoped that Johnson would read it before going to the session with Acheson and the study group. An hour before the meeting took place, Admiral Arthur C. Davis, the Director of the Joint Staff for the Joint Chiefs of Staff, told General Bradley that it seemed to him the State Department had been "railroading" its own views through the joint study group, and that Burns and Halaby had not protected the interests of the Defense Department there. Johnson and Bradley rode together to the meeting. Whether Bradley conveyed Davis' appraisal of the paper, in turn, to Johnson, the committee members never knew, although they found no reason to doubt that he had.[38]

The meeting was held in Nitze's office, next to Acheson's. Johnson would not come in the front door of the State Department building because, as he said, the attention that would be focused as a result on the meeting would encourage news leaks about it. Instead, he was escorted in secretly through the underground garage and up a private elevator. Besides Acheson, Johnson, and Bradley, Burns, Halaby, and Landon were there from the Defense Department, Matthews, Nitze, and Tufts represented the State Department, and Admiral Souers, the President's consultant on national security matters, was there from the White House staff.

The State Department contingent came united, for the dissenters were not there to dispute. Acheson had favored the study, and had kept an interested and sympathetic eye on its preparation, although he felt some doubts about its value. Nitze had been the major force behind it; now he was its rapporteur. Tufts had provided a skill in drafting and an expertise in economics. Matthews was a career diplomat with long and varied experience in the State Department, who must have been more skeptical than Acheson (though not so much as Kennan) about the value of such an undertaking. Responsible for liaison with the Defense Department, however, he should have been pleased with the concerted effort to reach an understanding with Johnson over major policies.

The Defense Department contingent had no such common view-

[38] Interviews.

point. Landon, Burns, and Halaby, the Defense Department members of the State-Defense committee, were committed to the enterprise and the product. Johnson had already made clear his objections to free contacts between the State and Defense Departments, and had committed himself to lower defense expenditures. Bradley, as Chairman of the Joint Chiefs of Staff, was subject not only to many of the same economic pressures to which Johnson had bowed, but also to others generated by the planners and operators of the services and the JCS in the opposite direction. Souers had been only an observer in the study group, but he had committed himself to the procedure in principle in December 1949 when he had recommended to the National Security Council the making of a general strategic appraisal.

The meeting began with Nitze briefing Johnson and Johnson reading the two-page summary. The abruptness and severity of his reaction startled everyone present, even though there had been forebodings of it. He questioned the authority under which the study was made. He charged Burns with failure to perform his duties as the Defense Department's contact man with the State Department, and all present, particularly Nitze, with scheming to undermine his policies. In a slap at Landon, he instructed Bradley to inform the Joint Chiefs of Staff and the study group of the procedure for State Department–Defense Department relations. He pointed out that the paper conflicted with established policies, and he indicated his contempt for it. The scene ended almost as abruptly as it had begun, with Johnson storming out into Acheson's office to talk the matter over privately, leaving surprise, anger, humiliation, and dismay behind. In private, Acheson pointed out to Johnson that the study group had worked under instructions from the President, and that he was going to see the President about it. In fact, he did not do so. But Admiral Souers did, and received Truman's permission to continue the work.[39]

Among the group left in Nitze's office, the State Department officials were disappointed, but not alarmed. Assured of Acheson's support, they knew their actions would withstand Johnson's criticisms. The Defense Department officials had no comparable grounds

[39] Interviews.

for reassurance, either that they would be vindicated, or, indeed, that their positions remained tenable. Although Burns was an old friend of Johnson—he had served as the latter's Executive Officer when Johnson was Assistant Secretary of War—his first thought was to resign, for he felt that the personal relationship upon which his position in the office of the Secretary of Defense was based had been destroyed by suspicion.[40] (He did not resign, but remained with Johnson until the latter left the Pentagon the following September.)

FINAL DRAFTING AND CLEARANCE OF THE POLICY PAPER

After the meeting with Johnson, the study group prepared a draft of the paper which was circulated more widely. In the State Department, where it was assured of support from the Secretary, it was shown to very few people, only the Under Secretary and the Assistant Secretaries, for the most part. In the Defense Department circulation was extensive. Furthermore, it occurred mostly in Johnson's absence, for he was away from Washington from March 28 to April 3 attending the NATO Defense Ministers' Conference at The Hague. All the civilian Secretaries, down to and including the Assistant Secretaries of the three services, were given an opportunity to read the paper and offer suggestions about it, perhaps in an effort to build up support to counteract Johnson's opposition to it. On the military staff side, on March 31, 1950, following unanimous approval of the paper by the Joint Strategic Survey Committee, it was submitted to the Joint Chiefs of Staff. Each of the three members of the JSSC had undertaken to brief the planner and the Chief of his service ahead of time, so that, for instance, General Landon briefed General Vandenberg, the Chief of Staff of the Air Force, General Norstad, the Acting Vice Chief of Staff, and General F. F. Everest, Norstad's assistant. The JCS approved the paper by April 5. Before the Joint Chiefs as a corporate body considered the paper, each of the Chiefs (except, presumably, General Bradley, the Chairman) had approved it individually on the basis of the briefing he had received from his service's member of the JSSC. Although this was not extraordinary staff procedure in the JCS, and the document was not a regular JCS

[40] Interviews.

paper anyway, it does denote a degree of care in the handling of JCS clearance which was not entirely routine.[41]

The document reached Johnson's desk two or three days after his return from The Hague with eight endorsements on it from within his own department—the three service Secretaries, W. Stuart Symington of the Air Force, Gordon Gray of the Army (both soon to retire), and Francis P. Matthews of the Navy; the three service Chiefs, General Hoyt S. Vandenberg of the Air Force, General J. Lawton Collins of the Army, and Admiral Forrest P. Sherman of the Navy; the Chairman of the Joint Chiefs of Staff, General Omar N. Bradley; and Johnson's adviser on atomic energy (as Chairman of the Military Liaison Committee to the Atomic Energy Commission), Robert LeBaron.[42] Were he to disapprove the paper, he could be sure that Acheson would take it to the President anyway. He may not have cared to risk the showdown between Acheson and himself which would thus have been precipitated. Besides, since the paper was only a general statement of policy, he was conceding nothing concrete. Later there would be ample opportunity to challenge concrete proposals for carrying out the new policy objectives and to take his stand against expenditure requests. After all, these signatories were not, for the most part, prominent among the economy-minded group in the administration, and the economy people had theretofore been in the position of dominant influence. Finally, it is not clear that Johnson had become the boldest supporter of the administration's drive for economy in government out of personal conviction. He had, for instance, obtained an increase of $500 million from the President in his first defense budget (fiscal 1950). No doubt the joint study group paper challenged his public stand on economy, but he may still have found approving it a personal satisfaction.

For whatever reason, Johnson did approve it. So did Acheson. It went to the White House over their signatures, dated April 7, 1950,[43] as a fulfillment of the request made in the President's letter of January 30.

[41] Interviews.   [42] Interviews.   [43] Interviews.

IV *Submittal to President Truman*

The fact that President Truman had authorized the joint study and had, following Johnson's blowup, agreed that it should be completed, was no assurance that he would approve it. His decision might turn on the views of the White House staff and the Bureau of the Budget, both of which were potential opponents of the study. On the whole, the White House staff were oriented more to domestic politics than to foreign affairs. National security matters usually by-passed them. Admiral Souers, the Executive Secretary of the National Security Council until January 1950 and, after that, consultant to the President for national security matters, briefed Truman every day on national security developments. National Security Council papers went directly from Souers to the President; no one else on the White House staff cleared them first, unless in Souers' judgment they had domestic implications. The main source of the information the White House staff received and the influence it exercised in this area during the initial years of the NSC was Clark Clifford, the Special Counsel to the President. Clifford moved out easily among the Cabinet members and had regular contacts with Forrestal. His resignation in the fall of 1949 marked the beginning of a period of diminished knowledge and influence on national security matters because his successor, Charles Murphy, did not develop, before the Korean War overtook all relations with military affairs, commensurable interests or sources of information and influence. Consequently, the White House staff was not as well informed on foreign and military matters during the drafting and initial clearance of NSC-68 as it had been earlier. It tended to look upon these matters even more as the province of Admiral Souers and the newer staff arrangements.[1]

[1] Interviews.

The Director of the Budget, Frank Pace, also emphasized domestic considerations. In fact, Pace was probably the clearest expositor of "domestic objectives first" in the administration, for he reduced this emphasis to a kind of simple arithmetic. He began with a ceiling for the national budget, based on "what the economy could stand in taxes," that apparent economic justification for an essentially political concept. From this he subtracted "essential" domestic expenditures and foreign aid. What remained was what could be spent on the Defense Department, which was usually somewhere between $11 and $13 billion.[2] Unless he were to change his approach, Pace could hardly be expected to view favorably a policy paper which directly challenged his own approach by insisting that the Federal taxes and expenditures could be more than doubled without causing national bankruptcy, and that expenditures for national security were not to be determined by what was left over from everything else.

The joint State-Defense study group, evidently hoping that the President would approve their paper outright, attempted to minimize the obstacle to Presidential endorsement by briefing the Special Counsel to the President, Murphy, and the Budget Director, Pace. The two men reacted quite differently to the paper, despite the fact that both were inclined to have a "domestic affairs first" viewpoint. Murphy was greatly impressed with the line of argument followed in the paper. He had accepted the claims of Pace, and the Budget Director before him, James Webb (who was now Under Secretary of State and a supporter of the joint study group paper), that there was an economic basis for budget ceilings. And he had accepted as a matter of course the priority of domestic needs over national security needs. The picture of the Soviet threat painted by the study group paper alarmed him, however, and economic arguments of the paper made him doubt that the economic limits of Federal expenditures had been reached. Murphy assured his briefers that the President would see their report.[3]

Nitze discussed the study group paper with the Budget Director. Pace's position remained unaltered by it. Reportedly, he quoted to

---

[2] Interviews.   [3] Interviews.

Nitze Bureau of the Budget figures on how much the economy could stand in the way of Federal expenditures, and how necessary expenditures on other things besides foreign and military affairs were.[4]

Within the bureau, another kind of opposition also developed to the document. The intention had been to make it a comprehensive appraisal of national strategy, focused on no particular geographical area and on no individual government function or agency. It was easy, therefore, to challenge the paper on procedural grounds. Had all the agencies with whose functions it dealt participated in its drafting? If not, had they all cleared it? Since they had not, what was its status? What was the reason for submitting it to the President? [5]

The views of other members of the White House staff besides Murphy seem to have ranged between Murphy's alarm over the Soviet threat and Pace's faith in the current rationale of fiscal policy. But even for those in the White House and the Budget Bureau who, with Murphy, had come to fear Russia and doubt that fiscal policy was rational, a final step was usually missing in their thinking which was necessary to make them, with Nitze and Landon, for instance, wholly committed to the study group paper. The missing step can best be illustrated by Senator Walter George's reaction to the document. Under Secretary of State Webb, though he agreed with the analysis made by the study group paper, was particularly conscious of the limitations which Congress was likely to impose upon its implementation. He thought that Senator George, then the Chairman of the Senate Finance Committee, senior Democratic member of the Foreign Relations Committee, and a highly respected Senator, was the key to the Congressional viewpoint. Reportedly, he arranged for George to come over to the State Department and be briefed on the paper by Nitze.[6] George did not disagree with the development of the argument in the paper, and after two days of discussions with Nitze he was presumably familiar with it. But he remained uncon-

---

[4] Interviews.   [5] Interviews.

[6] Interviews. Webb may have chosen George because as Director of the Budget he had developed a close connection with George on the Finance Committee. Or he may have wanted George to see NSC-68 because it might induce him to minimize his opposition to foreign aid, particularly MDAP appropriations.

vinced. His attitude seemed to be, "It is logical, but . . ."—a skepticism about any single line of rational inference which he shared with others who were oriented to the inhibitions of political accountability.

The comparable reaction among members of the White House staff and in the Bureau of the Budget was to ask precisely what had to be done and what it would cost. For instance, even Murphy's alarm did not carry him into strong advocacy of the document, for he wanted to know what it would cost before he committed himself.[7]

On April 12, 1950, evidently acting on the recommendation of James Lay, who was the Executive Secretary of the National Security Council, President Truman signed a letter to Lay referring the study group paper to the NSC. The letter indicated that the President particularly desired to know what program was envisaged in the report and what it would cost. It specified that the NSC subcommittee he anticipated would work on it should include representatives of the Economic Cooperation Administration, the Bureau of the Budget, and the Council of Economic Advisers, in addition to the statutory membership of the NSC. Upon referral, the paper received the file number NSC-68.[8]

What did the President's action mean? He had not specifically approved the document or any part of it. He had committed himself only to see that the concrete implications of the paper would be worked out by his staff. For the moment, the only thing that had been decided was that work on planning the new policy would continue through the process of establishing programs for it and estimating their costs.

[7] Interviews.   [8] Interviews.

v Preparing the Programs for NSC-68 before the Korean War

THE PRESIDENT'S OUTLOOK

Between April 12 and June 26, 1950, the administration was moving in two different directions in its national security policies. One was toward the expanded effort for which NSC-68 argued, for the document was under consideration with Presidential blessing. The other was a program to hold the line or retrench on defense expenditures. The Bureau of the Budget and the Office of the Assistant Secretary of Defense (Comptroller), headed by Wilfred J. Mc-Neil, wanted to keep the Defense Department budget from exceeding $13 billion. Talk of even a $10-billion budget ceiling for fiscal 1952 was serious enough to have prompted preliminary soundings on it. Just how close Johnson stood to McNeil and the Budget Bureau through April, May, and June is not clear, as will be explained more fully later.

Evidently President Truman was aware of these diverging trends.[1] Evidently, also, he was in no hurry to reconcile them or to choose between them. Of the two, however, the economizers had the initiative: Not choosing meant staying on the economy track, which seemed to fit the President's disposition. In his press conference on May 4 he stated that foreign technical and economic assistance would make possible a smaller military budget for fiscal 1952 (the beginning of which was more than a year away, but the initial preparations for which had already begun).[2]

[1] Interviews.
[2] Alsop column, New York *Herald Tribune,* May 5, 1950.

It should be noted that Truman's statement differed with NSC-68 both in the magnitude of the defense expenditures he anticipated and, at least by implication, in his assumptions about the nature of the Soviet threat. NSC-68 had rejected the notion that the U.S.S.R. could be contained with economic and technical assistance. Judging by this statement, the President had certainly not committed himself to the document. Yet, later on he seems to have had second thoughts. In his press conference on May 25, responding to further questions about future budget planning, he stated that a ceiling had been placed on the defense budget, but he could not go into it until all the facts and figures were in.[3]

If, however, the administration was hedging or beginning to turn about in the spring of 1950, the signs of any change are remarkably obscure. Defense appropriations were increased for the following year, but not through administration efforts, although the administration followed along as gracefully as it could. After the House Appropriations Committee cut the defense budget by $200 million, Carl Vinson, the dean of House military experts, led efforts to get $583 million more for the Air Force, and General Eisenhower, as a private citizen, testified in support of a $500-million increase from the House cut. Eisenhower's statement put Johnson in a difficult position. The previous autumn Eisenhower had, as unofficial chairman of the Joint Chiefs of Staff, approved a budget for fiscal 1951 totaling $14.6 billion. Johnson, however, had been calling the $13.5-billion budget, which he supported, "Eisenhower III," the effect of which was to associate the reputation of the eminent General with Johnson's budget. Eisenhower's recommendation of a $500-million increase in the budget undermined that association and posed for Johnson the choice of either giving up the support of the Eisenhower reputation or accepting an increase in the budget. He chose the increase.

After referring the proposed increase to the Joint Chiefs of Staff for study, Johnson supported a $350-million increase and a restoration of the cuts, and gave his assurance that the economy program still stood.[4] Congressman Mahon, the Chairman of the Appropriations Subcommittee, yielded to the pressure and accepted an increase

[3] *Ibid.*, May 26, 1950.   [4] New York *Times*, April 27, 1950.

of $385 million. The House passed the total figure of $13.8 billion. The Senate had not acted when the Korean War began.[5]

To supervise the programming for NSC-68, Lay, the Executive Secretary of the National Security Council, organized an ad hoc committee of the NSC on the Senior Staff level. The committee was noteworthy for the number of members it had from agencies not normally represented in NSC deliberations at that time. It included, besides Lay, Nitze from the State Department, Burns from the Defense Department, Richard Bissell from the Economic Cooperation Administration, Leon Keyserling, the new Chairman of the Council of Economic Advisers, and representatives from the Bureau of the Budget, the Central Intelligence Agency, and the Treasury Department. General Bradley attended the early meetings, probably until JCS guide lines for Defense Department estimates had been established, as will be explained below.[6]

Before the beginning of the Korean War, the committee did little besides put pressure on its Defense Department members to produce price figures for their consideration. In early meetings the Bureau of the Budget representative again raised the question of the status of NSC-68. It had never been adequately cleared, or "staffed out," he indicated, and until it was, the NSC could not appropriately consider it. (Presumably, the President could not appropriately consider it or refer it to the NSC either.) It is unclear whether or not this was an obstructionist device used by the bureau.[7]

One member of the committee came as a partisan in support of the economic viewpoint expressed in NSC-68. Keyserling had already

[5] Vinson's move can be traced more to the "Unification and Strategy" inquiry conducted by his committee the previous October than to any obvious underlying shift in administration policy, although it is evident that he had become uneasy about the general magnitude of defense expenditures. On the floor of the House on April 4 he attacked Johnson's economy program for having "weakened the national security in very important respects." Of the $565-million increase he proposed, $385 million would go to naval aviation. *Congressional Record*, XCVI (April 4, 1950), 4680–84.

[6] Interviews.   [7] Interviews.

begun to argue against the prevailing notion that there was an absolute upper limit, which had been reached, at which government expenditures could be sustained over the long term. It is not clear, however, to what extent he raised and argued this point in the committee prior to the beginning of the Korean War. He certainly did so afterward.[8]

Evidently the ad hoc committee was established to settle questions raised in programming for NSC-68 and to integrate various programs with each other. Whether or not these tasks, as contemplated, amounted to an exaggerated expectation of the role which other agencies besides the Defense Department could play in programming and pricing for NSC-68, in fact the main burden of that programming and pricing fell to the Defense Department.

The joint study had recommended beginning the needed build-up at the "center" of free world strength—the United States. This meant that the Defense Department budget was the key to the first step in programming for NSC-68. For particular reasons, European rearmament, which would be the next phase, was difficult to project into the National Security Council framework. The Mutual Defense Assistance Program was the obvious base from which to plan the new rearmament there. But this program was still in its formative stages, so much so that it was difficult to distinguish between what NSC-68 would require in American military assistance to Europe, particularly in its initial phases, and what any other program based on different premises would require. Congress had approved MDAP, with an initial authorization of $1.3 billion, only in October 1949 after long and trying hearings. While most of the money was obligated before the Korean War began, only a trickle of finished materials had come through. Shipping did not begin until March 1950; by the end of June, a mere 134,000 tons of military equipment, almost entirely from existing military stocks, had reached our European allies, and only $52 million—5 percent of the authorization for that fiscal year—had been expended.[9]

[8] Council of Economic Advisers, "The Annual Economic Review," in *The Economic Report of the President,* January 12, 1951, pp. 80–83.

[9] *Mutual Security for Fiscal Years 1948 to 1959,* Committee Print, Committee on Foreign Relations, United States Senate, 85th Cong., 2d Sess. (Wash-

An integrated defense plan, a statutory prerequisite imposed by Congress for the expenditure of MDAP funds, was not approved by the NATO members until April 1, 1950, at a meeting of their defense ministers. When their foreign ministers met in mid-May, the inter-relation between strategy (such as the defense line to be held), and the size, kind, and extent of international integration of their forces, supporting activities, and respective fiscal policies, had become more than clear, for initial projections of force requirements from the agreed defense plan were obviously beyond political and economic realities. For the Mutual Defense Assistance Program, NSC-68 seemed in the spring of 1950 logical, but useless. The need for a European build-up appeared obvious; those officials in the United States government who were involved in the early development of MDAP did not need the arguments of NSC-68 (or so it seemed) to justify the initial costs of that program, although later, the document might prove to be valuable to justify continuing expansion to a high level of preparation and expenditure. For this reason, programming for MDAP in the special subcommittee of the NSC seemed irrele-vant. For another, it seemed impossible: Programming for NSC-68 involved the establishment of demands upon American resources. These could be determined for MDAP only in conjunction with establishing the capabilities (in the largest sense) of our allies to share the total burden. Western European and American officials completed estimates of Europe's total capital equipment needs for rearmament in the summer of 1950. Not until October 20 did they derive American expenditures from these totals for clearance with the Defense Department and the Economic Cooperation Administra-tion.[10]

The implications of NSC-68 for the American foreign economic aid program were easier in one sense and more difficult in another to determine than MDAP needs. The European Recovery Program had begun two years earlier than MDAP. By 1950, many of the prerequisites for future planning had been achieved, including the

ington, 1958), p. 2; Department of Defense, *Semiannual Report of the Secre-tary of Defense, January 1 through June 30, 1950* (Washington, 1950), pp. 10–11.

[10] Interviews.

assembling of a skilled and experienced staff. On the other hand, NSC-68 and the programming for it primarily involved military capabilities, and only secondarily the economic program they would affect. The officials of the Economic Cooperation Administration who oversaw the programming for NSC-68 considered its impact to be indirect. American military supplies for our allies would not themselves have a substantial impact upon the European Recovery Program. Any important effect would come from the complementary programs of expanded effort by recipient nations. Larger military expenditures would threaten to unbalance national budgets, cause inflationary pressures, and increase balance of payments problems. These effects would be substantial, and ECA would be concerned with them; but they would be the result of military build-up programs as yet undetermined, which would be, in turn, geared in with, and to some extent determined by, an expanded American military aid program, also as yet unknown.[11]

At least, then, in the initial phase of planning, the fears of Kennan, the career diplomat, were justified. He had doubted the advisability of the whole study group effort because of the likelihood that its effect would be to emphasize military factors to the exclusion of other equally, or more, important ones. Certainly military planning dominated the programming for NSC-68 which preceded the outbreak of war in Korea.

DEFENSE DEPARTMENT PROGRAMMING

Secretary Johnson Supports NSC-68

As Secretary of Defense, Louis Johnson had undertaken to carry out the economy objectives of the administration with an enthusiasm which James Forrestal had never shown, an enthusiasm which had put him in the forefront of the spokesmen for economy in government. This he had done as a loyal supporter of the administration program. Stripped of the fervor of the moment, his complaint against the study group paper had been an important procedural one: He had originally directed that all Defense Department contacts with

[11] Interviews.

other agencies be cleared through General Burns because he had found that often his own position as Secretary of Defense was undercut by clearances with the working layers of the Defense Department.[12] Operating with perhaps unrealistic expectations about how much an executive in the American government can impose his policies on his subordinates in spite of their own views, he had thus hoped to identify more clearly the military factor in policy-making. The study group paper, NSC-68, was everything that he had objected to: a major policy position established by the working layers in the State and Defense Department (or at least in the Defense Department), which reached him as a fait accompli. Nitze had initiated the briefing of Johnson before the document was completed so that Johnson would not be confronted with a fait accompli. But in fact it already was one, for its main lines were already well drawn and all the major issues already argued out.

A possible reversal, or modification, of the President's commitment to low defense budgets was now to be anticipated. Following an NSC meeting in mid- or late April 1950, probably the meeting on April 20, Johnson stopped in to see the President. When he came out, he stated privately that his economy program was dead, and that he had shaken hands with the President on it.[13]

Eisenhower's testimony in favor of an increase of $500 million for the defense budget had come at the end of March, a week before Johnson put his name to NSC 68. On April 26, when Johnson appeared before appropriations subcommittees of both houses to propose an increase in aircraft contract authorizations and for Navy antisubmarine work, and to modify (or qualify) his stand on defense economies in the light of NSC-68, his prepared statement was both an attempt to reconcile previous with current defense policies and with the anticipated, though unknowable, future, and a general description of the current outlook which had led to a reconsideration of policy. It deserves extensive quotation:

[12] Johnson's account of the origins of his clearance directive appears in *Military Situation in the Far East,* Joint Hearings before the Committees on Armed Services and Foreign Relations, United States Senate, 82d Cong., 1st Sess (Washington, 1951), IV, 2595, 2687–88, 2690.

[13] Interviews.

In beginning my discussion of this subject, I would like to go back to last September. Immediately after the President's announcement on September 23 that there had been an atomic explosion in the USSR—which was a date somewhat in advance of the date we had anticipated—we began a reevaluation of our own military requirements. Almost simultaneously with this development, the President directed the Secretary of State and the Secretary of Defense, as a working committee of the National Security Council, to conduct a broad reevaluation of our national program, in the light of our international commitments and in the light of the constantly changing world situation.

Some of the results of the reevaluations mentioned above are already known to this committee. Specifically, the President's decision to proceed with the construction of the H-bomb was based in part on the studies described above.

In addition, many of the steps we have taken in furtherance of the North Atlantic Pact and the military-aid program implementing that pact have been based on the continuing studies I have already mentioned.

I would not like to leave the impression that these studies are completed. Indeed, in the broad sense, studies of this nature are never completed, for both the State and the Defense Departments must continuously review foreign policy and the military strength that goes hand in hand with it.

In making continuing reviews of this type, we have the advantage of the very excellent organizational arrangements Congress has provided through the vehicle known as the National Security Council—and I refer particularly to the language used by Congress in assigning to the National Security Council the duty "to assess and appraise the objectives, commitments, and risks of the United States in relation to our actual and potential military power, in the interest of national security."

The point at which we have arrived at the present time can be described as follows: Based on the work already done by the Council of Foreign Ministers, by the Council of Defense Ministers, and by the Chiefs of Staff of the North Atlantic Pact nations, we have for the first time, a fairly clear picture of the collective military requirements of the North Atlantic community of nations. We have also appraised recent events which make it entirely possible that appropriations in excess of those which have been requested for the current year will be required in succeeding years, not only for our own military forces but also for the military-aid program. Just as it is possible that in future years this Nation will have to devote an increased percentage of its total budget to these items, it is also possible that our partners in the North Atlantic Pact will be required by the force of events, and by the force of our collective planning as well, to take similar action. The events to which I allude include the Soviet atomic explosion, the fall of China, the serious situations in southeast Asia, the break in diplomatic relations with Bulgaria and deteriorating relations with other satellite countries, the Soviet assumption of control over the armed forces of Poland, Soviet naval expansion, the increased Soviet pressures in Germany, the recent attack on a naval aircraft in the Baltic, and the recent Soviet demands relative to Trieste.

None of this presents a happy prospect; but the "cold" war is not a happy circumstance. The only satisfaction that I can personally derive from the situation lies in the fact that our own Military Establishment is well on the road to becoming a stronger and more powerful organization, and one which, as circumstances require, can utilize increased appropriations in a manner which will provide substantially increased combat effectiveness, whereas, even as recently as 1 year ago, large sums of money out of any increased appropriations would have been drained off in the form of unnecessary overhead. It is particularly important that the armed forces maintained by the United States shall at all times provide a sound base on which can be built a Military Establishment of increased size, should circumstances so require—for our mobilization in time of emergency depends for its success upon the soundness of the forces in being which constitute our mobilization base.

Speaking to this point in chapter IV of the semiannual report which I submitted to Congress on February 28, I said: "Before the services could make effective use of their money, therefore, it is essential that they 'get into condition.' Even if additional amounts of money had been added to their budget, large percentages of it would have been to produce added military strength. . . . Our watchword must be economy and efficiency in every activity—with the size of our Military Establishment as stable a basis as possible, subject to such increases or decreases as the international situation may warrant."

In this connection, I should like to stress the fact that the economy programs, far from being laid aside, is made even more necessary by the world conditions and circumstances to which I have referred, to the economy program, on which we are all engaged as a team, and on which we have had such excellent cooperation and support from this committee, is to be carried on with undiminished vigor because we can continue to eliminate overhead in applying our resources to buttress up combatant forces. Indeed, the economy program—which has been misinterpreted and misconstrued in some quarters—is one of the principal tools used by the Department of Defense in channeling funds into the combatant forces where such funds can be used to give us added strength, and away from such wasteful expenditures as unnecessary overhead, costly duplication, and unwarranted overlaps.[14]

Referring to the above statement, Johnson made even more direct
reference to NSC-68:

. . . we give you there, for the first time officially announced, the fact
that some months ago the President of the United States directed the
Secretary of State and the Secretary of Defense to make a study for him
of this whole situation. The items that entered into our concern are listed
categorically in here, and it is as a result of these conclusions that we ask
this money. . . .[15]

It would be misleading to take Johnson's private statement that
his economy program was dead too literally, for throughout May and
June 1950 he continued to take a familiar position that funds were
sufficient and might possibly be cut later.[16]

Johnson was in real trouble, and not entirely of his own making.
Truman had decided to go along with the prevailing views about
government expenditures, and had charged Johnson with carrying
them out in the Defense Department. Johnson had gone his chief
one better and had seen these policies become identified with himself. Now, however, he found the President hedging and the public
mood shifting. The only rational thing for him to do was to hedge,
too, which is precisely what he did throughout the spring of 1950.

How the programming was carried out

Johnson assigned to General Burns his responsibilities for seeing
that NSC-68 was programmed and priced. Assistant Secretary of the
Army Tracy Vorhees purportedly suggested to Burns that the establishment of requirements be handled through special channels because the regular procedures in the Department of Defense for
determining them were not very effective. Burns evidently did not

[14] *Department of Defense Appropriations for 1951,* Hearings before the Committee on Appropriations, United States Senate, 81st Cong., 1st Sess. (Washington, 1950), pp. 843–44; also, *Department of Defense Appropriations for
Fiscal 1951,* Hearings before the Committee on Appropriations, House of Representatives, 81st Cong., 1st Sess. (Washington, 1950), pp. 2–3.
[15] *Department of Defense Appropriations for 1951,* additional Supplemental
Hearings before the Committee on Appropriations, House of Representatives,
81st Cong., 1st Sess. (Washington, 1950), p. 8.
[16] For example, Alsop column, New York *Herald Tribune,* June 23, 1950.

disagree with Vorhees' observation. Indeed, he had been aware of the inadequacies of Army procedures for determining requirements in both world wars. But he decided to use regular channels because he believed that they *ought* to be effective, and this would be one way to improve them. The result was not what he had hoped. No single official in charge of estimating requirements could be turned to in the Office of the Secretary of Defense, although the budget estimating process was centralized through the Defense Department's Comptroller, Assistant Secretary of Defense Wilfred J. McNeil. Hence, once the guide lines for NSC-68 were set by the Joint Chiefs of Staff, programming for it became part of the budget planning process, indistinguishable from planning for fiscal 1952 in the Defense Department. In effect, then, the setting of requirements as a process separate from the fixing of prices was accomplished only by the Joint Chiefs of Staff, and, after that, "programming" NSC-68 was handled by the budget makers in the course of performing their own duties.[17]

Johnson's memorandum on Defense Department programming for NSC-68 reflected this close relationship to budget estimating for fiscal 1952. The memorandum set a schedule of deadlines as follows:

July 1   Flash estimate of NSC-68 cost.

August 1   JCS analysis upon which more methodical study could be based.

October 1   Completion of preliminary estimates.

November 1   Completion of final money and force estimates for NSC-68.[18]

The deadline for the fiscal 1952 budget was December 1, so there would be a month in which to reconcile the two programs. But other points of reconciliation were anticipated, for Johnson's order dealt with the relationship of the two throughout the schedule it established. It provided that the fiscal 1952 budget and NSC-68 should be constantly related to each other, and in fact that NSC-68 should be related to current budget policies. How could a program as divergent as NSC-68 was from current budget policies and plans be "related" to those policies without destroying the meaning of at least

[17] Interviews.   [18] Interviews.

one of them? It is possible to see in Johnson's instructions a desperate attempt to equivocate. But evidently another explanation can be made. The letter did not assume that an expanded military program was approved, nor did it approve in advance the programming for NSC-68. But it did assure that the possibility of future expansion would be taken into account in the operation of the department and in the estimating of future budgets.[19] The practical effect of such account-taking could be only marginal, however. The two divergent programs remained unreconciled.

The joint State-Defense study group had viewed its work as a significant departure from existing policies, and the State Department reaction had been largely to agree. Acheson's reservations were not to the extent of that departure. He only doubted its relevance to political facts.[20] But in the Defense Department, as we have noted, the document, or at least its implications, seemed to be less radical.

When the Joint Chiefs of Staff proceeded to fulfill their obligation to provide guide lines for NSC-68, including general estimates of requirements, they divided the world into regions and estimated requirements by geographical areas. However, this procedure led to the usual difficulties. When these estimates were added together, they proved to be too much, and were cut back by the Joint Chiefs of Staff before submittal to the Office of the Secretary of Defense or the services. The Joint Chiefs of Staff were unable to work without some preconceived force limitations in mind. What was true for them was true elsewhere in the planning and control offices of Military Establishment administration. Although for its civilian sponsors, unencumbered by day-to-day political pressures, NSC-68 was a significant new appraisal of the strategic situation, to many in the Defense Department it was a special performance of a comparatively routine function. The Joint Chiefs of Staff, as we have seen, had found it impractical to produce strategic appraisals which were not conditioned by political considerations—at least those concerned with budget levels. Moreover, they were often forced, by the persuasive logic that budget cuts would be more painful if left to others, and by the requirement of loyalty to the civil power, to modify substantially an original appraisal without changing explic-

[19] Interviews.   [20] Interviews.

itly its frame of reference, with the result that what was eventually approved by the administration, although it usually bore little relationship to the original appraisal, still carried the approval of the Joint Chiefs of Staff.

Experience thus counseled a relativistic approach to national strategic estimating, a mixture of healthy skepticism and tired resignation about the objectivity or correctness of their own so-called military judgments. This relativism was magnified by lack of agreement among the services over even the elements of a common strategy. Granting each service the assumption which it employed in its own strategic planning, and allowing these assumptions to be projected into national dimensions, questions about strategy and national requirements could be answered with some definiteness. The answers needed, however, were not those for each service, but common answers for all three. By 1950, only a few interservice techniques had been developed to give a common meaning to the question of how much was enough. Consequently, the answer remained only relative.[21]

To the relativism of military planning which resulted from unsolved and inherent problems related to it was added budget relativism, based on the same kind of immeasurables and imponderables. The Military Establishment, with its long-, medium-, and short-range estimates, plans, and budgets, its "purely" military estimates and their many modifications, and its programming at several alternative budget levels, did not see NSC-68, on its face, as anything extraordinary. Rather than a chance to think through the general strategic situation in a fresh way, it was a problem in estimating the relevance of many positions identified and marked out in the course of planning and budgeting. For the planners of all three services, as a practical matter, it amounted to estimating at what overall dollar level approval of the Joint Chiefs of Staff could be secured. Previous experience indicated that that level was about $18 billion. Significantly, this was the approximate figure the Army and Air Force planners, Gruenther and Norstad, had in mind during the drafting of NSC-68 in February and March.

As Johnson's July deadline for flash estimates drew near, events

[21] Interviews.

in Korea changed the whole frame of reference for Defense Department budgeting and to a lesser extent for national strategic planning. On the evening of June 26, responding to reports of crumbling resistance in South Korea to the attack from the north which had begun early that day (American time), President Truman ordered United States naval and air forces to give assistance to the Republic of Korea. Four days later American ground forces were committed to the Korean Peninsula.

At the beginning of the Korean War, the Defense Comptroller, McNeil, had what he reportedly regarded as order of magnitude estimates, but nothing particularly precise. The Joint Chiefs of Staff produced as flash estimates for their July 1 deadline a supply program for military build-up with a procurement figure for first-year orders totaling $50 billion. It anticipated a steep schedule of expansion of military readiness, based initially on the reactivation of existing bases and equipment, and included an expanding schedule with monthly goals. Initiation of the program was to be achieved within a year, during which time, at the least, direct economic controls would have to be exercised by the government.[22]

It would be easy to exaggerate the significance of these figures. They were, for the most part, unscreened estimates based on unilaterally determined service force levels and included as well sums to cover the Mutual Defense Assistance Program and civil defense. Apparently the $50-billion figure was summed up for the JCS flash estimates from separate service figures between June 26 and the July 1 deadline. McNeil's office viewed the figure as having practically no real meaning. A similar view was taken in the Bureau of the Budget, which was represented on the NSC subcommittee.[23]

The $50-billion estimate, as Johnson's memorandum had provided, was the beginning, not the end, of Defense Department programming and pricing for NSC-68. The President referred it to the NSC subcommittee, but it also served as the highly tentative first step in defense programming.

[22] Interviews.   [23] Interviews.

THE CONDITIONS FAVORABLE TO A COMMON VIEWPOINT

When the Korean War began, NSC-68 remained unprogrammed and unapproved. Although President Truman had quite plainly withheld his approval of the document pending the development of some specific programs, some kind of favor (at least that he would consider it further) was implied by his referral of it to the National Security Council for the development of those programs. Officials in the Defense Department Comptroller's Office considered the $50-billion estimate so unrefined as to be practically useless, and in the Bureau of the Budget this figure was considered—when it was considered at all—much higher than was justifiable. At best, the status of NSC-68 was tentative at the time events in Korea altered the whole frame of reference for American military policy.

Yet, NSC-68 had much to recommend it. It had avoided, as we have seen, entanglement with questions which involved interservice disputes, such as the delineation of service roles and missions or the uses and limits of strategic air power. Moreover, it provided something for everyone and in a way that was palatable. Economic growth is a way to moderate problems of distribution. Similarly, proposals for the general expansion of national security activities, economic, military, and otherwise, would seem to offer the prospects of reduced friction among the rival claimants for resources to carry them out. Undoubtedly friction would be greatly reduced if it were certain that the proposals were going to be accepted. Without that assurance, however, such proposals offer the threat of reopening settled disputes over allocation, as well as the hope for general gain by all claimants.

The experience of the three services over the previous three years before the spring of 1950 supported this conclusion. The prospects for general increases in defense expenditures which took shape in March 1948 soon became an opportunity for the Air Force to promote its own case at the expense of the Army and the Navy. Considering new expenditures meant considering new ways of spending on defense. The argument for more funds for air power became, as the defense budget pressures increased after the 1948 election, arguments for less sea and land power. The Army and the Navy might have felt the pinch anyway, but, quite clearly, the fortunes of the Air Force took a turn for the better during the short expansive period in 1948, and the Air Force remained ahead of the Army and the Navy when retrenchment set in. The lesson to learn was not a new one. Indeed, the Army had known it in 1917 when it opposed the expansion of its own air arm in the face of a strong public sentiment. A similar reaction among all the services evidently affected the fate of the Gaither Report in 1958 when it reached the National Security Council. Although all three services knew they stood to gain if the report were adopted, each also feared that it might lose out, at least in relation to its sister services, if less than the whole were adopted.[1]

However, in the particular circumstances the prospects of a general expansion in the national security field assuaged more fears than it aroused. Characteristically, it offered more for everyone: more for the military departments, more for foreign military aid, even more, as we shall see, for economic aid. The conflicts which might have developed over the expansion envisaged are clear enough: The expansion of our own military capabilities is bound to compete for scarce resources and limited budgets with foreign

[1] For a description of interservice rivalry over budgets and air power in 1948 and 1949 see Hammond, "Supercarriers and B-36 Bombers: Appropriations, Strategy, and Politics," in Casebook, Twentieth Century Fund Study of Civil-Military Relations, in press. A revealing description of the Gaither Committee and its work can be found in Morton H. Halperin, "The Gaither Committee and the Policy Process," *World Politics*, (April, 1961), 360–84.

economic aid and military aid. It may also, as we have suggested, make the future less certain in the long run for individual services. But where the interests of the American armed services might have conflicted with the interests of American allies in a sustained level of military assistance, the fact that the allies, under the Mutual Defense Assistance Program, already expected to get substantial support, and that the services expected to give it, practically nullified the conflict. The conflict, that is to say, was there without NSC-68.

The services therefore took some assurance from the statement that free-world strength should be built from the center (meaning the United States) outward. On the other hand, because MDAP clearly fit into the scheme of NSC-68, gaining support from the breadth of its argument, the supporters of foreign military aid in the government were justified in viewing the document as an asset to *their* aspirations. Similarly, although military expansion would normally compete for resources with economic aid, the European Recovery Program was entering a stage where it was, by the early promises of its sponsors in the Truman administration, supposed to be phasing out. Furthermore, it was already up against the competing demands of MDAP for both American and European funds. On the defensive anyway, its supporters could hope for assistance from the broad perspective of NSC-68. They had, that is to say, nothing to lose; yet they might gain from the integrated approach.

Immediate circumstances also moderated interservice rivalry among the American armed forces posed by the possibility, without the assurance, of their expansion. The document had avoided figures, so that no fixed point presented itself upon which expectations and fears could be focused. The future was as indefinite as any proposal for expansion could make it. But suffering, as the services were, the stringencies of an economy program of the character of the American defense budget in the spring of 1950, with the expectations of further cuts to come, the uncertainties of a new program were far less to be dreaded than the uncertainties *and* the certainties of the present course.

The severe economy program in the Defense Department, the

declining expectations of foreign economic aid, and the beginning of a military aid program were all circumstances which could ease the way to a common viewpoint in the American government. When the Korean War broke, the considerations which made each of these circumstances important for the acceptance of NSC-68 were substantially reinforced. The objectives of economic and military aid might be abandoned if there were not some general plan of action, such as NSC-68. The American commitment to Europe as the decisive theater, a principle of American strategy since before World War II, might be threatened by the military challenge which had been accepted in Asia. The military services themselves could not look upon Korea as either a valid test of their capabilities or an objective which justified committing their full capabilities. They, too, needed an overall plan in order to keep their balance. NSC-68 might be that plan.

The State Department, both before and after the Korean War broke, was a definable interest which might have looked upon NSC-68 as a threat to its own status and objectives. Indeed, if the difference between Acheson and Nitze on the one hand and Kennan and Bohlen on the other was representative in any way, State Department personnel were divided over the value of NSC-68. Some of them must have supported it because they were alarmed with the state of American defenses or because, like Acheson, they had come to believe that improving military capabilities was the primary need of American diplomacy, and they expected that the State Department would somehow maintain its status in the Executive branch. Those who opposed it feared, like Kennan, that the State Department would be thrust aside in the rearmament effort envisaged by NSC-68.

Once the Korean War had broken, however, the opposition was considerably weakened. Those who feared the dominance of military considerations in American foreign policy could point out that arming to fight in Korea was quite different from the general rearmament triggered by the Korean War, and that the less armament the better. But the rearmament was based on a plan, which was more than simply a military reaction to a particular military move. For the State Department opponents of NSC-68, the choice of tactics was not an attractive one after the Korean War began: favoring and opposing NSC-68 seemed about equally unappealing. For those who already supported it, on the other hand, the Korean War was reassurance that the Department's identification of military capabilities as the primary need of diplomacy had been correct. On the whole, therefore, the interests and perspectives of the State Department were not antagonistic to NSC-68.

These institutional interests, moreover, were supplemented by considerations of personality and political responsibility. Once the Korean War had broken, it was expedient for the administration, particularly its members who were known specifically as supporters of vigorous budget-cutting in the Defense Department, to stress the prominence of NSC-68. The administration, particularly the Secretary of Defense, Louis Johnson, was under attack for lack of preparedness because of the poor showing of American arms in Korea (or so it appeared), but also because of the abruptness of the reversal of policy, from downward trends in defense expenditures to towering increases. NSC-68 now represented the continuity which was so apparently lacking in defense policy, and the evidence that the turn of events had not been unanticipated.

Witnesses made direct (though not specific) reference to NSC-68 in the first supplementary budget hearings in July and August 1950. "The plans covering the build-up of our forces," Secretary Johnson told subcommittees of the House and Senate Appropriations Committees on July 25,

are based upon studies which began immediately after the President's announcement of the Soviet atomic explosion last September. You will recall that I discussed these studies when I testified here on April 26.

Because of the events in Korea the minimum desired forces which these studies showed to be required—normally a matter that would have been provided for in next year's budget—are being requested at this time.[2]

---

[2] *Supplemental Appropriations for 1951*, Hearings before the Committee on Appropriations, United States Senate, 81st Cong., 2d Sess. (Washington, 1950), p. 39. [Hereafter cited as *SCA, Hearings 1951 Supplemental Appropriations Bill.*] See also *The Supplemental Appropriations Bill for 1951*, Hearings before the Committee on Appropriations, House of Representatives, 81st Cong.,

Johnson linked the expansion program brought on by the Korean War with the earlier economy program with which he had become identified by referring to his comments on the State-Defense study before the House committee exactly three months earlier, when he had concluded that the Military Establishment was, under his leadership, much more capable than ever before of expanding efficiently.[3]

Frank Pace, Johnson's recent appointee as Secretary of the Army, and former Budget Director, also made particular reference to NSC-68 in his opening statement. "One thing that I do not think has been sufficiently emphasized to this committee is the fact that this program which has been presented to you, which was prepared in a very hurried fashion, is nonetheless based on a well-integrated and well-coordinated plan."[4] General Bradley, the Chairman of the Joint Chiefs of Staff, referred to NSC-68 from another viewpoint. "I would like to emphasize," he testified,

> that this program of requirements has not [been] devised on short order. The Joint Chiefs of Staff have been considering the build-up of our armed forces as part of a long-range plan which is still in effect and which is only accelerated and enlarged by the present action in Korea.[5]

Later, as newspaper columnists were to reveal more of the background of NSC-68, these remarks by Johnson, Pace, and Bradley were to be associated with the newly revealed information to create an exaggerated view of the direct importance of NSC-68 to the planning of the Korean mobilization. NSC-68 was hardly the blueprint of the Korean rearmament. Its role was an important one, however, though subtle and usually indirect. To the difficult task of determining what that role was we now turn.

2d Sess. (Washington, 1950), pp. 7–8. [Hereafter cited as *HCA, Hearings 1951 Supplemental Appropriations Bill*.]

[3] *HCA, Hearings 1951 Supplemental Appropriations Bill*, pp. 1 f.; *SCA, Hearings 1951 Supplemental Appropriations Bill*, p. 32.

[4] *SCA, Hearings 1951 Supplemental Appropriations Bill*, p. 46.

[5] *HCA, Hearings 1951 Supplemental Appropriations Bill*, p. 21.

THE USES OF NSC-68 IN THE REARMAMENT

After June 25 the demands of the Korean War immediately launched the services into expansive planning, in the expectation that the sooner the increases in military forces could be initiated, the better. The first step in the Korean rearmament, therefore, was designed to cope only with the most pressing foreseeable demands. Yet it had to rest on some kind of assumptions; those which it used it took largely from NSC-68.

On July 6, the Army sought, and quickly got, approval for an increment in its authorized manpower strength by 50,000 "spaces," as the planners termed it. A few days later it obtained approval for another increase, this time of 60,500 "spaces." The immediate problems were somewhat different for the Navy and the Air Force. They began bringing equipment out of mothballs and accelerating procurement orders. Yet they, too, soon faced the prospect of exceeding their manpower ceilings. On July 19, the day of the President's message to Congress, legislation was introduced and soon passed which suspended for four years the statutory limits on the manpower ceilings of the three services.[6]

In the meantime, plans were afoot for a supplementary budget. The fiscal 1951 budget was ultimately to authorize a total of $48.2 billion for the military establishment. The President had originally asked for $13.5 billion. Still under consideration when the Korean War broke, the original defense budget did not actually pass Congress until late July, as part of an omnibus general appropriation bill.[7]

It was widely believed that the President would ask for a supplement of $5 billion[8]—the same amount Gruenther and Norstad had anticipated as a reasonable figure for implementing NSC-68. The

[6] *SCA, Hearings 1951 Supplemental Appropriations Bill,* p. 58; HR 9178, 81st Cong., 1st Sess. (Washington, 1950), introduced, *Congressional Record* XCVI (July 19, 1950), 10618; Public Law 655 (approved August 8, 1950).

[7] For a thorough description of trials and tribulations of this legislation *en passant* see Dalmas H. Nelson, "Omnibus Appropriations Act of 1950," *Journal of Politics,* May 1953, pp. 274–88.

[8] New York *Times,* July 19, 1950.

President did not even disclose to his own Cabinet, in a discussion which he held with them on the eve of his message to Congress, the sum he was going to request.[9] The following day, July 19, 1950, he asked for $10 billion for the Defense Department, in addition to the pending regular appropriation. Between then and July 24, when the estimates were given final approval in the White House and submitted to Congress, the services threw together their own more detailed supporting estimates. The Joint Chiefs of Staff modified the service figures very little; the White House made only "minor" changes in them, even though the final total exceeded Truman's announced sum by a half-billion dollars.[10]

The hearings began immediately, on July 25, and stretched out through August. They were to show that all of the services conceived of this supplement wholly as a stopgap measure, and so took pains to avoid committing themselves to a statement of needs which had any necessary validity beyond July 25![11]

The supplementary budget, General Bradley told the Senate Appropriations Committee, was intended to meet three requirements. As he put it:

First, in order to win the war in Korea, we must get more men and equipment over there as soon as possible. This means that the pipeline of essential supplies and personnel must be started flowing, and it must be kept flowing for as long as may be necessary.

Second, although the forces we have sent to meet the immediate threat in Korea still may be considered as part of our over-all defense, the effect is a reduction in that defense. We must therefore replace those units sent from other areas, particularly the United States, and thus restore our military capabilities.

Third, it is now evident that we must have an even greater flexibility of military power in the United States itself not only for our protection, but also to give us a ready, highly mobile standing force which we can bring to bear at any threatened point in the minimum time.[12]

The first two of these requirements could be regarded as Korean War expenses, the third as an attempt to implement NSC-68. These

---

[9] *Ibid.*

[10] *SCA, Hearings 1951 Supplemental Appropriations Bill,* pp. 48, 156 f.

[11] *Ibid.,* pp. 9–14, 157; *HCA, Hearings 1951 Supplemental Appropriations Bill,* p. 21.

[12] *HCA, Hearings 1951 Supplemental Appropriations Bill,* p. 20.

two purposes were evidently the basis for the estimates which were worked out as stopgap figures which would merely "get things going," while longer run requirements were being estimated. In the hearings, Secretary Finletter estimated that $6 billion of the $10.5 billion supplement was intended for general expansion (or the implementation of NSC-68); other testimony suggests that he might have been on the high side.[13] Thus, the initial defense cost of NSC-68 was a long way from the flash estimates of $50 billion prepared as the initial step in programming for NSC-68 pursuant to the President's directive of April 12.

The first supplement, nonetheless, bore some relationship to NSC-68, although there had not been time for critical appraisal of the document by the NSC subcommittee appointed for that purpose. For the first supplement was based on the four-year build-up schedule of NSC-68 and anticipated leveling off at just under $25 billion, with the peak, just over $26 billion, coming in 1952.[14] The second supplement, not introduced until December 1, 1950, afforded Pentagon officials more of an opportunity for relating budget requests with general policy.

By September 27, when Congress had approved the first supplement (which had been raised to $11.6 billion by the President with an additional request on August 4), a second supplement was already under way. Two weeks earlier, on September 13, the Secretary of Defense had directed the service departments to prepare justifications for a second supplement.[15] The following week, on September 21, the ad hoc subcommittee of the National Security Council which had been supervising the programming and pricing of NSC-68 completed the first major addition to that document, NSC-68/1. Nine days later it completed a second addition, NSC-68/2.[16]

Military budgets which provide for expansion are built upon force level targets fixed at some point in time, which are then costed in appropriate time phases. Had the Korean War not occurred, and the Johnson directive for budgeting for NSC-68 been carried through, by November 1, 1950, the Secretary of Defense

---

[13] *Ibid.*, p. 232.   [14] *Ibid.*, p. 270.
[15] *Semiannual Report of the Secretary of Defense, January 1 to June 30, 1951*, p. 30.
[16] The dates are from interviews.

would probably have had force level figures for each year up to and including three years hence (including the year of maximum peril identified in NSC-68, 1954) and budget estimates for the first year. Along with this information, the National Security Council might have had, by that time, further information about the economic impact of increased national defense expenditures. If the size of the defense estimates were great enough to warrant it (as certainly was the case with the initial $50-billion figure), the NSC subcommittee would have considered (if it had been forewarned) what economic controls would be necessary to achieve the force level targets.

The Korean War deprived all three of these tasks—setting force levels, costing the program to achieve them, and determining the economic policies necessary to meet the costs—of the special status distinct from immediate policy issues conferred upon them by NSC-68. The first two tasks became merged with the process of drafting the supplementary budget. Whereas before the war, the arrangement was that two different sets of figures would be developed—the regular budget and the hypothetical figures for NSC-68—now there would be only the estimates for actual budgets. Johnson's directive, moreover, had provided that first the Joint Chiefs of Staff would lay out guide lines, which would then be costed.

In an economy already growing taut from the first supplement and the expanding Mutual Defense Assistance Program, however, the end was selected with considerably more awareness of the extent of the means required than the Johnson directive had envisaged: the force level decision (the first task) was made after the costing (the second task) had been practically completed (as much as it was to be completed prior to its submittal to Congress). This reversal in the order of the planning process was no doubt due to the fact that what was being planned was a real, not a hypothetical, budget. The difference is noteworthy. In the preparation of the second supplement for the fiscal 1951 budget, during September, October, and November 1950, what it would cost was decided before the force level requirements were determined. Preparations for the second supplement began September 13, and it was submitted to Congress December 1, 1950. Yet not until November 19 did the

Joint Chiefs of Staff approve the force level goals for it, nor until November 24 did the President.[17]

This sequence makes evident the importance, under these circumstances, of capacity over desirability as a limiting factor. But taking capacity into account was the third task with which NSC-68 was concerned, the adjustment of means and ends through economic mobilization policies. The first two program additions to NSC-68, NSC-68/1 and NSC-68/2, both dated in September, were in fact concerned with the third task: with how steep and how fast the mobilization climb should be, as measured by its anticipated effects on the economy. The target date remained 1954. Mobilization was to be partial rather than total. Controls could be kept at a minimum. Whatever was done had to stand the test of the long pull. The Korean War had produced an important reversal in the relative emphasis on ends and means implied in NSC-68. But the result was all the more reliance upon a mobilization policy paced by the premises of time and size contained in NSC-68.

President Truman submitted the second supplementary defense budget to Congress on December 1, after the Chinese intervention in Korea. This budget provided for a Navy with 1,028 active ships, an Army with 16 full-strength divisions, and an Air Force with 68 groups. It had been prepared as the next step in a planned movement upward, as an interim budget in a four-year program of rearmament. As Robert Lovett described it,

This is not a war or a full mobilization budget. It is an initial step in a planned 4-year effort to restore our military posture in order to give us some measure of security against disaster and to put us in a better position to meet our obligations internationally. It is designed to provide a deterrent against aggression and to provide a base from which rapid build-up can be attained in case of all-out war. But it is obviously not a war-footing budget request. That would involve hundreds of billions of dollars. This aims at the creation of a Defense Establishment which can be maintained over a substantial period of time without excessive

[17] *Second Supplemental Appropriations Bill for 1951, Department of Defense* (Part I), Hearings before the Committee on Appropriations, House of Representatives, 81st Cong., 2d Sess. (Washington, 1950), pp. 20, 53–54. [Hereafter cited as *HCA, Hearings, Second Supplemental Appropriations Bill for 1951.*]

strain while providing the essential quality of quick build-up from a sound base.[18]

Like the first supplement, therefore, the second rested on interim judgments and agreements. Also like the first, but more clearly than it, the second supplement bore a discernible relationship to NSC-68. It was an attempt to schedule for the long pull and to keep the immediate imperatives of Korea properly placed in a larger strategic picture. Of the nearly $17 billion requested, $9 billion would be for major procurement items. Part of the latter sum would be for matériel expended in Korea, but much of it would be for general rearmament. Of the $9 billion, $4 billion were for Army tanks, guns, ammunition, and vehicles, and $2.1 billion were for Air Force plane procurement (bringing the Air Force total for aircraft procurement to $4.6 billion for fiscal 1951). Research and development would be stepped up with an additional $410 million. Procurement and production funds would be spent in such a way as to expand the mobilization base.[19]

The focus thus remained on a larger purpose for rearmament than the fighting of the Korean War. The Air Force, for instance, was being built up to a strength which had no relationship to the burdens directly imposed upon it by the Korean War. Although 99 percent of the Air Force effort in the Korean War was devoted to tactical uses, the major procurement expenditures for expansion were going for an increase in strategic air power—for relatively long-range air-atomic capabilities, rather than for ground support fighters.[20]

Perhaps the most striking indication of how much the broad perspective was maintained throughout this period was the attitude towards the Mutual Defense Assistance Program. Initial requests for MDAP for fiscal 1951 totaling $1.2 billion were augmented by a $4-billion supplement in July 1950. And over the last six months of

[18] *Ibid.*, p. 21.

[19] *Semiannual Report of the Secretary of Defense, January 1 to June 30, 1951*, pp. 30–32, 119–20; New York *Times*, December 2, 1950; HCA, *Hearings, Second Supplemental Appropriations Bill for 1951*, pp. 23–24; *Second Supplemental Appropriations, 1951*, Hearings before the Committee on Appropriations, United States Senate, 81st Cong., 2d Sess. (Washington, 1950), p. 1.

[20] *Semiannual Report of the Secretary of Defense, January 1 to June 30, 1951*, p. 198.

1950 deliveries of matériel to our MDAP allies doubled, despite the pressing demands in Korea for war matériel.[21]

Congress approved the second supplement to the fiscal 1951 defense budget on January 6, 1951. Before it did, however, on December 8, the National Security Council added a third "slant," or supplement, to NSC-68. A week later, on December 14, it added a fourth supplement to NSC-68. The contents of NSC-68/3 are unknown, although it probably had something to do with the speed-up of rearmament. NSC-68/4 brought to a conclusion the process of programming and pricing in the Defense Department for NSC-68 initiated by Johnson's May directive. It provided the initial guide lines for the fiscal 1952 defense budget.

The guide lines for the second supplementary budget for 1951 had not anticipated the massive Chinese intervention in Korea. Indeed, one major premise was that hostilities in Korea would continue at their mid-November tempo and would terminate by the end of the fiscal year. Furthermore, the pace of rearmament had been set at what the administration termed "partial" mobilization, which was considerably shorter of "total" mobilization than some critics of the administration advocated. It was also not so great as to require direct economic controls. The involvement of Red China in the Korean War immediately changed the administration's sense of urgency, although it could not implement the change instantaneously. Hearings on the second supplementary budget in early December indicated a determination to speed up the rate of rearmament beyond that envisaged in the budget requests then under consideration. In NSC-68/4, therefore, two purposes converged: one was the establishment of guide lines for the fiscal 1952 defense budget; the other, the acceleration of the planned rate of rearmament. It advanced the target date for rearmament from 1954 to 1952. It set a military manpower goal for fiscal 1952 at 3.5 million men, an increase of one million men in the next year. Production of major procurement items was also to be raised steeply. In a year, aircraft would be produced at five times the current rate, combat vehicles at four times, and electronics equipment at four and a half times. To

[21] New York *Times,* December 31, 1950.

achieve these rates, selective wage and price controls would be necessary.

President Truman spelled out the meaning of NSC-68/4 to Congressional leaders on December 13, the day before he approved it in the National Security Council. On December 15 he described it to the American public in an evening radio address.[22]

Thrust into the background was the question of how far to climb. The answers for each of the services came at different times. For the Navy, the most important answers came early. The first supplement, submitted in July 1950, provided that the Navy could go ahead to develop a new class of aircraft carriers which could handle heavier aircraft, and it also provided for substantial increases in authorized active ships by bringing vessels from the mothball fleet back into commission. The largest percentage jump in authorized active ship strength was provided in the first supplement, an increase from 657 to 912 ships.[23] The second supplement increased the strength another 112 ships, and the plans for the next phase, associated with the fiscal 1952 budget, were to increase it another 137 ships.

Army increases began with the addition of 1 division, and the bringing of the other 10 to full strength. The Army then went to 16 divisions. The next step, the figure associated with fiscal 1952, was to be 24 divisions. Air Force goals were raised from 48 to 62 groups in the first supplement for fiscal 1951, thence to 68 groups in the second supplement. The goal set in connection with fiscal 1952 was 95 groups or wings, a longer range target than comparable figures for the other two services. Indeed, this was the most striking feature of the build-up from the viewpoint of service interests.

Because each new goal was an increase over the last, and because Defense Department officials stressed the interim character of each, the competitive aspect of expansion could be minimized—until the goals of the Air Force moved further ahead and higher than did those of the Army and the Navy. Between 1951 and 1953, the

[22] The content of NSC-68/4 comes from *Semiannual Report of the Secretary of Defense, January 1 to June 30, 1951,* pp. 31, 103; *ibid., January 1 to June 30, 1952,* p. 4; New York *Times,* December 14 and 16, 1950.
[23] *HCA, Hearings, Second Supplemental Appropriations Bill for 1951,* p. 28.

number of active ships in the Navy remained exactly the same.[24] By the end of 1952, Secretary of Defense Lovett could report that the Army, the Navy, and the Marine Corps had almost achieved their partial mobilization goals. The Air Force, on the other hand, was only halfway to its projected goal. Like the Army and the Navy, it had roughly doubled, going from 48 to almost 100 groups or wings. But the goal established for it was 143 wings, three times its pre-Korean War strength.[25] In the spring of 1951 the prospects that the Air Force strength would rise so incommensurately above that of the other services became publicly known. By mid-June, this had become a serious matter of interservice discord.[26] Under heavy pressure from Lovett to keep the issue from becoming a public dispute, the Joint Chiefs of Staff approved the 140-group goal at the end of October 1951.[27] Their agreement was probably made possible, however, because budget plans then under consideration would stretch out Air Force expansion so that 95 groups would not be reached until 1953, and 140 groups would not be reached until 1957 or 1958.[28]

NSC-68 AS A POLICY STATEMENT
NSC-*141: The reappraisal of* NSC-*68*

In mid-1952 President Truman assigned to Secretary of State Acheson, Secretary of Defense Lovett, and Averell Harriman, the Mutual Defense Administrator, the responsibility for preparing a paper for the next administration which would be as clear and accurate a presentation as possible of the national security problem and of the programs necessary and appropriate to meet it. In effect, they were to direct a revision of NSC-68. These three officials assigned the task of drafting the paper to Richard Charles Noyes and

[24] *Semiannual Report of Secretary of Defense, January 1 to June 30, 1953* (Washington, 1953), p. 173.
[25] *Semiannual Report of the Secretary of Defense, July 1 to December 31, 1952* (Washington, 1953), p. 3.
[26] New York *Times,* June 15, 1951.
[27] *Ibid.,* September 30, October 3, 1951.   [28] *Ibid.,* November 16, 1951.

Paul Nitze of the State Department, Frank Nash of the Office of the Secretary of Defense, and Richard Bissell, an Assistant Director in the Economic Cooperation Administration. The paper which resulted received the file number NSC-141.

The foursome who drafted this document worked with a special eye for gaps in existing programs and changes of emphasis which were needed. The paper they produced held that a greater emphasis needed to be put upon the Middle East, Southeast Asia, and Africa than had been the case with American policy in the past. The preoccupation of the Truman administration with Europe could now be modified. It further asserted that the air defense of the United States, both active and passive, was entirely inadequate to cope with the growing Soviet nuclear capability which had to be anticipated in future years. The costs of continental defense would be in the billions. The necessary funds, furthermore, could not be cut out of other programs, but would have to be added as a net addition to the annual budgetary requirements for national security.[29]

The proposal for a moderation of the Air Force's emphasis upon offensive warfare capabilities did not come easily. Reportedly, Secretary of Defense Lovett and the Joint Chiefs of Staff were all reluctant to have an air defense program worked out in any detail,[30] probably because they feared a diversion of effort from objectives with higher priorities. The point in NSC-141 that expenditures for air defense had to be added to existing programs had a rather special meaning under these circumstances. It could mean that an increase in defense expenditures was imperative; but it could also mean, in the light of previous policies, that air defense, in particular, deserved only a secondary priority. The first meaning, however, was evidently now intended. The Truman administration was coming to an end. Before work on NSC-141 had been completed, the fact that responsibility for the Executive branch would pass to the other party, to the Republicans under Eisenhower, was settled.

There is no particular reason to believe that either those who drafted NSC-141 or those who approved it were recommending to

[29] Interviews; cf. Alsop column, New York *Herald Tribune,* May 8, 1953.
[30] Interviews.

the new administration things which they were unwilling to undertake themselves. Yet, in an indirect way NSC-141, when it is compared with NSC-68, did just that. NSC-68 had been shaped not only by the perceived thrust of logic, but as well by a sympathy for the circumstances under which it would be read by members of the Truman administration, whose support would be necessary for its implementation. Consequently, it was distinctive for what it did not say as much as for what it did say. In its foreign policies the Truman administration had conceived boldly, but had proceeded one step at a time—in order to proceed at all in the face of its critics and opponents. In NSC-68 the same tactic had been adopted. A central point of argument had been picked and hammered home. The purpose had been to make the point as strong as possible before practical considerations closed its readers' minds to sympathetic consideration of the line of argument. But this tactic also had the effect of leaving the administration free to proceed as it wished. Rather than emphasizing a carefully balanced or coordinated program, which might prove rigid or cumbersome, NSC-68 had emphasized a general objective, leaving Executive leadership the flexibility and discretion it would need to achieve that objective.

NSC-141, however, apparently from its terms of reference onward, was intended to emphasize coordination and balance, a less flexible program which would leave the new administration little room to maneuver in the interests of political leadership. The terms of reference for the preparation of these two documents, therefore, as interpreted by the drafting officials, differed in a crucial, though subtle and implicit, way. NSC-68 minimized wherever possible a concern with particular gaps or questions of balance, while NSC-141 was intended as a more ruthlessly logical product. The implicit difference was that officials of the Truman administration were less interested in considering the problems of political leadership which the new administration would face than they had been in taking into account the comparable problems of the administration which they served.

The practical consequence of this difference was probably negligible. The Eisenhower administration rejected NSC-141, not because it was less flexible than NSC-68, but because of its general support for larger defense expenditures. It is important here only because it lends perspective both to NSC-68 and to its first major revision.

The place of NSC-68 *in American policy development*

NSC-68 had major limitations. It was only a general statement of policy without a definite settlement of its meaning in terms of tangible decisions about budgets, procurement, and forces. Some who read it thought it was a scare document; others, that it justified any international commitments the government wanted to undertake; still others, that it only expressed the prevailing view. None of them were entirely wrong. In addition, NSC-68 was undoubtedly abused as well as used, for the number of people who saw it was strictly limited, yet it was referred to widely as the definitive statement of government policy.

The Bureau of the Budget was quite right in pointing out that the document, as it was submitted to the President in April 1950, had not been cleared with all of the agencies upon whose functions it touched. It had been drafted by a small group of people in the State and Defense Departments, and had not even been put through a thorough clearance in the Defense Department. It was not an organization product: Neither its preparation nor its clearance were routine. It was not the massive consolidation of organization viewpoints, not even a negotiated accommodation of official State and Defense Department viewpoints (although organization perspectives were not unrelated to its preparation). Indeed, it was never formally approved by the President beyond the qualified phrases of his referral of it to the National Security Council and his approval of NSC-68/4 as the basis for the fiscal 1952 defense budget. Undoubtedly, much of what was done in the Korean military build-up would have been done anyway. Yet, the existence of NSC-68 at the outset of the war contributed a particular quality to that build-up. From its beginning, and through its most frantic phases, the Korean War remained only a part of the larger picture of national strategy. For the small number of people in the Executive branch who had read it, and for a larger number who knew it by reputation, NSC-68 represented that larger picture.

It is easy for a crisis, particularly war, to break down the separate and conflicting views and interests of government and infuse them with a common purpose. The common purpose, however, may have to be oversimplified. For instance, one of the problems of assessing the political leadership of the United States in World War II, particularly in Soviet-American relations, is how to give proper weight to the objective of keeping the purposes of that enterprise simple enough to maintain united action, for many concessions were made to that purpose, and some of them were surely justified. NSC-68 provided a partial substitute within the Executive branch for the oversimplification of objectives in war. Before the Korean War had started, and, of course, without reference to it, a question had been asked and an answer provided which transcended organization perspectives and, when the time for implementation came, consolidated them. NSC-68 became a milestone in the consolidation of perspectives, establishing at least some kind of order of priority and magnitude between economy and security, domestic and foreign commitments, economic and military means, American and allied strength, and short and long-run national interests.

In this respect, it made an important difference. Aided by circumstances, to be sure, the existence of NSC-68 made it possible to move into a general program of rearmament with only a minimum of impedances and fumbling caused by the suspicions and misunderstandings of different agencies. How much the value of NSC-68 derived from the special circumstances surrounding its drafting and implementation, however, is a question which cannot be answered by examining only the one case. Yet it is worth ending this examination with the reminder that NSC-68 was valuable as much because of what—prudently—it did not attempt to do as for the thrust of the argument which it made.

VII Conclusions

Finally, it should prove helpful to draw some comparisons between the story of NSC-68 and the story of the fiscal 1950 defense budget and to discuss in the light of these comparisons the conclusions which Professor Schilling drew about the latter.

Both stories, it should be clear, are concerned with events about which one might expect, or at least hope, that certain rather obvious standards of rationality would have been met—for instance, that where one course of action is chosen, the choosers be aware of its probable outcome and costs and know what are the main alternative courses of action, their implications, and their costs. The fiscal 1950 defense budget was never expressed in terms of the strategies which it was intended to support, nor were alternative strategies and their costs described. By this standard, at least, the process by which NSC-68 was formulated was unquestionably more rational than was that by which the fiscal 1950 budget was formulated. Where the latter was means-oriented, NSC-68 was occupied first with the choice of appropriate objectives, and only then with the selection of the best means. It stated general premises and it examined general alternative courses of action, selecting among them the one most strongly supported by analysis.

In several respects, however, the terms of reference which made rational analysis more possible also made the immediate translation of the document's findings into public policy more difficult. To begin with, NSC-68 recommended the one thing which was prohibited at every step of the process of considering the fiscal 1950 budget, a substantial increase in the level of defense expenditures. Had the Joint Chiefs of Staff been asked to justify a defense budget for fiscal 1950 of $30 or $35 billion, they could have provided an explanation which would have appeared substantially more rational than was their explanation of the $13.5 billion allowed. The fact that they could not do so diminished the apparent rationality, not only of their own position, but of both the White House position and the defense budgetary procedures of Congress; for both depended, or so it was thought at that time, largely upon findings and judgments of the Joint Chiefs of Staff.

NSC-68, however, did not have to face such a severe test of its rational methods. Indeed, it did not have to face at all the test of relating military force levels to strategic requirements because of two rather important differences between the defense budget and the national security plan. The first difference was that NSC-68 did not have to cope with budgetary limitations. Those who wrote it were free to contemplate any force levels or expenditure levels which seemed to follow from its analysis. We have seen that in its initial formulation the document did not involve itself with even the most general estimates either of force levels or of annual expenditure levels. Nevertheless, it is significant that when its drafters thought in such terms they had in mind magnitudes quite similar to the estimates of the Joint Chiefs of Staff for fiscal 1950, which were made under roughly the same circumstances—without (or before) the imposition of a budget ceiling, or of the pressures which resulted from the threat of a budget ceiling. The State Department drafters of NSC-68 thought of it in terms of $30-odd billion—in the neighborhood of the initial estimates of the Joint Chiefs of Staff for fiscal 1950; and the Defense Department drafters thought in terms of the lowest figures to which the JCS could agree, around $17 or $18 billion. Neither figure was an important one. The lower one probably reflected more than anything else the difficulty which the military drafters had in throwing off the "climate of opinion" which prevailed. Yet, the two figures do indicate that, once the requirement to fit within a ceiling had been removed, the drafters of NSC-68 thought along lines quite similar to those which the Chiefs had adopted before the budget ceiling had been imposed for fiscal 1950.

The second difference between NSC-68 and the fiscal 1950 defense budget which made the meeting of rational standards, at least by appearance, easier for the drafters of NSC-68 involved the handling of details. As Professor Schilling has emphasized, the degree and multiplicity of detail with which the deliberations of the budgetary process become involved in the United States government is very high, and the discrimination with which details are selected for inspection, very low. This handling of detail, particularly in Congress, constitutes a major obstacle to the rational making of budget decisions (defense or others). Its effects run deep into the administration of the Executive departments and agencies; for no Executive official can ignore details. However unimportant they may seem to him, however inconsequential they are to the objectives of the programs which he administers, they can become the subject of intensive examination in Congress. The fiscal 1950 defense budget was prepared and presented with this problem in mind, and Congress examined it with its usual predisposition to miss the forest for the trees.

The contrast between the fiscal 1950 defense budget and NSC-68 in this respect could not have been greater. NSC-68 was not drawn to run the gamut of Congressional minutia-seeking, and it was certainly not burdened with the functions of an annual budget—at least not until it began to be used as the basis for the fiscal 1951 budget, well after the beginning of the Korean War. The original drafting of it was kept entirely free from details, both of cost estimates and of force requirements. The drafters were thus able to concentrate on general considerations of strategy, whereas the makers of the defense budget have ordinarily been overwhelmed with details about means, to the complete exclusion of any systematic treatment of ends and their relationship to means.

This lack of detail, in addition to avoiding the difficulties which detail had caused in the balance and breadth of the analysis in the fiscal 1950 defense budgetary process, also avoided a substantial additional obstacle to rational analysis in the case of NSC-68. At the time of its drafting practically no analytical tools were available for relating the military capabilities of each armed service to a common national strategy. In the absence of such tools, the Joint Chiefs of

Staff had been able in 1948 and 1949 to state an aggregate judgment about the forces needed to meet national security requirements, but the judgment was crude and general, and involved expenditures more than double the current (and the permissible) rate. When they were asked to relate a lower level of expenditures to scaled-down capabilities and requirements, the crudeness of their analytical methods became apparent. All they could do was to make rough guesses about *some* of the capabilities that could be bought with the sums under consideration. And those estimates were suspect for three reasons.

To begin with, the capabilities estimated—for instance, that $13.5 billion would allow only the mounting of an air attack from Great Britain, in response to Soviet aggression in western Europe—involved premises which were far from certain about the character of the military threat with which American forces would be required to deal. They were worst contingencies more than they were likely possibilities. It is true that no consensus about the range or configuration of probabilities existed among politically responsible officials to whom the military should have been able to turn for guidance on such matters. Under these circumstances, it seemed reasonable to the military to think in terms of worst contingencies. It is also true that their civilian overseers in the Executive branch and in Congress could not help them with their planning. Nevertheless, they had reason to doubt the value of the estimates provided by the military in the absence of adequate policy guidance.

Second, the President and the Congress could always doubt the accuracy of the estimating process itself. When they did, it was because they objected to "duplication" and "interservice rivalry," which meant, among other things, that estimates of capabilities were low and estimates of requirements were high because of competitive considerations among the services and because the services had, and wanted to maintain, overlapping capabilities. No doubt the whole unification movement, from its inception in the 1920's and its resuscitation in the 1940's, had rested partially on exaggerated estimates of the degree of duplication among the services and, hence, about the prospects for saving by various schemes of consolidation.

To the extent that, in the rhetoric of public discussion, "duplication" and "interservice rivalry" meant that wholesale economies were expected to follow from the next step towards unification, they were empty phrases. But when they were used to mean, as President Truman, James Forrestal, Louis Johnson, Carl Vinson, and a number of other Congressional and administration officials sometimes did when they used these or similar phrases, that they doubted the accuracy of estimates which related force levels, budgets, and strategic capabilities to each other, they reflected judgments which were, or could be, fairly rationally grounded. In 1948, 1949, and 1950, interservice rivalry had made it virtually impossible to determine those relationships. That rivalry had, on the one hand, made forces appear as ends themselves, which could be downgraded to means only at the risk of threatening the future of a military service. On the other hand, the rivalry had made impossible the development of a common currency of analysis among the services by which the forces of one service could be equated in their uses and capabilities with the forces of another. Without such tools, it was impossible to relate military budgets to strategic requirements with any degree of accuracy.

Finally, those responsible for the whole budget had to discount the claims and warnings of the departments and agencies of administration in the national government as tactics in the annual contest for appropriations. The resolution to discount could only have been strengthened by the open competition among the services for public support in evidence during these years.

Thus, the President and Congress could simply dismiss the one kind of estimate available which linked means with ends in the military sector of the government. Since there was no substitute for the rejected estimate, they had to find other ways to set the level of aggregate annual expenditure for military forces and allocate the aggregate sums among the various major forces. If more information had been available, certainly there would have been a more rational way to handle both kinds of decisions. But the problem they had to face was how to decide without more information. Possibly, more information was available than either the President or the Congress, or both, chose to acknowledge. Moreover, both the President and Congress would have appeared more rational had they been more explicit in insisting upon the development of the analyses necessary for ideally rational decisions. But the appraisals which they made about the availability of data and the conclusions which they reached about what to do in its absence were not wholly without rational foundation. Their refusal to try to solve their problem (the problem of producing a rational defense budget) by using analyses which posed alternatives and related means to ends was therefore not, in the sense in which we have used the term, irrational. Their greatest irrationality probably was their failure to appreciate the *possibility* of developing a more rational analysis of strategy. It was certainly not to act as though the analyses and the data were available when they were not.

Some practical considerations, therefore, explain, even if they do not wholly justify, the rough and crude methods used in the processes of the fiscal 1950 defense budget in the Executive branch and in the Congress during 1948 and 1949. The methods were adopted without any general and explicit agreement about the way to cope with the indeterminate and unknown elements, but as a series of unplanned adaptations to circumstances more or less individually perceived.

Moreover, the decisions made were, or were thought to be, real ones, hence the interests and pressures which had to be dealt with immediately were equally life-sized.

The drafting and initial clearance of NSC-68 did not have to cope with all of these difficulties because it excluded even general estimates about force levels and weapons and budget totals needed to carry it out, and because its clearance did not include its submittal to Congress as a part of the legislative program of the White House. The document itself concentrated upon the analysis and definition of national security goals. The breadth of its scope justified this initial trifling with practical considerations, and so did what NSC-68 achieved in its analysis of national strategy. Without a doubt it was superior to any analysis of national strategy which was involved in the fiscal 1950 defense budgetary process. It was systematic. It was comprehensive. It considered alternative courses of action by weighing their consequences and, in a very general way, their costs. The weight it carried was the weight of rational argument. Its prestige rested on the rational standards which it had visibly met.

But it had met these standards by avoiding practical considerations of two kinds: it had avoided dealing with concrete programs and it had ignored the problem of reconciling what seemed desirable with what was (or was thought to be) possible. As a consequence, until unforeseen events changed the whole frame of reference for policy, it was threatened with irrelevancy. Were it not for the start of the Korean War, its value would, very probably, have been only historical, to mark, but not to effect, a change in the climate of opinion in Washington and, possibly, the integration of the strategic views of several of the opinion elites in the government.

Further speculation about what relationship NSC-68 would have had to the policies of the United States government if the Korean War had not begun when it did would be fruitless. However, if one examines how various participants in the drafting and clearance of NSC-68 viewed its relationship, or potential relationship, to policy, one can at least find out something about the attitudes of government officials towards a process so obviously rational. Then those attitudes can be compared with the indifference, or seeming indifference, of the participants in the fiscal 1950 defense budgetary process to rational standards.

There is a striking contrast in the views of George Kennan and Paul Nitze, successive Directors of the Policy Planning Staff of the State Department. Kennan objected to NSC-68 and to the enterprise of drafting it—and presumably, therefore, to any organized rational procedures similar to the drafting of NSC-68—for two reasons. Even if the product was rational, he feared nonetheless that it would be perverted in application or misapplied. Beyond that, he believed that such procedures were bound to oversimplify the ends of foreign policy, if not their means, and to commit the nation unnecessarily to maintain them unchanged in the future. Nitze—and in this he was joined by Charles Bohlen—accepted such procedures as necessary, but was anxious to shape the product in order to cope with anticipated reactions (which Bohlen would not do). Bohlen wanted to make the draft at least more precise and accurate in the hope or expectation that greater accuracy in formulating the problem would result in more accurate conclusions, upon which policy could be based. Nitze adopted quite the opposite view. Anticipating that the military threat would be discounted, he wanted to sacrifice a degree of rationality in the analysis of NSC-68 in order to exaggerate the threat, with the hope that the reaction of opinion leaders would be commensurate with the threat—that is to say, would be rational as measured against the actual threat, though not against the portion of NSC-68 which purported to describe that threat.

Nitze had hopes that the policy statement could be turned into accepted policy. He wanted to bring into agreement the various policy-making elites within the government, and NSC-68 seemed an appropriate instrument for doing so. General Landon and his military associates in the Joint Strategic Survey Committee were less optimistic, at least in the beginning. They did not view the assignment to draft NSC-68 as anything extraordinary; for it seemed much like planning activities which were performed in the Defense Department as a matter of routine, work which normally was submerged in the budget-making process. What made the difference in their appraisal of the importance of the assignment was no doubt the perception that someone—the Secretary of State, possibly the President—really would be interested in the outcome of their work. Indeed, the very fact that someone in the State Department as well-placed as Nitze was interested in candid discussions about military requirements may have tempted them to believe that the "climate of opinion" was beginning to change. Had they not altered their initial appraisal of the joint State-Defense study group, and treated it instead from beginning to end as another rehashing of military requirements which was not expected to let the argument go where it led, there would have been ample reasons for justifying their actions. In that sense, Landon and his associates would have acted "rationally" if they had declined the invitation to define requirements, estimate costs, and explore alternatives.

If NSC-68 can be viewed as a rational activity so far as it went, then many government officials had only partial or ambivalent commitments to reason. Even Dean Acheson, the Secretary of State, who sponsored and endorsed it, stopped short of a full commitment to it. The fact that he recognized NSC-68 as a policy statement without official backing—indeed, one which was contrary to the administration's current policies—was not the basis for his ambivalence. Nitze in fact drew the same distinction. Acheson's commitment to NSC-68 as a rational process flagged when Nitze and Bohlen argued over their interpretations of the Soviet threat. "What difference does it make?" was, in effect, his response, as though the accuracy and internal consistency of the document were not important. Like Nitze, Acheson was more interested in the polemic value of NSC-68 than in its precise rationality. Evidently he saw it as a device for challenging established policies and premises which he thought needed reexamination.

President Truman's reaction was perhaps the most rational of all. He did not question the accuracy or validity of NSC-68, but he wanted to know what the cost would be to implement it before deciding what to do about it. Yet *was* this reaction entirely rational? As important as it may be to know the costs of alternative courses of action before choosing between them, the whole point of NSC-68 was that the danger was so great, the proper course of action so different from the one being followed, and the determination of costs so difficult and so unnerving that an important change needed to be made immediately without waiting for a costing of that change. The schedule adopted for estimating costs set July 1 as the deadline for flash estimates, and November 1 as the deadline for final costing. Hence, Truman rejected the proposal implicit in NSC-68 to choose without prices. All that he committed himself to was, in effect, that maybe he would decide what to do about NSC-68 later, when he could see what it would cost. Meanwhile, he had, for practical purposes, only decided to take it under consideration. Thus, he had ignored the urgency which was such an important part of NSC-68, while making no effort either to deny or to refute the arguments (some of them implicit, some explicit) in support of urgency. By his demand to know what NSC-68 meant in more concrete terms, therefore, we can say that his initial disposition of NSC-68 was rational, or quite the contrary.

We can say something similar about Louis Johnson. Of all the government officials whose views have interested us, Johnson's were the most negative to NSC-68, at least initially. He denounced the motives which prompted it and the procedures by which it was drafted. In the end, however, he approved it. We might therefore say that he was the most irrational of all with respect to it. He not only refused to consider it on its merits, but his reactions to it were contradictory. Yet it would have been difficult for him to have done otherwise than as he did. He had rested the conduct of his responsibilities as Secretary of Defense on the premise that he must accept the President's fiscal policies as a starting point. By early 1950 he had become so heavily committed to them that he could not gracefully reverse his position.

Perhaps in this incident there is a lesson that subordinates of the President should always hedge against the possibility of a reversal of Presidential policy. The lesson, however, is almost invariably missed. Students of American government who are interested in establishing rational norms usually identify compliance with Presidential decisions as the single most rational standard available, particularly in the field of foreign or national security affairs, where Hamiltonian principles have usually remained dominant. Whatever Johnson's reasons were, in the pursuit of the Truman economy program he was loyal to his chief. On the other hand, those who are interested enough to bother with such matters usually judge that the Secretary of Defense ought to be a spokesman at the White House for national security. Measured by this more particular standard, in his headlong pursuit of defense economies, by the spring of 1950 Johnson had been loyal to a fault.

To be aware of these conflicting standards of conduct, particularly in the light of experience with trying to apply them to more than one Secretary of Defense, is to question seriously whether there is any principle of rational procedure which, apart from the aesthetic standards met by its abstract symmetry, is of much use in the analysis of policy-making processes when it is defined apart from the substance of policies with which it deals. The problem is not simply one of constructing rational standards for judging the individual conduct of government officials. It also involves setting criteria to judge the rationality of a process of government as a whole in which each of these individuals plays his appropriate role.

As Warner Schilling's analysis indicates, it is not difficult to construct general criteria by which to judge the minimum rationality of a system, and it is possible, although it is a formidable undertaking, to carry out a comprehensive job of judging. The difficulty is in keeping our standards of rationality relevant. It is all very well to say that all the alternatives ought to be explored if choices involving them are to be rational. Yet, as Schilling has observed, when the President has decided upon a course of action, such as an Executive budget constitutes, his interest is in gaining Congressional approval of it, not in reopening all the questions which have been considered and settled within the Executive branch in the course of clearing the budget. In addition to this interest, he would have considerable evidence to induce a fear that reopening them in Congress would very likely lead to action which would be less rational than would be the general endorsement of his program, even though full disclosure and discussion in Congress would meet more fully an abstract notion of rationality. Full disclosure, we could anticipate from experience, would in fact lead to a host of unrelated amendments and the pressing of claims and arguments without regard to their proportionate weight in terms of any rational standard. Thus, the President may well be optimizing rationality by not making relevant information available to Congress.

The problem is the relationship of relevancy to rationality. The value of measuring a policy-making process of government against a general minimum standard of rationality should be evident from a reading of the first section of this book, the study of the fiscal 1950 defense budget. But the relevancy of that general standard for judging, or understanding, any *individual* action taken in the process under consideration is open to serious question because the relevant considerations for the participant at any specific point of choice cannot, in the real world, include what is identified by the question,

"If the system, and everyone involved in it, were rational, what ought I to do?" "If the system, and everyone involved in it, were rational," is so remote a contingency that for individual cases it is practically irrelevant for judging or deciding. Rather, the conduct of the individual who has a role in the process must be judged by less cosmic and more attainable standards. The opportunities for him to promote or apply rational standards are limited. His failure to heed these limitations would be irresponsible. Indeed, the more seriously he takes his responsibilities, the more difficult will he find it to make his policies, and particularly his manner of arriving at them, conform with any general standard of rationality.

One consequence of the fact that inhibitions against the pursuit of rationality accompany responsibility is that it may therefore be necessary to contrive the holding of rational deliberations under circumstances which insulate them from the forces which must ultimately be taken into account. Since, for instance, the deliberative procedures of the courts are thus situated, the framework for the study of modern American jurisprudence in its various schools rests on the insulation, on the one hand, and the ultimate adaptation to those forces, on the other. In administrative systems, similarly, it is the staff structures which are denied responsibility in order that they may probe for rationality more freely than can their bosses, ridden as bosses are with responsibility. Always, however, the insulation, the freedom to be rational, is purchased for a price. Advisers are without operating responsibility and are less in touch with administrative problems than are the officials who must deal with these problems directly. The responsible official may accept the rationality of his staff's plans, but he may nevertheless find them more or less irrelevant.

The contrived circumstances under which NSC-68 was drafted and initially cleared can be viewed in this same light, as an attempt to gain rationality at the cost of relevancy. It is notable that each of the main participants in the drafting and clearance of NSC-68 denied in some measure its rationality by questioning its relevancy. The State Department personnel involved who were without large domestic political responsibilities—notably Kennan, Bohlen, and

Nitze—dealt with the problem of relevancy in highly individualistic ways, which we have already discussed. Nitze would make the paper less rational in one direction in order to correct the irrationalities in another direction which he expected from its readers. Kennan objected to such a general policy statement because he thought it would inhibit future freedom of action and because it would place undue emphasis on the military instrument in foreign policy (which itself would add crude pressures and rigidities). Among them only Bohlen, in so far as the available evidence indicates, sought rationality simply by improving the rationality of the document itself— at least with respect to a small part of NSC-68, the definition of the Soviet challenge.

Landon and his colleagues saw NSC-68 as an oft-repeated procedure the relationship of which to rationality was in an important way unfathomable. They visualized themselves as professional military people playing their subordinate role in a government the ultimate authority of which, being civil, was distinct from the professional competence which gave them that role. Under these circumstances, they could not appropriately question the rationality of the system. They could only perform well the job assigned them. General Bradley's view of NSC-68, that the State Department had had its own way in drafting the document, reflects the same preoccupation with the playing of one's role and the doing of one's duty without reference to the virtues of the position one is defending or promoting that Landon had shown at first in the study group. Senator George's view of NSC-68 was not much different from President Truman's view of the high, early estimates of the Joint Chiefs of Staff for the fiscal 1950 budget; it was an interesting formulation, but his sense of reality made it difficult for him to take it seriously.

These were individual tactics for coping with the question of the relevance of NSC-68 to the real world of national security policy in the first half of 1950. In addition, however, for all participants the question of relevancy was raised by the possibility that the climate of opinion was changing, or could be changed.

No doubt, as Professor Schilling suggests, there is a "climate of opinion" sufficiently real to take into account. But, at least in the story of NSC-68, taking account of the climate of opinion was complicated by the difficulty of assessing its stability, which rested, in turn, on two conditions normally associated with instability—hence, indeterminacy at any specific time.

First, one cannot be certain how much the prevailing view rested on the incorrect premise that the economy could not stand any more of a burden of public expenditures, and how much the premise was asserted by unbelievers because they thought everybody else believed it—because, that is to say, the climate of opinion made it a weighty argument. Even in Forrestal's tenacious clinging to this simplistic version of economic analysis there was something in his manner—and in his hedging—less than the true believer, as though he were anxious never to let go of that special status which he had with the financial community of New York (which status, it should be added, was an important asset to his Washington career from the very beginning of his recruitment by Franklin D. Roosevelt in 1940 for a post in the White House) at the same time that he was willing to seek national security at some risk to fiscal soundness.

Second, in organizations there may develop a kind of inertia, what Schilling calls the gyroscopic effect, a continuation of policies while relevant circumstances are changing. If one of those circumstances is the climate of opinion about government expenditure policies, it can change very quickly—literally, overnight. At any *specific* time, therefore, the question is open whether the policies to which the government is committed reflect the climate of opinion or are out of phase with it. Or, to put it another way, at any particular time it may be quite possible to change policies which are substantially tied to the estimated climate of opinion. For although the climate of opinion may be a significant factor in the making of policy, it is always significantly indeterminate; and it is certainly unpredictable.

Specifically, in the spring of 1950 it was not clear how far complacency had shifted to alarm among the important opinion-forming elites for American foreign policy. The most obvious thing, at least to those who were alarmed, was that they would never find out how much the shift had occurred unless they adopted some extraordinary, even irrational, means for challenging established policies. Otherwise, they surmised, the inertia of the system would delay for too long the posing of alternatives to existing policies. In this way they attempted to cope with the problem of maximizing the rationality of their government in the real world of incomplete data and indeterminate inference where it is prudent to anticipate the non-rational actions of others, even at the risk of appearing irrational oneself.

THE "NEW LOOK" OF 1953

by Glenn H. Snyder

Contents

Introduction

The basic outlines of the Eisenhower administration's military policy were established during the second half of 1953 in a series of decisions which became known collectively as the "New Look." Although the term was first rather narrowly applied to a review of strategic plans and force requirements by the new Joint Chiefs of Staff— that is, simply to their act of "taking a new look"—it later came to denote the substance of the whole grand strategy evolved by the new administration in all its aspects—diplomatic and declaratory, military, and economic. The New Look was both a doctrine—that is, a set of ideas and concepts concerning the mobilization, deployment, and use of force as an instrument of deterrence and defense, and the striking of a balance between the competing demands of national security and economic welfare—and a set of actual changes and planned changes in the military establishment. The doctrine was most strikingly presented in the famous "massive retaliation" speech by Secretary of State John Foster Dulles on January 12, 1954. The changes in military capabilities were initiated with the defense budget for the fiscal year beginning July 1, 1954. The primary aim of this study is to tell the story of how the New Look doctrine and the initial implementing budget were formulated, with an eye to throwing some light on the process of policy-making for national security, especially on differences in attitude and approach manifested by participants of varying background and job responsibilities.

In terms of capabilities, the New Look meant a greater relative reliance on strategic nuclear air power and a de-emphasis of land, naval, and tactical air forces. The fiscal 1955 budget provided funds for expanding the Air Force from 114 wings [1] on June 30, 1954, to 120 wings a year later and eventually to 137 wings by June 30, 1957. It called for a reduction averaging about 13 percent in the manpower of the Army, the Navy, and the Marine Corps, with further cuts planned over the next two years. Since the Air Force build-up goal was lower than the 143-wing target which had been approved by the previous administration, the greater stress on air power was relative to the resources allocated to the other services, rather than relative to earlier Air Force programs. The improvement of the air defense of the North American continent also figured prominently in the New Look program, and certain changes were made in policies for stockpiling reserves of military equipment and for the maintenance of an industrial "mobilization base." In the fiscal 1955 budget, sent to Congress in January 1954, Congress was asked to appropriate $30,950,000,000 of new funds, a reduction of about $3,580,000,000 from the amount authorized for the previous year. This budget represented the first step in a three-year program designed to be completed by the end of fiscal 1957, when the armed forces were to reach the size and composition which was thought to be appropriate for "the long pull."

Associated with these budgetary and force changes was a doctrine of national security policy composed of a number of interlocking concepts and beliefs. The central problem was seen as the reconciliation of "security" with "solvency." The Eisenhower administration apparently believed that continuation of military expenditures at the rate reached in the latter years of the previous administration would eventually result in spiraling inflation or some other undesirable economic consequence, and that retrenchment to a balanced budget at reduced tax rates was imperative. Closely associated with the "solvency" theme was the concept of the "long haul," which envisaged an indefinite period of cold war during which defense preparations should be held to a moderate and steady level which the economy could support indefinitely without severe strain. The

---

[1] By the early 1950's, the designation of the basic combat unit in the Air Force had changed from "group" to "wing." For present purposes, the two labels can be considered roughly equivalent.

doctrine of "massive retaliation" emphasized deterrence by the threat of nuclear punishment, and also asserted "the initiative," which supposedly permitted a "selection" of weapons tailored to our own strategy, rather than to the moves or presumed intent of the enemy. A close corollary of this was the idea that nuclear weapons, applied either against the sources of the enemy's power at home or against his battlefield forces, could substitute for manpower in war. Another prominent motif was the "disengagement" of American ground forces from overseas positions, and their redeployment to a "central strategic reserve" in the United States, from which they would move swiftly to the support of allied forces in case of aggression.

NOTE ON SOURCES

The material for this case history was acquired very largely from personal interviews. Since a large proportion of the persons interviewed requested that their names not be mentioned, it was decided not to attribute any of the interview information, so as to avoid possible embarrassment to those few individuals who were willing to be identified. Material other than that obtained from interviews was acquired from published, unclassified sources, which, of course, are identified in the footnotes. Some secondary sources, such as magazine articles and unattributed newspaper stories, are cited, but only in cases in which the correctness of the information contained was verified by interviews with the governmental decision-makers involved.

Approximately fifty-five persons were interviewed over a period extending from the spring of 1957 to the summer of 1959. Most of those interviewed were past and present officials in the Department of Defense, both civilian and military. However, some former and present employees of the Department of State, the Bureau of the Budget, and the Treasury Department were interviewed.

1   *Policy Formulation*

The strategic and political concepts of the military New Look of 1953 were rooted deep in the tradition and ideology of American foreign and military policy. An exhaustive examination of the "roots" of the New Look is beyond the pretensions of this study. However, we may note in passing that air power has always held a special place in American thinking about military affairs. No doubt this reflects in part the American love for complex and powerful machinery, partly a reverence for "progress," and partly a deep aversion to the sacrifice of large numbers of American youth in war. Of course, the notion that "air power can do the job" gained much in plausibility and something in validity with the development of the atomic bomb. Also relevant is the American yearning for some single, simple solution to all the bothersome and frustrating complexities of living in a world of perennial conflict, a yearning which can be traced through the League of Nations, pacts to "outlaw" war, the United Nations, to "instant, massive retaliation." American conservative economic thought, with its stress on the dangers of excessive governmental spending, should also be mentioned as part of the intellectual background of the New Look.

In actual military policy, some of the tendencies which were manifested in the Eisenhower New Look had already been set in motion by the previous administration. Prior to the Korean War, although military budgets tended to be divided into three roughly equal proportions, by far the most significant part of the military establishment was the Strategic Air Command armed with the atomic bomb, and the foreign policy of the United States relied heavily on the deterrent effect of this capability. The administration during this period, not entirely successfully, resisted pressures to expand the Air Force—pressures exerted by Congress, by private air-power enthusiasts, and by the Air Force itself. But the Korean War, after first generating an increase in ground forces, also brought about official acceptance of a program for expansion of air power. On October 1, 1951, the Joint Chiefs of Staff approved an Air Force goal of 143 wings, replacing the previous target of 95 wings, which was to have been attained by the end of 1952. The Chiefs agreed also on an Army of 21 combat divisions and a Navy of 408 major combat vessels, with supporting forces—approximately the same as the ground and naval forces then in existence. In the JCS plans, this new program was to be completed by mid-1954, but President Truman "stretched out" the target date to December 31, 1955. The increased reliance on air power was reflected in the administration's request for new appropriations for the fiscal year 1953: $20.7 billion for the Air Force, $13.2 billion for the Navy, and $14.2 billion for the Army. The air power orientation continued to be reflected in the fiscal 1954 budget, which went to Congress just before the Democratic administration left office in January 1953. This called for new appropriations of $16.7 billion for the Air Force, $11.3 billion for the Navy, and $12.1 billion for the Army.

Although the priority of air power had been accepted, numerous influential persons and groups in both political parties still believed that the emphasis on air power was not being carried far enough—that too much was being spent on the Army and the Navy. Their arguments usually followed the line that the United States was trying to maintain an uneasy compromise between two distinct concepts of warfare and in so doing was in danger of falling between two stools. The two concepts were *deterrence* by threatening devastating nuclear punishment for aggression, and *containment* by being prepared to block Soviet and satellite aggressions with ground forces. The critics felt that the latter objective should be dropped or at least drastically minimized. These arguments usually were accompanied by a belief that the economy of the United States could not support, over a long period, an adequate implementation of both types of strategy.

This line of thought began influencing official policy in Great Britain earlier than it did in the United States. Upon taking over the government in 1951, the Conservatives under Churchill were faced with an economic crisis. One way to ease the strain, it was decided, was to reduce defense expenditures. Churchill summoned his Chiefs of Staff—Sir John Slessor, Chief of the Air Staff of the Royal Air Force; Sir William Slim, Chief of the Imperial General Staff; and Sir Rhoderick Robert McGrigor, First Sea Lord—and told them to reappraise Britain's defense policy, with an eye to cutting costs. At Churchill's suggestion, the Chiefs retired to relative seclusion, dispensing with staff assistance. In a period of several weeks they produced a paper whose central thesis was that the advent of atomic weapons had revolutionized the character of modern war, justifying primary reliance upon air power and substantial reductions in conventional surface forces. The paper urged that the Western powers declare that aggression would be resisted not only at the point of attack, but also by massive retaliation against the enemy's homeland. This, it was said, would deter future eruptions like the Korean War. In July 1952 Churchill announced a "shortfall" in the British rearmament program, based on "a new assessment" of British defense strategy.[1] Also in July, Slessor turned up in Washington bearing the paper which the British Chiefs had prepared. Slessor, in discussions with the American Chiefs, argued for adoption by the entire Western alliance of the strategy which the British Chiefs had worked out. He said the NATO force goal of about 96 divisions, which had been adopted at the NATO Council's Lisbon meeting in February, would place too great a strain on the fragile European economies. He urged a strategy of deterrence resting chiefly on American and British air-nuclear capabilities. Citing the apparent ebbing of the immediate danger of full-scale war, he argued for a reduction in the ground force goals of NATO.

Slessor failed to persuade the American Chiefs of Staff, with the possible exception of General Hoyt S. Vandenberg, the Air Force

[1] Charles J. V. Murphy, "A New Strategy for NATO," *Fortune*, January 1953, pp. 80–81. Also see Alastair Buchan, "Their Bomb and Ours," *Encounter*, January 1959, pp. 11 ff.

Chief of Staff. General Omar N. Bradley (the Chairman), General J. Lawton Collins (Army Chief of Staff), and Admiral William M. Fechteler (Chief of Naval Operations) insisted that the NATO ground forces be created on schedule. They admitted that the development of a variety of kinds of nuclear weapons for tactical use might eventually reduce somewhat the need for ground forces, but pointed out that the accumulation of such weapons in adequate quantity was still some years away.[2] In their view, the Slessor proposal was simply a rationalization of a British intent to renege on their NATO force commitment.

The Presidential election campaign in this country provided evidence, however, that Slessor's frustration might be only temporary. Much of the philosophy which later brought forth the New Look was expressed in campaign speeches by candidate Eisenhower and his Republican supporters. Even before his nomination, General Eisenhower had often spoken of the key importance of preserving the economic "solvency" of the members of the Western alliance, especially of the United States. His convictions on this point were of long standing, going back at least as far as his tour of duty as Chief of Staff of the Army after World War II, when he often preached to his colleagues the need for concern about "what the economy can stand."[3] His experience as Supreme Allied Commander, Europe, in 1951 and 1952, which brought him into close contact with the economic difficulties of the European allies in meeting their military commitments, probably reinforced this conviction.

At his famous Morningside Heights conference with Senator Robert A. Taft following his nomination, Eisenhower agreed with Taft's view that overall government spending, especially defense spending, should be drastically reduced.[4] During the campaign the candidate asserted that the largest savings in governmental expenditure would be made in the defense establishment, but without any reduction in defensive power.

"We must achieve both security and solvency," Eisenhower de-

[2] "Defense and Strategy," *Fortune*, December 1953, p. 82. Interviews.
[3] See Bernard Brodie, *Strategy in the Missile Age* (Princeton, Princeton University Press, 1959), p. 366.
[4] New York *Times*, September 13, 1952, p. 1.

clared. "In fact, the foundation of military strength is economic strength. A bankrupt America is more the Soviet goal than an America conquered on the field of battle." [5]

The candidate also called for a military program "that will keep our boys at our side instead of on a foreign shore." [6]

Taking up the theme of the "long pull," Eisenhower said his administration would call a halt to "stop-and-start planning" and would "plan for the future on something more solid than yesterday's headlines." [7]

Eisenhower proposed to appoint a committee of civilians to restudy the "operations, functions and acts of the Department of Defense," with a view to designing "an over-all scheme of national security best suited to our inventive, productive and military genius and to our geographic and strategic position in the world." [8]

Apparently the idea of "massive retaliation" to enemy aggressions in Europe and Asia did not hold a very prominent place in Eisenhower's precampaign philosophy of national defense. However, it was a pet concept of John Foster Dulles, Eisenhower's choice for Secretary of State. Dulles had written of "instant, massive retaliation" in the spring of 1952, using phrases almost identical with those in his famous speech of January 12, 1954. Even earlier, in December 1950, he had spoken of "the capacity to counterattack . . . by action of our own choosing" as the "ultimate deterrent" and the only "effective defense." [9] At Dulles' instigation, a reference to "retaliatory striking power" appeared in a draft of the Republican campaign platform. Eisenhower found the phrase offensive, however, and insisted that it be stricken out,[10] which was done. Yet, in a campaign speech on

---

[5] *Ibid.*, September 26, 1952, p. 1.   [6] *Ibid.*, September 17, 1952, p. 1.
[7] *Ibid.*, September 26, 1952, p. 1.   [8] *Ibid.*
[9] *Life*, May 19, 1952, pp. 146 ff.; *Department of State Bulletin*, January 15, 1951, pp. 85–89.
[10] The incident is described in C. L. Sulzberger, *What's Wrong with U.S. Foreign Policy?* (New York, Harcourt Brace and Co., 1959), pp. 41–43. It was Sulzberger who informed Eisenhower that the phrase was in the platform draft, and it was also he who transmitted to Dulles the candidate's wish to have it deleted.
Perhaps Eisenhower's initial negative reaction to the idea of massive retaliation can be laid in part to his recent experience as commander of the NATO ground and tactical forces in Europe. Logically, endorsement of the concept

August 24, 1952, the candidate made the following statement: "We must have security forces of mobility; security forces whose destructive and retaliatory power is so great that it causes nightmares in the Kremlin whenever they think of attacking us." [11]

THE HELENA CONFERENCE

In a dramatic gesture near the close of the campaign, Eisenhower had committed himself to visit the front line in Korea as part of his promised effort to bring that war to a close. On November 30, he took off from La Guardia Field, New York City, in fulfillment of that commitment, taking with him his Secretary of Defense–designate, Charles E. Wilson of General Motors, as well as his choice for Attorney General, Herbert Brownell. The trip was to be a significant one, not only from the point of view of its ostensible purpose—the termination of the war—but also from the standpoint of general defense policy, for it was to bring together for the first time the five personalities who were to be chiefly responsible for the formulation of that policy. When the Presidential plane stopped at Iwo Jima to refuel, Admiral Arthur W. Radford, the Commander in Chief of the Pacific Fleet (who had flown from Hawaii) joined the party. His presence had been requested by Wilson, who wished to meet him and measure him for a possible future role as a member or Chairman of the Joint Chiefs of Staff.

After the brief inspection tour in Korea, the group left for home aboard the cruiser U.S.S. *Helena.* The ship stopped at Guam on the return trip and took aboard a party of advisers who had flown from the United States—including John Foster Dulles and George M. Humphrey, Eisenhower's choices for the Secretaryships of State and the Treasury, and Joseph M. Dodge, the Detroit banker who was to be Director of the Budget. In the relaxed informal setting aboard

---

of massive retaliation in its full implications might have conflicted with NATO's "forward strategy" designed to hold European territory on the ground as far to the East as possible, as well as with the recently approved NATO ground force goal of 50 active divisions on the front line with a slightly smaller number of reserve divisions as a back-up.

[11] New York *Times,* August 25, 1952, p. 26.

the great ship, and stimulated by the electoral victory which had just been won, the men talked freely and expansively about broad aspects of policy. Matters of defense, and the problem of paying for defense needs, were prominent in the discussion. Many of the thoughts which were expressed had already been bruited publicly by these same persons and others, but in scattered form. On the *Helena* the ideas came together and the rough harmony which had been latent in them began to crystallize.

The two great military problems of the new administration, as the group conceived them, were to bring the Korean War to an honorable end and to evolve a defense concept which would permit the indefinite maintenance of a strong military posture without impairing the country's economic well-being and growth. On the Korean problem, the talk centered around a toughening of attitude—a show of force, a threat, discreetly conveyed—which would impress the Communist leaders with the determination of the United States to step up its military effort, or perhaps even to expand the war, unless the Communist negotiators ended their delaying tactics and agreed to a truce. Eisenhower's trip to Korea had intensified his determination to obtain a settlement.[12]

More relevant for our present purpose, however, was the discussion of overall defense and foreign policy. The President-elect dwelt at length on what he called "the great equation" of maintaining for "the long haul" a strong defense posture without bankrupting the country in the process.[13] Eisenhower's thinking was "heavily influenced by concern that any serious prolongation of the military programs of the kind then under way and in contemplation must inevitably turn the United States into a 'garrison state.'"[14] The military power of the United States, he stressed, rested on two pillars—actual fighting forces and a flourishing economy. Powerful armed forces were necessary, but they had to be weighed against

[12] Robert J. Donovan, *Eisenhower: The Inside Story* (New York, Harper and Bros., 1956), p. 17.

[13] *Ibid.*, p. 17.

[14] Quotation attributed to Robert Cutler, the President's Special Assistant for National Security Affairs, in Charles J. V. Murphy, "The Eisenhower Shift," *Fortune*, March 1956, p. 112.

the danger of inflation which could disastrously weaken the country.[15] These views were thoroughly in accord with those of Humphrey, but apparently Eisenhower, rather than Humphrey, took the lead in expounding them on the *Helena* trip.

Admiral Radford added some thoughts about strategy which fitted well into Eisenhower's general statement of the problem. According to Radford, American military power was overextended. Too many forces were committed to places, especially in Asia, where they could be pinned down. Radford favored greater concentration of American military power in a "mobile strategic reserve," stationed in or near the North American continent. Major reliance for local defense should be on indigenous forces, he reasoned, with the mobile power of the United States available as a deterrent and backstop in case of war.

Radford's ideas dovetailed with those of Dulles. The Secretary of State-to-be pressed his view that United States policy should be based on creation of a massive striking power, which would deter the Communists from aggression. Rather than attempting to contain communism all the way around its vast perimeter, the United States should concentrate on deterring attack by maintaining a massive retaliatory power capable of striking directly at the sources of Communist aggressive policy.[16] Dulles stressed another point: that all the great wars of history had resulted from miscalculation by the aggressor of the extent of resistance his attack would arouse. It followed that, to avoid war, it was necessary to inform the Communist leaders that the United States could be counted upon to resist any aggression and inflict damage in response which would far outweigh any possible gain.

THE FISCAL 1954 BUDGET

The most urgent problem facing the new administration after it assumed office was to revise downward the Truman administration's budget for fiscal 1954, which had been presented to Congress only a few days before Eisenhower's inaugural. This budget called for total

[15] Donovan, *Eisenhower: The Inside Story*, p. 17.　　　[16] *Ibid.*, p. 18.

expenditures of $78.6 billion and for new "obligational authority" of $72.9 billion.[17] For the military functions of the Department of Defense, it projected spending of $45.4 billion and asked new obligational authority of $41.2 billion. By far the greatest share of the new defense funds ($16,778,000,000) was programmed for the Air Force. It was clear that any substantial reduction would have to be taken very largely out of funds for national security.

Having come into power on promises of reduced government spending and an eventual balanced budget, the administration hoped to make a substantial cut in the estimated deficit of $9.9 billion for fiscal 1954 and to lay the groundwork for a balanced budget in fiscal 1955. To these ends, on February 3 Budget Director Joseph M. Dodge requested all departments to "initiate an immediate review . . . calling for recommendations on the downward adjustment of program levels and for information as to the probable effect of such adjustments on Government services." [18] The results of these reviews were to be used for making revisions in the inherited budget estimates for fiscal 1954, and for preparing estimates for fiscal 1955.

About a month after their receipt of this order, 45 government agencies had submitted revised estimates for the 1954 budget, but the results were not cheering to Budget Director Dodge. He reported to the Cabinet on March 6 that the economies suggested by the agency reviews were small, and that it might be necessary for the President to order further reductions.[19]

It was decided, at a meeting of the National Security Council on March 4, to initiate a second study which would explore the consequences of approaching a balanced budget in fiscal 1954 and achieving it in fiscal 1955. Each department was given certain "assumed" expenditure ceilings for each year. For the Department of Defense, these were $41.2 billion for the fiscal year 1954 and $34.6 billion for fiscal 1955.[20] These figures compared with the $45.4 billion which

---

[17] Roughly speaking, the term "obligational authority" refers to new appropriations of funds plus new authority to make contracts against future appropriations.

[18] Donovan, *Eisenhower: The Inside Story*, p. 55.   [19] *Ibid.*, p. 57.

[20] From an order sent to the Secretaries of the Army, Navy, and Air Force by Deputy Secretary of Defense Roger M. Kyes, March 9, 1953. The order is quoted in full by Drew Pearson in the Washington *Post*, March 21, 1953.

had been projected by the Truman administration for fiscal 1954.

The Department of Defense was directed to submit to the National Security Council by March 24 a statement of the program revisions which would be necessary to reduce expenditures to these levels, and "the effect of these revisions in relation to currently approved national security policies and objectives." [21]

Roger M. Kyes, the Deputy Secretary of Defense, asked the three military departments to make preliminary estimates of the forces which could be maintained at the given expenditure levels. Combat strength was to be maintained wherever possible, with the reductions coming out of "overhead personnel" and "less necessary projects." The Joint Chiefs of Staff were then to review the departmental estimates and provide the following:

(a) Recommendations regarding any adjustments within or between the military departments in the military composition or support of the forces proposed by the military departments which in their opinion would increase the ability of the United States to carry out its current policies and commitments within the total expenditure allocation to the Department of Defense.

(b) Evaluation of the capabilities of such forces to carry out presently approved policies and commitments.

(c) Evaluation of the nature and extent of the modifications that would need to be made in presently approved policies and commitments. [22]

The results of this study became available about March 24. At a meeting of the National Security Council, each member of the Joint Chiefs of Staff presented orally the conclusions pertaining to his own service. The gist of their presentations was that the proposed fiscal limits would seriously reduce the rate of build-up of military capabilities and would dangerously affect national security. [23] Although the council was not satisfied with either the quantity or the pertinence of the information which had been provided, it was able to

[21] *Ibid.*   [22] *Ibid.*

[23] Testimony of Secretary of Defense Charles E. Wilson and Assistant Secretary Wilfred McNeil, *Department of Defense Appropriations for 1954,* Hearings before the Committee on Appropriations, House of Representatives, 83d Cong., 1st Sess. (Washington, 1953), pp. 317 and 470–71. Hereafter cited as *HCA, Hearings 1954 Budget.*

decide that a balanced budget in 1955 was not feasible. The Joint Chiefs of Staff were then directed to make a further study which would indicate how much reduction could be made in the existing programs without damaging the security of the country.[24]

This additional JCS study, which was completed in one week, warned that *any* reduction in force goals would increase the calculated risk, and, in particular, that any cutback in the 143-wing target for the Air Force would increase the risk to national security "beyond the dictates of national prudence." The paper also stated that the years 1954 and 1955 represented the beginning of a potentially dangerous period during which the U.S.S.R. would have a substantial stockpile of atomic weapons and the improved ability to deliver such weapons.[25]

Obviously, if the budget were to be reduced, the Joint Chiefs of Staff would be of little use in providing the rationale. The civilian leaders in the Pentagon decided to take matters in their own hands. They were convinced that much "water" could be wrung out of the budget estimates without affecting either existing combat strength or the rate of build-up to approved goals. They initiated a searching review designed to eliminate inessential services and to correct inefficient procedures, rather than to revise strategy or force levels. The Department of Defense budget experts focused their attention on such things as supporting activities, lead times, bringing various related programs "into phase" with each other, personnel utilization, and contracting practices. As Deputy Secretary Kyes put it, the overriding aim of the review was to "go operational" in all the services— to avoid the spending of any money, or the letting of any contracts, in 1954, which could just as well be deferred until fiscal 1955.

The results of this review, which were submitted to Congress early in May, called for a reduction from $41.2 billion to $36 billion in the request for new appropriations (later reduced again to $35.8 billion) and a cutback in planned expenditures from $45.4 billion to $43.2

---

[24] *Ibid.*, p. 527.

[25] Testimony of General Hoyt S. Vandenberg, Air Force Chief of Staff, *Department of Defense Appropriations for 1954*, Hearings before the Committee on Appropriations, United States Senate, 83d Cong., 1st Sess. (Washington, 1953), p. 231.

billion. The most remarkable feature of the revised budget was the manner in which the reductions were divided among the three armed services. The Air Force, the most popular of the three services in Congress, suffered the heaviest reductions, being forced to reduce its planned new obligations from $16.7 billion to $11.7 billion. In addition, the Air Force's goal of 143 wings was replaced with an "interim" goal of 120 wings, with 114 wings to be operational by June 30, 1954. The Navy's new appropriation request was cut from $11.3 billion to $9.6 billion, while the Army's request rose from $12.1 billion to $13.6 billion. The figure for the Army would have been reduced by $1 billion had it not been for the inclusion of provision for additional military aid to South Korea and for combat consumption of ammunition in Korea at the prevailing rates for the entire year, two factors which had been left out of the Truman budget.

The large cut in Air Force funds aroused severe criticism on Capitol Hill, notably among Democrats and, in particular, from Senator Stuart Symington, a former Secretary of the Air Force. Administration spokesmen immediately sought—unsuccessfully, for the most part—to allay this criticism by explaining that the 143-wing goal had not been irrevocably abandoned, that it might be resurrected by the new Joint Chiefs of Staff, and that, in reality, the reduction in Air Force funds would not retard the build-up in that service. The Air Force could not obtain more than 114 wings by the end of fiscal 1954, or 120 wings a year later, whatever the appropriations, since the limiting factor was production capacity, not money. The budgetary cut reflected no change in strategic policy, it was said, but only the application of principles of efficient management. Secretary Wilson and Deputy Secretary Kyes explained that the cut was simply the "statistical result" of a management review applied equitably to all three services, that it had not, in other words, been planned that way. Kyes professed to have been "the most surprised man in the Pentagon" when he saw the results of the review.[26]

A good part of the reason for the Air Force cut, according to Wilson and Kyes, was a shortening in the lead time of manufacturers,

[26] *HCA, Hearings 1954 Budget,* p. 390.

which the Air Force planners had not considered in programming their contract obligations. This factor, combined with the considerable backlog of orders on the books of manufacturers, meant that many orders which were to be placed in 1954 could be deferred to 1955 with little or no deferral in delivery dates. Some aircraft production plans were curtailed to allow more time to work out "bugs" in the designs. There was some reduction in planned purchases of "support-type" aircraft such as helicopters and certain transport types. A slow-down in base construction and spare parts manufacture, to bring them into balance with aircraft production, accounted for part of the reduction. All except a small fraction of the reduction of $5 billion was accounted for by the tightening of financing procedures, it was said, with no effect on the rate of build-up.

In addition to such detailed explanations, it was pointed out by administration spokesmen that the Air Force was the only one of the three services which would continue to expand during 1954. President Eisenhower assured the nation that 60 cents out of every defense dollar would be devoted to air power and air defense.[27] The Army and the Navy were to remain at approximately their existing combat strength, although, like the Air Force, they suffered some reduction in "supporting services."

These data and explanations made a strong case for the administration's claim that real air power was not being reduced nor its build-up retarded, nor were future decisions regarding goals for air power being prejudiced. The savings resulted from elimination of overfinancing, balancing of procurement programs, and taking account of the realities of production feasibility—not from any changes in strategic plans. Nevertheless, the critics, ably led in Congress by Senator Symington, were not convinced. They asserted that a "stretch-out" had taken place; that the postponement of some contracting could not help but retard the build-up; and that the Air Force goal of 143 wings had been "abandoned."

These assertions received strong support from General Hoyt S. Vandenberg, Air Force Chief of Staff. Vandenberg appeared before the House Appropriations Committee and bitterly attacked the re-

[27] New York *Times*, May 20, 1953.

ductions in Air Force spending authority. He said that "no sound military reason has been offered to explain why the Air Force build-up to the agreed force level is again to be delayed." While agreeing "in general" that procurement of combat planes would proceed as previously scheduled, he declared that the reduction in other aspects of the program would inevitably reduce combat strength.

"Any one major element of an Air Force program is just as important as any other," Vandenberg declared, "and . . . so-called supporting elements cannot be sacrificed without crippling combat strength." [28]

Vandenberg went on:

> The numerous and somewhat contradictory administrative and fiscal actions of the past few months have caused the greatest amount of uncertainty and confusion in the Air Force and among allied activities that has existed since the demobilization after World War II. . . .[29]
>
> Once again the growth of American airpower is threatened with start and stop planning, and at a time when we face an enemy who has more modern jet fighters than we have and enough long-range bombers to attack this country in a sudden all-out atomic effort.[30]

But Vandenberg himself indicated that only $1.5 billion of the $5-billion reduction in the appropriations request represented a delay in the build-up of combat strength.[31] The administration, of course, denied that a delay of even this magnitude would occur.

Whatever the misgivings felt by the Congress about the strategic and security implications of the budget, they were overcome by the stronger Congressional desire to achieve economies in government spending. Congress even cut the budget more than the administration had proposed, trimming the new obligational authority to $34.5 billion in the final measure which passed on July 29. The division of funds between the services was left just about as the administration had requested.

---

[28] *Department of the Air Force Appropriations for 1954*, Hearings before the Committee on Appropriations, House of Representatives, 83d Cong., 1st Sess. (Washington, 1953), p. 961.

[29] *Ibid.,* p. 961.   [30] *Ibid.,* p. 963.   [31] *Ibid.,* p. 990.

THE "LONG HAUL"

At a press conference on April 30, the President announced a "radical" change in policy, the "essence" of which was as follows:

We reject the idea that we must build up to a maximum attainable strength for some specific date theoretically fixed for a specified time in the future. Defense is not a matter of maximum strength for a single date. It is a matter of adequate protection to be projected as far into the future as the actions and apparent purposes of others may compel us. It is a policy that can if necessary be lived with over a period of years.[32]

The President thus gave utterance to what was to become one of the major themes of the New Look doctrine, the concept of the "long haul." This concept had been adopted formally at a meeting of the National Security Council early in April and had been transmitted to the military services as guidance for requirements programming and budget-making. The idea had been discussed and recommended earlier in a report by the Advisory Council of the NSC—a group of seven prominent businessmen otherwise known as the "Seven Wise Men." [33] The report was incidental, however, because the concept had been germinating for some time in the President's mind and had already been seized upon by the new administration as the core of its defense philosophy.

As the President's statement (quoted above) indicates, the new Republican administration conceived of the "long haul" concept as a substitute for another concept which had to some extent guided military planning in the Truman administration—the idea of a "crisis year" or "year of maximum peril." In following the latter concept, Republican spokesmen said, the previous administration had picked a particular year in which the Soviets were likely to make war, and had planned to reach a peak of military expenditure in that year, to be followed by a decline if war did not occur. The trouble with this concept, its Republican denigrators (including the

---

[32] New York *Times,* May 1, 1953, p. 9.

[33] This group also recommended a stepping up of military operations in Korea—perhaps including the use of atomic bombs—with a view to bringing the war quickly to a conclusion. There is no discernible evidence that this part of the report had any influence on the Korean War strategy; the President had already decided not to use the atomic bomb.

President) claimed, was that no one could predict when the Soviets would make war, and the decline in military expenditure after the peak was reached and war did not occur would have disastrous economic consequences.[34] President Eisenhower said at a press conference that it was simply not possible to go from maximum production to zero.[35]

Under the "long haul" concept, on the other hand, there would be no attempt to estimate when war would take place, hence no peaking of expenditures. This concept, it was said, assumed that the Soviet threat was of indefinite duration and therefore called for the maintenance of a reasonably sturdy military posture over a long period of time. In contrast to the past "feast or famine" pattern of military mobilization, it would allow the maintenance of military strength at a steady level which the economy could absorb without serious strain.

The "radicalness" of the shift from "year of crisis" to "long haul" was very much exaggerated, perhaps partly because of an understandable desire of the new administration to show that fundamental changes were being made, but mostly, it seems, because of a real misunderstanding of the criteria for mobilization planning which the previous administration had used. This planning *had* postulated a year of maximum danger—a year in which the ratio of Soviet to United States capabilities would be most favorable to the former, in which the *probability* of Soviet attack would be higher than in any previous year. The year selected was 1954, although 1952 was used for a short time.[36] During the Korean War period, the Joint

[34] Secretary Wilson said later that if war did not take place in the crisis year, "we would have had a depression in this country, because we would suddenly flip from a high level of war production down to a lower production, and they would have laid off these people, and industry could not have absorbed them fast enough in other activities." *Department of Defense Appropriations for 1955*, Hearings before the Committee on Appropriations, House of Representatives, 83d Cong., 2d Sess. (Washington, 1954), p. 113. [Hereafter cited as *HCA, Hearings 1955 Budget*.]

[35] New York *Times*, May 1, 1953.

[36] Apparently the "crisis year" concept had first appeared prominently in NSC-68, a document considered by the National Security Council in the spring of 1950. This paper had predicted that the Soviet Union would have the capability to launch a devastating nuclear attack on the United States by 1954. The resulting neutralization of the atomic advantage of the United States, combined with the Soviet Union's continuing superiority in conventional arms,

Chiefs of Staff recommended that the planned build-up of United States forces be completed in the crisis year, in order to minimize the danger of attack and to be in the best possible fighting position should the attack occur. The force levels reached in that year would then be maintained.

The "year of maximum danger" concept was somewhat suspect in that it just happened to correspond roughly with the lead time for attainment of the force goals which the Joint Chiefs of Staff recommended in October 1951. Whatever the intent of those who evoked the concept, it did provide an excellent argument for justifying the force goals and the rate of build-up before Congressional appropriations committees. Nevertheless, there were fairly solid reasons for selection of the year 1954 as a crucial year, reasons which General Omar N. Bradley expounded as follows:

(1) The Soviets would attain a nuclear capability in 1954 substantial enough to do serious damage to the United States. This followed from considering that the United States had taken five years to build its atomic stockpile from negligible to substantial proportions and the Soviets had exploded their first atomic weapon in 1949.

(2) The NATO nations planned to reach their force goals—established at the Lisbon Conference in February 1952—in 1954. The Soviets would know that their chances of successfully overrun-

---

would pose a grave threat to the security of the United States and its allies unless something were done about it beforehand. The paper had proposed to to something about it in the form of an expansion of the conventional military capabilities of the United States and the free world, thus avoiding the crisis by countering the Soviet area of strength before or about the same time that the Soviets countered ours.

The recommendations of NSC-68 were largely realized as a result of the stimulus provided by the Korean War. In the early part of that war, the Joint Chiefs of Staff moved the assumed "year of crisis" up to 1952, apparently because of fears that this limited aggression might expand into, or be soon followed by, an all-out war. Later, after the Korean War had stabilized and the chances of global war seemed to have diminished, the date was extended again to 1954. Paradoxically, while the "crisis year" concept had been tied, in NSC-68, to a proposal for expansion of ground forces, it was most often used by the Air Force during the latter part of the Korean War period as an argument for speedy attainment of its cherished goal of 143 wings, and against President Truman's "stretch-out" of the target date to 1955 or 1956. Cf. Paul Hammond, *NSC-68, supra.*

ning Europe would have considerably lessened after the completion of this build-up.

(3) The Soviet Union had produced enormous amounts of military equipment in 1946 and 1947, after which military production had declined. Since military equipment tends to become obsolete in about eight years, the equipment produced right after World War II would have to be used in 1954 or 1955 if it was to be used at all.

(4) The rebuilding of Russian industry, and relocation of much of it beyond the Urals, would have been largely completed by 1953 or 1954.

(5) Russia's modernization of her own and the satellite forces, and the training of those forces "will reach a high point of veteran experience and knowledge, and a good point of material and equipment supply, in the area of time centered around 1954. After that, if sufficient means are provided, our relative capability will get closer and closer to that of the Soviets, and eventually minimize the risk of war." [37]

Even if it be argued that these reasons contained a generous sprinkling of rationalization and salesmanship, this would be considerably beside the point. The important point is that the mobilization policy of the latter years of the Truman administration was essentially a policy of the "long haul," with the "year of crisis" idea serving to dramatize the target date for completion of the build-up. After attainment of the scheduled force goals, plans were to level off and maintain approximately this level of forces indefinitely. There was no assumption that the Soviets *would* attack in the crisis year. Nor did the plans contemplate having in hand by the crisis year sufficient active, mobilized forces to defeat the Soviets in all-out war.[38] It was a "partial" rather than an "all-out" mobilization, aiming

[37] *Department of Defense Appropriations for 1953*, Hearings before the Committee on Appropriations, United States Senate, 82d Cong., 2d Sess. (Washington, 1952), pp. 332 ff.

[38] To some military extremists, the "year of maximum danger" concept did signify the total acquisition of all requirements for all-out war by the crisis date. But this interpretation was never accepted at the higher levels of authority in the Pentagon, although it might have had something to do with the very large budgetary requests which were generated by the armed services for the fiscal years 1952 and 1953—requests which were cut drastically by the Secretary of Defense and his staff.

at attainment of a moderate level of active military capabilities, supplemented by an industrial "mobilization base" (including active and stand-by production facilities and reserve stockpiles of materials, spare parts, and machine tools), which could produce a rapid expansion of active forces in a crisis. The policy explicitly recognized that the threat was going to be of long-term duration, that while a sturdy military posture would have to be continued indefinitely, the forces should not be so large that their maintenance would endanger economic stability or cause excessive civilian sacrifice.

None of the responsible leaders of the new administration ever claimed in so many words that the previous administration had intended to reach a peak of *capabilities* in the crisis year and then drop down to some lower level if war did not materialize. However, this was strongly implied, and the phrase "peaking of forces" was sometimes used to describe the kind of thing the new "long haul" concept was to banish.

A more explicit charge against the "crisis year" concept was that the shift from build-up to purely maintenance and modernization expenditures would entail such a sharp decline in military *spending* as to cause serious economic dislocation. It is true that the Truman administration had planned for such a decline. President Truman stated in his budget message early in 1953 that expenditures would begin declining after reaching a high point of $45.4 billion in 1954 and would eventually reach a sustaining rate of $35 billion to $40 billion. But a decline of such magnitude (even if it were to take place in one year, which the Truman administration did not intend) surely would not have meant going from "maximum production to zero," nor does it seem to justify Secretary Wilson's claims that it would have caused a depression.

Thus, the idea of "preparing for the long pull," of avoiding sharp peaks and valleys of capability and expenditure, did not originate with the new administration.[39] However, the abandonment of the

---

[39] As early as 1949, General Bradley wrote "Our way toward security lies not in any sudden burst of activity, but in the steady, unwavering, purposeful application of energy over a long period of years. . . . We are in for a long pull." General Omar Bradley, "This Way Lies Peace," *Saturday Evening Post,* October 15, 1949, p. 33.

"year of maximum peril" as a justification or rationalization for a target date does seem to have had some effect on military planning procedures. According to Admiral Radford, it made "a great difference in military planning." [40] Of course, the difference was not in the abandonment of target dates as such—these are an obvious requirement of orderly planning. The Eisenhower administration adopted its own target year—1957—marking the time at which it expected to complete its changes in the military establishment and level off for "the long pull." [41] Apparently the "great difference" of which Admiral Radford spoke was primarily psychological—elimination of the sense of urgency which had surrounded the build-up target date when it was rationalized as a "year of crisis." Henceforth, target dates were not to have any particular significance except as administrative guide lines. Moreover, they were to be moved ahead each year: there was to be a "floating D-Day" instead of a "fixed D-Day." The armed services would continue to develop D-Day "requirements," but the substitution of the assumption of an "extended period of uneasy peace" for a "year of peril" foreclosed them from arguing that these requirements *had* to be on hand by a particular date.

Thus, one effect of dropping the "crisis year" concept was to subtly shift the balance of power in the annual budgetary reviews to the disadvantage of the military services and to the advantage of the Department of Defense Comptroller and the Bureau of the Budget. Another effect was to encourage balance in military procurement. According to Wilfred J. McNeil, the Department of Defense Comptroller, when the "fixed D-Day" or "year of crisis" was used as a procurement and planning criterion, the armed services tended to purchase equipment rather indiscriminately, aiming only to have all their "requirements" on hand by D-Day, rather than attempting to maintain balance among the various elements of their

[40] *HCA, Hearings 1955 Budget,* p. 120.

[41] Ironically, the administration's reduction of military appropriations from the Truman request of $41.2 billion to $36 billion may have contributed something to the economic recession of 1953–54. Thus, the effort to retrench to the "long haul" level of military financing may have had some of the same effects that the alleged Truman "peaking" policy supposedly would have caused.

program year by year. In consequence, D-Day goals were approached more rapidly for the easy-to-get items than for those more difficult to procure, even though the latter were often the more critical items. Elimination of the fixed D-Day, and the special urgency which the "year of crisis" idea associated with it, encouraged the services to preserve overall balance in their programs by gearing procurement rates for all types of supplies and equipment to the availability of the items which were the hardest to buy or which had the longest lead times.[42] Still another effect was to reduce a previous tendency to place contracts hurriedly, before designs had been completely worked out or before new models had been thoroughly tested. The new approach also tended to inhibit the purchase of fast-obsolescing items. Under the concept of the "floating D-Day," a decision whether to continue buying an old model, to buy a new model not yet thoroughly proven, or to wait until the new model had been completely tested was more likely to be resolved in favor of the latter alternative.[43]

The concept of the "long haul" was introduced almost immediately into NATO planning. When the NATO Council met in Paris on April 23–25, Secretary of State Dulles informed the Allies of the change in United States defense philosophy and recommended that it be adopted as a guide to the defense planning of the alliance as well. Dulles said the United States administration had decided that the progress already made in the NATO build-up justified some reduction in current defense burdens, in view of the economic strains which they entailed for some members of the alliance. The Council approved Dulles' recommendation and agreed to a slow-down in the NATO military build-up. It was decided that, henceforth, the emphasis in the mobilization programs of all the Allies would be on "quality" rather than "quantity." [44]

OPERATION SOLARIUM

During his campaign, the President had promised to appoint a civilian group to make a thorough examination of the broad politico-

[42] *HCA, Hearings 1954 Budget*, pp. 445–46.   [43] Interviews.
[44] New York *Times*, May 3, 1953, IV, p. 1.

military strategy of the United States. As a starting point for such a study, the President had received from the previous administration a report on the overall national security problem over the signatures of Dean Acheson, Robert Lovett, and Averell Harriman, the outgoing Secretaries of State and Defense and the Mutual Security Administrator, respectively. Prepared specifically for the guidance of the new administration, and bearing the designation of NSC-141, the report generally viewed the Soviet threat with alarm and urged that the military build-up goals be maintained. It recommended an increase of some $7 billion to $9 billion in defense expenditures, mainly for air defense, and urged an increase in military and economic aid to the Middle East and the Far East. Obviously, this study ran sharply against the economy predilections of the new administration, so it was shelved and a decision was made to undertake a completely new appraisal.

The Eisenhower reexamination got under way on the afternoon of May 8, in the White House sun room or "solarium," where the President met with four of his most trusted advisers: General Walter Bedell Smith, Under Secretary of State; Robert Cutler, Special Assistant to the President for National Security Affairs; Allen Dulles, director of the Central Intelligence Agency; and C. D. Jackson, Chairman of the Psychological Strategy Board. As a result of preparatory work, principally by Cutler, the group had before it three alternative lines of politico-military policy. These were as follows:

(1) Continue the "containment" policy substantially as it had been inherited from the previous administration.

(2) "Draw a line" around the entire globe and inform the Soviets that if they moved over this line they could expect to be severely punished. As compared with containment, this policy would extend the geographical commitments of the United States and would threaten a more severe response to aggression. The phrase "instant, massive retaliation" was not used, but global "deterrence" by the threat of nuclear punishment was the implicit essence of this proposal.

(3) Substitute a policy of "liberation" for containment; undertake a vigorous program of political, psychological, and economic war-

fare, along with certain para-military measures, such as infiltration of agents and saboteurs, designed to "roll back" the frontiers of the Communist orbit.

Although each of these alternatives dealt primarily with foreign policy, they had obvious military implications. A policy of containment, effectively pursued, would mean being ready to block and push back Communist aggressions on the ground at the point of attack, and thus it implied substantial ground forces. The second alternative implied primary reliance on nuclear air power and was not so much concerned with holding the Communist forces should they attempt to cross the line as with deterring them from the attempt by the threat of punishment. The third alternative implied the adoption of guerilla-type techniques of violence, and the encouragement and support of revolutionary activity within the Soviet orbit.

It was the President's wish that each of these proposals be studied by a separate "task force" and that each task force would attempt to make the best possible case for the alternative assigned to it. The purpose of the exercise was not to select the best of the three alternatives, nor even to achieve a synthesis of the three. Rather, it was to highlight three dramatically different policy lines and to develop thoroughly the implications of each, as background material for a later policy determination by the regular agencies of the government. The leaders and members of the task forces were chosen from persons whose backgrounds indicated they would be competent advocates of one of the three alternatives. For example, George Kennan, a principal architect of the containment policy, was selected as chairman of the "containment" group. General James McCormack, Jr., of the Air Force, was chosen to direct the study of the "drawing the line—deterrence" alternative. Admiral Richard L. Connolly, then President of the Naval War College, headed the group which developed the argument for "liberation." The President asked Smith and Cutler to exercise overall control of the project, and also appointed an interdepartmental "steering committee," under Lieutenant General James H. Doolittle, a vice-president of Shell Oil Company and one of the President's favorite informal advisers, to lay down a "frame of reference" for each task force. The whole project was given the code name "Operation Solarium," after its place of origin.[45]

The steering committee developed an elaboration of about 250 words for each of the lines of policy to be studied and also suggested a fourth alternative: to undertake active negotiations with the Soviet regime under a definite time limit of two years. The significance of the time limit was that during this two-year period the United States could expect to enjoy a great preponderance in nuclear striking power as the result of its development of the hydrogen bomb, but that after two years this superiority would probably decline as the Soviets developed their own H-bomb. Thus, the Soviets would know that if they did not agree to terms within the time specified, they would be risking general war with the United States at a time when the United States had a vast advantage in striking power. However, this was academic, since the proposal was not considered acceptable by Smith and Cutler, apparently because it smacked too much of preventive war, and it was dropped from further consideration.[46]

The three task forces established themselves in the National War College and worked up their respective cases during June and July. Late in July, the reports were sent to the President, who turned them over to the Planning Board of the National Security Council with instructions to take the best ideas from all of them and incorporate them into a single basic policy paper. By October, the Planning Board had resolved the issue pretty much in favor of the first alternative—a continuation of the policy of "containment"—with some slight modification in the direction of the second alternative. That is, the board concluded that the basic objective of policy must be to prevent further expansion of the Communist orbit, but that the growing air retaliatory capacity of the United States would be an important deterrent to attempts to expand. The board's failure to incorporate any part of the third alternative marked the end of the policy of "liberation," so highly touted during the campaign of 1952.

[45] See Charles J. V. Murphy, "The Eisenhower Shift, III," *Fortune,* March 1956, p. 234. Interviews.
[46] Interviews.

An important feature of the Planning Board's paper—which was designated NSC-162—was its assessment of the Soviet threat as "total" and severe and likely to continue indefinitely. Although the paper saw little danger of war in the immediate future, it took a grave view of long-term prospects. It concluded—probably chiefly as a result of the Soviet hydrogen explosion in August—that the Soviets had the capacity to make an effective nuclear attack on the United States. Consequently, its reasoning went, national security had to take first priority over all other objectives of policy. Because of its support of the idea of containment, and its somber assessment of the external threat, this paper implied strongly that there should be no reduction in military forces, particularly ground forces. It also indicated that greater effort was necessary in the field of air defense in view of the growing capability of the Soviets to attack the United States directly. Although the paper did make passing reference to the need to preserve economic stability in the United States and the free world, its dominant emphasis on the seriousness of the enemy threat provided no encouragement to those in the administration who hoped for substantial reductions in defense expenditures.

NEW JOINT CHIEFS OF STAFF

In the early months of 1953, the continued presence in the highest councils of the new administration of military leaders appointed by a Democratic President constituted a disturbing anomaly to many Republicans. It was illogical, it seemed, for an administration and a party committed to a balancing of the Federal budget, which would inevitably mean a considerable reduction in military spending, to rely for military advice primarily upon military men identified with the programs to be cut. Moreover, there was a feeling in Republican circles that the incumbent Chiefs were not really the neutral experts that, as professional military officers, they might be expected to be. The Chiefs had frequently spoken in support of the former administration's broad politico-military policies. The Republican distrust focused on General Omar N. Bradley, the JCS Chairman, some of whose public utterances had seemed (to the critics) to be excessively partisan in tone and to touch on matters of foreign policy outside the proper competence of the professional soldier. Senator Taft had declared in 1951 that the Joint Chiefs of Staff were "absolutely under the control of the Administration. . . ." During his campaign for the Republican Presidential nomination, Taft had said that he had "lost confidence" in the Joint Chiefs of Staff and would replace Bradley if he were elected. Taft was especially disturbed by Bradley's condemnation of the "Gibraltar theory of defense" and his reiteration of the necessity for being prepared to defend western Europe with ground forces, views which conflicted rather sharply with those of Taft.

The terms of office of two members of the Joint Chiefs of Staff were not to expire until August 15,[47] so they could not conveniently be replaced until then. In April, some powerful Republicans in Congress, with Taft a prime force, had begun urging the immediate appointment of a new set of Chiefs on a stand-by basis. This new group, before taking office formally, would undertake a full review of all the strategic decisions of the incumbent Chiefs, the results of the review to be used in developing the defense budget for fiscal 1955. These Republican leaders hoped that the new Chiefs would come up with an entirely new grand concept of defense strategy which would guide future defense and foreign policy.[48] Presumably, Senator Taft wanted a fresh and sympathetic hearing for the concept of defense emphasizing sea and air power based in the United States and at strong points on the periphery of Eurasia, a concept of which he himself was a foremost advocate. Taft and other Republican leaders wished the survey to be completed, or well advanced, by August 1.

President Eisenhower discussed the proposal with Republican leaders on April 24, and decided then, or soon after, to carry it out. The new appointments were disclosed on May 12. Admiral

[47] The two were General J. Lawton Collins, Chief of Staff of the Army, and General Bradley. The term of General Hoyt S. Vanderberg, Chief of Staff of the Air Force, was to expire on June 30 and that of Admiral William M. Fechteler, Chief of Naval Operations, had two more years to run.

[48] New York *Times,* April 22, 1953, p. 1.

Arthur W. Radford, Commander in Chief of the Pacific Fleet, was named Chairman. Admiral Robert B. Carney was moved from his position as Commander in Chief, Allied Forces, Southern Europe, to the post of Chief of Naval Operations to replace Admiral Fechteler. General Matthew B. Ridgway, who had served most recently as Supreme Allied Commander in Europe, was named Chief of Staff of the Army, to succeed General Collins. The appointment of General Nathan F. Twining, Vice Chief of Staff of the Air Force, to replace General Vandenberg as Chief of Staff had been announced a week earlier.

The President had left to Wilson the selection of the Chairman, and Radford was Wilson's personal choice. According to some reports, Eisenhower would have preferred Admiral Carney for this post and had some reservations about Radford, stemming principally from the latter's leading role in the "revolt of the admirals" in the B-36 controversy of 1949. However, Eisenhower also reportedly wanted the Chairman to be an officer who was in sympathy with an active policy in Asia, to satisfy Republican complaints that the previous administration had concentrated too much on Europe and too little on Asia.[49] Both Eisenhower and Wilson had been favorably impressed by Radford on the *Helena* voyage. Radford also had been mentioned among Republicans in Congress for the post of Chairman. His general strategic views, stressing the importance of sea and air forces, and with a strong orientation toward Asia, were known to be similar to those of Taft.

Whatever the President's personal feelings about Radford, his appointment represented a sizable payment on Eisenhower's political debt to Taft. Before announcing the appointments, Wilson invited Taft to his apartment at the Wardman Park Hotel in Washington and showed him the list. Over scotch-and-sodas, the two men discussed the names and Taft approved them all.

Apart from the special significance of the appointment of Radford as Chairman, it appeared that a major criterion in the selection of the new Chiefs was breadth of experience, in terms of both geography and command. All the men had served in both the European and

[49] Donovan, *Eisenhower: The Inside Story,* p. 19.

the Pacific areas. Thus, as Eisenhower said, they could be expected to have "global outlooks," apparently as compared to the previous Chiefs' identification primarily with Europe. In addition, all of the new Chiefs had headed large unified commands—on this account, perhaps, their service biases might be expected to be minimal.

Early in July, the new military leaders were summoned to the White House for a briefing on what was expected of them. For about half an hour, the President talked of some of the ideas that had been growing in his mind. He outlined the global commitments of the United States and told the new Chiefs he wanted them to make a complete survey of the nation's military capabilities, in the light of these commitments.[50] They were to consider military policy in all its aspects—weapons systems, strategic doctrine, service roles and missions, force and manpower levels, the military role of allies—*and* relate the whole not only to the foreign policy, but also to the fiscal policy of the government. Most importantly, they were given to understand that they were dealing with the President's "great equation"—how to strike the proper balance between a strong military posture and the risk of economic "bankruptcy." Borrowing an idea from his friend Sir Winston Churchill, Eisenhower directed the Chiefs to work without benefit of staff. He stressed that he did not want a long, exhaustive staff study, but the personal views of the Chiefs themselves, based on their own great collective experience.[51] Later, at the annual conference of military leaders at Quantico, Virginia, Eisenhower also told the new Joint Chiefs of Staff that he wanted no "split papers," only unanimous decisions.[52]

The four men began their study on July 13 in a conference room near the office of the Chairman of the Joint Chiefs of Staff. As the President had directed, they worked alone, eschewing any staff assistance, with the exception of a single aide who provided pencils, large yellow scratch pads, and occasional pots of coffee.[53] Periods of study and discussion alternated with periods of travel to military installations within the United States.[54]

[50] General Matthew B. Ridgway, *Soldier* (New York, Harper and Bros., 1956), p. 267.
[51] *Ibid.* Interviews.   [52] Interviews.   [53] Interview.
[54] Ridgway, *Soldier*, p. 267.

By early August, they had made some progress, but were finding it difficult to keep themselves isolated from the pressures of service rivalry and other Pentagon distractions. In order to escape these distractions, Admiral Radford asked for and obtained the use of the Navy Secretary's yacht, the *Sequoia*. On August 6, the group began a two-day cruise on lower Chesapeake Bay, during which time they agreed upon some of the general outlines of future strategy.

Soon after this cruise, the Joint Chiefs of Staff made their first report to the President and the Secretary of Defense. This paper, which was unanimously approved by the Chiefs, made no recommendations for specific force levels or manpower strengths. It was a statement of general strategic principles and premises which were to guide future determination of force requirements. Furthermore, it was not considered definitive, but only a "study" to be used as a working paper for future discussions. Its chief conclusions were substantially as follows:

(1) There should be no change in basic service roles and missions.

(2) The two most important military problems facing the United States were defense of the continental United States and creation and maintenance of the capacity to retaliate massively and swiftly.

(3) Our military forces were overextended; some of the forces overseas should be redeployed back to the United States. In this connection, United States forces in Korea and Japan should be withdrawn.

(4) Local defense should be the primary responsibility of indigenous forces, backed up by United States air and sea power.

(5) United States forces should be given maximum mobility.

(6) Manpower reserves should be increased in efficiency and readiness.

Although no specific forces were recommended, the new Chiefs did discuss alternative levels of manpower and dollars—mostly lower than those currently in force—and related these to the capabilities and strategy which they could support. These figures were generated by the Chiefs themselves and represented their attempt to carry out the President's directive to keep in mind the economic capacity of the country in formulating their program. The Chiefs felt that the strategic reorientation which they tentatively proposed could be supported without economic strain.

The *Sequoia* program was conditional on certain assumptions— principally that international relations would not deteriorate and that the build-up of Korean and German forces would proceed on schedule. Ridgway and Carney, at least, felt that if these assumptions proved too optimistic, the *Sequoia* program would be invalid.[55]

Meanwhile, events were occurring which carried major significance for future military policy. The first of these was the termination of the Korean War with the signing of the armistice at Panmunjom on July 27. Of course, the immediate relevance of the armistice to general military policy was that it reduced combat requirements and seemed to promise a reduction of force levels, including manpower.

Another event of transcendent importance was the explosion of a hydrogen bomb by the Soviet Union on August 12—less than ten months after the United States' first thermonuclear explosion. Its major significance was to remind the world that the Soviet Union was well on the road to developing a nuclear capability comparable to that of the United States in its military and political significance, if not in quantitative size. To many thoughtful persons, this presaged a dangerous weakening of the deterrent capacity of the United States.

PRELIMINARY DEVELOPMENT OF THE FISCAL 1955 BUDGET

The separate armed services had begun preparing their budget requests for fiscal 1955 early in the spring of 1953, in accordance with the usual budget cycle. This early work was more or less technical in nature and was not significantly affected by the higher administration's determination to reduce spending and its casting about for ways, means, and rationalizations for doing so.

The administration had reluctantly concluded in March, after a National Security Council study, that early hopes of balancing the Federal budget in fiscal 1955 were not to be fulfilled. On April 29, the President approved a National Security Council paper which

[55] Interviews.

established a "projected level" of defense expenditure for 1955 of $40 billion—a figure which, at then current tax rates, would have involved a budgetary deficit. This paper also established military personnel ceilings for the armed services, to be reached by June 30, 1954: 1,423,000 for the Army, 981,870 for the Navy and Marine Corps, and 960,000 for the Air Force—a total of 3,364,870. These figures represented an overall reduction of about 145,000 from the active manpower at the beginning of calendar 1953, including a reduction in the Army of about 87,000. There were to be further reductions in Army, Navy, and Marine Corps manpower if the Korean War should end during the year.

Apparently as a result of its painful education in the difficulties of budget-cutting, the administration also decided to hold the line on tax reduction, temporarily at least. The President was firmly opposed to any large tax cuts before a balanced budget was achieved. In his tax program offered to Congress on May 19, the President called for a six-month extension of the excess profits tax, repeal of a scheduled 5 percent reduction in the corporate income tax, and postponement of a scheduled reduction in excise taxes.[56]

But within the inner councils of the administration the issue was far from resolved. George Humphrey, the persuasive Secretary of the Treasury, continued to urge an early tax reduction *and* a balanced budget in fiscal 1955. Joseph M. Dodge, the Detroit banker who held the post of Director of the Bureau of the Budget, was Humphrey's fervent supporter. Their chief opponent was Wilson, who knew, of course, that balancing the budget would have to be done chiefly at the expense of his department. On the evidence available, the President took a middle position, holding that defense economies were possible without loss of combat strength, but refusing to accept the drastic surgery advocated by Humphrey.

The day after Wilson had informed the House Appropriations Committee of the results of the NSC study previously mentioned, Humphrey publicly contradicted Wilson and the NSC study, claiming that a balanced budget *was* feasible in 1955 without jeopardizing national security.[57]

At a Cabinet meeting on May 22, Humphrey proposed a target

[56] New York *Times*, May 20, 1953, p. 1.   [57] *Ibid.*, May 13, 1953.

of $60 billion in Federal expenditures for fiscal 1955. This would have meant a reduction of almost $12 billion from the expenditure estimate for fiscal 1954. Humphrey told the Cabinet that some such drastic action was necessary to make possible a tax reduction during the next session of Congress.

After Humphrey had spoken, Wilson remarked that Humphrey's proposal implied a further reduction of nearly $10 billion in the Defense Department's budget. With the Korean War continuing, he said, this would be next to impossible.

At this point, the President entered the discussion. He said he was much disturbed by suggestions of additional heavy cuts in the defense program. The people, he said, should be made to realize that national security must not be endangered just for the sake of a balanced budget. If balancing the budget was so important, the President asked, why should it be the military programs that were sacrificed? Why shouldn't the sacrifice be spread among veterans' benefits, farm programs, grants-in-aid to states, and so forth? He maintained that if there had to be reductions, it would be better to apply them almost anywhere else than in national security programs.[58]

The issue was joined again during July in an exchange of letters between Dodge and Wilson. In a letter to Wilson on July 10, Dodge asked that the Department of Defense budget estimates be presented to the Bureau of the Budget by September 15. Dodge stated: "The fiscal year 1955 budget will have to show further substantial reductions from the fiscal year 1954 revised figures. These reductions will have to be at least equal to and may have to be greater than those already made in the fiscal year 1954 budget."

Since the new administration had reduced the Truman defense budget for fiscal 1954 from $41.2 billion to $35.8 billion in "new obligations," the Dodge letter implied a maximum of around $30 billion.

On July 23, Wilson replied, somewhat acidly, that since a "sound military budget" must rest on a "sound military plan," it was "not feasible to issue instructions for preparation of the 1955 budget before the basic military program is presented to the NSC." He

[58] Donovan, *Eisenhower: The Inside Story*, pp. 58–59.

added that "until the completion of the review of the military plan by the Joint Chiefs, it would appear undesirable to make an estimate as to the amounts required. . . ."

Thus, Wilson at this point took a stand firmly for the priority of military security considerations over fiscal ones. The Joint Chiefs of Staff, he felt, should not be forced to wear economic blinders in taking their "New Look." Only after an objective determination of military requirements by the military leaders should the civilians presume to establish economic limitations. Apparently Wilson did not consider the NSC's "projected expenditures" to be definitive ceilings.

Dodge then sought to circumvent Wilson by going to the service Secretaries. On August 5 he urged the Secretaries to reduce expenditures in order to "encourage a favorable public attitude toward the budgetary and fiscal problems inherited by this administration." He stated that "in view of the concern about the 1954 Congressional elections," every effort should be made to reduce defense spending. Congressional support of defense reductions could be construed, Dodge said, as indicating that Congress was convinced it "knows better than the agencies what the people expect. . . ." Deeper cuts were necessary, he said, "to meet public demand." He pointed out that Congressmen tended to be "sensitive" in an election year.

Apparently as a result of Wilson's letter, Dodge extended his deadline for submission of the Department of Defense estimates to October 5 so that they might reflect new force levels to be determined by the new Joint Chiefs of Staff. These figures were to be "flash" estimates—that is, not definitive and not in detail.

THE "INTERIM LOOK"

Thus, when the new Chiefs were formally sworn into office on August 16, they found that their most pressing order of business was the recommendation of force levels [59] to be used for preparation of the fiscal 1955 budget. Their preliminary study, completed on the

[59] The term "force levels" in Pentagon parlance means numbers of "major combat units" in each service: divisions in the Army, wings in the Air Force, and major combat vessels in the Navy.

Sequoia, was of no use for budgetary purposes because it did not recommend specific force levels and manpower levels. Moreover, it had not been concerned with fiscal 1955, but with a period some three years in the future. The Chiefs expected to continue this broad-gauge, long-range study, but did not expect to finish it for several months. Consequently, a quick "interim look" was required to meet the inexorable demands of the budget cycle. Secretary Wilson gave the Chiefs until October 2 to complete this task.

Of course the Chiefs were aware of the administration's desire to reduce defense spending as much as was safely possible. The NSC's earlier "projected expenditure" meant a reduction of $3.2 billion from estimated expenditures in fiscal 1954. Other, more informal, emanations from the Budget Bureau had indicated figures somewhat less than $40 billion in actual expenditures and a target in the neighborhood of $30 billion for new appropriations.[60] All four members of the Joint Chiefs of Staff often were invited to attend National Security Council meetings (in contrast to the practice of the previous administration, in which, normally, the Chiefs were represented by their Chairman), so that they were brought into direct contact with the development of fiscal policy and also with the charm of George Magoffin Humphrey, whose attendance at council sessions had become so regular as to make him almost a permanent member.[61]

But the Chiefs were also keenly aware of another trend of thought within the administration which was opposed to the economy motif —that which was to produce such grave appraisals of the security threat as NSC-162. Although this paper was not considered by the NSC itself until October 7—after the Chiefs had already made their force level recommendations—the Chiefs knew of it, and indeed participated in its preparation through their representative on the Planning Board.

The Chiefs were thus caught between the economizers and the viewers-with-alarm. But their professional inclination was toward

[60] Charles J. V. Murphy, "Defense and Strategy," *Fortune,* September 1953, p. 75.
[61] Austin Stevens, New York *Times,* September 28, 1953.

the latter, for the Chiefs could see little in the external situation to justify retrenchment. True, the Korean War was over, and this reduced requirements for certain support forces and for the "pipe line" of combat replacements. But there was no assurance that the war would not explode again. Political conditions elsewhere in Asia, particularly in southeast Asia, were unsettled. Above all, there had been no reduction in United States commitments; if anything, commitments were on the upswing because of the more active policy the government was following in the Far East. The Soviet hydrogen explosion, earlier than expected, seemed to argue against defense cuts. Finally, the Chiefs were not sure they could count on making use of the enormous fire power which was distilled in the atomic and hydrogen bombs. The decision whether to use the bomb was the President's to make in time of war, and there had been no firm indication as to what that decision would be. Consequently, military planning had to embrace the possibility that a future war—even a general war—might have to be fought entirely with conventional weapons. This consideration, of course, worked against any reduction in ground forces and reserve stockpiles of conventional equipment.

An important additional factor was the administration's hardening commitment to a greater effort in the field of continental air defense. In the final months of the previous administration, several scientific study groups, notably the Summer Study Group of Project Lincoln at the Massachusetts Institute of Technology, had recommended a substantial expansion and improvement in the air defense system. But the subject was controversial, and not only were responsibilities for air defense split among the three armed services, but they were also considered by each service to be secondary responsibilities, competing for the budget dollar with major missions. The previous administration had failed to resolve the controversy before leaving office. The new administration had picked up the subject, and several ad hoc groups had studied it during the spring and summer of 1953: the Kelly Committee, chaired by M. J. Kelly, President of Bell Telephone Laboratories, which had been appointed near the end of the previous administration; a committee under Lieutenant General Harold "Pinky" Bull, President Eisenhower's wartime operations chief; and a military committee under Lieutenant General Idwal Edwards. The Kelly Committee had reported in May, rejecting the crash program proposed by Project Lincoln, but recommending, nevertheless, a considerable improvement in the system.[62]

Also, the National Security Council itself had considered the Project Lincoln findings in April or May, and the result was a policy paper generally favoring a build-up of air defense, but making no firm decision. The Joint Chiefs of Staff had considered the problem of air defense in their *Sequoia* study.

Technological improvements—notably increases in the efficiency of the DEW Line early warning system in the Arctic and developments in electronic computers which made possible the SAGE system for tracking hostile aircraft—were among the factors favoring more spending for air defense. But the decisive impetus was provided by the Soviet Union's explosion of a hydrogen bomb on August 12, along with intelligence estimates indicating a growing fleet of Soviet long-range bombers. There were further discussions of the subject in the National Security Council during September, as a result of which the Chiefs were given firmly to understand that they were expected to recommend an expansion in air defense in establishing force levels for fiscal 1955.[63]

Weighing all these considerations, the Joint Chiefs of Staff concluded that they could not recommend a reduction in the military establishment for 1955. It was reported, also, that the Chiefs had decided not to produce a definitive New Look until after the NSC had clearly marked out United States commitments, and that they did not expect to be able to come up with such a definitive statement until well into 1954, too late to affect the 1955 budget. Reportedly the Chiefs, including Admiral Radford, were not yet convinced that the imminent availability of atomic weapons in quantity justified any major change in strategic concepts.[64]

According to Admiral Radford, the Chiefs "considered it absolutely mandatory that we not make any recommendations for radical

[62] Department of Defense, Press Release No. 513–53, June 3, 1953; also New York *Times,* June 4, 1953, p. 4.
[63] Interviews.   [64] "Defense and Strategy," *Fortune,* November 1953.

changes—especially not on an overnight basis." [65] Such changes might be desirable eventually, but they should be decided upon only after careful and thorough deliberation and should be carried out gradually. Radford said Secretary Wilson had "agreed that the best defense plans and programs will come about through evolution, if we plan deliberately and with wisdom." [66]

Although the Joint Chiefs of Staff were agreed that there should be no reduction in the existing forces, a disagreement was precipitated by the Air Force's demand that the Chiefs approve a long-range goal of 137 wings to be reached at the end of fiscal 1957. This program had been developed by the Air Force as a substitute for the 143-wing program, which had been put in abeyance pending completion of the JCS long-range review. General Twining wished this new program to be given JCS approval so that certain items with long lead times required to meet the 1957 goal could be included in the 1955 budget. The 137-wing program, besides being smaller in size, was somewhat different in its internal composition than the previous long-range goal. Roughly, it involved slight declines in both strategic and tactical air power, a substantial increase in air defense wings, and a large reduction in planned troop carrier facilities. The entire reduction of six wings in the overall goal could be accounted for by the decrease in planned troop transport strength —a fact which stimulated Army opposition to the program.

In asking approval of the new goals, Twining argued that the Russian hydrogen explosion, presaging a greatly increased strategic striking power for the enemy, underlined the urgency of shifting to a new strategic concept which would emphasize air striking power and air defense. The members from the other services resisted this view, arguing that the Joint Chiefs of Staff had no authority or basis for recommending a new strategic concept until certain fundamental decisions about commitments and weapons had been taken at higher levels.

The result was a split paper, with the Air Force in the minority.

[65] Address to the American Ordnance Association, December 2, 1953, Department of Defense, Press Release No. 1136–53.
[66] *Ibid.*

In the paper the Air Force stated that, although it really needed considerably more than 137 wings to carry out its mission, it was willing to settle for that number of wings as a "minimum requirement." The Air Force recommended that the basis for the 1955 Air Force budget be the 137-wing program. The Army, the Navy, and the Marine Corps took the position that acceptance of the 137-wing program would result in violation of the personnel ceilings and projected expenditures for 1955 which had previously been approved in the National Security Council. These services believed that the established personnel limits should be exceeded only for cogent reasons—reasons that would effectively persuade the National Security Council to approve the recommended force levels. Their paper noted that the Air Force proposal would raise Air Force personnel above the ceiling of 960,000 which had previously been established by the Secretary of Defense for the end of fiscal 1954. Finally, it stated that JCS acceptance of the 137-wing program should await completion of the full-scale strategic review then in progress.

The Air Force rebutted these arguments by saying that the NSC figures which the other services conceived as "limits" or "ceilings" were intended only as "interim guidance." They were clearly not intended as hard-and-fast limits on JCS deliberations and recommendations, but were subject to change as a result of JCS recommendations. Furthermore, the Air Force argued, the current JCS deliberations on force levels for 1955 were not separate from, but were a part of, the overall New Look review; therefore (it was implied) there was no point in waiting for completion of the entire review before considering changes for 1955.

The force recommendations of the Army, the Navy, and the Marine Corps took as a starting point the personnel ceilings previously established—about 3,365,000 aggregate for all three services—and added increases for continental defense and for maintenance of combat forces substantially at the fiscal 1953 level. The total came to slightly more than 3,500,000. It was recommended that this be the force level target for the end of fiscal 1955 and that this figure be used also as a basis for planning for 1956 and 1957 pending completion of the strategic review of the Joint Chiefs of Staff.

These services made it clear, however, that the forces they were recommending (on the basis of the ceilings) were below what they considered necessary to meet national commitments and the national objectives established in NSC papers. It was said that acceptance of these forces would involve a number of risks. There would be insufficient forces to fight a limited war in any theater other than Korea without withdrawing forces either from Korea or from Europe. The forces in Korea would be inadequate to achieve a military decision there should war flare up again in that area; a decision would depend on the shift of forces from Europe. If general war should occur in Europe, the Army would be unable to fulfill its NATO force commitments. In substance, the Army said that unless its stated manpower strength of 1,423,000 men, by the end of fiscal 1954, was substantially raised, high-level policy decisions reducing Army responsibilities and overseas deployments were required.

Whether or not as a result of civilian urging, the Joint Chiefs of Staff were able to resolve their differences about a week later. On October 2, they produced an agreed paper calling for no change in the forces already in existence or authorized except for moderate increases for continental defense. Agreement was reached on an Air Force goal of 120 wings by the end of fiscal 1955 and 127 wings by the end of fiscal 1956. It was noted that the Chief of Staff of the Air Force desired recognition of an ultimate goal of 137 wings, but that the JCS had taken no position on this demand and would not do so until they had completed their overall review. It was also noted that completion of this review required the making of certain decisions by higher authority. The paper stated that the reasons why no changes were recommended in existing or authorized force levels were that no reduction had occurred in the threat to the national security of the United States, there had been no change in foreign commitments, and no new decisions had been taken regarding the use of atomic weapons.

The Chiefs recommended that the Army continue at its existing size of 20 divisions, with some increase in anti-aircraft battalions to meet its increased responsibilities in continental defense. The manpower requirement for this force was set at approximately 1,500,000. The Navy was to increase its total number of active ships from 1,130 to 1,163, the entire increase being accounted for by additional destroyer escorts and mine sweepers for continental defense. The Marine Corps was to remain at three divisions and three air wings. The Chiefs recommended that work be started on a third Forrestal-class, 50,000-ton aircraft carrier. The Air Force was to expand, as described above, from the 114 wings scheduled for the end of fiscal 1954 to 120 wings the following year, with a commensurate increase in personnel. The aggregate manpower requirement for this program was placed at about 3,500,000, well over the existing ceiling.

In sum, the Joint Chiefs were standing firm against the pressures for economy, following instead the logic of the external threat and the existing national commitments, including the new commitment to a greater effort in the continental defense field. With General Twining relaxing his position to make possible a united front, the Chiefs were in effect saying to the civilian leadership that if cuts were made, they, that is, the civilian leaders, would have to take the full responsibility for making them, and that reductions would be justified only after a retrenchment in policy goals and/or a lifting of restrictions against planning for the use of nuclear weapons.

On October 5, each of the armed services submitted a rough estimate of the cost of implementing the program the Chiefs had recommended. The total bill came to about $42 billion in actual expenditures during 1955, with required new obligational authority of about $35 billion. [67] These figures compared with the $41.5 billion in estimated expenditures and $34.5 billion in new appropriations which Congress had approved for fiscal 1954. The difference was accounted for almost exclusively by a $500-million increase for continental defense. This increase, incidentally, was considerably lower than amounts contemplated by several of the previous studies of the problem of continental defense and air defense. Apparently the Chiefs were inclined to be "evolutionary" in the programs to

[67] Austin Stevens, New York *Times*, October 9, 1953.

be increased as well as in those to be reduced for "the long pull." They may have been partial also to the view which regarded air defense as a kind of "Maginot-mindedness." As Admiral Radford was to put it later in explaining the "Interim Look": "We want to see approved programs consummated at high priority. At the same time, we want to guard against a tendency to over-commit resources to purely defensive measures which would detract from other essential security programs." [68]

Secretary Wilson and his fiscal aides made no attempt to pare down the service estimates before presenting them to the National Security Council, nor did Wilson present them as approved Department of Defense estimates, but rather as tentative figures. Apparently Wilson, noting the large gap between these figures and the administration's fiscal goals, wished to shift to the NSC the responsibility for resolving this conflict.

The National Security Council, with Treasury Secretary Humphrey and Budget Director Dodge present, got a look at the Interim Look on October 13. Wilson, Radford, and Wilfred J. McNeil, the Defense Department's Comptroller, made the presentation. When McNeil suggested that the program would mean expenditures in the neighborhood of $42 billion in 1955, Humphrey and Dodge reacted with surprise and dismay. They had hoped for a figure some $6 billion or $7 billion less. For Humphrey, defense expenditures of $36 billion or below would mean at least the possibility of balancing the "cash budget" in fiscal 1955.[69] The program indicated a requirement for new obligational authority of about $35 billion, again several billion more than the amount hoped for by the administration. Most of those present, including the President, had expected that the end of the Korean fighting, combined with the substantial savings which Secretary Wilson and his civilian aides claimed to be effecting by increased efficiency and reduction of service support structures, would make possible at least some reduction from the 1954 budget.[70]

[68] Address to the American Ordnance Association, December 2, 1953, Department of Defense, Press Release No. 1136–53.

[69] The cash budget includes net changes in the Social Security account, which usually shows a "profit."

[70] Stewart Alsop, the Washington *Post*, December 6, 1953. Interviews.

Upon Radford fell the burden of defending the strategic basis of the estimates. His remarks summarized JCS thinking as outlined above, but especially stressed that, lacking an authoritative determination of the extent to which the military might plan on the use of nuclear weapons in war, the Chiefs were forced to plan for several contingencies—all-out nuclear war or conventional general war; limited nuclear war or limited conventional war. To prepare for every conceivable kind of war was necessarily costly. If the military were told what kind of war they were to prepare for, and, in particular, if they were given permission to use nuclear weapons whenever it was technically advantageous to do so, the Admiral pointed out, then the costs of defense could be lowered. The enormous fire power of the new weapons would permit reductions in conventional forces, especially in manpower.[71] Ridgway and Carney were later to dispute this view, but the unanimously approved Interim Look paper had stated that one reason forces could not be reduced was that there had been "no new decisions" regarding the use of atomic weapons. Radford did say that the change should come about gradually.[72] He also pointed out that as long as United States forces were deployed overseas in their present quantities, it would be difficult to achieve any substantial reductions in manpower.

Radford's little speech was sympathetically received and was later to have significant effects. Nevertheless, the overall reaction of the National Security Council to the program which had been submitted was decidedly cool. It was neither approved nor disapproved. Instead, Wilson and Radford were told to take it back to the Joint Chiefs of Staff for further "refinement." [73] The general impression received by the representatives of the Department of Defense was that the President and the council expected a reduction to be made, and also wished the Chiefs to proceed quickly with their general strategic reassessment, so that its results could be reflected in the 1955 budget. Evidently the President and the civilian leadership expected this review to point to significant downward adjustments.[74]

At a press conference after the meeting, Wilson said the force and

---

[71] Joseph and Stewart Alsop, "New Look: Secret History," New York *Herald Tribune,* February 22, 1954.
[72] "Defense and Strategy," *Fortune,* December 1953, p. 78.
[73] *Ibid.* Interviews.   [74] Interviews.

budgetary figures he had shown to the National Security Council represented only a partial completion of the plans of the Joint Chiefs of Staff for 1955 and that the final figures would not be determined until the end of December. He indicated that since time was running short, he intended to submit only a "one-line estimate"—that is, an overall total for the Department of Defense—in the January budget, with the break-down by services to come later in the spring. Wilson's chief reason for desiring this delay was to allow the Chiefs the time they thought they needed to complete their long-range strategic review—the New Look proper.

However, Wilson was soon instructed in the National Security Council that a "one-line estimate" would not do. It was considered bad politics; if Congressmen were not furnished with details until the last minute, they would tend to think something was being put over on them.[75] Consequently, Wilson had to direct the Joint Chiefs of Staff to speed their timetable for completing their "long haul" review so that its results could be brought to bear on the 1955 budget.

THE "BASIC DECISION"

After the NSC meeting on October 13, further planning in the Pentagon went ahead on two separate lines: the individual services developed their budget requests for fiscal 1955, and the Joint Chiefs of Staff continued their review of strategy and determination of force requirements for the "long haul." Although the administration leadership clearly expected the latter study to justify some budgetary reductions in 1955, the two lines of activity remained divorced for almost two months, only to be traumatically wrenched into consistency at the last minute by action at the Cabinet level.

Secretary Wilson forwarded a budgetary directive to the armed services on October 16, requesting completion of their estimates by December 5. In spite of the very cool reception which the JCS-approved force levels had received in the National Security Council

[75] Hanson Baldwin, New York *Times*, October 28, 1953, p. 16. Also interviews.

three days earlier, the services were told to continue planning on the basis of these same force levels. No doubt this was necessary, simply because no other authoritative determination of force levels was available, but it did mean that service budget preparations until early December, when new force levels were finally decided upon, were quite unrealistic. The service departments were also directed to use the same budgetary assumptions which had been used in pricing the October 13 "interim" program. According to these assumptions, the primary budget objective for fiscal 1955 was "to provide strong military forces while at the same time fully recognizing the urgent necessity for assuring the maintenance for an indefinite period of time of a strong economy." The estimates were to reflect the concept of a "floating D-Day," rather than the older concept of "building up to a maximum attainable strength for some specific date theoretically fixed for a specified time in the future." Adequate recognition was to be given to the cessation of hostilities in Korea, and equipment and supplies in that theater were to be counted as being available to meet D-Day requirements. As compared with 1954, "additional economies and increased efficiency should be contemplated and costs projected accordingly on a somewhat lower basis." [76] Thus, the services were exhorted to achieve reductions from the 1954 cost figures, but on the basis of force levels which had already been priced higher than the 1954 forces.

On the same day, October 16, the Joint Chiefs of Staff approved the appointment of a special ad hoc committee to continue the "long haul" review which the Chiefs had begun during the summer. The initiative in setting up this committee came from Secretary Wilson, after private conversations with Admiral Radford. The committee had two members from each armed service, with Air Force General Frank F. Everest serving as Chairman. Everest at the time was Director of the Joint Staff, the planning group which serves the Joint Chiefs of Staff. The committee's instructions were to recommend a strategy consistent with NSC guidance and a broad

[76] Memorandum from the Secretary of Defense to the Secretaries of the Army, Navy, and Air Force, October 16, 1953. In *Study of Airpower,* Hearings before the Committee on Armed Services, United States Senate, 84th Cong., 2d Sess. (Washington, 1956), II, 1642–43.

outline of the composition of the armed forces in 1955, 1956, and
1957. The only limitation of substance which Wilson imposed was
that the manpower strength to be reached by the end of fiscal 1957
be somewhere between 2.5 million and 3 million men. There was no
specific fiscal guidance, but the committee was directed to get economic data from other agencies, from which it was to work out its
own fiscal limitations. The committee's report was due on December
1, only four days before the service budget estimates were to be
submitted.[77]

Consistent with his instructions to the Everest Committee, Wilson
directed the Joint Chiefs of Staff to broaden their military outlooks
to include "a wide range of economic and political factors," as well
as the latest technological developments.[78] The initiative on this
came from the President, who believed that the Joint Chiefs of Staff
had to be made to recognize that they could not make military
decisions in a political and economic vacuum.[79] In its economic
implications, at least, the directive from Wilson constituted a rather
significant revision in the role of the Chiefs, as their role had developed in the later years of the Truman administration. In the days
of tight budgetary restrictions prior to the Korean War, the Chiefs
had simply been given a budgetary ceiling and had been told to

---

[77] Interviews.

[78] *Department of Defense Appropriations for 1955,* Hearings before the Committee on Appropriations, United States Senate, 83d Cong., 2d Sess. (Washington, 1954), p. 81.

[79] The President had already enjoined the Chiefs to broaden their thinking
when he gave them their initial instructions for their "New Look" study in
the summer. Apparently he felt they had to be reminded in view of their
failure to come up with any reductions in their force recommendations for
1955. Incidentally, the President's thinking on this point contrasted rather
starkly with some remarks he had made during the campaign, praising the
Joint Chiefs of Staff for limiting themselves to the "strategic" aspects of international problems. Regarding the JCS recommendation of 1948 to withdraw
American combat forces from Korea—a decision for which Eisenhower himself
was criticized, having himself participated in the recommendation—Eisenhower
said during the campaign that it would have been "improper" if the Chiefs
had considered factors other than the strategic importance of the area. (New
York *Times,* April 23, 1953, p. 16.) Ridgway was reminded of watching Eisenhower, as Chief of Staff in 1947, testifying before a Congressional committee
that as a professional military man he could not be held responsible for any
judgments other than what military forces were necessary for national security.
Ridgway, *Soldier,* pp. 287–88.

work out the best defense program possible within the funds allotted. When fiscal inhibitions were relaxed during the Korean War, the Chiefs were allowed to estimate "requirements" based on their professional judgment of the military forces required to meet the commitments outlined in national policies. These estimates usually were cut sharply by the civilian leadership on fiscal and economic grounds, but the Chiefs were not asked to participate in assessment of the economic impact of their estimates or in determination of the allowable economic sacrifice. Such economic and fiscal judgments were considered to be the responsibility of the civilian leadership.

But now the Joint Chiefs of Staff were told that, since a "sound economy" was itself an aspect of "national security," it was a proper subject for military appraisal. The new frame of reference had the advantage of increasing the "realism" of JCS deliberations and recommendations, meaning correspondence with what Congress and the administration were likely to be willing to provide, but it tended to widen the professional role of the members into areas where their competence was questionable. Of course, from the viewpoint of the administration leadership, it had the merit of giving military sanction to a choice between military and nonmilitary values, a choice which could be politically embarrassing if made entirely at the civilian level. From the point of view of the JCS members, the new directive provided a legitimate reason for giving such sanction without violating their professional consciences. Nevertheless, the reaction to these instructions by the members of the Joint Chiefs of Staff was mixed. They were accepted enthusiastically by Radford, who had long been arguing that the state of the economy was a factor in military security and thus properly a subject for consideration by military men. Carney and Twining felt much the same way, but on the more generalized ground that it was only common sense for the Joint Chiefs of Staff to take account of all factors bearing on their problems. Ridgway reacted much differently, believing that the directive was an attempt to corrupt the professional integrity of the Chiefs. He did believe that the JCS should be "realistic" in their recommendations—meaning that they should keep in mind some outside limit on the funds that were likely to be available—but he did not believe that "realism" included the making of any substantive judgment about how much military expenditure and procurement the economy could support. For the Chiefs to make such an assessment, he felt, would be dangerous because it would deprive the civilian leadership of undiluted, objective professional judgment on the military factors.

Even as the JCS and the Everest Committee were being told to use their own judgment in establishing economic limits for the New Look, they were also casually informed of what the result of that "judgment" was expected to be. For example, the Office of the Comptroller at one point told the Chiefs that a "reasonable" sustaining budget for the "long haul" (to begin in fiscal 1957) would be around $35 billion. Why this guidance was necessary in addition to the economic data provided to the Everest Committee, which carried within it an implicit ceiling, is unexplained.

Further guidance was provided for the Joint Chiefs of Staff in a paper approved in the National Security Council late in October— after it had first been submitted to and approved formally by the JCS on October 27. The paper stated that a sound economy and a system of private enterprise were the foundation of free-world defense. Avoidance of recession in the United States was described as essential to free-world security. The document noted that, under existing law, substantial tax reductions would occur in January and April, 1954, and that it was contrary to administration policy to attempt to substitute other taxes for the ones reduced. Large deficits were forecast for fiscal 1955 and 1956. The paper concluded that requirements for national security must be considered in the light of these prospective deficits.[80]

Having the Joint Chiefs of Staff assume formal responsibility for weighing the economic risks and sacrifices of military programs, and impressing them with the seriousness of these risks and sacrifices, was evidently intended to persuade them to restrict their force recommendations to the fiscal boundaries which the administration had in mind—short of the crude application of budgetary "ceilings." But this did not remove the basic tension between the economy

[80] Interviews.

drive and the external threat as appraised in NSC-162, along with the national commitments in the face of the threat. This tension, and the urgent need to resolve it, produced a turbulent debate about the very fundamentals of grand strategy during the month of October.

Admiral Radford had suggested a way to resolve the tension: make a firm decision that nuclear weapons would be used in future wars. This suggestion had a strong appeal to those who believed that the main reason why the military services continued to generate high force requirements was that they were attempting to maintain a "dual capability." Secretary Humphrey reportedly stated at one point that the principal fault in the military planning of the previous administration was that it had attempted to be ready for six kinds of wars—two for each service.[81] President Eisenhower, Humphrey, Secretary of State Dulles, and Deputy Secretary of Defense Roger Kyes were among those who felt that it was necessary to "select" a single strategy from all those available and pursue this one efficiently, avoiding trying to "do everything at once." The strategy they had in mind, of course, was one based heavily on nuclear weapons— strategic nuclear air power in general war and the use of nuclear weapons tactically in limited wars. This view was also heavily influenced by the idea of keeping up with technological progress— embracing the new and throwing out the old. Kyes succinctly stated this theme when he said on October 18:

We must reassess our strategic planning and logistics in the light of technological advances, and have the courage to discard the outmoded procedures and weapons which will no longer serve more than tradition. We no longer can afford to prepare for every conceivable kind of war. . . .[82]

Humphrey spoke in a similar vein a few days later:

There would be no defense but disaster in a military program that scorned the resources and problems of our economy—erecting majestic defenses and battlements for the protection of a country that was bank-

[81] Charles J. V. Murphy, "The Eisenhower Shift, III," *Fortune*, March 1956, p. 112.
[82] Speech to the Women's National Press Club, quoted in the Boston *Herald*, October 19, 1953.

rupt and a people who were impoverished. We know that a sick American economy would fulfill the Communist dream of conquest just as surely as disaster on the battlefield. . . .

We live in an age witnessing a revolution in scientific and production techniques. In such an age, the surest formula for defeat would be a static defense, committed to old-fashioned strategy, served by obsolete weapons.[83]

These views were not shared by either the civilian Secretaries or the military chiefs of the Army and the Navy. Secretary of the Navy Robert B. Anderson said that nuclear weapons might act as a deterrent to their use by either side in war, in which case "the emphasis would immediately be restored to the capability of conventional weapons as the basis for military decision." [84] Anderson asserted that a strategy built around the capabilities of a single weapon system and limited in its application to the circumstances under which that weapons system might effectively be employed was a dangerously narrow concept upon which to base the security of the nation.[85]

Robert T. Stevens, the Secretary of the Army, was just as plainspoken. It was not yet time to put all the defense eggs in one basket, said Stevens.

Nobody has yet produced an adequate substitute for a well-trained ground soldier. . . . The necessity remains for the maintenance of military forces whose successful employment has been proved. Our plans must be flexible and must prepare us to meet any type of emergency, for we can hardly count on the cooperation of the aggressor. As long as the initiative remains with him, he is likely to attempt to avoid our strength and exploit our weaknesses.[86]

Besides being opposed to extreme reliance on strategic air-nuclear power, neither Admiral Carney nor General Ridgway believed that the use of nuclear weapons tactically would reduce the need for manpower in the Army and the Navy. It is clear that when Admiral Radford suggested a shift to a nuclear strategy, in the NSC meeting of October 13, as a means of reducing costs and manpower requirements, he was speaking only for himself and was not presenting an

[83] New York *Times,* October 21, 1953.
[84] *Time,* September 30, 1953, p. 14.
[85] New York *Times,* October 27, 1953.
[86] *Army-Navy-Air Force Journal,* October 31, 1953, p. 272.

agreed position of the Joint Chiefs of Staff. Ridgway, in fact, fought hard against the adoption of Radford's suggestion and refused to recognize many of its alleged implications after the Radford proposal was approved in the National Security Council.

The Department of State did not play a very active role in this debate. Curiously enough, Secretary of State Dulles, whose doctrine of massive retaliation provided an important philosophical rationale for those who wanted to shift strategy in the nuclear direction, did not feel competent to advocate particular military means and methods for implementing the doctrine. He felt that his proper role was limited to that of general theoretical conception. The State Department participated in the weapons debate largely through its Policy Planning Staff and particularly through the Staff's Director, Robert Bowie, who sat on the Planning Board of the National Security Council.

The Policy Planning Staff tended to support the Army's position. That is, it tended to resist extreme proposals to adopt a nuclear strategy for all but the most minor aggressions, and to insist on the need for maintaining substantial conventional ground forces. Nevertheless, the Staff was not willing to go all the way with the Army, which (the Staff felt) was unrealistically basing its case on the possibility of an all-out conventional war of the World War II variety. The Staff did not think this contingency very likely, but it did believe that there might be a considerable range of limited aggressions, larger than the "brush fire" type, to which a nuclear response would be too costly and too risky. The Staff felt that the Army's case would have been much stronger if the Army had "cut its losses," by giving up the idea of all-out conventional war and basing its arguments on the more solid ground of limited war. Before the Army could make any headway against the dominant trend toward nuclear weapons, they had to scotch the idea, which was prominent in the President's mind, that they wanted to "fight World War II all over again"; failing this, the Army was defeated before it started.[87]

[87] In fairness to the Army, one must note that the Army's position was more complex than simply an insistence that all-out conventional war was possible. At least as prominent as this argument was the assertion that, even in nuclear war, large ground forces would be required to obtain a decisive victory. The

The issue which aroused the most concern in the State Department was the question of the deployment of United States ground forces in Europe. Some reduction in this force commitment was favored by leading officials in the Department of Defense, including Secretary Wilson, Deputy Secretary Roger Kyes, and Admiral Radford. The public received an inkling of this when Wilson remarked at a press conference that new weapons might reduce the need for United States forces overseas, and Kyes said in a speech that a reappraisal of NATO requirements was in order.[88] These statements, particularly Wilson's, set off a flurry of anxious queries from Allied capitals, and both Secretary Dulles and the President found it necessary to proclaim that the United States had no plans to withdraw its troops from western Europe.[89] Dulles and the Policy Planning Staff opposed any redeployment out of Europe mostly on political grounds; they feared lest such a move would suggest that the United States was losing interest in Europe. It was on this issue that Dulles played his most active role in the behind-the-scenes debate; his success in blocking retrenchment in Europe was perhaps his chief contribution of specific substance to the New Look decisions.

The turning point in the debate came on October 30, when the President approved NSC-162/2, a major NSC paper which laid down the essential policy basis for what was later to be known as the "New Look." The paper attempted to resolve the fiscal-strategic conflict substantially along the lines which had been urged by Admiral Radford at the October 13 NSC meeting, by decreeing that the Joint Chiefs of Staff and the military services could plan on using nuclear weapons, tactical as well as strategic, whenever their use would be desirable from a military standpoint. While the President retained in his own hands the authority specifically to order the use of nuclear weapons, the new directive constituted, in effect, a

---

weight of the evidence suggests, however, that in advocating conventional forces primarily for limited wars, the Policy Planning Staff was well ahead of Army thinking, which did not fully develop a doctrine of limited war until perhaps two years later. Interviews.

[88] New York *Times*, October 20, 1953, p. 1, and *Army-Navy-Air Force Journal*, October 24, 1953.

[89] New York *Times*, October 21, 1953, p. 1; *ibid.*, October 29, 1953, p. 1.

promise, or at least a formal assumption, that such a Presidential order would be forthcoming if requested by the military.

The intent of this decision was to foreclose any of the services—in particular the Army—from generating large requirements for manpower and conventional equipment based on an assumption that large-scale conventional war was possible. Henceforth, any wars larger than small "brush fires" or "border incidents" were to be considered nuclear for planning purposes. There was to be no repetition of a conventional limited war on the scale of the Korean War, and no conventional "general war." Of course, the fundamental assumption behind the new directive was that the fantastic fire power concentrated in atomic weapons would reduce manpower requirements and overall costs. Technologically, the decision was supported both by the arrival of "atomic plenty" and by the progress which had recently been made in developing "small" atomic weapons for tactical use.

Although the decision just mentioned was primarily intended to legitimize the concept of tactical nuclear warfare and to rule out all but very small conventional wars, the document also gave official sanction to the doctrine of "massive retaliation," which Secretary of State Dulles later expounded in his widely quoted address to the Council on Foreign Relations in January 1954. The paper stated, in somewhat more moderate terms than were used later by Dulles, that the basic objective of national security policy was to deter Soviet aggression and that the major deterrent was the massive retaliatory capability of the United States.[90]

[90] This point generated considerable argument, both in the Joint Chiefs of Staff and in the National Security Council. Early drafts of the paper referred to massive retaliatory capacity as *the* deterrent. At the insistence of the Army and Navy members of the Joint Chiefs of Staff, this was changed to read "a major deterrent" in the draft that went to the National Security Council. This gave effect to arguments of the Army and the Navy that their forces, such as troops stationed at potential trouble spots abroad, but also including Army and Navy capabilities generally, made some contribution to deterrence. At the NSC meeting at which the paper was discussed, this wording was questioned, but Secretary Wilson vigorously supported it as an agreed position of the Joint Chiefs of Staff. The President became annoyed at Wilson's position and stated that the wording failed to meet a primary objective, which was to establish a clear priority among the various kinds of military force. Wilson capitulated, and the President changed "a" to "the," making it read "the

The document did not specify what sorts of aggression would set off "massive retaliation" and what enemy moves would incur a more limited response. It did say, however, that the United States and its allies must have sufficient ground forces, suitably deployed, to deter or counter local aggression and to discharge the initial tasks in the event of general war. For countering local aggression, stress was laid on the necessity for greater reliance on the indigenous allied forces. The major contribution of the United States to free-world defense, it was said, should be its nuclear capability. The paper called for diplomatic action to convince the allies of the logic and feasibility of this division of tasks and to gain their approval of some redeployment of United States overseas forces to the United States.

The paper gave firm approval to an increase in the continental defense program. It stressed also the danger of weakening the economy of the United States by excessive military expenditures, and it referred to an idea which by this time had become a firm tenet of the administration's defense ideology—that military forces and expenditures should be restricted to a level which could be maintained steadily over "the long pull." [91]

Approval of this document undoubtedly did constitute a "basic decision," as Secretary Dulles later called it, but its real effect on

---

major deterrent." The word "major" was left in as a partial concession to the Army and Navy views.

This discussion was not as picayune as it sounds, for it reflected a basic philosophical conflict within the administration, between "absolute priority" and "relative priority" thinking. The "absolute priority" group, which included most of the Air Force leadership, many of the top civilian officials, including the Secretary of the Treasury and the President himself, tended to argue that the requirements of the first priority (long-range air–nuclear power, of course) should be entirely fulfilled before any resources were allocated to lower priorities. The "relative priority" group, led by the Army and the Navy, while recognizing the importance of an adequate retaliatory capability, asserted, in effect, that at some point before total requirements for this capacity (as stated by the Air Force) were reached, increments to surface forces began to assume greater (or equal) utility than further increments to air power. This was the basic philosophical content of the slogan "balanced forces," in its more sophisticated meaning. The "relative priority" people feared that the "absolute priority" doctrine was accompanied by an overpessimistic view of the capacity of the economy to absorb military expenditure, and that, therefore, if the latter philosophy were accepted, there would only be some very small crumbs left for the Army and the Navy. Interviews.

[91] Interviews.

military planning probably was somewhat less than had been anticipated. The decision did foreclose any planning for a long conventional general war, a contingency which the Army, at least, had previously included in its criteria for estimating requirements. Thus, it tended to reduce the size of the "mobilization reserves" of conventional equipment which the services could legitimately claim. But it did not bring total harmony within the Joint Chiefs of Staff, or between the Army and Navy and the administration leadership, because these two services did not agree with the fundamental assumption behind the decision—that the tactical usage of atomic weapons would significantly reduce manpower needs and costs. Both Admiral Carney and General Ridgway publicly stated their disagreement with this thesis soon after the decision was made, and neither of these men changed his opinion regarding the size of the ground and naval forces required.[92] Perhaps the most important effect of the decision was to provide Secretary Wilson and Admiral Radford with a formal justification for reducing these forces. The President, for whose military judgment Wilson had the greatest respect, had now put his name to a policy obviously intended to stress air power

[92] The Army and the Joint Chiefs of Staff had been considering for some time the impact of atomic weapons on future land warfare. As early as October 1949, General Bradley had written that "the A-bomb, in its tactical aspect, may well contribute toward a stable equilibrium of forces, since it tends to strengthen a defensive army"—implying that the future development of tactical weapons *would* reduce manpower needs. (General Omar Bradley, "This Way Lies Peace," *Saturday Evening Post*, October 15, 1949, p. 170.) Early in 1951, a scientific study group known as "Project Vista" was established at the California Institute of Technology to study tactical nuclear warfare. Its report had recommended "bringing the battle back to the battlefield" and diverting a larger portion of the nation's nuclear resources to the production of tactical weapons. (See General James Gavin, *War and Peace in the Space Age* (New York, Harper and Bros., 1958), p. 134.) The idea that a wholesale shift to an atomic strategy, including tactical nuclear warfare, was the only way the United States could avoid the alternative disasters of "bankruptcy" or "military ruin" had been powerfully stated by Senator Brien MacMahon, Chairman of the Joint Committee on Atomic Energy, in a speech of September 18, 1951, which had stimulated considerable discussion of the subject, both inside and outside the government. (New York *Times*, September 19, 1951.) Apparently the doctrine that tactical nuclear weapons, although useful, would *not* reduce requirements for manpower, did not develop in the Army and the Navy until about 1953. One may speculate that its development then was considerably stimulated by the threat to the Army and the Navy posed by the economy drive of that year.

and to justify Army and Navy cutbacks. On November 10, Wilson forecast that "new strategic plans" might bring an end to the "balanced forces concept," and he predicted that the fiscal 1955 budget would emphasize air power and air defense.[93] During the ensuing month, both Wilson and Admiral Radford were to exert much more active pressure than they previously had exerted upon the uniformed chiefs of the Army and the Navy—particularly upon General Ridgway—to persuade them to reduce their estimates of force requirements.

NEW LOOK: FINAL STAGE

The decision of the National Security Council on nuclear weapons applied more appropriately to the long-range JCS study—now "bucked down" to the Everest Committee—than to the fiscal 1955 budget, since tactical atomic weapons would not become operational in any great quantity during fiscal 1955. The committee did consider the decision in its deliberations, since it regarded its own work as the strategic implementation of the "national policy" contained in the NSC document.

Having temporarily shifted the drafting of the New Look to subordinates, the Joint Chiefs of Staff left separately for tours of United States overseas installations. By agreement among themselves, they each went to a different area. General Twining went to air bases in Europe and Africa, Admiral Radford inspected the bases under construction in Spain, and General Ridgway and Admiral Carney visited Army and Navy installations in the Far East. At least one purpose of these trips was to see what economies could be made in overseas operations and to explore the feasibility of reducing overseas deployments.

The Chiefs returned about mid-November, and about December 1 they received a report from the Everest Committee. The report contained four separate views—that is, the committee had been unable to agree. There was agreement on one point, an overall personnel strength of 2,750,000 by the end of fiscal 1957, but this

[93] New York *Times,* November 11, 1953.

figure apparently represented an arbitrary halfway split between the minimum and maximum limits which Wilson had given the committee. The committee had obtained various kinds of economic data from other agencies, pursuant to its instructions. The Council of Economic Advisers provided projections of gross national product through 1957. The Treasury Department furnished an estimate of tax rates which assumed they would be reduced somewhat over the next three years, and provided the further assumption that the overall Federal budget was to be balanced. The Bureau of the Budget provided estimates of expenditure requirements for non-security programs and for security programs—such as atomic energy and military assistance—not included in the Department of Defense budget. At the Everest Committee's request, economists were assigned from these agencies, as well as a man from the staff of the Defense Department Comptroller, to help evaluate these data.

The economic calculation which was then performed had two steps: first, a combination of the estimates of gross national product with the assumed tax rates to obtain an estimate of governmental revenue for the fiscal years 1955, 1956, and 1957; then, a subtraction of the projected expenditures of other agencies from the estimated revenue to find the "remainder" available for the military budget. The remainder turned out to be $34.8 billion for 1955, $32.8 billion for 1956, and $33.8 billion for 1957. The controlling figure was the one for the "level-off" year of 1957, which was the target year used by the committee for determining force requirements. However, the committee had not been able to get its force level recommendations within the fiscal limit. Each service made a separate recommendation, not only for itself, but for the strength of the other services as well, and their "price tags" ranged between $34 billion and $38 billion. Each recommendation, as was natural, favored the service which made it. The Army thought the Air Force should have only 120 wings by fiscal 1957, the Navy was willing to allow 127, and the Air Force wanted 137. The Army wanted 14 divisions, but both the Navy and the Air Force thought 12 would be enough. The Navy recommended more ships than either the Army or the Air Force were willing to allow.

The $33.8-billion figure which the Everest Committee had deduced from its fiscal guidance was thereafter considered by Secretary Wilson and the administration as the controlling figure for military expenditures in 1957. It seems that General Ridgway was the only one of the Chiefs who viewed this figure as a flatly imposed "ceiling," the others apparently believing, or having been led to believe, that since it had been produced by a military committee (albeit with outside assistance), it was not a "ceiling" or "directed verdict," at least not in the usual sense of these terms. Nevertheless, the Chiefs gained from Secretary Wilson and Admiral Radford the clear understanding that they were to pare down the Everest Committee's figures to something under this amount. The committee's manpower figure of 2,750,000 also was treated as an upper limit by Wilson.

By the first week in December, the Joint Chiefs of Staff were close to agreement on a revision of the Everest figures. Admiral Radford told Secretary Wilson that unanimous agreement could be reached if Wilson would raise the manpower ceiling from 2,750,000 to 2,815,000, an increase of 65,000, of which 50,000 would be allocated to the Army and 15,000 to the Marine Corps. Wilson agreed to this change, and the Chiefs then agreed to a total manpower strength of 2,815,000, with a one-million-man army, to be reached in fiscal 1957.

However, the agreement was predicated upon a long list of assumptions or conditions. Among the more important of these were: (1) that there would be no new outbreak of war in Korea, (2) that the political situation in Korea would become stabilized, (3) that the build-up of the German, Korean, and Japanese armed forces would proceed on schedule, (4) that the war in Indo-China would be ended and the political situation there would be stabilized, (5) that the European Defense Community plan would be ratified, and (6) that there would be no further deterioration in international political conditions. These assumptions were made by the Joint Chiefs of Staff without consultation with the State Department or any of the political organs of the government. It was assumed, further, that force levels would be reviewed every year in the light of conditions then existing.

Ridgway and, to a lesser extent, Carney had insisted upon these assumptions. For Ridgway, they were necessary conditions for his approval of the "long haul" program. If any of the assumptions should fail to be realized by fiscal 1957, the "recommended" program would be null and void, in Ridgway's understanding—greater forces would be required. Thus, while the program did carry the formal approval of all the Chiefs, the agreement was synthetic, at best. The assumptions were, in effect, a device for preventing a split in the Joint Chiefs of Staff. They were not real predictions of what conditions actually would be like in 1957, but, rather, a set of highly optimistic hypotheses which permitted Ridgway and Carney to put their signatures to a document which they could not otherwise have approved without violating their professional consciences—a document which in reality only gave effect to budgetary and personnel ceilings imposed by the administration.

As Ridgway himself put it, these force levels for 1957 were not "freely arrived at." He agreed to them, he said, only "in the sense it was the best you could do within the limitations given, and only on the basis of the stated assumptions." [94] The importance of the assumptions in Ridgway's mind, and their true nature as a device for obtaining synthetic agreement, is revealed in the following comment by Ridgway: "In order to carry out what we conceived to be the missions of the Army, or, in other words, in order to meet the Army's commitments if we were called upon to do so, we could not do it with one million men." [95]

THE FISCAL 1955 BUDGET

But the agreement on conditional level-off targets to be reached in three years did not solve the more urgent problem of the fiscal 1955 budget. The ponderous budgetary machinery of the separate armed services had been grinding along during the fall according to established procedures, quite divorced from the discussions of grand strategy which had been taking place in the Everest Com-

[94] *Department of Defense Appropriations for 1957,* Hearings before the Committee on Appropriations, House of Representatives, 84th Cong., 2d Sess. (Washington, 1956), p. 610. [Hereafter cited as *HCA, Hearings 1957 Budget.*]
[95] *Ibid.*

mittee, the Joint Chiefs of Staff, and the National Security Council. The services used as guidance the "interim" force levels which had been approved by the Chiefs in October, along with Secretary Wilson's budgetary guidance of October 16 which, while urging the utmost economy, had not been significantly restrictive. It was clear that, unless some restraining action was taken at a higher level, the services would produce budgetary estimates well exceeding what the administration was willing to accept.

Wilson was not among those who expected large reductions in 1955. In mid-November, he predicted that defense expenditures in 1955 would be around $40 billion.[96] This indicated that, although some progress may have been made in whittling down the estimates of October 13, a gap of several billions still separated the Department of Defense from the more fervent economy advocates. Secretary Humphrey made it known at a press conference about the same time that he favored a $5-billion reduction in defense spending during fiscal 1955, to around $37 billion.[97]

Still abhorring the blatant application of "ceilings," the administration passed down to the services certain suggested fiscal "targets," but these, not being mandatory, were largely ignored. The real pinch was to come in manpower, not dollars. Early in November, through his Assistant Secretary for Manpower, Dr. John A. Hannah, Secretary Wilson proposed a 10 percent cut in the manpower of the Army, the Navy, and the Marine Corps during fiscal 1955. This figure had been rather arbitrarily selected by Wilson, who later called it a "nice, round number to set for a target." [98] However, the general idea of a further reduction in manpower seems to have originated with the President, who believed it was justified by the ending of the Korean War and by the NSC decision of October 30 integrating nuclear weapons unequivocally into military planning.[99]

The 10 percent reduction was to be calculated against the authorized strengths for the end of fiscal year 1954. A considerable reduction of the military personnel of the Army, the Navy, and the Marine Corps had already been ordered as a result of the trimming of the

[96] *Wall Street Journal*, November 20, 1953, p. 1.   [97] *Ibid.*
[98] New York *Times*, December 10, 1953, p. 1.   [99] Interviews.

fiscal 1954 budget. The Army was due to come down to 1,423,000 by June 30, 1954, a cut of 110,000 from a year earlier. The Navy and the Marine Corps were scheduled to drop about 60,000 men in fiscal 1954, leaving a total of 975,000. A further reduction of 10 percent would cost the Army another 140,000 men and the Navy and Marine Corps about 97,000. In the proposal circulated by Hannah, the Air Force would increase its military personnel from 960,000 to 970,000 during fiscal 1955, in line with the projected expansion of its unit strength from 114 to 120 wings.[100] It was unofficially estimated that the proposed reduction in the surface forces would save at least $1 billion annually in personnel costs, plus several hundred million indirectly, for example, in closed facilities and reduced needs for supplies and equipment.[101]

On November 25 Hannah stated that the cutback was not mandatory, but that the Army, the Navy, and the Marine Corps had been asked to make an "honest-to-goodness" effort to reduce their requirements by the specified amount. He paraphrased the instructions to the services as follows:

You see what you can do within this number of men. Then bring in your figures, and if you can't do it within this number, give us some priority on the activities that would have to be discontinued and we will look at it and then come up with a figure.

It was believed in the Office of the Secretary of Defense, Hannah said, that the full 10 percent reduction could be taken without any impairment of combat strength. In other words, the cut could be taken in the "supporting forces." [102]

The Army, which stood to suffer most, took the lead in resisting the proposed reduction. Both General Ridgway and Secretary Stevens protested strongly in several meetings with Hannah, Kyes, and Wilson.

Ridgway's arguments boiled down to two fundamental points. First, a reduction of the size contemplated would "strike at the spirit of complete loyalty" in the Army, reducing its effectiveness

[100] New York *Times*, November 26, 1953, p. 1.
[101] *Army-Navy-Air Force Journal*, November 21, 1953, p. 337.
[102] *Army-Navy-Air Force Journal*, November 28, 1953.

by destroying its prestige and its morale. Secondly, such a reduction would make the Army incapable of carrying out its world-wide missions and commitments.[103] Ridgway told his civilian superiors that they were wrong in believing that a 10 percent reduction could be absorbed entirely in supporting forces and that combat strength would not thereby be impaired. Combat strength *would* be impaired, he said, therefore the reduction would be dangerous unless a corresponding retrenchment were made in the Army's overseas commitments.[104] He told Wilson that if the cuts were ordered, Wilson would have to direct the Army where to apply them so that the Department of Defense, rather than the Army, would assume the responsibility for the consequences.[105]

A good deal of argument took place about the nature of a "commitment" and about the proper basis for reasoning from commitments (however defined) to force requirements. The subject was discussed in meetings of the Joint Chiefs of Staff, as well as in talks between Wilson and Ridgway. Ridgway defined commitments simply as promises to defend certain areas, as expressed or implied in treaties, international agreements, and formal unilateral declarations of national policy. He asserted that enough military force should be available to defend successfully all the areas we were committed to defend, in case they were attacked. Wilson, Radford, and others, notably in the Air Force, said the only "military commitments" were agreements to send specific numbers of military units to defend allies. The only place where such a force commitment, or "earmarking," existed was in the NATO area. This group refused to recognize as "commitments" general promises to defend as contained in treaties. Most of these promises were too vague, they argued, to be used as any sort of criterion for planning. There was no way of telling, before an ally was attacked, how much force would be needed to defend it, Wilson said; therefore, he claimed, Ridgway's view that there was some sort of logical, calculable relationship between commitments (Ridgway's definition) and force requirements was a specious one. Even if Ridgway's definition were accepted, certainly all of our commitments were unlikely to be challenged at once; to maintain

[103] *HCA, Hearings 1957 Budget*, p. 561.   [104] Ridgway, *Soldier*, p. 288.
[105] *Ibid.*, p. 288.

enough forces for such a contingency, which seemed to be Ridgway's position, would not only be excessively costly, but would also represent an extreme of prudence. A certain amount of "calculated risk" would have to be accepted. Finally, in Wilson's view, a promise to defend a country did not necessarily mean a promise to defend it on the ground. These pledges could be carried out with air and sea power, or, better still, attacks could be deterred by the threat of using air and sea power with nuclear weapons.[106]

Ridgway agreed that the power of swift and devastating retaliation by air was a necessary part of the defense arsenal, but he insisted that the capability for successful action on the ground was also necessary to prevent the conquest of allies' territory and eventually to bring the enemy to defeat. Ridgway declared the foot soldier was still the "ultimate weapon," indispensable for obtaining final victory, which could ultimately be achieved only by wrenching control of territory away from the enemy.[107]

When it was suggested that tactical nuclear weapons, by greatly increasing the fire power available to ground troops, reduced the need for manpower, Ridgway made three main points: (1) such weapons were not yet available in sufficient quantities to make much difference,[108] (2) it was not at all clear that the use of nuclear weapons on the battlefield would reduce manpower needs, and (3) in any case, the enemy would have the new weapons, too; force levels should be determined primarily by the enemy's capabilities, not by unilateral calculations concerning the substitution of fire power for manpower.[109]

Another argument made by Wilson was that the reserve components of the armed forces soon would be large enough and strong enough to warrant cutting down the number of men on active duty. Ridgway replied that the speed of modern war made reserves of dubious value, even under the most optimistic estimates as to their readiness. He said the forces the United States would need in the initial stages—perhaps the first six months—of a future war would have to be forces on active duty.[110]

Another argument for reducing the Army's manpower centered on

---

[106] Interviews.   [107] Ridgway, *Soldier*, p. 290.   [108] *Ibid.*, p. 291.
[109] HCA, *Hearings 1957 Budget*, p. 619.   [110] Ridgway, *Soldier*, p. 291.

the prospect that a West German army of 12 divisions would soon join in the defense of Europe. Ridgway asked, "Where are they?"—and pointed out that the speed of creation of this force was problematical.[111]

In his book, *Soldier,* General Ridgway speaks of the "pressure" that was exerted upon him to agree to the proposed cutback. He recalls that Secretary Wilson urged him to reduce the strength of combat forces overseas to 85 percent, and to inactivate some units, putting them on a cadre basis.[112] Although Ridgway was willing to maintain units in the continental United States at something less than full combat strength, he vigorously opposed weakening any units which were "under the gun" of the enemy. This applied even to Korea, from which Ridgway believed all American forces should be withdrawn, except for a military mission. He insisted that if it was decided to keep some fighting units there, these should be kept at full combat strength.[113] He told Wilson that he would not reduce the strength of any combat units overseas, unless he had "clear, specific and direct" orders from the Secretary to do so.

Wilson then told Ridgway that the suggestion to reduce unit strength came directly from the President. The President was a man of considerable military experience, Wilson reminded Ridgway, and to oppose his wishes would put the Army Chief of Staff in the position of taking issue with his Commander in Chief. "And that would not be good," Wilson added.

Ridgway replied that he had profound respect for the military judgment of the President, but that he would heed his own deepest convictions until purely military arguments proved them wrong. He said he could not be induced to change his professional judgment by arguments that what he advocated was politically unacceptable or that its cost was greater than the administration felt the country could afford.[114]

President Eisenhower publicly declared his support for a reduction in Army manpower at his news conference on December 2. He declined to specify a percentage, but asserted that reductions could

[111] *Ibid.,* p. 291.   [112] *Ibid.,* p. 286.   [113] Interview.
[114] Ridgway, *Soldier,* p. 287.

be made in supporting forces as a result of the ending of the Korean War. Units closest to hostile positions would not be reduced, he said, until political considerations made this possible.[115]

The "agreement" by the Joint Chiefs of Staff on force levels for fiscal 1957 provided a further argument for those who wished to reduce manpower in 1955. In the Office of the Secretary of Defense, especially in the Comptroller's office, it seemed that the reduction to the agreed 1957 levels should proceed gradually, with the "phasing down" process beginning immediately, in fiscal 1955. The 10 percent reduction in manpower was viewed as the logical first step in this process. To do otherwise, that is, to continue at current levels and then suddenly drop down to the "long haul" goals in 1957, would be extremely disruptive, if not impossible, it was contended. It was even argued that the agreement of the Joint Chiefs of Staff on the 1957 figures constituted implicit approval of an orderly phasing down to these targets, and that Ridgway, in opposing the proposed reductions for 1955, was reneging on the earlier agreement.

For Ridgway, on the other hand, his qualified agreement to the 1957 force levels did not include or imply any commitment as to the rate of progress toward those goals. He insisted that the rate of reduction should be premised, not on administrative smoothness, but upon external political conditions, that is, upon the rate at which the world progressed toward the hypothetical conditions which formed the political framework of the 1957 goals. He argued that none of the assumptions attached to the 1957 targets had yet become actual and that no cuts were justified until they had. The future of Korea and Indo-China was still highly problematical, the willingness of the Germans and the Japanese to rearm was becoming increasingly questionable, and the general international political situation was not getting any better. True, the Korean War had ended, but Ridgway argued that this called only for a redeployment, not a reduction, of American ground forces. The commitment of the United States to fight in Korea and elsewhere in the Far East remained unchanged, he pointed out.[116]

Carney, like Ridgway, had based his approval of the 1957 forces

[115] New York *Times*, December 3, 1953, p. 1.   [116] Interview.

on an appended list of political assumptions, and he felt that no reductions should take place until these assumptions actually had materialized. He also argued that the Navy had acquired additional commitments and, in fact, required more forces rather than fewer if these commitments were to be met. They might be met with the same or lesser forces, but this would mean that the ships would have to stay away from home ports longer, which would be bad for morale. However, Carney did not resist the proposed reductions for 1955 as vigorously as did his Army colleague. He recognized that the final determination of Navy force levels was subject to factors beyond the competence of the Navy to assess; for example, intelligence possessed by the Central Intelligence Agency and the President bearing on the probability of war. Although Carney did formally express his opposition to the proposed reduction for 1955, he confined himself largely to clarifying the effect of the reduction on naval combat capabilities, especially making sure the administration realized that the Navy would not be equal to its assigned tasks should war occur. Carney believed strongly that it would be silly for the military to ask for more than they could possibly get, but that the civilians should be made aware of just what could be accomplished militarily with given force levels.

The controversy over the 1955 force levels came to a head when the services submitted their budget requests on December 5. These amounted to $35,901,230,614 in requested new obligational authority, about $6 billion higher than the figure hoped for by the administration. Naturally, these figures caused some concern in the Office of the Secretary of Defense and the Bureau of the Budget, although they could have been foreseen, considering the promises upon which the budget staffs of the services had been working.

Meanwhile, the services had come up with reports, which Wilson had requested earlier, showing the effect of the proposed manpower reduction on their combat capabilities. Both the Army and the Navy stated that combat capabilities would be reduced below minimum requirements. While the requested statements of priority among the activities to be reduced were not as clear as had been hoped for in Wilson's office, it was nevertheless possible, as one high official put it, to "read between the lines" and deduce that some reductions could be taken without cutting into actual fire power, but that the services would not accept responsibility for making them; they would have to be ordered. The service studies also indicated (although again, not explicitly) that combat strength could be maintained with reduced personnel if overseas deployments were reduced.[117]

On December 6 or 7, after consulting with the President, Wilson ordered a reduction of approximately 10 percent in Army, Navy, and Marine Corps manpower. Obviously, this order made obsolete the budget estimates of all the services. A "flap"[118] ensued, caused by the necessity to hastily revise all the estimates in time for the scheduled consideration of the budget by the National Security Council on December 15.

In ordering the cutback in manpower, Wilson ruled that it be taken out of supporting elements rather than combat forces, despite the statements of the services that some reduction in combat strength would be inevitable.[119]

NEW LOOK: THE RESULTS

On December 9, Wilson received from Admiral Radford a document containing the results of the "New Look" of the Joint Chiefs of Staff—that is, a strategic reappraisal and set of force requirements to be reached by the end of fiscal 1957. At the same time, he received documents showing "interim" manpower levels for the armed services for the fiscal years 1955 and 1956. However, the latter were not JCS documents; they had been prepared by Admiral Radford and General Everest, with assistance from the Office of the Comptroller. The 1955 paper put into effect the manpower reduction in the surface forces which had been ordered by Wilson and also suggested some further reduction in Army personnel. The 1956 figures indicated another phase-down of Army, Navy, and Marine Corps personnel toward the 1957 target. From the absence of any formal objec-

[117] Interview. [118] Pentagonese for "crisis."
[119] John G. Norris, Washington *Post*, December 9, 1953, p. 1.

tion, Wilson gained the impression that the latter documents, like the New Look document, had been unanimously approved by the Joint Chiefs of Staff.[120] As will be seen, however, this interpretation did not coincide with Ridgway's and Carney's conception of their action on the 1955 force levels.

The general strategic appraisal in the New Look paper closely followed the lines of the conclusions which the Joint Chiefs of Staff had reached earlier on the *Sequoia* cruise. It also echoed many points of NSC-162/2. In broad outline, the Chiefs stressed the importance of maintaining a massive retaliatory power as a deterrent to major aggression against the free world and as the means of fighting a general war. However, they also recognized the possibility of limited aggression. To meet such lesser enemy moves, most of the necessary ground forces should be provided by allies, with the United States participating only in a marginal way, with mobile ground forces and sea and air power. The major contribution of the United States to the defense of the free world should be its massive retaliatory power, the Chiefs said. Tactical atomic weapons should be used whenever militarily desirable, either in general war or in the case of local aggression.

The paper strongly recommended the redeployment of some overseas forces to the United States, in order to achieve greater flexibility, reduce support costs, and minimize manpower requirements. A strategic reserve, mostly on United States territory, should be maintained, with sufficient readiness and mobility to move quickly to trouble spots. The paper recognized, however, that United States forces abroad had strengthened the determination of our Allies to resist communism and to build up their own forces; any withdrawals in the near future, it went on, could be interpreted as a decline in United States interest in their defense and might threaten the cohesion of our alliances.

Although it noted the need for maintaining some forces in the general area of the Far East, the paper recommended the complete withdrawal of combat forces from Korea. The threat of nuclear retaliation should be considered the main deterrent to future aggres-

[120] *HCA, Hearings 1957 Budget,* p. 45. Interviews.

sion in Korea, the Chiefs said. Indo-China was singled out as an example of an area which the United States would defend with force, even though it had no treaty commitment to do so. An attack on such an area would be met either locally or by strategic attacks against the centers of the aggressor's power.

The Chiefs recognized that, because of political as well as military factors, ground forces of the United States probably would have to be maintained in western Europe beyond the end of fiscal 1957. However, they also recommended an "educational program" to convince the Allies that United States redeployment to a strategic reserve, with reliance mainly on local forces for countering local aggression, would be beneficial to all. After completion of this educational program, action should be taken to reduce the force commitments of the United States to NATO, the Chiefs recommended.

The Chiefs said their recommended program would be sufficient for defense in fiscal 1957 and thereafter as far as the situation could be predicted. The recommendations were based on the assumption that the existing degree of international tension would continue to prevail. Any deterioration in the world political situation, or substantial change in the United States–U.S.S.R. power ratio, would require a new appraisal. Contrary to Ridgway's public testimony, there were no other assumptions, specifically stated as such. However, some of the assumptions which Ridgway recalled were stated as "implementing actions." For example, it was *recommended* that the Germans and the Japanese be *encouraged* to build up their military forces, rather than assumed that these build-ups would proceed on schedule. Apparently, the assumptions recalled by both Ridgway and Carney were considered as such during the deliberations—or portions of these deliberations—of the Joint Chiefs of Staff, but for some reason they were not stated as assumptions in the final document, but rather as desiderata to be worked toward.

To support their outline of strategy, the Chiefs recommended force levels for the long pull, to be reached by the end of fiscal 1957. In terms of manpower the level-off strength was set at 2,815,000, approximately 540,000 less than the total personnel strength scheduled for June 30, 1954, with the Army absorbing about 420,000 of the reduction. The Army was to have one million men, the Navy, 650,000, the Marine Corps, 190,000, and the Air Force, 975,000.

The projected changes in manpower over the three-year period are roughly summarized in Table 1 (omitting the figures for fiscal 1956).

Table 1. Recommended Force Levels, 1954–57

	December 1953	June 30, 1955	June 30, 1957
Army	1,500,000	1,281,000	1,000,000
Navy	775,000	670,500	650,000
Marine Corps	230,000	207,000	190,000
Air Force	945,000	970,000	975,000
Totals	3,450,000	3,128,500	2,815,000 [121]

In terms of major combat units, the Army was to go down from 20 to 14 divisions, the Navy from 1,126 to 1,030 fighting ships, the Marine Corps was to stay at three divisions and three air wings (but with reduced manning levels), and the Air Force was to expand to 137 wings. The Chiefs estimated that these forces could be maintained with an annual military budget of just under $33 billion.

In an economic annex, the Joint Chiefs of Staff outlined the fiscal considerations which had guided their thinking. These were essentially the same projections of Federal receipts and expenditures, through fiscal 1957, which the Everest Committee had worked out with expert assistance from other agencies. As previously indicated, subtraction of the projected expenditures of other agencies from the total expected revenue left a "remainder" of $33.8 billion for the Department of Defense in fiscal 1957.

Meanwhile, the services and the budget review officers in the Department of Defense, with assistance from the Bureau of the Budget, were busy completing the budget for fiscal 1955. By December 15, they had whittled approximately $4.7 billions off the earlier service estimates. Table 2 campares the service requests for new appropriations with the estimates which finally went to the Bureau of the Budget.

One significant change was made in this program at a meeting of

[121] Hanson Baldwin, New York *Times*, December 13, 1953, IV, p. E5. Confirmed by interviews.

Table 2. Comparison of Requests for New Appropriations with Estimates Submitted to the Bureau of the Budget, December 1953

Office of the Secretary of Defense and Interservice Activities	Service Request (Dec. 5, 1953)	Submission to Bureau of the Budget
	$ 795,403,000	$ 811,000,000
Department of the Army	10,075,297,614	8,211,000,000
Department of the Navy	11,515,868,000	9,878,000,000
Department of the Air Force	13,514,662,000	11,200,000,000
Total, Department of Defense (including minor amounts for liquidation of prior contract authority and for later transmission.)	35,901,230,614	31,200,000,000 [122]

the National Security Council on December 11: a more rapid reduction in the Army. The Army was directed to pare down to 1,164,000 men by the end of fiscal 1955, as compared with the 1,281,000 which had been decided upon earlier by Secretary Wilson. This lower figure may have been mentioned in the documents which Wilson received from Radford on December 9, or it may have originated with the President, who did not believe the 10 percent reduction announced earlier fully reflected the end of combat in Korea. The Army was also directed to reduce faster in fiscal 1954, to 1,407,000 men at the end of June 1954 instead of the 1,423,000 earlier planned. With these additional cuts, the Army was to shrink in manpower by about 24 percent during the two fiscal years 1954 and 1955, with about 18 percent of the reduction coming in the latter year.

The strategic precepts of the New Look, plus the force levels for 1955, 1956, and 1957 and an outline budget for 1955, were given formal and definitive approval by the President at a meeting of the National Security Council on December 15.

Although the major decision of substance had gone against him, Ridgway later managed to salvage a minor technical victory in a determination that the Army would reduce its *unit* strength from 20 to 17 divisions over fiscal 1954 and 1955. Wilson had wanted the number of divisions to remain unchanged, with the personnel reductions coming out of supporting structures. Ridgway had insisted that

[122] Office of the Secretary of Defense, Comptroller, EISED-215, May 1, 1956.

the cutback would weaken combat capability, and he wanted this fact to be fully registered in the Army's divisional structure. He deplored any attempt to create a false impression of strength where strength did not exist, and he felt that this was just what the administration was trying to do.[123]

The first dramatic application of the New Look was a decision to reduce United States ground forces in Korea. On December 26, the President announced that these forces would be "progressively reduced" and that as an initial step, two divisions would be withdrawn. This would release about 32,000 men from the Korean theater and would reduce the United States ground forces there to six divisions.[124] In making this announcement the President recalled a recent statement by the nations which had fought in Korea, that "the consequences of . . . a breach of the armistice would be so grave that, in all probability, it would not be possible to confine hostilities within the frontiers of Korea." Eisenhower also cited the increased capabilities of the Republic of Korea forces and noted that "our growing national air power possesses greater mobility and greater striking force than ever before." Henceforth, United States forces in the Far East would feature "highly mobile naval, air and amphibious units," the President said.[125]

[123] Interviews.

[124] Felix Belair, Jr., New York *Times*, December 27, 1953. The two divisions were later disbanded as part of the planned reduction in the Army.

[125] *Ibid.*

Public Presentation

The military budget which went to Congress in January 1954 was presented as embodying the first stage of a projected three-year program which would put into effect the strategic decisions made by the Joint Chiefs of Staff. It asked for new obligational authority of $30,993,000,000. Expenditures for the year were estimated at $37,-575,000,000. Of the new obligational authority the Army was to get $8,236,000,000, the Navy, $9,921,000,000, and the Air Force, $11,206,000,000. The projected expenditure budget apportioned $12,084,000,000 to the Army, $10,632,400,000 to the Navy, and $16,194,000,000 to the Air Force. Table 3 shows changes in new obligational authority and expenditures for the three services as compared with the fiscal 1954 budget estimates.

Table 3. Budget Requests for Fiscal 1955 as Compared to Fiscal 1954 Budget

	1954	1955	Change
New Obligational Authority			
Department of the Army	12,776,981,000	8,236,000,000	−4,540,981,000
Department of the Navy	9,600,064,000	9,921,000,000	+ 320,936,000
Department of the Air Force	11,416,896,000	11,206,000,000	− 210,896,000
Expenditures			
Department of the Army	12,909,460,876	12,084,000,000	− 825,460,876
Department of the Navy	11,322,400,000	10,632,400,000	− 690,000,000
Department of the Air Force	15,461,000,000	16,194,000,000	+ 733,000,000

The total number of military personnel was scheduled to be reduced from 3.3 million on June 30, 1954, to a little over three million by June 30, 1955, the major part of the reduction, of course, coming out of the Army. Correspondingly, planned expenditures for personnel costs were to decline by approximately $600 million from the $10.9 billion estimated for 1954. The cost of operation and maintenance of the existing military establishment was to be reduced slightly, to about $8.7 billion, and major expenditures for new procurement were slated to fall about 15 percent from the 1954 levels, to $14.5 billion. However, within the procurement account, the rate of spending for new aircraft was to remain practically stable at $8.3 billion. Aircraft procurement accounted for 22 percent of the total expenditures budget for 1955, compared with 20 percent in 1954, 17 percent in 1953, and 13 percent in 1952.[1] The objective was to increase the total of active aircraft in all three services to 40,000 (24,700 in the Air Force) by the end of 1957, with more than half of these being jets. At the end of the 1953 calendar year, there were approximately 33,000 operating aircraft, with only one-third of them jets.[2]

The Army

The Army's budget reflected the planned reduction in manpower from 1,481,200 at the end of calendar 1953 to 1,164,000 on June 30, 1955.[3] The existing 20 divisions were to be reduced to 17, but all of the 18 regiments and regimental combat teams were to be retained, and the anti-aircraft forces were scheduled to increase from 117 to 122 battalions.[4] Two more National Guard divisions were to be added, bringing their total from 25 to 27, and the National Guard anti-aircraft battalions were to increase from 101 to 112. The increase in anti-aircraft capability reflected the increased emphasis on continental defense.

[1] *The Budget of the United States Government for the Fiscal Year Ending June 30, 1955* (Washington, 1954), p. M45. Cited hereafter as *U.S. Budget, FY 1955.*

[2] *Ibid.*, p. M44.

[3] The end-strength was later increased to 1,172,700 as the result of a decision to absorb 8,700 more ROTC graduates.

[4] *Department of Defense Appropriations for 1955*, Hearings before the Committee on Appropriations, House of Representatives, 83d Cong., 2d Sess. (Washington, 1954), p. 116. Hereafter cited as *HCA, Hearings 1955 Budget.* Volumes of hearings on appropriations for the separate services will be cited as *HCA, Hearings 1955* [name of service] *Budget.*

The Navy and Marine Corps

During fiscal 1955, the Navy was to reduce its personnel from 740,600 to 688,900 men and its active fleet from 1,126 to 1,080 ships. The latter figure included 404 major combat vessels, reflecting a planned inactivation of five ships, including a cruiser. The Navy and Marine Corps active aircraft inventory was slated to fall from 13,285 to 13,191 planes. Nevertheless, the Navy would continue to maintain 16 carrier air groups (75 to 100 planes each) and 15 carrier anti-submarine squadrons (12 or more planes each).

The Marine Corps would continue to maintain three divisions and three air wings, but would suffer a reduction in manpower from 225,000 to 215,000 during the year ending June 30, 1955.[5]

The Air Force

The Air Force reappeared as the principal arm of the military establishment after its seeming eclipse in the 1954 budget. From 115 wings at the end of June 1954, 120 wings were to be operating a year later, with 137 wings as the goal by the end of fiscal 1957.[6] Much of the increase for 1955 was to go into fighter-interceptors, again reflecting the greater emphasis on continental defense. But there was a considerable reduction in troop transport capabilities (from 16 to 13 wings) and some decline in tactical air forces. A comparison of the longer term 137-wing program with the 143-wing program which had guided Air Force planning in the Truman administration revealed similar tendencies. The 137-wing program called for 54 wings for the Strategic Air Command, 34 wings for air defense, 38 wings for the Tactical Air Command, and 11 troop carrier wings. This contrasted with the earlier goal of 57 wings in the Strategic Air Command, 29 air defense wings, 40 tactical air units, and 17 troop carrier wings. The 6-wing overall reduction in the goal could be accounted for entirely by the elimination of 6 troop carrier wings—actually a reduction in ground strength rather than air power.

[5] *Ibid.*, pp. 116–17.
[6] The size of a wing varies approximately from about 30 to 75 planes, depending on the type.

The manpower of the Air Force was to increase from 955,000 to 970,000 during the fiscal year 1955.[7]

Mobilization reserves and mobilization base

The 1955 budget and explanatory statements by administration spokesmen revealed several changes in policies concerning the accumulation of "mobilization reserves" of military equipment and supplies for combat replacement and supply of newly activated forces in the early months of a war, and also in the related policies for maintaining an industrial "mobilization base" for quick expansion of production of matériel. Mobilization reserve requirements were reduced by the decision to use nuclear weapons in wars larger than police actions and also by the planned reduction in the standing army. The rate of accumulation of the lower reserve requirements was reduced by adoption of the "long haul" concept, which reduced the urgency of building up the reserves and discouraged the stockpiling of fast-obsolescing equipment. Mobilization reserve goals for equipment and supplies widely used in the civilian economy (for example, passenger cars, pencils, soap, and so forth) were either eliminated or sharply reduced, on the assumption that these could be obtained by requisition from industrial inventories.[8] There were plans for a reduction in the "active mobilization base" by concentration of procurement in fewer plants, but this policy was largely reversed after public criticism of the cancellation of certain aircraft and tank contracts.

In general, the administration attached high importance to maintaining an industrial mobilization base which could convert to production of military supplies fairly quickly after the outbreak of war. Such an industrial base was considered essential even for the fighting of a general nuclear war.[9] This view, and the related one that

[7] *HCA, Hearings 1955 Budget,* p. 117.

[8] For example, the previous administration had built up a reserve of 23 million rolls of toilet paper, which was reduced by the new administration to three million. Harold Pearson, Deputy Under Secretary of the Army, stated: "My judgment is that we can acquire from new production in industry this type of material quicker than we can acquire the men who will generate the need for our having this type of material." *Ibid.,* p. 225.

[9] As late as January 1955, President Eisenhower told Secretary Wilson that retaliatory power and air defense were of highest priority to "assure that our

weapons and materials could be successfully transported to overseas areas during an all-out nuclear war, now appear to have been somewhat anachronistic in view of what is known about the destructive potentiality of atomic and hydrogen weapons.

Manpower reserves

The new policies for the mobilization reserve and the mobilization base had their parallel in the field of manpower. It was emphasized at the hearings that a reorganization of the manpower reserve programs for all the services to make the reserves larger, more efficient, and more "ready" was an essential part of the New Look. The constant theme of administration spokesmen was that the reduction of the standing forces, especially of the Army, would be largely offset by the increased readiness of the reserves. Secretary Wilson insisted that this involved no reduction in national security, since the rate of movement of men to the battlefront was limited anyway by the existing transportation facilities. There was not much use, he said, in having more men on active duty than could be moved during the time it took the reserves to mobilize.[10]

It was estimated that between December 31, 1953, and June 30, 1955, reserve personnel on active drill-pay status would increase from 621,600 to 832,100. In the budget this was reflected as a $105-million increase in planned expenditures, to a total of $675 million, during fiscal 1955. Apparently, these estimates were based primarily on the planned increase in the rate of outflow of men from the services, rather than upon changes in the reserve program itself.[11] However, such changes were contemplated, in terms of increasing both the numbers of reservists and the degree of their readiness. The plans had not been completed by the time of submission of the budget to Congress, but studies were under way. The future was to illuminate not only the high degree of importance which the Pres-

---

industrial capacity can continue throughout a war to produce the gigantic amounts of equipment and supplies needed."

"We can never be defeated so long as our relative superiority in production capacity is sustained." Letter, President Eisenhower to Secretary Wilson, January 3, 1955, printed in *Army-Navy-Air Force Journal*, January 8, 1955.

[10] *HCA, Hearings 1955 Budget,* p. 63.

[11] See testimony of Brigadier General Herbert B. Powell, USA, in *HCA, Hearings, 1955 Army Budget,* p. 125.

ident and the Department of Defense attached to the modernization and readying of the reserve forces, but also the difficulty of getting the consent of Congress for the necessary changes.

Continental defense

The improvement of the air defense of the North American continent figured strongly in the New Look program. In the study which they submitted early in December 1953, the Joint Chiefs of Staff laid great stress on continental defense, recommending a stepped-up program and laying out in considerable detail measures to be accomplished over a three-year period.[12]

Greater effort in the air defense field was a logical complement to the strategy of "instant, massive retaliation," for the credibility of such a threat would be small indeed if the United States were to leave itself wide open to retaliatory air attacks by the Soviet Union's long-range air force. Also, it squared with the shift in emphasis from mobilization reserves to mobilization base. Obviously, the value of a ready industrial mobilization base would have to be discounted by its vulnerability. In the words of Secretary Wilson, the New Look included "a recognition of what our greatest deterrent to war is: a recognition that above all things we must protect the industrial complex of the North American continent. No one can finally win a world war unless they destroy our will to fight and our industrial potential here in this country." [13]

The budget document for fiscal 1955 did not reveal the exact extent of the greater efforts in continental air defense, since appropriations and expenditures for air defense were not stated as a distinct category, but were submerged in the budgets for the individual services. It did say, however, that expenditures in this area would be higher than in any previous year.[14] Informed guesses placed the increase in new obligations at about one billion dollars over the previous year. The Defense Department estimated that on a narrow construction of the meaning of "continental defense," approximately 10 percent of total defense expenditures in fiscal 1955

[12] See testimony of Admiral Radford in *HCA, Hearings 1957 Budget,* p. 279.
[13] *HCA, Hearings 1955 Budget,* p. 67.   [14] *U.S. Budget, FY 1955,* p. M41.

would be for this purpose.[15] Some of the projected measures have already been mentioned under other headings. The Army was to add 5 anti-aircraft battalions and the National Guard, 11. The number of battalions equipped with guided missiles was to be increased "substantially." [16] A good part of the expansion in the Air Force in 1955 and during the next two years was to be in fighter-interceptors of advanced design. There were to be increased expenditures for radar warning and control, as well as communications networks.[17]

Nuclear Weapons

Consistent with the budget's shift in emphasis to the "full exploitation of airpower and modern weapons," expenditures by the Atomic Energy Commission were to be higher in fiscal 1955 than in any previous year. Expenditures for military research and development were scheduled to decline, however, from $1,425 million to $1,350 million, and requested new appropriations for this purpose, at $1,352 million, were about the same as the previous year.[18]

DOCTRINE

The general philosophy behind the New Look military program was gradually revealed during the winter and spring of 1954 in a series of statements by leading officials. The first and most inclusive statement was that made by Secretary of State Dulles before the Council on Foreign Relations in New York on January 12, 1954— a speech which probably will be regarded by historians as one of the most remarkable policy utterances in United States history. This was followed by the statements of Secretary Wilson, the Joint Chiefs of Staff, and other Department of Defense officials to the House and Senate Committees on Appropriations. Further contributions were made by the President's Budget Message to Congress and by press conferences held by the President and various other leaders. The section which follows will attempt to analyze the doctrine expressed in its component parts, show the relation of these parts to each

[15] *HCA, Hearings 1955 Budget,* p. 86.   [16] *U.S. Budget, FY 1955,* p. M44.
[17] *Ibid.,* p. M41.   [18] *Ibid.,* p. M45.

other, and relate the doctrine to the forces which were provided for in the budget.

"Instant, massive retaliation" and the doctrine of deterrence

In his "massive retaliation" speech before the Council on Foreign Relations, Dulles said that the collective security of the free world could be made more effective and less costly "by placing more reliance on deterrent power, and less dependency on local defensive power. . . ." Although local defenses "will always be important," they must be reinforced "by further deterrence of massive retaliatory power. A potential aggressor must know that he cannot always prescribe battle conditions that suit him. . . . The way to deter aggression is for the free community to be willing and able to respond vigorously at places and with means of its own choosing."

"So long as our policy concepts were unclear," Dulles continued, the military leaders could not be "selective" in building military power. That is, as long as the enemy was allowed to pick the time, place, and method of warfare, we had to be prepared to fight in many different places and with a variety of old and new weapons. But now a "basic decision" had been made in the National Security Council "to depend primarily upon a great capacity to retaliate, instantly, by means and at places of our choosing." This permitted the Joint Chiefs of Staff to "shape our military establishment to fit what is our policy, instead of having to try to be ready to meet the enemy's many choices. That permits a selection of military means, instead of a multiplication of means. As a result, it is now possible to get, and share, more basic security at less cost."

Dulles drew an analogy between this policy of reliance primarily on central deterrent power and normal police practices in local communities:

This is accepted practice so far as local communities are concerned. We keep locks on our doors; but we do not have an armed guard in every home. We rely principally on a community security system so well equipped to punish any who break in and steal that, in fact, would-be-aggressors are generally deterred. That is the modern way of getting maximum protection at bearable cost. What the Eisenhower administration seeks is a similar international security system.[19]

The speech implied that the United States might respond with strategic nuclear air power against the Soviet Union itself, or perhaps against Communist China, in the event of Communist aggression anywhere against the free world. Since the previous administration had apparently intended to reply with "massive retaliation" to a major Soviet ground attack in Europe, the only thing new about the Dulles statement was the implied application of this threat to lesser contingencies—for example, lesser Soviet or satellite moves in Europe or satellite attacks in Asia. However, Dulles did make reference to the importance of "local defense" and said that "at some times and at some places there may be setbacks to the cause of freedom," implying that in some cases limited defeat would be accepted in preference to retaliation. He also indicated that the maximum return expected from the policy was that it would "deter such aggression as would mean general war . . . ," which would seem to limit its applicability to major aggressions in western Europe.

But these qualifying phrases were generally lost sight of in the storm of criticism which followed. The critics saw in the speech either an intent to transform every incident or "brush fire" into all-out war or a gigantic bluff so transparent that it would not only fail to deter, but would also weaken allied confidence in the integrity of American policy. In view of the planned reduction of ground forces, it seemed to many that the United States was being placed in the uncomfortable position of having to choose between thermonuclear incineration or inaction when faced with a Communist military challenge.

Dulles sought to rebut some of these criticisms in a number of subsequent statements. He pointed out, for example, that he had not said we *would* retaliate instantly in all cases of aggression, but that we should have the *capacity* to do so.

"The question of circumstances under which you retaliate, where you retaliate, how quickly you retaliate is a matter which has to

[19] New York *Times*, January 13, 1954.

be dealt with in the light of the facts of each particular case," the Secretary said. It was wrong to assume, he continued, that the new doctrine posed a choice between either all-out war or no action in cases of limited challenge. Illustrating, he said that in the event of renewed Communist aggression in Korea, retaliation would not "necessarily" mean the dropping of atomic bombs on Peiping or Moscow, but "does mean that there are areas of importance to the aggressors in that vicinity which may have an industrial or strategic relationship to the operation which would no longer be what General MacArthur called a "privileged sanctuary." [20] The heart of the matter, Dulles said in a magazine article, was that "a potential aggressor be left in no doubt that he would be certain to suffer damage outweighing any possible gains from aggression." [21] Although this called for a strategy based on the free world's "special assets," including air and naval power and a wide variety of atomic weapons suitable for both strategic and tactical use, this strategy and these forces must be capable of "various responses." The free world "must not put itself in the position where the only response open to it is general war." [22]

But despite the qualifications, Dulles kept returning to his basic thesis that "the main reliance must be on the power of the free community to retaliate with great force by mobile means at places of its own choice," since it would be impossible to maintain sufficient local defenses at every threatened point around the 20,000-mile periphery of the Soviet orbit.[23] If we attempted to do this "on a basis of man-for-man, gun-for-gun, and tank-for-tank . . . we are going to go bust," the Secretary insisted.[24]

Other administration spokesmen also denied that the new doctrine ruled out the "little war" or the need for forces to deal with such wars. Admiral Radford was the most explicit, declaring in language somewhat clearer than that of Dulles that the military task consisted of "two principal requirements." These were: to be ready for "tre-

---

[20] *Ibid.*, March 17, 1954.
[21] John Foster Dulles, "Policy for Security and Peace," *Foreign Affairs,* April 1954.
[22] *Ibid.*   [23] *Ibid.*   [24] New York *Times,* March 17, 1954.

mendous, vast retaliatory and counteroffensive blows in event of global war" and also for "lesser military actions short of all-out war." United States military forces were designed not only to deter aggression, but also to "provide the basis for winning a war—an all-out war or a limited war—if war is forced upon us." [25]

The qualifications and explanations constituted a disavowal, not of the retaliation thesis as a whole, but only of the more extreme interpretations which might be drawn from the rather ambiguous phrasing of the original speech. No doubt the speech was deliberately ambiguous so as to force the enemy at least to ponder the possibility that the most extreme interpretation *might* represent real intent. It seems clear—both from the public statements and from what we know of the development of the doctrine within the administration—that there was never any intent to turn every limited enemy action into all-out war. Nevertheless, the sum total of the administration's utterances gave the distinct impression that there had been a shift of policy in the direction of *deterrence* by the threat of nuclear punishment, with the "punishment" graded according to the degree of the "crime." The essence of the doctrine was that the enemy was to be made to perceive that any aggression would produce costs for him greater than his possible gains. Thus, the conception included deterrence via the capacity or threat of limited, or "selective," retaliation as well as "massive" retaliation.[26] On the whole, it was a distinct shift (but not a complete shift) away from the idea implicit in the earlier doctrine of "containment": that the enemy would be blocked from making territorial gains. The emphasis shifted from blocking to deterrence by the threat of unacceptable punishment. The punishment motif, and the rejection of containment of Communist aggression at every point where it might

[25] *HCA, Hearings 1955 Budget,* p. 121.

[26] Indeed, it appears that "limited retaliation" comes closer to describing the Dulles conception than "massive retaliation." The word "massive" appears in the original speech of January 12 only once; in subsequent statements Dulles took great pains to point out that the retaliation did not have to be massive, but only sufficiently punishing to assure an aggressor that he would lose more than he would win. Close associates of Dulles have confirmed, in interviews, that what he had in mind was a whole spectrum of possible degrees of retaliation.

break out, was neatly illustrated in the parallel drawn by Dulles between the new doctrine and the domestic security systems which do not maintain "an armed guard in every home," but instead "punish any who break in and steal. . . ."

Yet it would be going too far to say that, in the Dulles doctrine, threats of nuclear punishment (massive or otherwise) were to be made only for deterrent effect and did not represent real intent. Not only were air power and nuclear weapons considered the primary instruments of *deterrence,* they were seen also as the most efficient means of *defense*—that is, of actually fighting a war for the control of territory.

This was illustrated by a shift of emphasis in NATO strategic doctrine. Before 1953, the application of strategic air power against the Soviet homeland in a European war was conceived of as a kind of "holding action"; it would delay the Red Army's advance long enough to permit the mobilization and transportation of sufficient ground forces to stop it.[27] It was the ground forces which would be decisive, with air power playing a supporting role. But in the early years of Eisenhower's Presidency, there developed a doctrine which reversed these roles, which held that strategic air power would be the decisive factor, with the ground "shield" playing the role of "holding" the Soviet ground forces until the strategic bombardment produced victory.[28] This shift of emphasis may have been justified, of course, by the development of hydrogen bombs.

A remarkable aspect of the whole debate on massive retaliation was the fact that the debaters on both sides really failed to recognize and confront their opponent's basic premises. Dulles based his thesis almost entirely on the deterrent effect of a *capability* to retaliate, and he tended to ignore the possibility that the enemy would not believe that we really intended to retaliate when the retaliation

[27] For a statement of this doctrine, see testimony by Gen. Omar Bradley in *Department of Defense Appropriations for 1952,* Hearings before the Committee on Appropriations, House of Representatives, 82d Cong., 1st Sess. (Washington, 1951), I, 205.
[28] The best statements of this doctrine are by General Lauris Norstad, Supreme Allied Commander in Europe. See especially his testimony in *Mutual Security Act of 1958,* Hearings before the Committee on Foreign Relations, United States Senate, 85th Cong., 2d Sess. (Washington, 1958), p. 187.

could be answered in kind. Dulles' critics, on the other hand, stressed heavily the enemy's appraisal of our *intentions*, and they tended to ignore the possibility that the enemy might retain some fear of our capability to retaliate, on the chance that he might have guessed wrong about our intentions. In retrospect, one can realize that the debate would have been strikingly illuminated if both sides (or even one participant in the debate) had recognized that deterrence is a function of the enemy's appraisal of both capabilities and intent; that low credibility in a retaliatory threat might be offset by the prospect of *possibly* very severe costs, just as the deterrent value of a capability to retaliate must be discounted in some fashion by some factor representing the enemy's doubts whether retaliation will occur. In short, the debate was frustrating and inconclusive because both sides were using inadequate, single-factor theories of deterrence which yielded opposite conclusions. The opposing arguments needed to be synthesized, but no synthesizer appeared.

Substitution of air power and fire power for manpower

The New Look rested heavily on the assumption that nuclear weapons created "new relationships between men and matériel which emphasize airpower and permit economies in the use of manpower." [29] Actually, the administration justified its reduction in active military manpower, especially Army manpower, in four different ways. First was the argument that nuclear weapons had increased the effectiveness of strategic air power relative to land power. In war, it was believed, fire power wielded from the air against the enemy's sources of power at home could take the place of substantial numbers of ground troops. Secondly, progress in development of tactical nuclear weapons had greatly increased the fire power available to surface forces, and this permitted some reduction in personnel. Thirdly, most of the manpower reduction was to come out of other than combat forces, it was stated. According to Secretary Wilson, only 103,500, or about one-third, of the Army personnel reduction by the end of fiscal 1955 was to be combat manpower. Of this number, 51,000 represented the "pipe line" of men in transit

[29] *HCA, Hearings 1955 Budget,* p. 2, statement of Secretary Wilson.

to or from Korea, which, of course, could be eliminated with the end of the war, and 52,500 reflected the elimination of three combat divisions. The rest of the reduction, 213,700, was to be taken in "supporting," or noncombat, units. Secretary Wilson said that, considering the continued maintenance of three Marine combat divisions, there was to be only a 10 percent reduction in active ground combat strength,[30] even though total Army manpower was to be reduced about 20 percent.

The fourth reason given was grounded less in logic or fact than it was in tradition. It was said that the manpower of the United States was "limited," that we could not hope to compete with the Russians in the mobilization of raw manpower, and that we should concentrate instead on our "long suits" (as Admiral Radford phrased it), that is, upon our superior technology and industrial capacity. Said Secretary Wilson: "I think it is clear to all Americans that we do not expect to fight with land armies in our country. It is going to be pretty late if we ever get around to that." [31]

The "sound economy"

The administration made no secret of the fact that a desire to economize and eventually to balance the Federal budget had been a major determinant of the New Look program. But its spokesmen denied that it was the *only* determinant, or that security was being sacrificed on the altar of economy. On the contrary, the New Look program would provide *more* security than heretofore, while at the same time saving money. Apparently the claim of "more security" rested chiefly on the decision to embrace a nuclear strategy for a wider range of contingencies, thus enhancing both defense and deterrent capabilities by a multiplication of fire power. Moreover, it was said that a "sound economy" was an aspect of national security, not a consideration opposed to security.

At what level of military expenditure or overall government spending or taxation the economy would become "unsound," and what the nature of this condition would be, were never made very explicit. Often the statements seemed to imply that once the danger point

[30] *Ibid.*, p. 62.   [31] *Ibid.*

was exceeded some dire catastrophe would take place. Dulles spoke of the danger of "bankruptcy" and Wilson of "wrecking our economy." Admiral Radford said that "economic collapse" would follow any attempt by the United States "to station combat-effective units of superior strength every place where aggression might occur." [32]

It would be most logical to assume that the kind of catastrophe symbolized by these words would be severe uncontrollable inflation. Yet, Radford's particular fear was of depression. He said:

I honestly felt and still feel that the economic stability of the United States is a great factor of military importance over the long pull. I know from traveling abroad that our allies are almost as afraid of a depression in the United States as they are of a Communist attack. In other words, they realize that if we were to have a severe setback in this country, we would curtail our military aid programs and we would be forced to take other actions, all of which would be, in their opinion, very dangerous.[33]

Radford did not explain why excessive military spending might cause a depression. Nor did he explain why a depression might cause us to reduce our expenditures for military aid, a program which, one would think, would help to stimulate business activity.

Perhaps the most reasonable and explicit statement of the economy theme was the following one by Secretary Wilson, stressing the possible effect of defense spending in retarding economic growth.

The cost of national security will remain high for many years. This cost must be bearable not only in the sense that the burden can be carried without wrecking our economy but also be within the limits of what can be supported without retarding the future growth of our country. Over the long pull, economic strength is an indispensable prerequisite for military strength. . . . This strength, together with our faith in our free society, is the real source of our military power.[34]

At the hearings, the three service Secretaries, as well as Admiral Carney and General Lemuel C. Shepherd, Jr., Commandant of the Marine Corps, also referred in their prepared statements to the

[32] For Radford's statement, cf. *ibid.*, p. 121.
[33] *Department of Defense Appropriations for 1955*, Hearings before the Committee on Appropriations, United States Senate, 83d Cong., 2d Sess. (Washington, 1954), p. 83.
[34] *Ibid.*, pp. 4–5.

importance of weighing defense needs against the need to preserve a healthy economy. General Ridgway, under questioning, said he agreed to this thesis, but he denied the competence and responsibility of military men to consider this factor.[35]

The "long haul"; gaining the "initiative"

President Eisenhower opened the "national security" section of his budget message with the following statement:

This budget is based on a new concept for planning and financing our national security program, which was partially applied in the budget revision recommended last spring for the fiscal year 1954. Our military planning in previous years had been based on several successive assumed fixed dates of maximum danger, which were extended from time to time with procurement and personnel plans focused to achieve maximum readiness by each such date. This budget is aimed instead at providing a strong military position which can be maintained over the extended period of uneasy peace.

Later, the President said:

The previous history of our military budgets has been one of feast or famine, depending upon the state of world affairs. In peacetime, appropriations have customarily been much reduced. In wartime, financial considerations have been largely ignored. Our present budgetary plans represent a departure from these practices. They provide for the continued maintenance of a strong military force which is within the financial capability of a sound economy. We cannot afford to build military strength by sacrificing economic strength. We must keep strong in all respects.[36]

This was one of the clearest expositions of the rather vague concept of the "long haul." As we have pointed out earlier, the administration greatly exaggerated the degree of change involved in substitution of this concept for that of the "crisis year." Nevertheless, the new concept and its explanations by various spokesmen were rich in associations, implications, and overtones which it is instructive to explore.

A primary association was that of the "sound economy." It was

---

[35] For Ridgway's statement, cf. *HCA, Hearings 1955 Army Budget,* p. 90.
[36] *U.S. Budget, FY 1955,* pp. M38–M39, and M40.

asserted over and over that a "sound economy" was an essential aspect of national security. A policy of the "long haul" would preserve the health of the economy in two ways. First, it would hold military spending down to a level which the economy was *capable* of supporting for an indefinite period of time. The administration apparently believed that the level of security expenditures which the economy could sustain over a long period of time was much lower than the expenditures which could be supported in a short period—for example, during a war. Secondly, it was said that the "long haul" policy would avoid another kind of economic catastrophe, the depression that would result from building up fast to maximum military strength, then suddenly reducing expenditures. This would have been the result of following the previous administration's "crisis year" or "D-Day" concept, it was claimed.[37] By stretching out the build-up, thus smoothing the change from build-up to maintenance rates of expenditure, the "long pull" idea not only protected the stability of the economy, but also was said to allow the preservation of an "active" industrial mobilization base.

Further benefits would accrue, it was said, from the elimination of the "feast and famine" cycle which had characterized American military and mobilization policy in the past. The gains envisioned here were partly in terms of less risk and partly in terms of cost reductions through increased efficiency. The following statement by Admiral Radford admirably summarizes the "feast and famine" argument.

In analyzing these peaks and valleys of military preparedness we find that they are most expensive. Waste and inefficiency under such circumstances are the inevitable result. Besides being more expensive, such a system is dangerous. Planning based on such programs can no longer be accepted as a justifiable risk, because never again in a global war will we have the same amount of time which we had in World War II to build up our forces. Another serious disadvantage that adds to the infeasibility of such a system is that these valleys of preparedness constitute an invitation to aggression.[38]

[37] Secretary Wilson said the "D-Day" concept posed the alternatives of "disastrous war or depression." *HCA, Hearings 1955 Budget*, p. 113.

[38] *SCA, Hearings 1955 Budget*, p. 80.

The "feast and famine" thesis tended to focus attention on the fact that the administration intended to maintain a military force larger than had ever before been supported by the United States in peacetime, a point which was often made explicitly by administration spokesmen.[39] This was true, of course, but it tended to obscure the fact that United States military capabilities were being reduced from what had been maintained and planned by the administration's predecessors. What Admiral Radford failed to mention was that "famines," if not "feasts," had already been rejected by the Truman administration—a permanent high level of mobilization had become a firm commitment of policy at least a year and a half before the Eisenhower inaugural.

The "long haul" idea also symbolized a deep, emotionally grounded, desire for *stability* in the new administration's foreign–military policy ideology. The commitment to stability was accompanied, perforce, by a belief that military policy could, and should, be determined with less regard for changing external events than had been the case in the past. In President Eisenhower's words, military policy in the future would depend less "upon the state of world affairs." In the Republican image of the former administration's foreign and military policies, these policies were characterized by frantic makeshift reactions to Soviet "initiative," reacting to events rather than controlling events, an inability to formulate a long-term policy which would be able to ride out a variety of different kinds and degrees of crisis without fundamental change.[40] In his "massive

[39] In stressing that the "long haul" military program would be the largest ever maintained by the United States in peacetime, Roger M. Kyes, the Deputy Secretary of Defense, saw this as a sort of quid pro quo for the administration's demand that the military consider the economic results of their recommendations. "As civilians, we must cease to cut the military to the bone in time of peace, while on the other hand, we permit them to utilize our resources unnecessarily in time of war as a result of inflated requirements. If we insist that the military abandon their present attitude as claimants for absolute requirements without responsibility for economic consequences, we should also insist that the civilian attitude of irresponsibility between wars should be abandoned." *Department of Defense Appropriations for 1954,* Hearings before the Committee on Appropriations, House of Representatives, 83d Cong., 1st Sess. (Washington, 1953), p. 489.

[40] During his campaign, President Eisenhower had asserted the need for a "new administration that will call a halt to stop-and-start planning; an admin-

retaliation" speech Secretary Dulles mentioned several instances of "emergency action, imposed upon us by our enemies" during the Truman administration. These were the decision to fight in Korea, the Marshall Plan, and the military build-up during the Korean War. Such "emergency measures," Dulles said, "are superficial and they imply that the enemy has the initiative. They cannot be depended on to serve our long-time interests." [41]

The explanation of the "long haul" concept implied that American military policy was no longer to be merely a series of improvised reactions to enemy "initiative," but was to be formulated in greater degree according to criteria indigenous to the United States— notably the "health" of the American economy and the state of development of American weapons. The military establishment would be maintained at a more or less steady level, regardless of short-run indications of changes in Communist intentions. Thus, the "long haul" purported to wrench "the initiative" from the Soviets in the field of *preparedness policy,* just as the idea of planning to retaliate "by means and at places of our own choosing" asserted the initiative of the United States in *action policy.*

In deemphasizing external and emphasizing internal criteria for determining preparedness policy, the "long haul" concept minimized the importance of the traditional bases for the determination of requirements by the military: enemy capabilities and United States commitments. This made it more difficult for a military man to argue that a certain level of force was "required" in the face of a civilian's claim that the country could not "afford" a force of this size. Besides shifting the psychological balance of power in favor of the economy-oriented civilian, the "long haul" concept also had the perhaps beneficial effect of encouraging balance in procurement, since it tended to orient procurement around *supply availabilities,* with the buying of all items geared to the availability of the scarcest ones, rather than to a schedule of externally determined "requirements."

---

istration that will not demobilize and then hurriedly mobilize; an administration that will not swing from optimism to panic; and an administration that will plan for the future on something more solid than yesterday's headlines." New York *Times,* September 26, 1952, p. 12.

[41] *Ibid.,* January 13, 1954.

Assessment of the enemy

The "long haul" idea was closely related to the administration's image of the intentions of the Soviet enemy.[42] According to this image, the Soviets were always "one up" on the United States because their short-term foreign policy moves were guided by a long-range strategy. This long-range plan gave flexibility to Soviet policy in the short run: they could shift policies quickly, retreat in the face of opposition, and not become overly committed to some short-term goal. It gave the Soviets "the initiative," and these cool and calculating opponents used their initiative to manipulate the United States, to trick the United States into making short-run moves which were against its long-run interests, for example, "crash" programs of military build-up, "tying down" forces in Asia, and so forth. To compete successfully with such an antagonist, it was necessary for the United States to base *its* day-to-day or month-to-month policies on a long-range plan. As Secretary Dulles put it: "The Soviet Communists are planning for 'an entire historical era' and we should do the same." [43] Thus, a policy of the long haul would remain relatively unruffled by specific Soviet moves in the short run, but rather would focus on the long-range Communist objectives and seek to maintain a relatively steady level of military strength consistent with the threat represented by these objectives.

This image of an enemy who combined great patience, cleverness, and relentless pressure is well illustrated in the following quotation from Admiral Radford:

We are already in a period of tension. It could last 10 or 20 years or more. The Communist world has no time limit for the accomplishment of its objectives. Their goals are so long-range in concept that they can attempt to achieve them at any time it is expedient. In addition, it is characteristic of the Soviet strategy to try to create situations which pose to us courses of action, all of which are unpleasant or which have definite disadvantages for us. . . .

[42] Admiral Radford noted this connection when he said that "it was in recognition of the Communist objective and their methods for attaining it that the President directed that military planning no longer be based on the year-of-crisis theory, but on preparations for the long pull." *SCA, Hearings 1955 Budget,* p. 81.
[43] New York *Times,* January 13, 1954.

My own feeling is that the Soviets do not want a shooting war at this time. They prefer tension and discord, hoping that we will destroy ourselves. At the same time, such a dictatorship can make sudden, and sometimes illogical decisions. What it boils down to is that we have to be ready for almost anything, anytime.[44]

The unpredictability of Soviet intentions was stressed heavily by administration spokesmen, usually in derogation of the "year of maximum peril" concept which, according to them, had postulated that the Soviets were likely to make war in the "crisis year." Since predictions of Soviet intentions were futile, it followed that they should be left out of the military policy calculus. The most obvious alternative criterion would, of course, be Soviet *capabilities,* but to try to match Soviet capabilities on the ground would lead to "bankruptcy." The only reasonable course, therefore, was the policy of the "long haul"—that is, maintain the maximum military force which the country could "afford," while at the same time creating conditions (in the form of a ready mobilization production base and well-trained reserves) which would allow quick expansion to the required force should the enemy begin clearly to exhibit warlike intentions.

One of the leading aims of the Soviets, according to administration doctrine, was to entice the United States into excessive military expenditures, leading to "economic collapse," thus, as Admiral Radford put it, "attaining their objective without firing a shot." [45] One of the clearest statements of this dogma came from the President:

It has been coldly calculated by the Soviet leaders—by their military threat, they have hoped to force upon America and the free world an unbearable security burden leading to economic disaster. They have plainly said that free people cannot preserve their way of life and at the same time provide enormous military establishments. Communist guns, in this sense, have been aiming at an economic target no less than a military target.[46]

There is no record of any administration spokesman citing a specific source in Communist doctrine to support this belief. Secretary Dulles (without mentioning his documentary source) did claim that

[44] *United States News and World Report,* March 5, 1954, pp. 48–55.
[45] *SCA, Hearings 1955 Budget,* p. 80.
[46] From a radio speech, May 19, 1953. New York *Times,* May 20, 1953.

Lenin had said communism should seek to overextend capitalist nations in efforts which were "beyond their strength, so that they come to practical bankruptcy," at which point "our victory is assured." [47]

Incidentally, Dulles implied in his "massive retaliation" speech that in adopting a policy good for the "long pull," the shoe would be placed on the other foot: in avoiding "economic bankruptcy" we would force the Soviets into "political bankruptcy." Dulles said:

If we persist in the course I outline we shall confront dictatorship with a task that is, in the long run, beyond its strength. For unless it changes, it must suppress the human desires that freedom satisfies—as we shall be demonstrating. If the dictators persist in their present course then it is they who will be limited to superficial successes, while their foundation crumbles under the tread of their iron boots.[48]

While maintaining that the *long-term* threat of Soviet aggression continued unabated, the administration also said that the danger of war in the *near-term* had declined. One authoritative statement to this effect followed a meeting of the North Atlantic Council in December 1953. The council decided (in the words of Secretary Dulles) that "Soviet armed aggression is less likely than it seemed several years ago," although, in the long run, "the Soviet threat persists and probably will long persist." [49] Dulles said these statements coincided with his own views. Secretary Wilson also spoke more than once about the decrease in international tension. There have been no clear statements indicating specifically upon what this intelligence estimate was based. Secretary Wilson said it was "because of the increased strength of the free world." [50] It would seem, however, that two other factors must have been at least as important, namely, the death of Stalin in March 1953 and the rel-

[47] *Ibid.*, January 13, 1954. Research for the present study did not include any attempt to discover such an aim in Communist doctrine. It is well known, however, that this doctrine does stress a theme which is exactly opposite to the one mentioned above; namely, that capitalist nations need high military expenditures to *support* their economies and avoid periodic or chronic depression.
[48] *Ibid.*
[49] Richard P. Stebbins, *The United States in World Affairs, 1953* (New York, Council on Foreign Relations, 1954), p. 443.
[50] *HCA, Hearings 1955 Budget*, p. 102.

atively "soft" policy followed by his immediate successors, and also the Communist decision to agree to an armistice in Korea.

The reassessment of Soviet intentions was accompanied by a downgrading of Soviet capabilities, at least in the minds of the civilian leaders in the Pentagon. Deputy Secretary of Defense Roger Kyes described some of the intelligence documents on Russian capabilities as "sales promotion intelligence," that is, exaggerated estimates of Soviet strength designed to "sell" service budgets.[51]

Secretary Wilson seemed to share this skepticism about the estimated Russian capabilities, deploring (in his characteristically colorful prose) the idea that "the Russians are ten feet tall." It was also reported that some military men, particularly in the Navy, were of similar opinion. It was felt, apparently, that past intelligence appraisals, in the absence of absolutely reliable information, had tended to estimate Soviet capabilities on the high side, whereas a more rational procedure would have been to strike a median between the highest and lowest possibilities.[52]

Disengagement: A central strategic reserve

The geographic concentration of surface forces was a leading element in the new strategy. The motif of redeploying United States forces from outlying positions, particularly in Asia, to a "central strategic reserve" was most prominent in the statements of the military leaders, especially in those of Admiral Radford. This seemed to be one point upon which all the military men, including General Ridgway and the Army, could agree in general, although there were some differences in degree. This concept—perhaps it would be more accurate to call it a tendency, or a fundamental inclination—had always been prominent in American military thinking, and to some extent in civilian thinking as well.

The stationing of American forces abroad in the years prior to 1953 had always been undertaken reluctantly by the American military, under the pressure of overriding political factors. Especially was this true with respect to deployments in Asia; the intense military desire to withdraw American combat units from South Korea

[51] Hanson W. Baldwin, *New York Times*, December 13, 1953.   [52] *Ibid.*

in the early postwar years, eventually satisfied in 1949, may be well—and perhaps regretfully—remembered. But even when the decision was made in 1951 to send four additional American divisions to Europe, military spokesmen repeatedly referred to this deployment as temporary, to last only until the Europeans were able to "take care of themselves," and General Eisenhower stated that "our great strength lies in our central position with our ability to move in the directions that we see require it." [53]

This particular aspect of the New Look seems to have been derived from four motivations. First was the desire to get United States forces deployed in the best possible positions for the contingency of general war. Obviously, in the event of general war, the United States would want to concentrate its forces in the decisive theater, which would certainly not be in Asia.

Second came the desire to obtain more "flexibility" in the United States military posture. This was a more arguable point. The idea seemed to be that troops in a "central strategic reserve" could more easily respond to aggression anywhere in the world, whereas forces committed at distant points would have to fight where they were located or not at all. As Secretary of the Army Robert T. Stevens stated succinctly, ". . . to whatever extent we will have divisions return home from the Far East available for use here in the Zone of the Interior, by that extent we will improve our capabilities of reinforcing NATO." [54]

The third reason given was political: redeployment would help to refute Communist charges of United States "imperialism." This reason was given, however, only by Secretary Dulles; [55] it was mentioned by none of the military leaders.

The fourth reason was economic: having ground forces centralized in a strategic reserve would reduce support costs.

It was mentioned occasionally at the hearings that part of the justification for redeploying troops to the United States was that

[53] *Assignment of Ground Forces of the United States to Duty in the European Area*, Hearings before the Committees on Foreign Relations and Armed Services, United States Senate, 82d Cong., 1st Sess. (Washington, 1951), p. 18.

[54] *HCA, Hearings 1955 Budget,* p. 39.

[55] New York *Times,* January 13, 1954.

indigenous troops had become stronger or would become stronger through United States military aid. The Republic of Korea Army was the principal exhibit; its growing strength was claimed to justify the plan to withdraw two United States divisions. Secretary Wilson pointed out that the cost to the United States was much less to maintain indigenous forces than to station United States troops on foreign territory.[56]

Although General Ridgway presumably had approved the concept of the strategic reserve in the study made by the Joint Chiefs of Staff, his remarks at the hearings did not reflect any great enthusiasm for it. He indicated his approval of the decision to withdraw the divisions from Korea, on the ground that in case of general war, it would be difficult to extricate these forces for quick employment in some more vital theater. On the other hand, Ridgway made this comment:

From this brief resume of the Army's assigned tasks, I believe that you will agree that there is an existing requirement for the overseas deployment of Army forces in significant numbers, as well as for the maintenance of forces in the United States to support them, to reinforce them as necessary, and, should the need arise, to provide a base for rapid mobilization. I believe that the presence of United States Army forces in sensitive areas on our security frontiers has contributed materially to such military stability as exists in the world today, and that they continue to strengthen the peace.[57]

A Navy man provided a sidelight on the matter of redeployment—its relation to morale in the armed services. Vice Admiral James L. Holloway, Jr., Deputy Chief of Naval Operations (Personnel), said: "The big thing which affects morale nowadays, and it is indigenous to the great responsibilities our country has taken on, is the amount of distant service required of all services which separate the members from hearth and home." [58] This was as close as any witness came to saying that disengagement from overseas positions would tend to

[56] *HCA, Hearings 1955 Budget,* p. 60.
[57] *HCA, Hearings 1955 Army Budget,* p. 44. Apparently the "sensitive areas" to which Ridgway referred did not include Korea, for, as noted earlier, he wished to withdraw all Army combat forces from Korea.
[58] *HCA, Hearings 1955 Navy Budget,* p. 113.

stimulate reenlistment, with consequent economies. Presumably, this consideration added to the attraction of the "central strategic reserve" idea.

The "central strategic reserve" concept, at first blush, would seem to be in conflict with Secretary Dulles' notions about "drawing a line" and clearly letting the enemy know that if he stepped across the line, he would be in for trouble. In other words, the latter idea would seem more congenially linked with the idea of "trip-wire" overseas deployment, to make it necessary for the enemy to attack United States forces if he moved across a boundary, thus triggering a more "massive" United States response. Since Dulles was heard to espouse the "strategic reserve" idea in some of his statements, the contradiction apparently did not exist in his mind. The most plausible reason for this is that, in Dulles' mind, "drawing a line" to prevent miscalculation was almost entirely a verbal gambit. We would simply tell the enemy that if he stepped over the line, he would be at war with the United States, and this would be sufficient to deter him. Also, of course, the central strategic reserve was a logical corollary of another facet of the Dulles doctrine: the necessity to seize the "initiative"; to avoid fighting at times, places, and circumstances of the enemy's choice.

Mobility

The words "mobility," "mobile readiness," and the like, appeared frequently in the administration's explanations of its new military program. There were frequent references to "mobile sea and air power" and "hard-hitting, mobile" ground forces. The impression created was that although United States military forces were being cut down in quantity, the ones that were left, besides wielding tremendous fire power, were going to be able to move around very fast. The idea of the "central strategic reserve" depended for its validity, of course, upon mobility; if the central reserves were unable to move to battlefronts in time to affect the outcome, they might better have been left at the potential battlefront in the first place. The general statements of the administration witnesses left the impression that, besides being more centrally located, United States ground forces were going to be able to move faster to "hot spots" anywhere in the world. Admiral Radford said, for example, that "we must have strong, mobile, combat-ready units capable of being projected wherever required."[59] Concerning the Navy, Admiral Carney said: "Mobility enables us to make a major military effort in one area, and at the same time be capable of redeploying promptly to another. It enables us to concentrate superior strength in critical areas more quickly."[60]

An alert Congressman, Representative Robert L. F. Sikes (Georgia) exposed the reality of the Army's highly advertised new "mobility." Sikes got Secretary Stevens to admit that additional "mobile readiness" would be effected primarily by geographic redeployment, rather than by faster means of locomotion, such as airlift.[61] In other words, when administration spokesmen applied the word "mobile" to the Army or to ground forces, they were not using the word in its ordinary sense, but rather to refer chiefly to the strategic advantage of central location. Later, however, under further questioning by Sikes, Stevens said the concept of "mobile readiness" did include airlift in the sense that "we can also, I think, airlift them much more quickly from here than we can from some places at which they are currently tied down." He also stated that "with every year that goes by we hope we will have a greater capability of airlift."[62]

Stevens' "hope" certainly was not encouraged by the budget which he was defending. The budget actually reduced the Army's capacity for strategic movement by air by cutting the Air Force's air transport strength from 16 to 13 wings. Under the 137-wing program to be reached in 1957, it was scheduled to go down further to 11 wings. The only concrete indication of greater mobility for the Army in fiscal 1955 was in the field of *tactical* mobility—faster locomotion on or near the battlefield. One regular infantry division and two National Guard divisions were to be converted to armor during the year.

Apart from such improvement in the Army's battle theater mobility, the references to increased mobility apparently referred to the build-up in air power and to the *intention* to place more reliance

---

[59] SCA, *Hearings 1955 Budget*, p. 90.
[60] HCA, *Hearings 1955 Navy Budget*, p. 38.
[61] HCA, *Hearings 1955 Army Budget*, p. 39.   [62] *Ibid.*, p. 56.

on "mobile air and naval forces," to deter aggression and support the local defenses of threatened areas.

Balanced collective forces

The principle of "balanced collective forces" figured quite importantly in the official explanations of the New Look. It might be described as an application of the economic principle of "comparative advantage" to the security policy of the entire free world. Each member would contribute to the common defenses that which it could provide most efficiently. Because the United States possessed superior industrial and technical capacity, and only a "limited" supply of manpower, it should concentrate on providing air and naval power, complex equipment and weapons, and "highly mobile offensive combat forces," rather than manpower in the mass. Other nations, poorer in industrial capacity and technical skills, should provide the bulk of the ground troops needed to defend their territories, as well as bases from which United States air and naval power could be applied.[63] Admiral Radford, who stressed this concept strongly in his public statements, said that it replaced the old idea of "balanced forces" *within* the United States military establishment, that is, a roughly equal distribution of the defense budget among the three services. In his words, the Joint Chiefs of Staff had adjusted "the balance of United States forces so as to fit into the larger system of collective Allied forces." [64] Although "for the long pull," the emphasis had shifted away from ground forces and toward air power in the United States forces, this did not apply to "collective allied forces throughout an actual global war." In such a war, Radford said, the total of the ground forces needed would be "as large as any time before. . . ." [65]

[63] Secretary Wilson said: "I think it is clear to all Americans that we do not expect to fight with land armies in our country. . . . It is also clear that our country can supply the material for war better than we can the men, and many of our allies can supply the men better than they can the material. So the defense of the free world has to be worked out on an international balance and not on a national balance, if I make my point clear." *HCA, Hearings 1955 Budget*, p. 62.

[64] *SCA, Hearings 1955 Budget*, p. 84.

[65] Interview in *U.S. News and World Report*, March 5, 1954, pp. 48–55.

"Balanced collective strength" therefore was complementary to the idea of the "central strategic reserve." The local ground defense of the allies would take the initial shock of the attack, and, assisted by the efforts of the United States air and naval forces, would hold off the enemy until a contingent of "hard-hitting, mobile" ground forces from the central strategic reserve of the United States arrived on the scene.

It was also said that the military capabilities of the allies had improved and that this justified, in part at least, the reduction of United States ground forces.[66]

A "natural evolution"

Almost at the same time that the administration was advertising its defense policy as a brand-new Republican model, representing a sharp break with the outmoded or wrong-headed policies of the past, it also, somewhat inconsistently, described it as a "natural evolution" of policy, something that would have occurred at this particular point in history whatever the political complexion of the administration or the personal identities of the Chiefs of Staff. The evolution was said to have been the result of changes in external conditions—notably the end of the Korean War, the build-up of the NATO and Republic of Korea forces, and the receding of the immediate threat—and advances in technology which promised soon to make available large quantities of nuclear weapons in a variety of sizes. Both Radford and Wilson stressed this theme—no doubt in part to help counteract the wave of criticism which followed the Dulles "massive retaliation" speech.[67] The President also emphasized the evolutionary character of the new policy when he said at a press conference that it was only "an attempt by intelligent people to keep abreast of the times." [68]

[66] Department of Defense, *Semi-Annual Report of the Secretary of Defense, January 1 to June 30, 1954* (Washington, 1954), pp. 1–2.
[67] SCA, *Hearings 1955 Budget*, p. 4 and p. 81.
[68] New York *Times*, March 18, 1954, p. 14.

III   *The Ridgway-Wilson Misunderstanding*

In his State of the Union Message, delivered on January 7, 1954, President Eisenhower made the following statement, which had been checked and approved by Secretary Wilson: "The defense program recommended in the 1955 budget . . . is based on a new military program unanimously recommended by the Joint Chiefs of Staff and approved by me following consideration by the National Security Council."

Wilson told the House Appropriations Committee that the budget reflected the "fiscal year 1955 phase" of the "carefully considered and unanimously agreed long-range plan of the JCS. . . ." Admiral Radford said the program had the "full endorsement" of the Joint Chiefs of Staff. The Chiefs of the Navy and the Air Force made similar unequivocal statements. Ridgway, under questioning, affirmed that the program had the "unanimous endorsement" of the Chiefs, but added that the endorsement was "on stated assumptions and limitations."

As Ridgway's testimony progressed, however, it became quite clear that the phrases "unanimously recommended" and "full endorsement" did not accurately describe his position on the fiscal 1955 program. He asserted repeatedly that ground forces were the decisive element of warfare and denied by strong implication the administration's basic thesis that developments in air power and nuclear weapons had substantially reduced the need for manpower. He said the combat capability of the Army was being reduced, when there had occurred no corresponding reduction in the Soviet threat and no change in the nation's commitments or the Army's responsibilities for meeting this threat. The military capabilities of the Communist bloc actually were on the increase. There had been no increase in allied forces sufficient to justify a smaller United States Army.

When asked for his views on Secretary Dulles' "massive retaliation" doctrine, Ridgway indicated skepticism, although, interestingly enough, on political, rather than military, grounds. "I think it will raise serious apprehensions in the minds of many segments of foreign populations, notably those of the Western world presently allied with us," he said. He prefaced this statement, however, by noting that this was only his "personal view" which he hoped would "not be in the slightest degree considered as a criticism of a statement by one of our constitutional authorities." [1]

Several times during his testimony, General Ridgway referred to "ceilings" and other "limitations" which had been imposed by higher authority in preparation of the budget. These references brought moderate protest from Secretary Stevens. The Secretary said that "while the word 'ceiling' is used, actually I do not consider that any official ceiling was imposed, but that we were given targets to shoot at and we were shooting at them and trying to hit them." [2]

Ridgway thus made it perfectly clear that he disagreed with the budget and its underlying philosophy, particularly as they affected the Army. Nevertheless, he exhibited great reluctance to say outright that he opposed the program, even when pressed with point-blank questions. Under close questioning by Senator Burnet R. Maybank, he refused to say whether he was "satisfied" with the Army program or whether he had "recommended" it. He would say only that he "accepted" it. In explaining his reticence, Ridgway said:

It has been my unvarying position that when a career military officer receives from proper superior authority a decision, that regardless of his views previously expressed, he accepts that decision as a sound one, and does his utmost within his available means to carry it out . . . I accept this program as sound. . . . [3]

In his reluctance publicly to disagree with official policy, Ridgway stood in remarkable contrast to the Air Force Chief of Staff, General

---

[1] *HCA, Hearings 1955 Army Budget*, p. 84.   [2] *Ibid.*, p. 59.
[3] *SCA, Hearings 1955 Budget*, pp. 43–44.

Vandenberg, whose frank and vigorous assaults on the revised 1954 budget had seemed uninhibited by any considerations of professional or administrative propriety.

Later, after his retirement had released him from such restraints, Ridgway published an autobiographical book in which he said he had never felt a "greater sense of surprise and shock" than when he read the President's 1954 statement that the 1955 military budget had been based on a program "unanimously recommended" by the Chiefs.

As one member of the Joint Chiefs of Staff who most emphatically had not concurred in the 1955 military program as it was presented to the people, I was nonplussed by this statement. The fact is the 1955 budget was a "directed verdict," as were the Army budgets for 1956 and 1957. The force levels provided in all three were not primarily based on military needs. They were not based on the freely reached conclusions of the Joint Chiefs of Staff. They were squeezed between the framework of arbitrary manpower and fiscal limits, a complete inversion of the normal process.[4]

This assertion, plus similar statements made by Ridgway in a magazine article published about the same time, caused something of a stir in the press and in Congress. As a result, both Ridgway and Wilson were questioned about the matter by the House Appropriations Committee at the hearings on the military budget for fiscal 1957. At these hearings, Ridgway made the following unequivocal assertion:

In all matters on which the Joint Chiefs of Staff reached unanimous agreement in the last half of calendar year 1953, there was none which recommended personnel ceilings for the several armed services for fiscal year 1955. The agreement reached in December, 1953, which was unanimous, dealt with fiscal year 1957, not fiscal year 1955, and it was the one which had preset manpower and dollar ceilings and was qualified by a series of stated assumptions and conditions. . . .[5]

Ridgway also said that personnel levels for 1955 and 1956 were not even discussed by the Joint Chiefs of Staff during the fall of

[4] General Matthew B. Ridgway, *Soldier* (New York, Harper and Bros., 1946), pp. 288–89.
[5] *HCA, Hearings 1957 Budget,* pp. 560–61.

1953—meaning, apparently, after the JCS recommendation of 1955 force levels in October. These figures were obtained in the Office of the Secretary of Defense, he said, by a process of "extrapolation" between the 1957 goals which the Chiefs had approved and the forces then in existence. Ridgway said he "never for a minute subscribed to either the method or the intermediate figures obtained thereby." [6]

Wilson made the following statement:

I got a paper from [Admiral Radford] which had no objection from any members of the Joint Chiefs of Staff. But that covered a longer planning period than one year. The first year of it involved the 1955 budget, and I have every reason to think there was no disagreement on that. [7]

The reasons for this misunderstanding, as best they can be pieced together from the often conflicting memories of the principal actors, add up to a miasma of faulty communication, wishful thinking, semantic confusion, and avoidance of responsibility. In the first place, the President's statement in his State of the Union Message might be superficially justified by noting that he did not say specifically that the Chiefs had agreed on the 1955 program, but only that this program was "based on a program" which had been unanimously approved by the Joint Chiefs of Staff. The "long haul" program, starting in fiscal 1957, *had* been approved unanimously, and the 1955 program *had* been derived from this program, although not by the Chiefs. This technical justification, of course, does not satisfy Ridgway and Carney, who note that the President's statement did give the impression that the Chiefs had positively and unanimously approved, even originated, the budget and program immediately at issue, namely, the 1955 program. They point out, further, that the statement ignored the fact that JCS approval of the 1957 program was conditioned on a set of hypothetical assumptions which were far from being realized. [8]

Inclusion of the words "based on a new military program" indicated to Ridgway that Wilson, and perhaps the President,

[6] *Ibid.*, p. 600.   [7] *Ibid.*, p. 45.
[8] While deploring this omission, Carney was much less exercised about it than was Ridgway.

although aware that the Chiefs had not unanimously approved the 1955 force levels, were seeking for a way to give the impression of such unity without technically violating the truth.

But, as we have already pointed out, Wilson and Radford apparently did believe that the 1955 program had been approved by all the members of the Joint Chiefs of Staff. Their reasons for believing this were chiefly two. One was that when the Army and Navy Chiefs had agreed to an end-target for 1957, they also had agreed implicitly to a gradual phasing-down of their forces during the intervening years. Another was that all of the Chiefs had had an opportunity to register a formal dissent against the 1955 program and had failed to do so. We have already discussed the "phasing-down" argument and Ridgway's answer to it. The second reason—the lack of any formal objection from the individual Chiefs—is perhaps the more substantial one. Wilson later expressed his philosophy on this point as follows: ". . . if a man feels strongly enough about it then there is a disagreement. If there is no disagreement stated you have the right to believe that the men are in agreement and everything considered this is the right thing to do." [9]

Admiral Radford apparently held a similar view. He said (although not with regard to this particular decision) that "if there is no indication of a disagreement we send the paper up as a recommendation of the Joint Chiefs of Staff, which means all of them." [10]

Ridgway's reason for not dissenting formally was that he believed his position had already been made clear, that the decision had already been made over his objections, and that therefore dissent at this late stage would be pointless. Ridgway had expressed his opposition to the original 10 percent cut in manpower several times, and in writing, during the five or six weeks prior to December 9 when this proposal was under discussion. Apparently he believed that when Wilson ordered a reduction of this amount on December 8, the argument was closed, and in failing to object formally after this point he was simply "accepting" the program as determined by his superiors, indicating implicitly his willingness, as a "good

[9] *HCA, Hearings 1957 Budget*, p. 128.   [10] *Ibid.*, p. 274.

soldier," to carry out the order.[11] Perhaps he had in mind also the President's injunction at the Quantico Conference the previous summer that he wanted only unanimous decisions from the Joint Chiefs of Staff.

Perhaps it should be marked against Ridgway that he did not make clear that his failure to dissent meant only "acceptance," not something more positive, such as "agreement." [12] At any rate, it *did* become something more positive in the minds of Radford and Wilson, under their interpretation of the meaning of "no dissent" as mentioned above, and perhaps also because of their understandable desire to present a united military front to the President and to Congress. They, as well as Ridgway, were aware of the President's dislike of split papers, and they also knew that disunity in the Joint Chiefs of Staff would tend to generate doubts in Congress and public opinion about the military viability of the program. But these two men must have known that a technical interpretation of Ridgway's lack of objection as "agreement" did not coincide with Ridgway's real views.

[11] At the hearings on the 1955 budget, Ridgway refused to say in open session whether he had "approved" the program, but said "I accept this program as a sound one." *SCA, Hearings 1955 Budget,* pp. 43–44. Later Ridgway said the "soundness" of the program resulted from its having been "announced as an official decision by a properly constituted official." *HCA, Hearings 1957 Budget,* p. 597.

[12] That Ridgway learned his lesson well is indicated by his actions the following year when force levels and manpower strengths for fiscal 1956 were under discussion. In that year the pattern of the previous year repeated itself: The Joint Chiefs of Staff had agreed on a set of force levels, but Radford and Wilson then privately drew up a different set, which Radford then asked the Chiefs to approve. This time Ridgway put in a formal dissent, and the result was a split paper. Interviews.

IV   *Conclusions*

The New Look was certainly no revolutionary upheaval in American military policy. The actual changes were less than were implied by their verbal explanations. Both the innovations themselves and the tendency to overadvertise them can be partly related to the fact that this was the first change of administration in the "cold war," indeed, the first Republican administration in 20 years. Understandably, the new administration felt a strong need to innovate, to differentiate its own policies clearly from those of its predecessor. Understandably also, this desire was felt most strongly in the field of military policy, not only because, in budgetary terms at least, this must be the primary concern of any administration, but also because it was in the military area that the new President could claim a special wisdom and wielded enormous prestige.

As compared with the policies prevailing at the end of the previous administration, the "newness" of the New Look in terms of forces or preparedness policy lay chiefly in the reduction of Army and Navy manpower and the increased effort in air defense. Offensive air power was *not* to increase over that scheduled by the previous administration; in fact, the build-up goals for both strategic and tactical air power were reduced slightly. Thus, the shift in emphasis in favor of air striking power and away from surface power was relative, not absolute. In terms of "action policy"—intentions regarding the use of forces—the change was somewhat sharper. The New Look included a determination to use nuclear weapons, especially nuclear air power, in a wider range of contingencies than those for which the previous administration had firmly planned. "Declaratory policy" featured a much greater stress on threats of nuclear retaliation—massive or otherwise—to deter aggression. Speaking broadly, the policy highlighted the objective of "deterrence" and played down the objective of "defense at minimum cost." Whether it actually was more effective in deterrence than previous or alternative policies were can only be conjectured. What is certain is that it accepted the risk of greater costs *in* war in return for a reduction in the cost of preparing *for* war. Force goals, action intent, and threats were justified and explained in terms of a doctrine which, while hardly new in its component parts, was new in the combination of those parts and in the striking presentation of the ensemble as a new direction in policy.

As we have indicated, the administration was of divided mind as to whether the New Look was a "natural evolution" resulting from changes in the external political and technological environment or whether it was the result of new concepts and new methods for dealing with the environment. The latter thesis was useful for indicating that "something new" had been added; the "natural evolution" idea was useful for rebutting opposition claims that the "new" was "bad." There is considerable plausibility in the idea that something like the New Look probably would have occurred even if there had been no change of administration in 1953. Certainly the idea of "taking a New Look" was nothing new as far as the organization of the Joint Chiefs of Staff was concerned. The broad outlines of strategy and forces had periodically been "reappraised" by the Chiefs during the Truman administration, and the middle of 1953 would have been an obvious time for "another look." With the end of combat in Korea, it would have been logical to expect any set of Chiefs to recommend *some* reduction in Army and Navy manpower to take account of reduced needs for personnel replacements and combat supplies. The fact that small "tactical" atomic weapons were just becoming available in significant quantities about that time would have had to be considered, as well as the imminent development of a thermonuclear arsenal on both sides.

The Soviet hydrogen bomb explosion *might* have been interpreted by another set of Chiefs as indicating an imminent decline in the effectiveness of the United States nuclear deterrent and as requiring stronger ground *defense* forces as a substitute, but this is problematical. Certainly the Soviet explosion would have increased the urgency of air defense, and, in any case, a need for greater effort in this field was on the way to being recognized when the Truman administration left office.

Not only the end of the Korean War, but also the death of Stalin and the softening of the Soviet foreign policy line which followed that event, would have stimulated considerable popular pressure for retrenchment. As already noted, the previous administration had planned to maintain a steady level of armed strength "for the long pull." The military leaders of that administration, even those of Army background, were not committed to maintaining indefinitely an army of the size attained during the Korean War—in fact, they were sometimes heard to speak in favor of a smaller standing Army, supplemented by a strong reserve program.[1] The ideas of "disengagement" of forces from distant theaters, of redeployment in a "central strategic reserve," and of substituting "mobility" for mass have always had a certain amount of intrinsic appeal for American military men.

Yet, the New Look cannot be explained entirely as a natural response to external and technological changes. The new leadership brought to bear on the defense problem certain special attitudes which made the shift in strategy and forces somewhat sharper than is likely to have occurred as the result of environmental factors

---

[1] For example, at the height of the Korean War, General Bradley said: ". . . I think we face a period of tension for a long time, and I would think that the only way to solve that is by some long-range policy, military policy, . . . so that we can eventually reduce the size of our active forces that we have to keep on daily duty. It is very expensive to keep troops on active duty the way we have—three and one-half million of them—for an indefinite period of time. Not only is it costly in money, in taxpayers' money, but it means that more people have to stay away from home in the service than we would like to have over a long period.

"If we could work out some long-range military policy whereby we could have a certain number of units readily available, quickly available, and the rest of our forces to come from well-trained reserves . . . in my opinion we would be much stronger." *Military Situation in the Far East*, Hearings before the Committees on Armed Services and Foreign Relations, United States Senate, 82d Cong., 1st Sess. (Washington, 1951), pp. 884–85.

alone. Preeminent among these attitudes, of course, was the commitment to a balanced budget at reduced tax rates, along with great concern about the stability of the economy under the impact of prolonged defense spending at the level of the recent past. However, it would be wrong to say (as has been said) that the economy motif was the exclusive controlling factor in the development of the New Look. There were two other sets of attitudes which, while conveniently complementary to the idea of saving money, cannot be dismissed simply as rationalizations of the latter. One of these was a preoccupation with technological progress which took as its basic premise the idea that innovations in weaponry would inevitably—despite the experience of the Korean War—be incorporated in strategy. From this stemmed an impatience with the concept of limited war, with the idea that the enemy might refrain from using his most powerful weapons if we did likewise. In the context of this attitude, it was simply nonsense not to throw out "outmoded" weapons and strategies and incorporate the newest and most powerful weapons, changing strategy to allow the use of those weapons in the most efficient way. This attitude tended to focus attention on the means of policy—specifically on the maximization of fire power —and to divert attention away from policy ends. Simply maximizing fire power at least peacetime cost—"more bang for a buck," as it were—was deemed the overriding objective of military policy, not the maintenance of a reasonable level of "security"—with "security" including some calculation of the consequences of using various possible gradations of fire power in war.

The third set of attitudes might be described, not too inaccurately, as a modern version of isolationism, or at least as a thought pattern which grew from the same emotional soil which fostered the isolationism of the past. Of course, the New Look did not reject peacetime alliances or the idea—by this time almost universally accepted—that the United States did have vital interests overseas which would have to be defended against aggression. Indeed, the increase of foreign policy commitments of the United States during the Eisenhower administration suggests a positive liking for "foreign entanglements." The New Look was not isolationist about the *ends* or objectives of policy, but rather about the *means* and application of means for supporting these objectives. One rather obvious evidence of this was the constant stress placed on the *deterrence* of war, as opposed to *defense,* and preparation for effective defense, should aggression occur. One way for America to stay out of war was to persuade the enemy not to start wars. Paradoxically, although the emphasis on deterrence was consistent with a deep-seated yearning to avoid involvement in foreign wars, it was also consistent with the expansion of America's formal alliance commitments, which took place in the early years of the Eisenhower administration. Deterrence required that definite lines be drawn so as to make clear in advance to the enemy that his aggression would trigger a response by the United States.

Another aspect of means—isolationism was the upgrading of nuclear air power to the position of the "decisive" instrument of *defense* should the enemy not be deterred. If wars could be won from the air, Eisenhower's wish "to keep our boys at our side instead of on a foreign shore" might be satisfied. A close corollary was the easy acceptance of the dubious notion that the use of tactical atomic weapons would significantly reduce the numbers of American boys who would have to fight and die on "foreign shores." The policy of pulling American troops back from distant deployments to a "central strategic reserve" had a clearly isolationist connotation, although it was also consistent with the ancient military principle of "concentration of forces." In passing, it may be noted that all of these ideas happily implied a reduction in defense costs.

The basically isolationist or unilateralist attitudes of the New Look architects were revealed in the fact that no aspect of the New Look decisions—except possibly the short-lived proposal to reduce United States ground forces in Europe—was cleared or discussed to any significant degree with the other NATO Allies until after the decisions had been taken. Such decisions as the adoption of the "long haul" concept and the determination to plan on using nuclear weapons in some limited wars found expression in NATO policy statements, but to a large extent as United States faits accomplis.

The New Look carried a somewhat more subtle isolationist connotation in the concept of "seizing the initiative." The American tradition of noninvolvement was based not simply on an aversion to the shedding of American blood in (supposedly) other peoples' interests, but also on a deep emotional yearning to be free to determine our own policies without regard to the policies of others. This hankering to be left alone, to be allowed to live our own life according to our own lights, had been repeatedly frustrated by the obvious fact that our own foreign and military policies were determined in large degree by actions of the enemy. This popular frustration came to a boil as a result of the Korean War and the Congressional hearings concerning the ouster of General MacArthur. Republican campaigners during 1952 continually reiterated the theme that the Soviets, simply by giving the nod to a satellite, could "tie us down" or "bleed us white" in interminable struggles in out-of-the-way places, or, by alternating threatening gestures and peaceful moves, could seduce us into frittering away our strength in a series of "crash" mobilizations.

The New Look doctrine proposed to end all this; in a sense it was a "declaration of independence" from the Soviet Union. Although the enemy could still determine the *timing* of war (since American principles rejected "preventive war"), henceforth we, not the enemy, would call the tune regarding *how* and *where* the war was to be fought. Thus, our *action policy* was to be founded on a determination to retaliate "by means and at places of our own choosing." This idea of seizing the initiative, not the idea of retaliation per se, was the basic underlying theme of the "massive retaliation" doctrine. The importance of nuclear retaliation in that doctrine was largely that it provided a plausible strategy by which the United States might escape being restricted to fighting wars on terms established by the enemy's initiative.

Our *preparedness policy* was to be based on the concept of the "long haul," which tended to reject enemy actions and predictions of enemy intent as determinants of the level of our military forces. Preparedness policy was no longer to consist of a series of improvised "emergency" reactions to Russian "initiative," but was to be formulated according to criteria which *we* would determine—criteria which would not ignore the *long-run* nature of the external threat, to be sure, but which would take short-run provocations in stride without fundamental change. The "initiative" was asserted also in the policy of redeploying to a "central strategic reserve" where our forces could not be "tied down" by enemy action, thereby allowing the maximum freedom of choice in determining the extent of involvement of American troops in war.

In a broad sense, the philosophy of the New Look tended to dissociate military policy from both the external threat and external objectives (including in objectives the minimization of the cost of war) and to substitute internal criteria for its determination. The primary internal criteria were the capacity of the economy to support military expenditures and the availability of "new weapons." The formulation of the policy did not run from statements of "policy objectives," to "strategy," to "capabilities," but the other way around. Statements of "national policy," such as the Dulles "massive retaliation" speech and NSC-162/2, were not so much statements of policy objectives as they were determinations of the military strategy and means for supporting unstated or vaguely stated objectives.

As Dulles said, the *object* of the "basic decision" made in the National Security Council was to "permit a selection" of military means instead of a "multiplication" of means. Obviously, one reason why a "selection" of means was necessary was that a "multiplication of means"—which would be the result of tailoring preparedness to the Russian initiative—would cost too much. Thus, there was a very close relation between the means–isolationist and the economy themes of the New Look. Secretary Wilson expressed the connection very well when he described "economy in planning" as "devising a strategy which permits the selection of those force elements and weapons systems which provide the greatest combat effectiveness." [2]

Thus, the administration's policy reasoning started from the internal objective of economy and the balanced budget, moved from there to the idea that significant economies could be made only by a "selection" of military means (it being understood by all

[2] *HCA, Hearings 1955 Budget,* p. 4.

that "selection" meant nuclear weapons and nuclear air power), from there to the need for devising a strategy which would permit such "selection," and, finally, to the need for a "national policy" directive sanctioning such a strategy. The likelihood that such "selection" would reduce our means for supporting our real policy objectives—the holding of certain vital interests abroad at least cost in war—was either ignored, or disbelieved, or obscured by the emphasis on deterrence and the unqualified acceptance of air power and nuclear weapons as the decisive instruments of defense.

A corollary of the means orientation of the New Look doctrine was the tendency to find absolute limitations in the means available. The most important case of this was the assumption that the economy could not "support" expenditures beyond a certain level. Another case of "absoluteness of means" was Wilson's idea that the amount of shipping available to move troops overseas in the early stages of a war placed an absolute limit on the size of the standing army required. The possibility of building and stockpiling more troop transport capacity apparently was not considered. This particular notion, incidentally, Wilson seems to have picked up from President Eisenhower.[3] Another example was a consequence of adoption of the "floating D-Day" as a planning criterion: that the rate of procurement of all items would conform to that for the "hardest to get" items. The rate for the scarcest items was spoken of as an absolute, not something that might be increased by the "breaking of bottlenecks," construction of new production facilities, and so forth.

It is instructive to contrast this "absoluteness of supply" approach with Ridgway's policy calculus, which might be described, not too inaccurately, as an "absoluteness of requirements" approach. Ridgway started with "commitments"—that is, policy ends—and enemy capabilities to challenge the commitments, and reasoned thence to force requirements. Although he admitted under questioning that

[3] In a letter to Wilson dated January 5, 1955, the President said: "In view of the practical considerations limiting the rapid deployment of large military forces from the continental United States immediately on outbreak of war, the numbers of active troops maintained for this purpose can be correspondingly tailored." *Army-Navy-Air Force Journal*, January 8, 1955, p. 1.

deviations from the "requirements" might be countenanced provided the responsible authorities were thoroughly aware of the risk being taken, the dominant tenor of his remarks on the subject was that rather specific "requirements" followed logically from a given set of external conditions and commitments and that the professional estimates of these requirements should be the primary criterion for the formulation of military policy. Wilson's counterargument that requirements could not be deduced from commitments, and his narrow definition of a "commitment," not in terms of a policy intent, but in terms of written promises to supply specific numbers of troops, reflected the dominant means orientation.[4] So did the thesis which held that once force goals had been established for fiscal 1957, the rate of approach to those goals was more dependent on considerations of administrative efficiency than on the degree of external threat.

A concomitant of the focus on internal factors was a tendency to minimize the importance of the enemy's capabilities in the selection of appropriate means. In other words, attention was directed to what *we* could do to the enemy and tended to ignore what *he* could and would do to us in return. Thus, the decision to substitute tactical nuclear fire power for manpower was taken with apparently little consideration being given to the probability that the enemy would soon have tactical nuclear weapons, too. But perhaps the most remarkable exhibit in this connection was the adoption of deterrence by "massive retaliation" as a central element in policy at the very time when this concept should logically have been going into eclipse—that is, just at the time when the Soviets had produced evidence that they would soon be able to punish us in kind. There is no evidence that anyone, even the Army, saw in the Soviet hydrogen bomb explosion the probability that threats of nuclear punishment might soon lack sufficient credibility to deter, and that if

[4] This interpretation of course limited United States "commitments" to those undertaken in support of NATO. According to General James M. Gavin, Wilson even argued that there was no commitment at all to NATO and "by juggling words, and finally by a change in NATO's standards of readiness, he made it stick." General James M. Gavin, *War and Peace in the Space Age* (New York, Harper and Bros., 1958), p. 156.

actually applied, the consequences via Russian counterretaliation might be disastrous for the United States. It might have been foreseen that this event augured the decline of strategic nuclear deterrence as a sufficient answer to any but the most serious challenges and indicated a need for greater, rather than less, reliance on ground forces for the actual defense of territory. But instead, the only effects of this momentous occurrence were to stimulate a marginally greater effort in continental air defense (which was logical) and to provide another argument for shifting the emphasis in United States strategy toward air power and nuclear weapons.

While the New Look had isolationist overtones, it also might be placed in relation to some very activist traditions in American foreign policy thinking. One of these might be called the "reformist–pacifist" approach: that which periodically generates schemes for doing away with "power politics" and substituting some form of world organization which would dispense "collective security." In this tradition are the League of Nations, the United Nations, and the various proposals for World Government. The essence of the security feature of these plans is that any prospective aggressor is to be deterred by the certainty of "massive retaliation" by all the other members of the community, acting collectively. The New Look and the doctrine of massive retaliation simply applied this principle unilaterally, with the immense destructive power of nuclear and thermonuclear bombs taking the place of the overwhelming force of the community. We may recall that Dulles drew an analogy between the principle of deterrence by massive retaliation and domestic security systems based on the organized police power of the community.

There is no contradiction in saying that the New Look can be related both to the tradition of isolationism and to the tradition of "reformist–pacifism," since both of these traditions are themselves closely related. The one wishes to withdraw from power politics, the other, to do away with power politics by reforming the international system in the image of a national community.[5] Both reject

---

[5] This relationship is one of many striking ideas which I absorbed from Professor William T. R. Fox during my graduate work under him at Columbia University.

the concept of applying power in limited, calculated ways so as to promote a configuration of power in the external world most favorable to United States security interests. Americans have traditionally been impatient with the complexity, the inconclusiveness, and the restraints implied by this concept and have yearned for some single panacea which would relieve them of the need to engage in such frustrating activity. The New Look to some extent reflected this yearning. We may also note that Americans, when forced to war, have generally not prosecuted the war with the aim of bringing about the most desirable set of external power relations, but rather with the aim of punishing the enemy thoroughly for his transgression of civilized norms. And, with the exception of the Korean War, the punishment has always been "massive"—that is, applied to the full extent of the resources and capabilities available. The New Look might be seen, in part, as a reversion to a deeper tradition in reaction to the frustration experienced during the Korean War, the nation's first major attempt to apply its power in the restrained, limited, calculating way mentioned above.

Of course, the fact that the New Look doctrine was in line with certain deep-seated tendencies in American thought is not sufficient to condemn the doctrine as completely wrong-headed. There was much in it that was good. Any rational calculus for national security policy would have to consider the economic consequences of allocating resources to military use. There *are* limitations on means which must be weighed against the imperatives of policy objectives, although in general the relevant limitations are not absolutes, but the existence of values which must be sacrificed in greater or lesser degree in order to free resources for national security use. Deterrence by the threat of "massive retaliation," and the capacity to carry out such retaliation, perhaps still has a legitimate place in national security policy. A rational formulation of national security policy might be visualized as the selection of an appropriate combination of deterrence and defense (with "defense" defined as the capacity to hold objectives at minimum cost), the choice taking account of the chances that the deterrent will fail to deter, of the consequences should it fail, and of the cost—in terms of sacrificed nonsecurity values—of maintaining various alternative combinations of capabilities for deterrence and defense. If there is a very good chance that the threat of punishment will succeed in deterring, then it may be rational to economize on capabilities for the defense of territory. Or it may be rational to accept less overall security if this makes possible a more-than-offsetting saving in nonsecurity values.

The idea of maintaining a relatively steady level of mobilization "for the long pull" and refusing to be easily thrown off this steady pattern by enemy feints or minor or temporary changes in the external environment also is commendable. But the value of steadiness must always be weighed against the possibility that the moves of the enemy are not feints or that the changes are more than minor or temporary.

Although the doctrine did have its praiseworthy and rational aspects, one receives the distinct impression that it reflected an emotionally derived craving for an ideal state of affairs as much as it did a realistic analysis of the national security problem. This impression is reinforced by certain inconsistencies in the doctrine itself, and between the doctrine and the forces provided. Although it was apparently assumed that the nuclear exchange in the early phases of a general war would be decisive,[6] this was contradicted by the Chiefs' recommendation for, and the administration's acceptance of, a policy of building an industrial mobilization base for producing equipment over an extended period during such a war. Although the doctrine stressed the mobility of United States ground forces, the Army's mobility was reduced by the reduction in air transport facilities. Although "emergency actions" were deplored and supposedly were to be avoided in the future, statements that "another look" would be taken if the international situation "deteriorated" seemed to imply that emergency actions were still possible.

ROLES IN THE FORMULATION OF THE POLICY

We may usefully discuss the process of formulating the New Look from the point of view of the "roles" played by the various

[6] Gavin, *War and Peace in the Space Age*, p. 152.

participants. The concept of "role" is a rather complex one in the growing literature on "decision-making"; however, we define it here rather simply as having only two dimensions—"range of competence" and "range of discretion." A man's role in the "range of competence" dimension refers to the breadth of subject matter which he takes into account in making judgments or that he thinks he *should* consider, or is responsible for, considering. The "range of discretion" dimension roughly describes his degree of authority or influence in decision-making. It extends from no participation at all (or participation but no influence—for example, when a person's views are given no consideration) to the actual making of a decision.

We shall be most interested in two intermediate points on the "range of discretion"—the "neutral expert" role and the "policy advocate" role. As a neutral expert, a participant merely states the consequences of alternative lines of policy, for the information of a higher authority who makes the decision. As a policy advocate, he positively recommends a policy. We shall use these rather rough-hewn concepts primarily to discuss the role played by the Joint Chiefs of Staff in the formulation of the New Look.

The Joint Chiefs of Staff

Probably the most conspicuous change which the New Look made in the process of formulating defense policy was the manner in which the demands of security were reconciled with the administration's fiscal goals—particularly the way in which the latter were introduced into the deliberations of the Joint Chiefs of Staff. As we have already mentioned in the narrative, the Truman administration had tended to introduce fiscal limitations externally—before Korea by applying firm ceilings *before* the Chiefs calculated "requirements," during part of the Korean War period by chopping down requirements *after* they had been calculated by the military. In both practices, the responsibility for finally striking the balance between security and economic sacrifice clearly lay with the civilian leadership.

In the first year of the Eisenhower administration, however, an attempt was made to "internalize" this choice within the Joint Chiefs of Staff—to make the Chiefs responsible, in other words, for making this choice in their own deliberations. Fiscal "targets," "orders of magnitude," "projected levels" of expenditure, and verbal exhortations were used to steer the Chiefs and the armed services in the direction of retrenchment, but no firm "ceilings" were applied, in the sense of firm, mandatory money figures. In other words, the Chiefs were made clearly aware of the size of the program, in money terms, which the administration expected them to produce, but they were expected to make a judgment of their own about the proper balance between security and the values to be sacrificed for security.

However, the Chiefs probably did not make any such judgment because the data which they were given as raw material for making it carried an implicit ceiling, requiring only a rather simple arithmetical calculation to make it explicit. Even so, the Everest Committee as the agent of the Joint Chiefs of Staff found that it could not, or would not, make this calculation itself, and requested expert guidance from the proper civilian agencies and from the spokesman for nondefense values within the Defense Department—the Office of the Comptroller. Thus, the "consideration of the economic factor" by the military consisted in their being apprised of the data which went into the determination of a ceiling and in their being corporeally present when the calculation was made. Whether the result was the same as a flat ceiling would depend on whether or not the Chiefs regarded as mandatory the controlling assumptions in the data—no tax increases and a balanced budget.

General Ridgway believed that the Chiefs had, in effect, been given a ceiling. Of the other Chiefs, at least Admiral Radford seems to have believed that they exercised some degree of choice. This belief might mean that they gave active consideration to the data and the reasoning which went into the calculation of a "remainder" for the Department of Defense, and that they felt they had been free to give greater or less weight to this reasoning and to recommend forces costing more than the "remainder" if they chose. Or, even if they had regarded the remainder as a firm limitation, they might have considered and fully approved the controlling fiscal policy assumptions behind it.

For Admiral Radford, the crux of the issue was whether the Joint Chiefs of Staff had been ordered to consider the economic data, or whether they had done so voluntarily; it was "whether we agreed to accept the fact that the national economy over the long pull is a military factor, and therefore the Chiefs would get estimates of the national income and make an assumption as to the amount that might be allotted for defense, or whether in so doing we were in fact accepting a directive to follow that procedure." [7]

I honestly felt and still feel [Radford went on] that the economic stability of the United States is a great factor of military importance over the long pull. . . . Without any reservation, I subscribe to the theory that as military men, in trying to work out plans for the long pull . . . we must take economic factors into consideration. I did not feel in this case that we were operating under a ceiling or directive. We were merely taking notice of what we thought could be made available without any assurance, of course, that we would get it.

From figures that we obtained on prospective national income over the long pull, we eliminated the more or less fixed expenses, and within the remaining estimated amount, we did feel—at least I did, and I thought the others did—that we came up with a military program adequate for the security of the United States. The question as to whether we did that voluntarily or under a directive I think is the real point at issue.[8]

It is clear that the Chiefs *were* given a directive to consider "the economic factor," but that such "consideration" involved merely their being allowed to participate in the manipulation of certain data which carried within it an implicit "ceiling." Thus, Ridgway's description of what had taken place as a "directed verdict" was much closer to the truth than Radford's version.

At any rate, by ostensibly giving the Chiefs the responsibility for marking out their own fiscal boundaries, the administration leadership shifted over to the Chiefs a greater share of the responsibility for the final product than if mandatory ceilings had been applied. Broadening of the Chiefs' "range of competence" into the economic sphere also made it possible for them to accept this responsibility with minimum injury to their professional consciences.

The Joint Chiefs of Staff also brought international political

---

[7] SCA, *Hearings 1955 Budget*, pp. 82–83.   [8] *Ibid.*, p. 83.

considerations into their professional deliberations and indeed made several recommendations of a political nature. In this connection we may recall the Chiefs' warning that redeployment of United States forces from overseas positions might reduce the cohesiveness of the alliances and their recommendation for an "educational" program to convince the Allies of the desirability of such redeployment. The first-mentioned was an assessment of the political *effect* of a military move; the second, a proposal for political *action* to reduce the undesirable effect. The Chiefs' recommendation of an eventual reduction of the United States ground force commitment to NATO certainly had strong political implications, which the Chiefs recognized when they said that "political" factors, as well as military ones, would require the maintenance of United States ground forces in Europe beyond fiscal 1957. Also, the observation that the United States would be compelled to react militarily in case of an attack on Indo-China was a statement of a foreign policy objective.

As between two possible roles in the "range of discretion"—that of neutral experts merely stating the military consequences of alternative lines of policy and the more positive role of *recommending* a single policy—the Joint Chiefs of Staff played both roles at different times, but leaned toward the latter. In the long-range New Look study the Chiefs played the more positive role—they were to recommend a strategy most appropriate for the long haul. In this case, since they were to recommend *a* policy rather than to state the consequences and risks of alternative policies, the administration felt it necessary to broaden their focus to include both sides of the "great equation" between national security and national economic solvency.

But on several other occasions, mainly concerned with the development of the budget for fiscal 1955, the Chiefs were asked merely to state the consequences of a hypothetical policy. The first occasion was in the spring of 1953 when they were asked to point out the military consequences of attempting to balance the budget in 1955. In the "Interim Look," completed in October, the Army and the Navy made an attempt to state the risks of alternative manpower levels. When the 10 percent reduction in manpower was being considered in November, the individual services were asked to state the consequences of such a reduction on their capacity to carry out their missions. It is interesting to note that in the first and third of these cases—which were more or less special studies requested by the civilian leadership—that leadership was dissatisfied with the lack of information in the resulting reports.

Apparently, the Chiefs found it difficult to play the role of the neutral expert or data-giver and felt compelled to take positive positions, for example, that balancing the budget would reduce national security "beyond the dictates of prudence" or that a 10 percent cut in manpower would make the Army and the Navy unable to carry out their assigned missions. A natural concomitant of taking a position either for or against a policy proposal was a failure of the Chiefs to provide detailed information which might lead the responsible leaders to some other conclusion. The Chiefs clearly showed that they were unwilling to leave entirely up to the civilian leadership the making of value judgments concerning how much risk the nation could accept or how much security it should have.

In the second case mentioned—the "Interim Look" in which the Joint Chiefs of Staff considered force levels for 1955—the Army, Navy and Marine Corps half of the initial split paper did set out the risks and consequences, in considerable detail, of two alternative manpower levels. It is notable, however, that the statement was definitely argumentative in tone, tending to imply that if the lower figures were to become policy, the country would be taking an unacceptable risk. The later paper which reconciled the split was simply a recommendation for certain force levels, with little information which might have enabled the leadership to assess their validity or utility, other than the general statement that force reductions were unwise, since no reduction had occurred in the extent of United States foreign commitments or in the external threat, and no new decisions had been made by the administration concerning the use of nuclear weapons in war.

Another interesting instance of the Chiefs' reluctance to relinquish all freedom of choice to the civilians was the Everest Committee's recommendation of a total manpower strength of 2,750,000 for fiscal 1957, after it had been given a ceiling of 3,000,000 men. One wonders why the committee did not take all it could get, unless it was motivated by a desire to assert at least some freedom of choice, even though in a downward direction. Another way of putting it is that the objective character of the military expertise—the presumed special ability of military professionals to determine just what was "required" for national security—might be thrown into doubt if military men simply asked for all they had previously been told they could have. A parallel phenomenon occurred later when the Chiefs recommended a program priced at slightly less than $33 billion for fiscal 1957 when their ceiling was $33.8 billion.

There were some notable differences among the members of the Joint Chiefs of Staff in their conceptions of the role they should play in policy-making. For the most part, the differences were between General Ridgway and the other members. Admiral Radford and Admiral Carney believed that the Chiefs should consider *all* factors bearing on military policy—the economic and political [9] as well as the military.[10] They believed that the military aspects could not be separated from the others. Therefore, if the Chiefs' recommendations were to be "reasonable," they would have to consider the whole problem, not just the "military" aspect. By considering "the economic factor," these men did not mean that the Chiefs should make any judgment of their own concerning "how much the economy could stand" in the way of military expenditure, but that they should give appropriate consideration to the judgments of those expert in the economic field and weigh these judgments against their own expert estimates of military requirements before making a recommendation.

Presumably the Chiefs also would say that the judgment of the Department of State in the political area should be given due consideration—although one receives the distinct impression that in the role images of all the Chiefs, including Ridgway, the line between the "political" and the military was much less distinct than

[9] As used here, the word "political" refers to international political factors.
[10] General Twining's views could not be ascertained in detail, but indications are that he stood generally with Radford and Carney on this issue.

the line between the "economic" and the military. That is, they would feel that their military role naturally encompassed certain international political considerations—especially those relating directly to the use or deployment of military force.

Ridgway believed the Chiefs should base their estimate of force requirements on military factors alone. He believed that it was possible to make a "purely military" recommendation of the forces required, by reasoning from enemy capabilities and United States commitments. He did not think "enemy intentions" should be part of the military calculus. However, Ridgway did think military recommendations should be "reasonable." By this he did not mean, as the others did, that the military range of competence should be broadened to include considerations other than military, but that military recommendations concerning force levels should be within some general "order of magnitude" that the civilian leadership might reasonably be expected to consider seriously. They should not be "fantastic," but "within a certain reasonable bracket." [11] It was then up to the civilian leadership to determine the precise balance to be struck between military needs and economic costs.

In the "range of discretion" dimension, it seems that all the Chiefs conceived of their role as encompassing both the "policy advocate" and the "neutral expert" dimensions. That is, the Chiefs believed they should *recommend* what they considered the best military program, and that the civilian authorities were then responsible for either accepting this program or proposing an alternative one. If their initial recommendation was rejected, the Joint Chiefs of Staff then should inform their superiors of the consequences of the reduction (or increase) proposed.[12]

But there was a subtle difference in emphasis between Carney and Ridgway. Ridgway seems to have felt a much stronger professional commitment to the initial recommendation than Carney did, as

[11] *Department of Defense Appropriations for 1957*, Hearings before the Committee on Appropriations, House of Representatives, 84th Cong., 2d Sess. (Washington, 1956), p. 602.

[12] Ridgway's views to this effect may be found in his address to his principal aides upon assuming office. See General Matthew B. Ridgway, *Soldier* (New York, Harper and Bros., 1956), p. 34f

indicated by the fact that Ridgway denounced the administration's Army reductions as motivated by "politics"—that is, considerations of domestic partisan political advantage—which Ridgway apparently regarded as nonlegitimate considerations.[13] Carney, on the other hand, reasoned that the rejection of his initial recommendation might have been the legitimate result of applying considerations beyond military competence, and he was content to lapse into the role of neutral expert, merely stating the military consequences of the reductions the administration had in mind. In a sense, Ridgway's position was less logical. Since he espoused a narrow "range of competence" for the Joint Chiefs of Staff, he should logically have been at least as willing as Carney to rationalize the decision as the consequence of the application of legitimate nonmilitary considerations.

Carney disagreed with Ridgway's view that the budget for 1955 and the New Look program "were squeezed between the framework of arbitrary manpower and fiscal limits, a complete inversion of the normal process." [14] Ridgway's use of the word "normal" was perhaps ill-advised, considering that, before the Korean War at least, it had been rather "normal" practice to impose a ceiling on the Chiefs before or during their determination of force requirements. Carney thought the New Look process of decision had been quite a normal one, except that the Chiefs had participated to a somewhat greater degree than usual in the development of the economic parameters for their decisions. The difference of opinion on this point might be attributable to the fact that Ridgway had had no previous experience with the budgetary process at the higher levels, while Carney had.

In general, Carney took a more relaxed and casual attitude toward the decision-making process, considering it more or less an attempt by a group of reasonable and well-intentioned men, all of them considering all the factors relevant to the whole problem, to reach a solution in the national interest. Ridgway's image was more rigidly "professional," featuring a sharp differentiation between civilian and military roles.

[13] *Ibid.*, pp. 291–92.   [14] *Ibid.*, p. 289. Interviews.

Our chronicle suggests considerable ambiguity in the decision-making process of the Joint Chiefs of Staff. The principal exhibit in this connection, of course, is the misunderstanding between General Ridgway, on the one hand, and Admiral Radford, Secretary Wilson, and the President on the other, as to what action Ridgway had taken on the 1955 military program. One source of this mis-understanding, as we have pointed out, lay in different interpretations concerning whether an individual member of the Joint Chiefs of Staff, in agreeing to a distant force level target, had also agreed implicitly to interim measures for phasing down (or up) to that target. Of course, there is much to be said, on administrative grounds, for gradual rather than abrupt change. And it was natural for the Office of the Secretary of Defense, with its prime interest in the management and financial aspects of defense policy (especially during Wilson's tenure), to favor a smooth phasing down to the 1957 targets. It was also natural for Ridgway as a military man to posit his estimate of military needs on external factors, such as the enemy's intentions and capabilities and the nation's commitments, rather than on desiderata of smooth internal administration. But the belief in the Secretary's office that in agreeing to force levels for 1957, Ridgway automatically agreed as well to force cuts in the intervening years which he had had no part in determining, seems remarkable, to say the least. Even if one were to grant that Ridgway implicitly agreed to *some* reductions in the interim years, this would not justify assuming his agreement to a particular program. Certainly there was some flexibility as to the degree of phase-down—there might have been no reduction at all in 1955 followed by substantial cuts in 1956 and 1957 rather than (as it turned out) a rather large reduction in 1955 and smaller ones in the subsequent years. As support for an assumption of Ridgway's agreement to the 1955 program, the "automatic phase-down" thesis is a specious one. But it is a commentary on the vagueness of JCS and Department of Defense procedures that such an argument could be made at all.

Another ambiguity concerns the lack of any clear distinction between passive acquiescence and positive "agreement" or "approval" of a program by a member of the Joint Chiefs of Staff. Both

Wilson and Radford felt that only two kinds of action were possible: either a member "agreed" or he "disagreed"—in the latter case he would have to express his disagreement in writing and the result would be a "split paper." This does seem to correspond roughly to normal JCS practice: if no objection is formally expressed, unanimity is assumed. But this interpretation left no room for the kind of action Ridgway apparently thought he was taking when he failed to object formally to the final determination of the 1955 force levels. He thought he was merely indicating his passive "acceptance" of a decision already made by higher authority. If this had been a JCS- or service-originated paper processed through normal channels, Ridgway probably would have realized that his lack of objection would be taken as indicating that he was compromising his views and "agreeing" in the interest of unanimity. But this was not a formal JCS paper; it had originated rather obscurely in consultations between Admiral Radford and the Secretary's office, and in any case it did not do much more than give effect to a decision which already had been transmitted to the services.

In indicating his "acceptance," Ridgway apparently did not make clear to his superiors that his action fell somewhat short of "agreement." The evidence we have presented in the narrative is admittedly sparse, but the whole incident does seem to indicate a need for more precise ground rules which would serve to distinguish between various forms of action by the Joint Chiefs of Staff—ranging on a spectrum between passive "acceptance" and positive "recommendation"—and would also make a clear distinction between "predecision" papers and those which merely give documentary effect to decisions already made by higher authority.

Still another source of confusion lies in the practice of attaching "conditions" or "assumptions" to documents of the Joint Chiefs of Staff. This is a rather usual practice made necessary by the obvious fact that military programs have to be decided upon several years in advance of the time when they will become operational. The legitimate function of assumptions is to resolve future uncertainty into certainty to the degree necessary for planning. In this function, the assumptions should, of course, be consistent with the best possible intelligence predictions. But assumptions may perform a somewhat different function, as they did in this case: the creation of a hypothetical set of external conditions in the context of which a recalcitrant member of the Chiefs could "approve" a program which he would not approve in the face of real conditions and probabilities. Ridgway and Carney were clear that the New Look assumptions were of the latter character, which made their "approval" of the program purely hypothetical. But the administration either considered them to be the former type—that is, real forecasts of future conditions—or chose to ignore them and thus felt at liberty to declare publicly that the program had been "unanimously recommended." Ridgway's irritation over the President's State of the Union Message therefore had a double basis: not only did it imply his approval of an interim program—the 1955 program—which he had had no part in formulating; it also implied, by its use of the word "recommended," that the New Look program itself—the 1957 targets—had been developed by the Joint Chiefs of Staff under no restraints from higher authority and had been approved by them without qualification or condition.

The hypothetical nature of the assumptions explains why they were not based on official intelligence estimates or on consultations with the Department of State: "objective" intelligence estimates were irrelevant, since the purpose of the assumptions was not to provide a foundation for a program yet to be determined, but to give synthetic validity to a program *already* determined by the administration's fiscal and manpower restrictions.

It is possible that Secretary Wilson and the President never saw the list of qualifying assumptions. As we have pointed out, all but one of them—that the international situation would not "deteriorate" —were either left out of the final New Look paper or were stated as policy goals rather than assumptions. We can only speculate about the reasons for this. Perhaps the assumptions were stated as such in Army and Navy working papers which were not attached to the document which Radford presented to Wilson. Or perhaps the assumptions appeared in the penultimate draft of the New Look document itself, but were omitted or obscured in a final rewriting of the document in the Joint Staff after it had left the hands of the Chiefs themselves. The fact that Ridgway is dead certain the assumptions did appear and that they clearly qualified his approval of the final paper would seem to support a hypothesis that the document was either redrafted or truncated without his knowledge before it reached the eyes of Wilson. Or possibly Ridgway failed to realize that when the assumptions were restated as policy objectives they lost all their force as conditions or qualifiers of the program and his approval of it. If we rule out deliberate chicanery by the higher authorities, or a massive lapse of memory on Ridgway's part, all we can say is that there was a definite ambiguity of procedure in the handling of these assumptions and a rather sharp difference of opinion as to their importance in the action of the Joint Chiefs of Staff on the New Look program.

This case illustrates a very tenuous relation between "high policy" and force level determination, and budget-making by the armed services. It is true that the year under study—1953—was somewhat atypical in that it brought into office a new administration dedicated to cutting costs and making changes in defense policy and also a new set of military leaders who assumed their positions when the budgetary cycle for fiscal 1955 was well under way. Nevertheless, it is a continuing Pentagon malaise that the budget-makers at the "Indian" level are out of contact with high policy formulation until the very last moment, when new policy and new force levels are suddenly determined, making obsolete many of the assumptions on which the earlier budget activity was based and necessitating frantic last-minute surgery on the child of perhaps over a year's budgetary labor.

What occurred in December 1953 was a rather extreme case of this general phenomenon. All through the summer and fall of 1953, the budget-makers at the lower levels went ahead on force level and personnel assumptions which everyone knew were very likely to be revised downward. The administration might have made the downward revisions rather early by applying ceilings, but it refrained from doing so, apparently because of the political pitfalls of this course. Before cuts were ordered it was necessary that the Joint

Chiefs of Staff produce a program which would serve to rationalize
the cuts. For 1955, the reductions could not be justified on purely
administrative grounds, as the 1954 revisions had been; strategic
changes were involved, so the sanction of the strategists had to be
obtained. The strategists dallied; they were prodded and did manage
to produce a program which (under a very loose interpretation)
was thought to justify mandatory application of a reduction in manpower which the administration had been considering for several
weeks. The political necessity of getting at least a semblance of
JCS approval thus was the cause of considerable inefficiency and
waste of man-hours.

The President

It is evident that President Eisenhower played a much more
active role in *originating* various aspects of the New Look program
than is generally believed. This is quite apart, of course, from his
ultimate responsibility for the decisions reached. It was natural for
the President to participate actively in military decisions, since he
felt a good deal more confident of his ability and wisdom in this
area than in civilian policy areas. Most of the concepts and attitudes
which were to comprise the New Look strategy had already taken
shape in Eisenhower's mind before his nomination for the Presidency.

His extreme sensitivity to the economic dangers of excessive
military spending deserves particular mention. He visualized the
national security problem as the reconciliation of two "great logics"
—strategy and economics. As a military man, fearing possible criticism for overemphasizing military security, he may have tended to
lean in the direction of "economic logic" in resolving his "great
equation." As for his origination of various tangible aspects of the
New Look policy and the 1955 budget, we may recall that the President apparently persuaded Wilson to reduce Army and Navy manpower, that he took the initiative in broadening the intellectual focus
of the Chiefs to include the economic impact of their recommendations, and that he decided (at Radford's suggestion, it is true) to
allow the military to plan on the use of nuclear weapons in both
limited and general war.

The Secretary of the Treasury

The image of George M. Humphrey as the main architect of the New Look, exerting his influence insidiously on the impressionable President on the quail marshes and the golf links, as well as in governmental councils, probably is overdrawn. The President's philosophy on economic matters, particularly the relation between economics and security, had been at least roughly formed before he took office. However, Humphrey's expounding of conservative economic doctrine, combined with the force of his strong personality, certainly was not without influence. Humphrey was the most able, articulate, and persuasive spokesman for this philosophy in the President's Cabinet; and the philosophy was shared by many of the leading figures in the Republican Party. Perhaps the President would have been more hesitant about pushing his own economic views had it not been for the ardent support of Humphrey, for whose opinions and general judgment Eisenhower had the utmost respect. In short, although Humphrey cannot be singled out as the "architect" of the New Look, he played an important catalytic role as the articulator of an economic doctrine which became the touchstone of basic administration policies.

The Secretary of Defense

When Charles E. Wilson assumed the post of Secretary of Defense, he conceived of the job primarily in administrative terms. He had come to Washington to put the Defense Department's house in order and to save money by applying principles of business efficiency. He preferred to leave questions of strategy and force requirements to his military subordinates. Thus, Wilson did not play a strong originating role in the formulation of the New Look. In the early stages—that is, prior to the "basic decision" of October 30—he resisted economy pressures from the Bureau of the Budget and the Treasury Department, taking the position that economies beyond those of the housekeeping variety would depend on the outcome of the JCS study and that any attempt to set budgetary targets or restrictions prior to its completion were premature. When questions of force levels and strategy were discussed in the National Security Council, he appears to have staunchly supported the views of the Joint Chiefs of Staff. Thus, in this period, Wilson acted as the more or less passive purveyor and representative of the military view—assisted, of course, by Admiral Radford—before the rest of the civilian leadership. However, after October 30, which marked the beginning of much more severe pressure from higher authority —namely, the President—for a budgetary reduction in 1955, Wilson reversed his role and became a primary agent for exerting such pressure upon the military leaders. Wilson seems to have been greatly influenced by two military men—the President and Admiral Radford. His role in relation to the Joint Chiefs of Staff shifted as Radford's shifted—that is, after the President's strong position became clear, they both played the role of interpreting and giving effect to the President's desires and impressing upon the service Chiefs the necessity for conforming with those desires. Although he followed the President's orders on matters of general policy, Wilson tended to take Radford's advice regarding the implementation of those orders.

The Chairman of the Joint Chiefs of Staff

Admiral Radford made the post of Chairman of the Joint Chiefs of Staff a much more independent and powerful one than its statutory basis suggests. According to the National Security Act of 1947, as amended, the Chairman is to serve as presiding officer of the Joint Chiefs of Staff, draw up the JCS agenda, assist the Chiefs in their work, and report disagreements to the Secretary of Defense and the President. Later, as a result of reorganization plans, the Chairman was given somewhat greater formal authority, including the management of the work of the Joint Staff. But Radford was much more than simply an administrator and occasional liaison man between the Joint Chiefs and their civilian superiors. He operated as a sort of executive vice-president for the President and the Secretary of Defense. In this role, and in the rather peculiar circumstances of the Eisenhower administration, Radford was as much an envoy of the President and the Secretary of Defense to the

Joint Chiefs of Staff as the other way around. Also, he played a rather substantial originating role, sometimes making policy recommendations on his own authority, without previous action by the Joint Chiefs of Staff as a group. His remarks to the National Security Council on October 13, suggesting a policy decision permitting more emphasis on nuclear fire power in military planning, and asserting that this would allow a reduction in military budgets, were actually contrary to the opinions of two members of the Joint Chiefs of Staff. Radford apparently had a great deal more to do with the formulation of the final program for fiscal 1955 than did the other Chiefs, who were presented with a fait accompli which had been devised in rather obscure ad hoc consultations at a higher level.

It is difficult to gauge Radford's contribution to the New Look doctrine, since his views, like Humphrey's, were similar to those already held by the President. The heavy stress on redeployment in the New Look papers of the Joint Chiefs of Staff seems to bear the Radford stamp. Radford's Asian orientation may be reflected in the recommendation for military action in Indo-China, for maintenance of enough United States forces in the Far East to defend the offshore island chain, and for eventual reduction of the United States force commitment to NATO. He was a thorough believer in the thesis that economic stability was an important aspect of national security which should be integrated into military judgments.

At least by the time of the final formulation of the New Look in December 1953, Radford had become convinced of the priority of long-range air power, a conviction which amounted to an about-face from the views he expressed some five years earlier during the Air Force–Navy controversy over the utility of the B-36 bomber. Radford's reasons for changing his mind were (1) that the Soviet development of nuclear weapons had forced the United States to place more emphasis on strategic air power to counter the Soviets and (2) his growing belief that because of economic and manpower limitations the United States could not hope to counter the Soviet ground forces locally at all points, but must rely on nuclear retaliatory power for some contingencies. It is reasonable to suppose that, in addition, his move upward to a military post not identified with a single service, a post which brought him into the highest policy discussions where the air—nuclear orientation was strong, made it easier for him to change his mind if it had not been changed already.

The Secretary of State

Secretary Dulles did not play an active role in the formulation of the New Look in its concrete force level and budgetary aspects. His main contribution in this respect was to resist firmly any tendencies toward withdrawal of American ground forces from Europe—tendencies which did appear on the military side. Apparently he did not resist the reduction of ground and naval forces; in fact, this reduction was consistent with his own views, which emphasized the deterrent efficacy of nuclear air power and the inability of the free world, for economic reasons, to match the Communist side in armed manpower. Dulles' role was chiefly that of conceptualizer, advocate, and synthesizer of the administration's national security doctrine. Apparently, he was able to convert the President to the "massive retaliation" doctrine, which Eisenhower had earlier found repugnant.

Parallel with the broadening of the role of the Joint Chiefs of Staff into the economic and political spheres, the civilian leaders concerned themselves to a considerable degree with the details of military policy. In the case of the President, of course, this was to be expected because of his military background. As we have already noted, the chief architect of the New Look was the President himself. With the President taking the initiative in originating basic military policy, the civilian leaders of the Department of Defense found themselves in the position of having to "sell" that policy to the Joint Chiefs of Staff. They were thus led to debate rather detailed and low-level questions of military policy with the Chiefs—particularly with Ridgway—in order to find a formula by which the Chiefs could conform. As a result, Wilson proposed to Ridgway that he reduce Army manning levels and deactivate some units, he made efforts to secure reductions in "supporting forces," and he claimed, in opposition to Ridgway's opinion, that such reductions could be made without reducing combat strength. Wilson's argument with Ridgway about the calculus for deducing "requirements" from "commitments" also brought him well into the domain of the military expert. We do not intend to imply that the legitimate role of a Secretary of Defense should not include taking the initiative on questions of strategic substance, or that he should act merely as the purveyor of the views of his professional subordinates to the National Security Council and the President.[15] But it does seem that the Secretary's role should emphasize matters of high policy choice rather than matters of policy implementation, and that Wilson delved farther into the latter area than he would have if he had not been cast in the role of salesman.

Other instances in which the civilian leadership tended to move into the military realm include the many public statements concerning the need to "select" a strategy, to make full use of "new weapons," to throw out "outmoded" techniques, and so forth. Even the Secretary of the Treasury was heard to speak in this vein.

By way of summary, we may say that a considerable "fusion" of roles occurred during the formulation of the New Look.[16] There was a general blurring of role boundaries between the civilian and military decision-makers, with the military bringing economic and political matters into their professional deliberations and the civilians generally feeling little hesitation about making judgments of a primarily military nature. We do not intend to infer that the line between civilian and military areas of competence has ever been sharp in the United States policy-making process, or that it should be. It does seem, however, that in the process of decision which we have described, the blurring or intermixing of roles occurred to an especially high degree.

[15] We may appropriately note that this rather passive role does roughly describe Wilson's behavior before the President began taking a firm hand in policy formulation, that is, before October 30.

[16] The concept of "fusion" has been used by Samuel P. Huntington to refer to a policy-making milieu in which military leaders drop a purely professional role and absorb into their own thinking the value preferences of their civilian superiors. The term is used here in a somewhat broader sense. Cf. Samuel P. Huntington, *The Soldier and the State* (Cambridge, The Belknap Press of the Harvard University Press, 1957).

In the case of the Joint Chiefs of Staff, as we have pointed out, the expansion of their role beyond the military sphere took place largely at the initiative of the civilian leadership, as part of an effort to get the Chiefs to agree unanimously on a program consistent with the administration's fiscal policy. In the case of the civilians other than the President, the tendency to move into the military area was stimulated by the President's leadership and his great military prestige and by the fact that the basic military decisions were made at the National Security Council level. But perhaps a more basic reason was the intense drive for budgetary reductions. The economy motive, and the general belief that the desired reductions could be made only by a strategy shift placing greater reliance on nuclear fire power, tended to lead civilian thinking into the area of strategy, just as the President's insistence that the Chiefs unanimously agree on a program satisfying the fiscal limitations of the New Look program forced a broadening of the Chiefs' role into the economic realm.

Probably General Ridgway was exaggerating a bit when he said later that the JCS "New Look" study was "merely an orientation exercise"—that "the size and strength of the Army—in fact the pattern of the whole military establishment under the new administration—had already been decided upon, in outline at least, long before" and that the Joint Chiefs of Staff were simply expected to give their unanimous assent to these "pre-set plans." [17] Nevertheless, these assertions do contain a large amount of truth. It is clear that the formulation of the New Look proceeded from the top down, not from the bottom up. Although the program may not have been completely jelled as to detail before the administration assumed office, or before the new Chiefs began their study, its evolution during 1953, in its essentials, occurred primarily in the mind of President Eisenhower, and this evolution seems to have been relatively little affected by advice received from the Joint Chiefs of Staff. The Chiefs were expected principally to ratify, not to advise. When it became clear that the Chiefs, left to themselves, would not provide this ratification, pressure had to be applied. The agents of its ap-

[17] Ridgway, *Soldier*, p. 289.

plication were Radford and Wilson, but its source was the President.

According to General Ridgway:

I learned . . . with a certain sense of shock, that sometimes I was not expected to present my reasoned military judgment to Secretary of Defense Charles E. Wilson. On the contrary, incessant pressure was brought to bear on me, seeking to persuade me to make my views conform to a preconceived politico-military party line. I also learned that no matter how strongly my views might differ from those of higher authority, it was not expected that I would let my nonconcurrence publicly be known. It was essential, I learned, that the policies of the Defense Department should be presented to the public as being the unanimous recommendations of the Nation's top military men.[18]

Of course, it is understandable that the President would have had a fairly clear idea of the kind of military program he wanted, without benefit of advice from his military subordinates. But it is somewhat less clear why the administration should have felt such a strong compulsion to secure unanimous approval of that program by the Joint Chiefs of Staff, in view of the President's own great military reputation. This effort to achieve unanimous military support appears even more remarkable in view of the President's tolerance of repeated instances of deviation by his subordinates in nonmilitary policy areas. One possible explanation is that the President felt his own prestige to be most deeply involved in military affairs. Disagreement with his own program by one or more of his highest military subordinates would have tended to undermine that prestige and would have cast doubt on his own military wisdom.

Eisenhower's abhorrence of conflict in the Joint Chiefs of Staff, and between himself and the Chiefs, might also be related to something broader than personal sensitivity—that is, to a conception of military policy as a problem in logic, to which there could be only a single correct solution—a solution to which all reasonable military men would be led unless they were biased. The President often spoke of his firm belief that there was a "great logic" in military affairs which paralleled an "equally great logic" in economic affairs. "If these two logical disciplines can be wedded," he said, "it is then

[18] General Matthew B. Ridgway, "My Battles in War and Peace," *Saturday Evening Post,* January 21, 1956, p. 46.

possible to create a situation of maximum military strength within economic capacities." [19]

It seems, however, that the President's great dislike of "parochialism" or "rivalry" among the armed services was probably at the bottom of his own desire for a unanimous JCS view. The President's concept of the military role emphasized the military man's responsibility to the whole nation rather than to his own service, and he was inclined to view any individual's deviation from official policy as special-interest pleading rather than sincere difference of opinion. In his view, the Joint Chiefs of Staff should divorce themselves entirely from their service interests and biases and, if they did so, they would find themselves in substantial agreement. This viewpoint, which found expression also in the concept of "teamwork" in the general ideology of the early years of his administration, obviously is related to the point mentioned above—a belief that there was only one correct solution to the economy–security equation and that this solution would reveal itself simply by the application of reason, if approached in good faith.

Whatever the reason, the attempts to force unanimity in the Joint Chiefs of Staff, and the attempts to create the impression that a unanimous decision had been reached on the fiscal 1955 program, constituted an attempt to "politicize" the Joint Chiefs of Staff. That is, at least in the case of Ridgway, it was an attempt to get the Chiefs to forsake their objective professional views and embrace other views, in order to enhance the political acceptability of the administration's military program. This is ironic, considering that the chief impetus for the appointment of a completely new set of Chiefs had come from a Republican protest against the supposed "politicization" of the former Chiefs by the Truman administration.

[19] New York *Times,* May 1, 1953, p. 9.

INDEX

Index